THE BIOLOGICAL CLOCK

THE BIOLOGICAL CLOCK

Reconciling Careers and Motherhood in the 1980s

Molly McKaughan

Doubleday

NEW YORK

1987

EL CAMINO COLLEGE
LIBRARY

Grateful acknowledgment is made for permission to reprint previously published material:

Quote from Tim Page on page 46 is reprinted by permission of The New York Times Company. Copyright © 1985 by The New York Times Company.

Quote from *The First Three Years of Life* by Dr. Burton White on pages 229–230 is reprinted with permission of Prentice Hall, Inc. Copyright © 1975 by Burton L. White.

Quote from Dr. Lee Salk on page 230 is reprinted with permission from *Esquire.* Copyright © 1984 by Harry Stein.

Quote from Dr. Benjamin Spock on page 230 is reprinted by permission of *People Weekly.*

Quotes on pages 232, 233, and 234 are reprinted from THE DAY CARE DECISION by William Dreskin and Wendy Dreskin. Copyright © 1983 by William Dreskin and Wendy Dreskin. Reprinted by permission of the publisher, M. Evans and Co., Inc., New York, NY.

Library of Congress Cataloging-in-Publication Data
McKaughan, Molly.
        The biological clock.
        Includes index.
        1. Working mothers—United States.   2. Childbirth in
middle age—United States.   3. Choice (Psychology)
I. Title.
HQ759.48.M25   1987   306.8'743   87-560
ISBN 0-385-23064-8

For my husband, Bill,
and my children, Nicholas and Samantha

ACKNOWLEDGMENTS

I'd like to thank Bill Gerin, Ph.D. and Jim Johnson, Ph.D. of Columbia University for their tireless and painstaking work on the data for the book; Irwin Merkatz, M.D., Chairman of the Department of Obstetrics and Gynecology at Albert Einstein College of Medicine, and two members of his faculty, David H. Barad, M.D. and Cassandra E. Henderson, M.D., for critiquing the chapters on the biological clock, infertility, and pregnancy; Nanette Santoro, M.D., a Fellow in Reproductive Endocrinology at Massachusetts General Hospital for her help with the chapter on the biological clock; and Alice S. Rossi, Ph.D., Harriet Martineau Professor of Sociology at the University of Massachusetts for her help with the chapter on nurturing; and Anne Mollegen Smith and Julia Kagan for publishing the survey that made this book possible. I'd also like to express my appreciation to Dr. Merkatz for his marvelous care and skillful delivery of Samantha Snow Plummer, the product of my biological clock, and Ruth Merkatz, R.N., M.S.N., and her nursing staff at Albert Einstein for such fine care during my hospital stay. I'd also like to thank my agent, Angela Miller, for her efforts on behalf of this book and my editor, Shaye Areheart, for her invaluable suggestions early on, and her skillful pruning of the manuscript into its final form. Last, I would like to thank my husband, Bill Plummer, for his moral support and good humor that helped me maintain my sanity throughout this long project, and most of all for hearing the loud ticking of my clock and understanding the depth of my lust for another baby.

Contents

Introduction

The idea for this book began with my own clock, which at age thirty-eight was suddenly ticking very loudly. I had a four-year-old son, and a husband who was reluctant to go through all the baby stages a second time. But I knew I wanted another baby, and as the months passed with no resolution of our impasse, this desire increased in intensity until I could no longer focus clearly on other plans for the future that had once seemed exciting. At the same time, women friends and colleagues who had not had any children were becoming acutely aware that time was running out.

I started to wonder why so many of us had waited to have children (I'd had my first at thirty-four), and why we were so suddenly consumed by the subject. Many clock-watchers were like myself—smitten by baby lust but unable to do anything about it. Others were caught in a whirlpool of indecision about whether or not they really wanted to become a mother, and their ticking clocks heightened their anxiety about making the right decision.

What was happening to us? Was it a physical phenomenon—our bodies telling us through our hormone systems to have babies before it was too late? Was it a contrary impulse on our part—wanting a baby just because the clock would soon say no? Were large social forces at work here, causing us baby boom women to behave in a particular way—a new sort of mid-life crisis following in the wake of the liberation movement? Or were all our clocks ticking in unison merely because very personal decisions made by us in our twenties had had similar, coincidental, repercussions in our thirties?

There seemed to be only one good way to find an answer to these questions. I did not think that interviewing an expanding circle of women friends would be sufficient; I wanted to produce more than an anecdotal record of this phenomenon. I also didn't want to rely solely on the big sociological picture of our generation that has been painted by the demographers. The solution I arrived at was to survey a significant number of women by means of a thorough questionnaire. This would allow me not only to compile basic information about their lives, but through interviews with many of the participants, to discover the stories behind the numbers.

I chose *Working Woman Magazine* as an appropriate place for such a survey because, like most women who were watching the clock, their readers had taken advantage of the terrific new employment opportunities that had opened up for women, and their concern with issues of career fulfillment and individual success, would logically put any desire for a family on the back burner, where it would stay until the inner alarm clock went off. In other words, the stories of these women's lives would be the stories of many clock-watchers—parables for our times.

I devised a four-page questionnaire with the assistance of William Gerin, Ph.D., a social psychologist and assistant professor at Barnard College. Entitled "How Do You Feel About Having a Child?" it sought to get at the root of the dilemma confronting clock-watchers everywhere. It asked why women had postponed, what was their attitude about becoming a mother when they were younger, how loudly was the clock ticking for them, and how much influence did their concern about their careers and their lifestyles have on their timetable. It dealt with practical matters—how to deal with a career after having a baby, what effect a child had on a career, how much maternity leave one could expect, what kind of child care to use, and how they envisioned the balancing act to follow. It explored the single mother option—who would consider it, how they would get pregnant, and what involvement from the father they wanted. And it asked for basic information about their life histories—age, educational level, marital status, whether their mother had worked, abortions, and birth control—and their attitudes—were they confident of their ability to be a good mother, how satsified were they with their lives today, how they would feel if they never had a child, and how they felt about motherhood.

The questionnaire ran in the May 1985 issue of the magazine. Almost five thousand women responded, many writing poignant letters about their lives and the importance that issue held for them. Dr. Gerin and I randomly selected a thousand of the responses to be analyzed for this book.[1]

Three quarters of the women who responded are childless, and over half of them are very aware that time is running out. This approaching biological deadline is making one of life's most important decisions even more difficult for many of them. These clock-watchers are the subject of the first half of this book. I also looked at women who became mothers late in life, and who currently have preschool-aged children—women who joined the "secret society" of motherhood after living successful, independent lives and can counsel the uninitiated on what membership is all about.

[1] The data was also the basis of an article for the magazine, which ran in the February 1986 issue.

Over 200 of the women who answered the survey told stories that seemed to belong in this book. I interviewed 103 of them through the fall and early winter of 1985–86. The interviews opened up to me a world of women at various stages in their thinking about motherhood. Their concerns are universal ones, repeated over and over in variations based on their personal experiences. They are not stereotypical hard-bitten career women whose closets are full of tailored suits and whose briefcases are permanently attached to their left hands. Instead, they are women of the 1980s who are involved in their work yet feel their private lives are as important as year-end profit and loss statements or climbing the next rung up the ladder.

Sixty-two of them were clock-watchers; forty-one were mothers, many of whom also heard their clocks ticking as they thought about having a second child. A number had made or were about to make major decisions about having a child. But others were still in the throes of indecision. Some, especially single women, found the subject so painful they burst into tears during the interviews. I would like to thank them all for their time, their openness, and their honesty in telling their stories for the benefit of other women who are hearing the same tolling of the bell. I have preserved their anonymity by changing their names and other identifying characteristics. The stories of their lives are interwoven throughout the book. The "Cast of Characters" (see Appendix) gives their names, ages, occupations, and vital statistics.

The book is divided into three sections. The first deals with the professional and personal reasons why women have postponed children. The second section describes the way married women have arrived at the decision to go ahead, the feelings of single women about becoming mothers on their own, how our hormonal clocks operate, the problem of infertility and age, and pregnancy for older first-time mothers. The third part of the book tells the story from the other side of the great divide, motherhood: how women feel about their babies; how they manage work, child care, and their private lives; what single mothers' lives are like; and, finally, how both mothers and nonmothers see children within the continuum of their lives. The book is concluded by an epilogue in which I tell the story of my own path to motherhood.

Molly McKaughan

PART I

TICKTOCK

1

Why We've Postponed
The Road Not Taken

We women of the baby boom generation who are now hearing our biological clocks are unlike any generation before us. We were raised in one of the most affluent periods in human history and had great expectations for ourselves and what we could accomplish in this world. We were given the best education money could buy, and told to use it. Twice as many baby boomers attended college as did their parents, three times as many as did their grandparents. With education came higher aspirations, aspirations that worked against our becoming mothers. Demographers have shown that the probability a woman will become a mother is substantially lowered by any education she receives beyond high school.

The clock-watchers who answered the survey support this theory. They are an elite and accomplished group: over 80 percent are college grads and 40 percent have an additional postgraduate degree. The more education these women have, the more likely they are to be watching the clock: only a third of the women who did not attend college are childless, whereas over half of the college grads are in this position and over two thirds of the M.B.A.s and women with Ph.D.s or M.D.s hear the clock ticking.

But it was not just our education that pulled us away from early motherhood. Our own mothers and fathers taught us from childhood that we were smart and could be independent, that we could achieve more in life than just being housewives and mothers.

"As I was growing up my mom and my dad really encouraged me to go to college, have a career and be very self-sufficient," says Barbara, twenty-nine, a dean of students at a small Midwestern college. "To me getting married and having a baby was the opposite of self-sufficient. I thought I'd be independent and take care of myself and not have a baby. I guess it was selfishness too—wanting things for me, and feeling I'd be restricted. I couldn't see how I could combine the two."

We also looked at our own mothers' lives, and often what we saw was that children were limiting. By avoiding motherhood, we could keep all our options open. Over 40 percent of the childless clock-watchers indicated that when they were young their dreams for the future rarely or never included having a child. "Maybe I would have been more strongly motivated to marry and have children if I hadn't from my earliest years been so eager to be free, to be able to explore the world, to learn and do all I could," says Ariel, thirty-eight, a programmer analyst who is still single. "I saw how totally unfree my mother was and I decided fairly soon that marriage and family would imprison me and I could lose the chance to do all I wanted to do. I remember my parents encouraging me in my belief."

This idea was reinforced and amplified by the women's movement which came to flower in the late 1960s and early 1970s when most of the clock-watchers were graduating from college. The Feminine Mystique was published in 1963; NOW was founded by Betty Friedan in 1966. "Remember, if you can," wrote Sara Davidson in "Having It All" in the June 1984 issue of Esquire, "the shocking and intoxicating rhetoric of the first women's liberation groups in 1968. 'Leave your husbands.' 'Avoid having children.' 'The nuclear family is oppressive to women.' 'Don't wear lipstick or shave your legs to please a man.' The ideal was to become 'independent,' 'whole,' a strong woman who was nobody's sex object and who found salvation through achievement in the world." This was the rhetoric we had all been waiting for. It reinforced our resolve.

Moreover, for the first time in human history, we didn't have to give birth to babies we didn't want. Avoiding pregnancy, or terminating it, had become exceedingly simple. The birth control pill came on the market in the late 1960s, and the IUD became available soon afterward. By 1975 three quarters of all baby boomer couples were using one or the other; 85 percent of the clock-watchers have used the pill at some time in their lives. In 1973 abortion was legalized by the Supreme Court, and two years later over a million legal abortions had been performed. Among the clock-watchers, 35 percent have had at least one abortion.

By 1978, a mere five years after the Supreme Court's decision, only 3 percent of middle- and upper-income women gave birth to babies who were not planned for. More often than not, planning leads to postponement: Dean, thirty-one, an M.B.A. who is a program officer with a New York foundation, says, "If I were to just get pregnant, I'd probably love it and everything would work out fine. But being on the pill gives me the opportunity to plan, and it makes it too precise. I'm a natural planner, an organization freak, and here it works against me."

Meanwhile, in our work we found good reason to postpone. Our education had opened up employment possibilities to us; more of us were working than ever before: from 1960 to 1979 the proportion of women aged twenty-five to thirty-four who worked outside the home almost doubled. Nearly 66 percent of the 33 million baby boomers in their twenties and thirties are in the work force. The clock-watchers who responded to the survey have taken advantage of these opportunities: more than half are in management positions, and almost a third are professionals. These jobs and careers gave us financial independence unknown to housewives and stay-at-home mothers. The clock-watchers make an average of $31,700 and 30 percent make more than $35,000.

But money wasn't everything. Many of us who married didn't work because we had to: we did it because we wanted to. Through our work, we gained a sense of wholeness that our mothers, who had devoted themselves first to their families and husbands, seemed to lack. In fact, according to sociologists, the more money our husbands make, the more likely we are to be employed. Over three quarters of upper-income families in this country have two wage earners. "My ego is really tied up in my work. I see myself very much in what I do," says Miranda, twenty-nine, a married advertising and sales promotion director, whose family income is close to $80,000 a year. "I get a great deal of satisfaction from doing a good marketing plan, or rolling out a great project and bringing in revenue for the business. I worry about being at home with a baby and having my husband come home after shooting four TV commercials and being all excited about what he's done. What would I say I'd done?"

As we moved up the corporate ladders or used our advance degrees to enter and become established in the professional ranks, more and more of us became attached to this new way of life; we didn't want to drop out to have children and lose the professional gains we had made, and we didn't see how we could squeeze them into already crowded lives. In fact, 34 percent of the clock-watchers surveyed list "worry about the effect on my career" as one of their top four reasons for still being childless. "I just know that if I were a parent, something would suffer," says Sally, thirty-six, who is a personnel officer for a large corporation. "I don't think I could do it all. I don't think I could remain in the job I'm in now in this capacity and also have a child. It's just too much responsibility. Something would have to give. I don't think I could give up working completely, but I wouldn't want the stress of both."

Career, not family, provided the continuity to our lives. "When I think back," says Kim, a head medical librarian who is thirty-five and married for the second time, "I see that my career has been a wonderful and interesting experience—that I love what I have done for the past thirteen years. It's been the solid foundation through several cities and two marriages and I think, 'I don't want to mess this up; I don't want to jeopardize this.' "

Our priorities were the opposite of those of our mothers: We put our personal fulfillment first. The "me decade" was born. "Me" did not so easily translate into "we." If we wanted autonomy, not dependence, it made it hard for many of us to accept being cared for by a man. We also didn't cotton to the self-sacrifice marriage requires, nor did we want to give up our individual freedom and self-expression, which we believed marriage would take from us.

So many of us did not marry, or postponed marriage in favor of remaining single. Diplomas in hand, we got jobs and lived on our own. In the 1970s the proportion of unmarried women aged twenty-five to twenty-nine doubled. By the mid-1980s there were twice as many men and women who had never been married as there were in 1970. Over a quarter of the clock-watchers are among them. For baby boom women who graduated from college, the marriage bust was even more pronounced. In fact, sociologists have determined that the more education a woman receives, the less likely she is to marry.

This scenario is certainly true of the clock-watchers surveyed: 42 percent of those with Ph.D.s, M.D.s, or other professional degrees have never married compared to only 20 percent of college graduates and 29 percent of those who did not attend college. Maggie, thirty, a social worker who has a master's degree and is still single, was engaged when she was nineteen and broke it off so she could continue her education—a step she now regrets. "My college days were in the early to mid-seventies—the height of feminism and just beyond the fringes of the sixties turmoil," she says. "One would think that I would have become a 'Southern Belle,' since most of my high school years and all of my college years were spent in Mississippi and Alabama. But no—I had to pursue my education and career. I could not see myself 'barefoot and pregnant' and putting my fiancé through pharmacy school, while working as a secretary. I do not regret what I've done with my life—I only regret the way I handled that relationship. I probably should have prolonged the courtship —and continued my education and career along with his."

Marriage was also postponed because it was no longer unsafe to have a sexual relationship outside of it. The new methods of contraceptive devices allowed us the freedom to establish the kinds of relationships with men formerly reserved for marriage. From 1970 to 1982, the number of couples without children who were cohabitating more than tripled. Such arrangements weren't necessarily trial runs before heading to the altar. "My boyfriend has moved back in with me again," says Diana, twenty-nine, the executive director of a human services agency. "This time I thought it was temporary, but it looks like it's probably a step forward. We've talked about marriage; we've gone around on the subject. I don't know. I think the only reason we would is to have kids."

Even if we want to marry, and by our late twenties or early thirties many of us do, we find ourselves with many fewer men to choose among. Traditionally, men have married down, and women up. But as women have received more education, gotten more interesting jobs, and gained financial independence through their careers, there are fewer and fewer men who have higher accomplishments than they do. Men to whom they might have been attracted if they had not done so well for themselves no longer seem worthy of consideration. Conversely, men who might have been attracted to them if they had stayed a few notches down the ladder are now threatened, or confused. Women also tend to marry men several years older than themselves, and for those born at the beginning of the baby boom, that means a smaller number of men because the birthrate during the Depression and World War II was considerably lower than during the boom years. Over fifty thousand potential husbands died in Vietnam and many men in our generation have declared a different sexual preference.

The result is that there are now 30 percent more available women in their thirties than there are men. New research by two Yale sociologists and a Harvard economist paints a grim picture of single women's marital prospects: If a woman is white and college-educated and is not married by the time she is twenty-five years old, she has only a 50 percent chance of ever marrying. If she reaches thirty and is still single, her chances of also reaching the altar drop to 20 percent. When she is thirty-five, they plummet to 5 percent. It's been estimated that 22 percent of all college-educated women born in the mid-1950s will never marry. The attitude of the single clock-watchers about their chances reflect these numbers—under half of them feel very confident about finding a mate. "I sometimes wonder if I am the only woman caught in the dilemma of having reached a satisfactory point in my career, but being unable to meet the right man," says Kyle, thirty-three, an ethics director. "I wonder if statistically I'm one of the leftovers nobody wants. I wonder if, because of my career goals, I've become too intimidating for the potential mates who are allegedly 'out there.' Or are they really there at all?"

Many of us who did marry did not stay married. Almost 30 percent of the clock-watchers have been divorced; 16 percent have remained single since then. The divorce rate doubled in the 1970s, a trend that some sociologists closely relate to women's increased economic power—we no longer had to stay in an unhappy marriage to be financially secure. In fact, sociologists have found that the higher a woman's income in relation to the total family income, the more likely she is to seek a divorce if things go badly. If we have not yet had children, it makes it even easier to escape.

When marriage was good, and work was economically rewarding, many of us saw no reason to rock the boat by rocking the cradle. Two thirds of the clock-watchers are very satisfied with their lives just as they are. "Sometimes we think it would be neat to have a family that is more than two people," says Mary, thirty, a sales and marketing manager who has been married for ten years. "But then we think, 'God, it would be so much work, and they are there all the time, and you'd have no free time, and how do you work and have a family without going crazy?' I come home from work now and I'm so beat I can't do anything but growl. The best parts of my life would change. I'm on the board of directors for a professional group. I play racquetball after work. I'm in a church choir. Would I resent giving up my activities?" In addition, the longer a woman is involved in a happy marriage, the more she worries about changing the equation by adding a child. Only 11 percent of the women surveyed who have been married less than two years expect to remain childless, but 39 percent of those married five to nine years feel this way.

The economics of having children have also played a definite part in our postponement. The more our wages went up, the more we considered the cost of having a child—including the lost income from staying home even for a year or two—the fewer of us who took the plunge. Candy, thirty, an executive assistant, finds herself and her husband in this boat: "I need to work because of the necessary income, but more than anything my husband and I want a child. This causes anxiety that is reflected at work, and the stress from work affects me emotionally. My biggest fear is to bear a child and have to work in a high-stress environment. But I cannot accept anything less because the pay is excellent, so my husband has taken on side jobs to help pad the bank account."

Then in the 1970s, double-digit inflation hit us, along with the additional whammy of astronomic interest rates and soaring housing prices. Many couples are only now finding themselves in a comfortable financial position, so the additional burden of a child—which in small middle-income families eats up more than 20 percent of annual income—seems like a sacrifice. "We have only recently reached a financial level that allows freedom not previously available—travel, investment, the purchase of a house," says Ellen, thirty-one, an artist and illustrator. "The addition of a child to our family at this point would result in less for all. Having grown up in the baby boom era with a great deal of material comfort, we both would like to be able to provide the same for our children. We don't feel we could offer that at this point and maintain our own freedom or pursue our short-term goals financially."

This financial bind afflicts substantial numbers of us. In 1970 only 14 percent of thirty-year-old white women were childless; by the end of the decade that figure had doubled, and the birthrate for women under thirty continued to decline from 1980 to 1985. It's estimated that by the end of the 1980s, 18 million women will face what some sociologists have called the Catch-35 dilemma.

Over 60 percent of the clock-watchers in this book are in their early thirties and find themselves in that position; another 12 percent are hearing the clock even before they hit thirty. But a quarter of them are past Catch-35 and looking Catch-40 squarely in the face. Almost 60 percent of these women have found that in the last few years they've experienced an almost complete turn around on the question of having a child. The existence of a cutoff may in fact be part of the reason for this change of heart since less than a quarter of the women who do not hear the clock ticking report the same shift in feelings.

In fact, two thirds of the clock-watchers say they want a child very much— yet many still find it impossible to decide that now is the time, so the months continue to tick by. The other third are still ambivalent about the proposition of making this lifelong commitment. What in their professional and private lives is causing this indecision?

2

The World of Work

Almost a hundred years ago, Elizabeth Cady Stanton, a seventy-six year old widow, wrote, "No matter how much women prefer to lean, to be protected and supported, no matter how much men desire to have them do so, they must make the voyage of life alone, and for safety in an emergency they must know something of the laws of navigation." Two things that can be said for the clock-watchers are that they not only have learned the laws of navigation, but also enjoy sailing. The employment opportunities that have opened up in the 1970s and 1980s have shown them an exciting new world, one where hard work breeds success.

Over 85 percent of the clock-watchers surveyed believe their work is a career, not just a job. They have good reason to feel that way: 28 percent have risen through the corporate ranks to top or middle management; 23 percent are in lower management or supervisory positions; and 30 percent are professionals (doctors, lawyers, teachers). To get there, they have worked hard through their twenties to educate and establish themselves.

According to John Naisbitt's *Megatrends,* 25 percent of all M.B.A. recipients are women; 33 percent of law students are women; and 50 percent of all students at the most prestigious law, medical, and architectural schools are women. Their training and the push to get ahead usually rules out becoming a mother at an early age. Carol, thirty-seven, is a good example. She grew up assuming she would get married and have children, but when she was still in high school she discovered she wanted to be a scientist, and she spent most of her twenties getting her Ph.D. in biology. She is now the coordinator of a university degree program. "I geared up my life to graduate school and a profession," she says. "I didn't see my education as precluding getting married or having a child, but it happened that way. A career has always been so important for me and my professional group. For us, instead of the obvious easy choice being to have a child, the easy choice was not to have one. Babies just weren't a part of it."

By this point in their lives, the clock-watchers are reaping the rewards of their efforts, and many find that their work is one of the cornerstones of their existence. "My career is so encompassing for me," says Cheryl, thirty-one, an assistant director of an industry council, who has been married for three years and who, until recently, had no desire to have a baby. "I'm on different boards and committees; I teach part-time at the college; I give seminars; I'm in demand as a consultant; and I have a full-time, very demanding job. It's very seductive. I love it."

Mothers and Daughters

In the fifties, when the societal pressure on women was to be a full-time homemaker, à la Donna Reed or the Beaver's mom in "Leave It to Beaver," and job opportunities for women were very limited, the clock-watchers often saw their mothers frustrated by their roles. Many of their mothers urged them to do more with their lives. "My mother never worked and I'm an only child so she devoted her whole life to raising me and didn't have much of a life for herself," says Jennifer, thirty, a public relations writer who recently left a large firm to start her own business. "She complained about it—although she never had any ambition to work. But it was clear to me that she felt there was more to life than just having a child. I can remember her pointing out a survey that one of the women's magazines had published that said the majority of mothers wished they hadn't done it . . . that it wasn't all it was cracked up to be. I grew up in a small town in New Hampshire and it seemed that more women than not got pregnant and then got married and stayed in the same town and never really did anything with their lives. My mother was very eager for me to have more. The signal was: don't get into this trap." The signal was received loud and clear. "When I was twenty-two or twenty-three I had a physician offer to sterilize me because I felt so strongly about never having children," Jennifer says. "I didn't take him up on his offer, but I used my feelings as a way of getting out of my first marriage. When my husband said he wanted them, I said I never would and he'd be happier with someone else." Only recently has Jennifer begun feeling more positive about having a child with her second husband—a change that amazes her.

Pam, twenty-eight, who is postponing children until she has established herself in a new career in public relations, received the same kind of message from her mother. "My mother married at twenty and had her first child at twenty-one. There was no question that she'd not work and just be a mother," she says. "She graduated from high school young and had always wanted to become a nurse. She was going to Mount Sinai nursing school when she met and married my father. Student nurses had to live in the dorm, and because of that rule she had to quit when she got married. So she never completed the professional training she had dreamed of, and she's always regretted it. She had three children, they grew up, and she found herself completely lost. She had no training; she had no education really. Every time we mention having a family she looks at me rather sternly and says, 'Get yourself settled first, before you do it, because you'll regret it.' It wasn't that she didn't like being a mother; she enjoys her children very much. But she always felt she had done this terrible disservice to herself."

But half of the clock-watchers had mothers who didn't fit the 1950s mold— they were working women when it was not "the thing to do" and provided strong role models for their daughters. "My mother worked from the time I was real small. I had an aunt without children who also worked. All my role models have been working women," says Nancy, a software editor. "I'm twenty-seven and having fast-tracked through a university, I just can't imagine not having a profession. When I review the lives of the women I know who don't work and have grown children, I don't understand it and don't relate to it. I'm just not interested in being a full-time homemaker. I love a lot of the homey stuff—designing clothes, baking, deciding how a room is to be arranged. But cleaning, pushing the vacuum cleaner—I can't stand it. There's not enough intellectual stimulation for me."

When Sadie, thirty-six, a financial administrator with two children, was growing up, she says she never knew that a mother wasn't supposed to work full-time. "I was very proud of my mother as she had her various successes in her career. I believe by working my mother made it easier for me to work and have a family. She paved the way. And even though she would have preferred I stayed home with her grandchildren for the first four or five years, she supported me when I made my decision to continue."

Roads to Success

Whatever their own lives held, these mothers raised ambitious daughters, and sent 95 percent of them off to college—81 percent of them graduated. Many of them began to formulate career plans in the college years—when they first had visions of themselves as serious working women. "I have planned every day of my life since I entered college, knowing that I wanted to be extremely successful: first in my career, then in marriage, and, finally, in my home life with children," says Evonne, twenty-eight, who has been married for four years and wants to have a child sometime in the next three. "Since graduating, I've grown with the same company from a department of one person—me—to a department of seven, plus additional responsibilities for a separate department of six people. I am a stockholder, and there is an opportunity to become the first female vice president within eight to ten years if all goes as it has."

Other ambitious women who are now established in successful careers didn't figure out what they wanted to do until they were through college. Often their majors were chosen with no career goals in mind; and they got little or no guidance from family or faculty about what to do with their lives. For those reasons, among others, the paths they took seem somewhat haphazard.

Dean, thirty-one, a program officer at a New York foundation, whose salary is approximately $40,000 a year, is one of them. "I graduated from college in 1975 with a degree in Spanish and got married a month later," she says. "Two months after that we moved to Indiana for my husband's job. I did substitute teaching two to three days a week. I was bored to death and he had this exciting new job. That was when I decided that I wanted a really good job. I had never thought about it before, coming from a traditional family and not getting guidance.

"I figured I could always start out doing secretarial work, but I didn't know shorthand, so I enrolled in a shorthand course at the local high school. When we moved east, I really cased the area for a job. I chose a boss whom I saw as someone who was interested in helping develop me as a person, and not just in having a secretary. The foundation he worked for was doing exciting things. It was like a think tank, an academic atmosphere. I worked there for two years and my boss suggested I get an M.B.A. I had taken a lot of math in college but I wasn't interested in pure math and nobody had guided me into statistics or computers. Business school had never entered my mind. I had very few supporters about the M.B.A. My husband thought I could rise through the ranks as he was doing, but I had no business background and also thought it was harder for a woman without a degree. I felt I could work my way up but it would take ten to fifteen years compared to two years for an M.B.A. So I got the degree. It got me the job I have today."

Sometimes careers have grown slowly out of hobbies that are unrelated to college degrees. That is the case with Mindy, thirty, a pilot with Northwest Airlines, who makes $65,000 a year. Her degree in microbiology would not have gotten her a job that was lucrative enough to pay for her flying lessons, so instead she worked as a waitress and at other odd jobs to support her hobby. "I liked to fly. I had a class in high school in aviation and it got me started," she says. "Initially, all I wanted to do was to get a license and fly my plane to go skiing or to another airport with a girlfriend for lunch. But I liked it so much I started putting more and more of my money and time into it. One of my instructors said, 'Wouldn't it be neat if you could do what you enjoy doing as a hobby for a living?' I agreed, but I never had any idea how much money airline pilots made, or time off or anything like that. So I hadn't considered it as a career.

"I also had a preconceived notion of airline pilots being men. My mom was pretty liberated and I guess I thought I was, but I had never pictured women flying for an airline. So I just started getting one license after another. First my pilot, and then my commercial, so I could take other people along for pay. Then I got my instrument rating so I could fly in the clouds, and eventually my flight-instructor rating, that's when they finally start paying you to fly for them.

"I got married ten years ago to a pilot. He helped me complete my first flying license. He jumped around the country after flying jobs and I just moved with him and found waitressing jobs and kept working on my licenses. When he was in Portland, Oregon, I taught flying. Then I got a job with the U.S. Forest Service flying over forest fires doing infared work. From there I put out a few applications with airlines, but I didn't have enough flying time until five years ago to be serious about it. When I had about two thousand hours, I put my applications in again and Northwest hired me as a flight engineer. Only then did my diploma help me get a job—a college degree was one of the requirements."

Most clock-watchers didn't spend a great deal of time thinking about children when they were figuring out their careers, and 42 percent of them say they had no interest in motherhood back then. But 58 percent were postponing motherhood for a career, and a few of them held a telescope up to the future—they chose their careers knowing they wanted to become mothers and didn't want to enter a field that would be in conflict with that. "One of the reasons I got into the computer business is because there are lots of free-lancers and part-time people and people who work funny hours," says Nancy. "I plan to work at home when we have a family. I'll free-lance for three or so years. I'm not comfortable about leaving a tiny baby with strangers. I wouldn't want the primary care functions taken from me."

Such a combination of work and motherhood was also envisioned by Eleanor, forty-six, who had her only child when she was forty-one. She had by then established herself as a psychotherapist in private practice and as a writer. "Over the ten years before I became a mother, I'd been consciously building my career with the idea of having a child. I put together a career that would make it much easier for me to have both at the same time than if I were otherwise employed," she says.

Elizabeth, thirty, a financial economist, was single when she went back to graduate school. In deciding what career direction to pursue, she had to put some big geographic limits on herself because she wanted to have children. "I come from a very large family and family was always important," she says. "I had been in the Peace Corps in Africa, and it reinforced those feelings. When I came back to the States, I went to graduate school and took my degree in international trade and finance and development economics. The career was important, but having a family was my ultimate goal. I was going in an international direction and I had to first understand that taking two-year tours here and there was not realistic. I would have enjoyed it, but it would have worked against building a family. The beginning of my last semester was the worst, with all the decisions floating around. I even contemplated going to Zaire or Uganda. I thought I could go for a couple of years, but I finally decided that wouldn't help me pursue my goal of having children. I tried the World Bank and other international organizations where I could be based here, but that didn't work out. So I finally pursued a government career so I could stay in Washington." That decision worked for Liz: she married a professor and is now the mother of a one-year-old daughter.

Some demanding full-time careers lend themselves to motherhood better than others because they can be left in the office. Picking one of them made sense to Kathleen, twenty-nine, a vice president of a large New York bank and the mother of a two-year-old. "I don't have to bring work home at night. That's why I'm a commercial banker and not an investment banker," she says. "It was a conscious career choice. I could go work twelve-hour days for an investment bank and earn $250,000 a year, but I've chosen this line of

business where I can get 99.9 percent of my work done in the office. I don't
have to take it home; I don't have to work on weekends."

Postponing Babies

Whether or not they chose careers to dovetail with motherhood, concern
about how a child might affect their careers is causing almost three quarters
of the married women to continue to postpone motherhood for at least a few
more years. For over a third of them, these worries are one of the top four
reasons they have remained childless.

The main concern voiced by almost 70 percent of these women is that they
want to be better established in their careers before going ahead. "We got
married when I was in my early twenties and I thought I'd be done with
having kids by twenty-five. But it didn't happen," says Mary, thirty, a sales
and marketing manager. "Part of it was that I didn't have my career where I
wanted it to be. I went to grad school, and I'd have a job for two years, and
then switch jobs and I kept feeling, 'Where's my career? I have to get this all
together; then I can think about bringing something new into my life, a new
responsibility.' I feel more settled now, but again I'm in a new job, which I
just began nine months ago."

Mary's feelings are echoed by a number of clock-watchers who are just
starting out with a company, or in their own endeavor. Victoria, thirty-two,
an anesthesiologist, says, "My career was a major force in our waiting as long
as we did. When we got married I was in my last year of medical school and I
really didn't want to have a baby during my residency. It's hard enough
without that. I barely had enough energy to make it home at night. Then
getting a practice established is another whole challenge. I didn't want to
walk into a practice and try to convince the men that I was really committed
to working as much as they were working, and that I was one of the guys, and
then get pregnant and have them think, 'Oh, here we go . . . This is exactly
what we expected.' I really felt the whole burden of the women's movement
on my shoulders for a while. I was established in my practice for a year when
I got pregnant, and by then I felt very comfortable."

How a child might affect their advancement is a major concern for over 40
percent of the clock-watchers. Priscilla, thirty-three, who recently sold a
word-processing business she had started and took a new middle-management job, voices feelings typical of many of them. "Right now it would be

pretty inopportune for me if I got pregnant," she says. "I want to give it a couple of years. I can also see reasons I'd want to postpone it then. The organization I'm in is very male-oriented, and most of the women are working to help support their families, not so much to further careers. When 5 P.M. comes, they are gone. They don't advance as quickly as women who don't mind the extra hours or coming in on Saturday. This makes me hesitant. It depends on how much advancement I see coming my way. If I saw a promotion coming in six months, I'd wait to get it before becoming pregnant."

Many clock-watchers who are concerned about their careers seem to be hoping that they can set a date, and when it arrives feel ready to go ahead with motherhood. Unfortunately, such epiphanies usually don't happen. Dean used to think that she'd feel ready "when I reached a point in my job where I'd done what I wanted to do and it was a natural transition point . . . get pregnant, have the baby, stay home for six months, and then look for another job. But now that I'm at that point, I think how much I really like my job, and how the foundation is a nice place to work, and it continues to be challenging and I feel myself growing in different ways. I'm still not ready."

If the perfect time never seems to arrive, some women give up waiting for it. That happened to Margie, thirty-seven, a Ph.D. chemist and middle manager with a Fortune 500 company, about four years ago. "The best thing I can say about timing is that it's never the right time," she says. "It finally got to the point that it was past when I thought we should have a child by several years, and I came to the conclusion that it was never going to be the right time so therefore now was the time." She is the mother of a three-year-old son.

But occasionally a woman does sense a "right time" in relation to her career. It seems to depend on how comfortable she feels. Anne, thirty, a director of marketing, has started feeling more positive about having a child for just this reason. "A lot of the major career issues are ironed out now," she says. "I've gotten to a certain level where I no longer feel that having a child will be an automatic threat. I've started to feel it's as much of a risk for my employer as it is for me. I have enough clout so that no one can fire me within days of learning that I'm pregnant. Also, as I've gotten more experience with working, nothing has seemed quite as dire. So, if it doesn't work out with this job for whatever reason, there are other jobs in the world, and now I feel I could get them. I'm no longer figuring out on a daily basis what it means to be a worker."

Babies versus Careers

For 30 percent of the married clock-watchers, waiting to have a baby will not make motherhood any easier. The nature of their work is simply incompatible with motherhood, and some of them are not—at least for now, maybe forever —willing to make the career sacrifice they think would be necessary to combine two lives. Beth, thirty-six, who has been married for eight years and says she would love to have her husband's child, is faced with this kind of situation. "I've been a flight attendant for fourteen years and plan on continuing this job. I do not think kids fit into this lifestyle. If I seriously wanted kids, I feel I would have to quit my job. I do not believe it would be loving to bring a child into the world with the intention of farming it out to other people to care for it. Children need good care and love and under the circumstances, I could not do it and will not do it. I also know myself well enough to know the whole situation would be depressing and frustrating and very stressful. You can't do it all, no one can, and this I've come to realize."

The conflict is similar for Jackie, thirty-five, a bureau supervisor for a police department. "I'm kind of career-oriented and I'm old-fashioned enough to believe that if you are going to have kids, someone ought to be there to take care of them, and I really disapprove of farming them out," she says. "It comes down to a choice of giving up the job, or my husband giving up his, and staying home and being more available. But I would find it difficult to stay home all day, and I can't effectively translate what I do into something I could do from home. What I do has more to do with management, and to be in management, you have to have people to manage. So, I'm leaning toward not doing it. But if we were to pick up and move back East in the next couple of years we might seriously consider it. However, I'm thirty-five and if we wait much longer than that, we probably won't. We have some business investments back there, and my husband has his retirement income from the Air Force and he could putter around managing those. Or he could stay in engineering and I could be home and go back to school or something. But we can't do it now with us both working."

Other women feel they will probably go ahead and have children because they are under much pressure to do so, even though doing so directly conflicts with their careers. Gerry, thirty-two, a stock market analyst who earns in the $40,000 range and whose husband very much wants a child, is caught in this bind. "My job pays too much to just quit, but flexible hours or part-time work just don't exist at my company," she says. Would she change jobs? She doesn't want to, so she worries about who would care for the child, and she has no role models who have done it the way she will have to if she keeps working. "Eight couples we know have had babies in the last year. The mothers have either quit their jobs to take care of the infants, or have one of the grandmothers baby-sit. My mother and mother-in-law live over fifty miles away from us so that would not be a viable solution."

Half of the clock-watchers who know their current situation is incompatible with motherhood are willing to make a change. And when a woman wants to have a baby very much, she is naturally more willing to do so than if she's ambivalent about motherhood. But if it isn't clear what that change should be, and she wants to get pregnant soon, the pressure can be tremendous. Sandy, twenty-seven, who has a demanding management job at a New York bank, worries constantly what to do about her career. "I have four hundred people in my division and I am totally responsible for their microsystems, their computers—buying, repairing, teaching. I work a lot of hours, and without warning I can be kept much later than I planned. People line up outside my office—'I need this . . . I need that . . . My computer broke . . . My printer broke.' Right now, my career is absolutely number one. And I, who want to have a kid so much, cannot imagine how I will manage my career and be a mother. I don't have to stay in this exact job, but I don't know what direction I want to head. The real dilemma is how to put motherhood into the equation of career/success/ambition—how to accomplish two lives at once."

Miranda, twenty-nine, an advertising and sales promotion director in a financial services marketing company, wants to start trying to get pregnant in six months, and the demands of her job put her in an even worse position than Sandy's. "This is a small company and I wear a lot of hats. I manage my clients like small businesses. There is no way to tell them that you are in only three days a week. I also bounce around—Buffalo, San Francisco, Oakland. I can't do that when I have kids. I don't see how I'm ever going to be able to have a job like that and a child. I seldom get home before eight or nine at night. How is it ever going to be flexible enough?

"My pet peeve with the women's movement is that it hasn't done anything to help us be mothers and career people at the same time. I'm really scared. I haven't come up with any way I can make the kind of change I want, but I know that not every working environment is as demanding as this. There are a lot of jobs that are nine to five. One possibility would be to go to work for one of my clients. But my ideal would be three days a week out of the house, a flexible environment in which I could set the working hours; feeling that I could do a good job in three days, that I could earn good money, that I could get credibility and respect. However, there's no precedent for this in my work world. I don't know what I'm going to do. The pressure is so great sometimes that I think of having a child as an escape. I'm going to stay home and raise the child and get away from the working world. But I also can't imagine staying home all the time."

Those Important Role Models

When clock-watchers have a hard time seeing themselves in the dual role of mother and career woman, finding other women on whom to model themselves is very important. Unfortunately, sometimes the mothers they see around them are not managing very well—they're exhausted, their careers are suffering, or they have no time for their families or themselves. This kind of "bad" example can put a real damper on any desire to become a mother. Abigail, thirty, an assistant manager in the regional office of a federal agency, says she works with such a woman. "She is very dissatisfied with her whole life: her job, her house . . . everything. She says she regrets having had two children. She wouldn't do it again. She's run ragged all the time to the point where she's sort of a space cadet: her job, his job, taking care of the house, the kids."

But sometimes clock-watchers look at their peers and see that motherhood has changed their attitude about work and about what is important in their lives. This change amazes some of the women who haven't taken the plunge, and, when it is positive, it can make it easier for them to consider motherhood. Suzanne, twenty-nine, who is single and totally committed to her career as a systems engineer, finds such an example in her sister. "My sister is thirty-eight and she has a one-year-old baby," she says. "She was essentially in the same position I am in now when she was in her late twenties. She went back to school and got an M.B.A. and had a very interesting career in social work. She met someone when she was thirty-three, and after the birth of her child she decided to quit. I can't believe she's changed her attitude so much. When she was my age, she was in the same frame of mind that I find myself in—gung ho career. She had every intention of going back part-time after the baby was a few months old, but then she decided not to. After listening to her I've decided to keep an open mind."

Kim, thirty-five, a head medical librarian, found a number of similar experiences among women in a kindred profession. "I ran across an article in the journal from the American Women's Medical Association about female doctors who have children. The women were surprised that they were perfectly comfortable about taking time off, about interrupting their careers for a few years, and they expected to feel more that they were being pulled in two directions. They were surprised to feel all these nice family feelings, and that everything was OK."

Unfortunately, many potential role models do feel that pull from two directions. Those who are still working full-time are caught in a very tight bind—wanting to keep up their professional endeavors, but also wanting more time with their baby. "Everyone I know who has done it says it's very difficult; that it's much more difficult than they anticipated," says Anne, who is planning on continuing full-time when she has a child. "I think they are all astounded at the compelling nature of motherhood, and how they feel about it, that they really do feel robbed by being at work, but staying home all the time doesn't look that attractive to them either. They are a lot more torn than anticipated. They'd love part-time jobs. It's sort of ironic that women have tried to be like men, and now they have to layer on these additional responsibilities, and it's very very hard on them."

When clock-watchers are committed to careers, such stories can make them very uncomfortable. But if they are able to find examples of women who are managing a career and motherhood in a way they themselves would like to do it, it can help them come to see that having a child can be a fulfilling addition to their lives. This happened to Jennifer. "I think some of my fears about what motherhood would do to my career were unfounded because I've seen examples of people managing it quite well," she says. "I didn't really have any role models for several years that I would have chosen. The mothers weren't also pursuing careers. Now there are mothers I know who are working part- to full-time and managing well and feeling satisfied."

Clock-watchers also look back to their childhoods for a positive example. If they feel that growing up with a working mother was good for them, this helps them see how they will combine working and child rearing. "My mother was a teacher and she went back after I was in kindergarten," says Evonne, who was the youngest child in her family. "She didn't get home until an hour after we got home. We thought that was the coolest thing. By the time we were in fifth or sixth grade, if we were sick, she'd put the TV tray by the bed and say goodbye in the morning. We loved it; we thought we were really mature. I think it made us all independent, and I don't think you hurt your kids by making them depend on themselves."

Sometimes role models show a clock-watcher that having a baby and a career can increase a woman's sense of well-being. "One of my friends was very career-oriented and since she has had her baby, she's just not so caught up in the career thing. She's very directed, but it's not everything. And that's been good for her," says Naomi, thirty-one, a marketing research consultant with her own business. "I also read an article about a woman who was working at home as a free-lance writer. She had the same kind of fears I do that people wouldn't take her seriously, especially working for herself. She said that once she had the baby, she felt even more motivated to keep her professional identity; the baby made her want to keep going. I had been viewing having a baby as all negative, that there would be no benefits. Those two women's experiences gave me two new viewpoints with possible positive aspects."

Planning for Motherhood

Over 40 percent of the clock-watchers indicate they would be very willing to make a career change in order to integrate a child into their lives. Some of them are even taking a different fork in the career road before becoming mothers. Often the decision to make such a change arises out of the realization that a current job is too demanding. "I used to work for a public relations firm in Washington and it was a lengthy commute and my day was a very long one. I couldn't imagine getting home at seven o'clock at night exhausted and trying to give quality time to a child," says Jennifer. "I began my own business partly because I knew I couldn't do it the other way. And it was time to try it on my own. It seemed like a logical step. Setting up the business was really a turning point in my thinking about having a child. Recently I've been offered some jobs with attractive salaries, but I can't give this up; I've got to take advantage of it while I've got it. It's the perfect, flexible career situation."

Motherhood is a lot easier to manage with some full-time jobs than it is with others. Dana, thirty, a corporate attorney who used to have her own practice in Houston, recognized that fact all too well. "I loved my work. I'd never had more fun in my life. It was crazy and wild," she says. "I'd get phone calls at 2 A.M. from people who wanted me to get them out of jail. Lunatics who were getting a divorce would wake me up in the middle of the night to tell me their husband just drove by and opened the garage with his garage door opener. The money was good. It was riotous fun. But I knew I couldn't do that with kids. I worked a twelve-hour day six days a week.

"So when we began to think about having children, I chose corporate practice because it is eight to five. There are times when I work on weekends, or have to travel, or stay in the office a little late, but 90 percent of the time I'm there only from eight to five. I regret having lost the independence, however. I had been my own boss. If I didn't like a client, I could tell him to go to hell. If I didn't want to take a case, that person could take a hike. Here I can't. If the company is doing something I don't like, there is nothing I can do about it. I really believe that at some point when my kids are less dependent on me, when they are in high school, I'll go back into private practice, because it was the most fun I ever had."

Other clock-watchers are planning for a change once they become mothers, even if that won't happen for a few years. Nancy is taking her first step toward self-employment by changing jobs for more money. "I'll be able to save *and* make a network of contacts so that in two years when we want to start a family I'll be able to free-lance. I'm also going to keep up my relationship with my current company by doing free-lance. It shouldn't be that difficult."

Occasionally, the decision to make a change comes from deep self-examination. This is the case with Hannah, twenty-eight, who is changing to a job selling real estate. "When I was younger, I pictured myself as a career woman. I was very ambitious," she says. "I wanted to get into a position of power and control. But I didn't progress in my career the way I wanted to. I went for counseling and I came to the realization that I don't function well in an environment where others can tell me what to do. I finally understood that the only one I needed to control was me and I began looking for a career situation in which this could happen. It meant fighting the traditional notions of success and failure, and it was very hard on me.

"All along I had mixed feelings about being a corporate career person and being a mother. I'm going into real estate, which will be a lot better for me and a child. The same kind of rewards are there for me, but it's at my own pace. I've got my license and a couple of sales under my belt. I'm anticipating leaving my job after the first of the year and going into real estate full-time. My baby is due at the end of May so I'll have some full-time experience before he or she is born. I'm hoping it will work for me. It's very satisfying already. If it doesn't develop too rapidly and require too much, I'll be happy with it."

Career Change Ahead

Whether they think they will make minor adjustments to their full-time schedules, start their own businesses, work part-time, or quit their jobs, most clock-watchers don't plan on doing anything about their careers until after they have a baby. What they do recognize in advance is that it won't be easy to balance two lives. Two thirds of them feel that the stress of having these two important commitments is one of the toughest aspects of the career-motherhood combination, and many no longer believe in the Superwoman who can "have it all." This new awareness demonstrates again that they are in the forefront of the "different breed" of women—those who are moving away from the position that a career must continue on the same course, come hell, high water, or a baby.

"Americans are typically extremists," says Helen A. DeRosis, M.D., author of *Women and Anxiety* and an associate clinical professor of psychiatry at New York University Medical Center. "The whole business of pushing all women into the belief that they must be out of the home and hustling when many feel that they have a greater obligation to their children is not in our best interests. I think it is the better part of wisdom to reexamine this assumption, as some women are doing today. We don't have to swing from one side of the spectrum to another. We can, for instance, entertain the solution of postponing motherhood until a career is established, then having children without expecting to continue the career at the same fast pace for a few years."

Despite her current commitment to her career, Cheryl agrees she will have to slow down, at least a little bit, if she has a child. "I use up a lot of my energy at work; I don't have that much left over now," she says. "I like my career so much. I'd have to go on working because I'd resent a kid if I stopped. But something will have to give if I become a mother. I can't imagine being Superwoman." She plans to give up her teaching and consulting and keep her full-time job.

Fifty percent of the clock-watchers share Cheryl's point of view—they want to continue with a full-time schedule after they become mothers. But many sense that the number of hours they put in, the pace of their careers, and even their commitment to work, will change; otherwise, the combination would be too stressful.

Kim is willing to make this kind of change. "I don't know whether I could do the quality job that I would want to do in less than full-time. But the extra time for a child has to come from some place, and part of it would probably come from work. I tend to work more than a forty-hour week now. I could probably cut that back to being right on the line, and still legitimately be full-time. It's funny, when I spend long hours at work, or bring work home, my husband asks me why women can't learn from seeing men spend too many hours at work and not enough with their families. 'You don't have to reinvent the wheel here,' he says. He's probably right."

Some of the clock-watchers don't worry so much about handling their work as about having time and energy for their families if they keep on with a full-time schedule. Forty-three percent would like to cut back to part-time for a few years in the jobs they have, or establish their own businesses where they will have control over their time. "I believe that women have to put a priority on either their career or their family, at least during a major chunk of their lives," says Judy, thirty-one, a public relations research assistant who wants to have a child in the next year or two. "Ideally, I would work part-time after having children. Unless absolutely forced to, I will not put that infant in day care in order to keep a full-time job. Once you drive home, read the mail, fix dinner, and clean up, how much 'quality time' can be left for your child and husband, not to mention yourself? I am a little afraid of feeling left behind or less professional than some of my friends, but my choice is clear and my definition of personal success is less material than what is usually touted."

The lives of the mothers she works with have helped to convince Sybil, thirty-six, a U.S. attorney who is wrestling with infertility and has had two miscarriages in the last year, that she does not want to continue full-time in her current job if she is able to have a child. "I really do enjoy my career, but I'm overworked," she says. "Our caseload in this office has gone up dramatically this year and we haven't gotten any extra help. There is no other lawyer job in this town that I'd want. Yet I can't see having a child, raising a child, and doing what I do. There are women in this office who are doing it and I can't imagine how. They are frazzled most of the time. If I did get pregnant, my fantasy is that I would go on a leave of absence for a year, or six months anyway, and start back part-time or begin teaching. My lifestyle is important to me, but I'd give up large chunks of it for a child."

Unfortunately, the corporate world is not yet on the same wave length as the mothers-to-be it employs. Part-time arrangements, including job sharing and flextime, are not a real possibility for most clock-watchers, although they may be for their younger sisters who are still five to ten years away from becoming mothers. A Louis Harris survey found that 70 percent of the major corporations in this country plan to adopt a job-sharing policy within five years, and a General Mills survey found that 66 percent of the 104 corporations it questioned expected to have maxi-flex programs within five years, allowing workers to log seventy hours every two weeks because computer technology would permit many of them to work at home.

But most of today's clock-watchers will not benefit from these changes. They will have to continue full-time in their present position, make a major career change, or even quit all together. This reality is underscored by the employment history of the mothers in this book: only 23 percent worked part-time after they had babies, and only 13 percent of those with children under six are now working thirty hours a week or less. Most of the clock-watchers seem to understand this reality. "Working part-time is a dream scenario," says Anne. "I doubt it would be possible in my current job, but it's always a question mark until someone tries it. And there is no one combining motherhood and a part-time job at my company."

Lana, thirty, a computer sales representative who is pregnant, can see a precedent in her company, but unfortunately that doesn't make it any more possible for her. "My company has only established one professional part-time position and they didn't give her a raise in two years because they didn't want to encourage it," she says. "We're going through some tough times in the computer industry right now, and my company has had a hiring freeze on for a year. I don't think I'm going to be in a position to ask for part-time. We can afford for me to stay home, but do I want to give up the $60,000 in income? It would be a lot easier if I were only making ten or fifteen."

Some part-time possibilities do exist. They usually require adjustments by both management and the women themselves. Sandy thinks she might be able to negotiate such a job. "My boss's coworker has been with my bank for fifteen years and has two children and works two to three days a week," she says. "She's even been promoted to vice president. So I think if I could convince them to let me hire two people to work for me, I could work three days a week. I don't know what they'd do with my salary. If they gave me three fifths of it and my husband maintained his, we would break even. But no furniture, no vacations, no dinners out."

The foundation where Dean works has told her she can work part-time in her current job, but she's not sure she would want to. "My current schedule is impossible," she says. "Yet it would be hard to continue part-time because of the commute, which is almost two hours each way. Also, I wonder if I can fulfill my commitment there part-time. We have a person on staff working a four-day week because she has children, and frankly it's sometimes difficult for the rest of us. Periodically I think that maybe I should look for a new full-time job close to home instead of in New York, and then try to negotiate a part-time job after I have a baby. Another option would be to just get pregnant, leave my job when the baby is born, and then look for part-time work near home when the baby is six months old. But that kind of job will be much harder to find."

One alternative to part-time office work is a business out of the house that will allow maximum flexibility. More and more women are taking this route in order to integrate two lives. In *Entrepreneurial Mothers,* Phyllis Gillis reports that almost six times as many women as men are starting their own businesses. Sandy not only thinks about negotiating a part-time job at the bank, but is considering the possibility of starting her own business. If she does go that route, she feels it is imperative that she get up and running before she becomes a mother. "I can teach anyone in business or at home to use any piece of software," she says. "I did consulting a couple of years ago when I knew a lot less about computers than I know now. I was making thirty dollars an hour and I hardly knew anything. I also want to learn programming, which I don't know, and with that you can make hundreds of dollars a day from home. The corporate world isn't something I have to have. I like the salary, the importance that goes along with it, but there are definite alternatives."

But a number of these women voiced concerns about working on their own at home that are strong enough to keep them from making plans in that direction. Dean says, "I like having an office to go to. I like having colleagues. I'm used to drawing up plans or projects and bouncing them off other people. It would be kind of lonely being home. I also worry about marketing myself —it would be like having constant job interviews. Having a job somewhere would be less stressful."

A small number of the clock-watchers—7 percent—don't see any of these solutions as viable for them. They want to be full-time mothers when they have young children. Even though she has a high-powered job as a vice president and commodities broker, Agatha, thirty-three, would leave it all without hesitation. "My job is just too stressful. If I got pregnant, I'd have to quit tomorrow," she says. "Plus, I'd like to be home. I think I'm the kind of person who wouldn't be bored. I'd just cart that kid all over creation. The child would fit into my life, rather than changing my whole life."

Some women would like to quit but find they can't afford to. "I always imagined having children and not working, staying home, and having a clean house and a cooked meal and plenty of free time to do things with the children. And I realize that may not be possible," says Renee, thirty-six, the regional administrator for a computer company. "I've had to decide whether

I want a child badly enough to sacrifice. It may not be perfect; I may not be able to be home all day with a child. I may have to work, and juggle money and my schedule. But I think it can be done. I don't want to give up having a child just because I have to work. If I have to, I'll do it. My stepdaughter is with us every weekend and every night until about 9 P.M. It's almost like full-time. I see that you do manage. You do get them off to school, and pick them up and cook supper. You're tired, but you do it."

A number of the clock-watchers have thought about the possibility of quitting, and their heads swirl with questions. Heidi, twenty-seven, an occupational health consultant, speaks for many of them. "I grew up in a nontraditional home. By nontraditional I mean we were expected to achieve regardless of sex. A college education and subsequent career were givens and I never questioned them," she says. "My mother was a 'traditional' mom for a shorter period of time than the moms of my friends. Both of my parents are professionals and completed their numerous years of education when they were forty-one. By that time all three of their children were quite grown up. So instead of joining car pools, our parents bought us a car. I believe my family structure showed me the great opportunities available in the world. My parents always believed that experience was an important investment. In other words, we didn't have a lot of material stuff and we certainly were not wealthy. Given all my grooming it is very difficult to consider the traditional way of raising a family. But a little voice inside of me is saying give it a try for a while. Yet I feel conflict and I wonder if I'll want to continue my career path. Full-time? Part-time? Will I be fulfilled at home? Will I feel guilty staying at home while my husband is working to support us? I don't know the answers to any of these questions. It makes it doubly difficult when they are intermixed with my longings to have a family."

For other clock-watchers, the stay-at-home option seems unattractive. Many think they would "go nuts"—that their self-image would suffer. "Now that I'm in my thirties, a lot of my friends who also postponed having children because of careers are starting their families. Most of them are planning on staying home," says Priscilla. "We don't have really good day care in Albuquerque and it's so expensive to get a housekeeper. Maternity leave is just about nil except for two major corporations. The expectation is that when a woman has a child she will quit and stay home. Right now I think of it as 'giving up everything,' and that attitude would really have to take a major swing if I were to stay home."

The long-term effect on their careers of quitting, or even going part-time, worries many of these women. Lester Thurow, the well-known economist, wrote in the New York *Times* that when women from age twenty-five to thirty-five leave the labor force or become part-time workers "the current system of promotion and skill acquisition will extract an enormous lifetime price." Cheryl has seen this with her own eyes. "I interview a lot of people for jobs and it's just staggering to me how many people there are in their mid- to late thirties who want a career change or want to reenter the work force," she says. "They're hurting. It's tough competition out there. I think it would seriously hurt my career if I dropped out for five years."

Evonne is also concerned. "If I miss that promotion to vice president, will there ever be another chance? If I make it to VP, will there be time for my family? If I work through my children's formative years, will I pay for it in their lack of adjustment?" These are the questions which seem impossible to answer.

3

Private Lives

Control . . . independence . . . autonomy—these are the clock-watchers' buzzwords. They have sought to take charge of their lives in ways that women of previous generations could not. Back then, marriage (followed almost inevitably by motherhood) was just about the only escape a woman had from the confines of her parents' house.

Not the clock-watchers. Successful in careers, married to men who accept their independence, joint owners of their houses, they've got their lives neatly packaged—financial freedom to indulge themselves and their spouses, time and energy to spend on travel and extracurricular activities. Yet they are still faced with the ultimate issue of control: If they have a child, will they forever give up a large portion of the independence they have gained?

Many of them find it easiest to avoid answering that question. They keep putting off motherhood, right up until midnight—the age at which they believe they should have a first child—or even beyond. Fifty-four percent of those who have three to four years until their cutoff age are waiting out those years. Sometimes they push that age upward in order to give themselves more time, and to allay their fears. "The only reason I'm saying five years from now is because I'm too scared to make a commitment now," says Cheryl, the assistant director of an industry council, who is thirty-one. "It seems off in the distance. My age is what would trigger me to go ahead. Right now I'm saying to myself that I'd like to have two children, a boy and a girl, but not yet. I think also that my husband's attitude would have a lot to do with it. If I felt he was supportive and excited about it, that would encourage me a lot, but I'm further along than he is."

Other women feel OK about postponing having children because the new medical wisdom no longer tells them they must have children by age thirty, and they see positive aspects about waiting. "I think the emphasis that age thirty-five is when you need to start worrying kept me from feeling panicky on my thirtieth birthday," says Daphne, thirty-two, an account supervisor in a market research firm, who didn't get married until she was thirty-one. "I knew I had at least until thirty-five. The fact that so many women were postponing having babies also made it easier."

Barbara, twenty-nine, a dean of students at a small Midwestern college, who recently married and plans to wait two or three years, says, "It doesn't concern me that I'll be fifty with a teenager on my hands because that's the way my parents did it. I felt I had an advantage over some of my other friends when I was growing up. My husband and I will be well-established when we have our children. We'll be able to provide things for them and go on vacations and do things that you can't do when you are struggling."

But by the time a woman reaches thirty-five, her timing does speed up: half of the women over this age intend to have a child in the next year compared to only 37 percent of those aged thirty-one to thirty-five. Yet her advancing age (and the length of her marriage) can also increase a woman's ambivalence. Only 40 percent of the clock-watchers in their early thirties aren't sure they want to have a child, whereas 70 percent of those thirty-six to forty feel this way. Thus, postponing having babies for a few years may turn out to be postponing it forever. "My first line was drawn at thirty: if I hit thirty and didn't have any children, I'd never have any," says Jackie, a bureau supervisor in the police department who is now thirty-five. "Now, it's if I hit forty and don't have any, I'll never have any. We tend to nudge it along. But I'm leaning toward not doing it."

Priscilla, thirty-three, a middle manager, also has found it easy to put off the question from year to year, but she is still tugged both ways. "It's something we're thinking about doing, but it's a difficult decision," she says. "A lot of it will be based on the age factor. My gynecologist is already saying that after thirty-five I can't hesitate anymore, that I won't be a 'spring chicken.' My clock ticks loudly sometimes. I go in and out of moods about it. It's hard when you get older. I made my decision a long time ago to postpone, and every year it seems to get easier to live with the choice. But the difficult thing is that a lot of my friends who postponed for careers as I did are now starting their families and I'm attending so many more baby showers. It really makes you take stock of what you are doing with your own life."

Going with the Flow

For the clock-watchers who have put off decision making, drifting through their twenties and early thirties, not planning this segment of their lives, not thinking long-term, the necessity of making a decision about having a baby can make them very uncomfortable. Betty, thirty-six, a business development representative who has been living with her partner for two years, finds herself suddenly caught in this time bind. "I was married for four and a half years and we were not ready for children then," she says. "Since my divorce at age twenty-six I have never been in a position to seriously consider parenthood. I suppose the key is that if I had been eager to have children I'd have tried harder for a relationship in which that would be possible. Or maybe I just always thought it would come with time. It seemed there would always be time. I wasn't consciously postponing motherhood as much as I was just not thinking about it. Now I'm thinking—a lot—and I'm very aware that I don't have much time to resolve my ambivalence, or for my partner to resolve his."

Carol, thirty-seven, a Ph.D. and coordinator of a degree program in biology, is just as ambivalent. She is involved with a man with two grown children who doesn't want any more.

"I guess if I think about it, I don't really want a child. But then sometimes, I'll look at my breasts and say, 'What are they for if I don't have a kid?' I was the youngest in my family. My friends were all the youngest, and there weren't any babies around. I never got used to babies. I think some of the three-year-olds I see are darling. But I don't know if I'd want one twenty-four hours a day. When you have waited this long you wonder: Do I really want to be tied down that much? Now that I'm used to living life a certain way, do I really want to change that?"

Although she has been married for her entire adult life, and thus in a position to make plans for a family, Sally, thirty-six, a personnel officer, didn't think much about it either. Still ambivalent, she looks back and wonders about her life course. "I've been married for fifteen years. I can remember when I was twenty-one, my husband and I may have said that we didn't want kids back then, but we never really discussed it. We have never laid out our lives. What I'm realizing now is that here I am, I'm thirty-six years old and my life has not really changed since I was twenty-one. I still have that twenty-one-year-old mentality. It's as if I haven't grown up yet. I have a responsible job as a personnel officer—in that area I've matured. But I still feel I haven't really grown up. I see all my friends, and they are having kids, and they're doing things as families with other families. They are acting older. I don't seem to be doing that. At times I think I'm very self-centered, and I don't like it. I'd love to talk to other people, people who have been married to the same person for as long as I have who have gone through life and don't have kids. I'd like to find out if they have any regrets."

The Life Plan Approach

Many of these women are not drifters, but natural planners. Just as they have established career agendas for themselves, they and their husbands have also set personal agendas they want to accomplish before starting a family. For them, the decision to have a child is similar to any other lifestyle decision—purchasing a house, going on a trip, buying a new car. It will be postponed until all the correct components are in place. They are able to plan with impunity because contraception today is so foolproof. This very quality can actually help undermine the best-laid plans. "It's funny that birth control makes it so easy to put off, and so hard to make a decision," says Cheryl. "I was talking with a woman at work who is in her fifties and has teenagers. I said, 'I don't know how you could just make that decision so easily.' She turned to me and said, 'There was no decision; all of my pregnancies were unplanned. We didn't have the pill, we had crummy methods. With my last child, I went to the doctor to see if I was physically able to have another child, and at that appointment I discovered I was already pregnant.' "

Over a third of the clock-watchers have gotten pregnant when they didn't mean to and have felt so strongly that a child did not fit into their life plan at that time that they terminated the pregnancies.

Myra, thirty-four, a marketing consultant with her own business, also chose an abortion, but more for her husband's sake than her own. "We've been the perfect couple—either he was down on one side of the baby issue or I was. We just kept flipping back and forth," she says. "At one point I was pregnant when I was about twenty-seven and we chose to terminate it. I would probably have ambivalently gone ahead with it, but my husband was very adamant about my having an abortion. I just felt, given where our relationship was, and given his strong feelings against having the baby, that I couldn't cope with it. I just wasn't willing to stand firm on the issue. I've always had second thoughts about it, but in retrospect I feel even more firmly that I made the right decision."

When the planners are ambivalent about making the big leap, they like to take a look at the total picture of their lives, and where a child would fit in. Mary, thirty, a sales and marketing manager, has established some financial goals she wants to reach by April 1988, and she now feels able to think about motherhood for the first time. "I feel like there is a financial commitment I have to make in order to have children," she says. "I'm trying to think through what I want from my life and where I want to go. And at this point kids are in the discussion. I won't say they are definitely in the plan, but they are in the discussion. My real dream is to make enough money to buy a ranch and have horses and maybe a batch of kids. Not necessarily even my own kids, but adopted ones. If I make the money I want, I can have the ranch, and I'll feel I'm ready to go for it."

Obviously, there are umpteen perfectly good, logical, justifiable reasons for postponing motherhood, and the clock-watchers are articulately at expressing all of them. In fact, they seem to have been rehearsing them in their heads for the last decade. Interestingly, these women do not take feminist or other philosophical positions against motherhood. Instead, their reasons are based on their own particular lives, backgrounds, and personalities, which they see with tremendous clarity.

Living the Good Life

Almost three quarters of the married clock-watchers are happy with their lives right now. It is therefore not surprising that 37 percent of them picked as one of their top four reasons for still being childless "like my life the way it is." Some of them feel this way more strongly than others: women who had no interest in motherhood earlier in life are five times more likely to give this reason as women who have been simply postponing children; those who are ambivalent about motherhood are three times more likely to feel this way than those who want a child; and those who earn a bigger income and are younger also give this reason more often.

Not only do they like their lives as they are, but almost a third of these women see the additional responsibility of a child as necessitating a sacrifice of things they enjoy. They ask themselves, "How can we handle anything more?" And the answer, at least for now, is that they can't and won't. "We got married back in 1970 and people kept asking us when we were going to have kids, and we kept saying, 'Oh, in about five years,'" says Emma, thirty-four, an advertising executive. "Five years came and went and we were still saying it. We just really didn't know if we were ever going to want to have children. I don't think I felt I was mature enough to have children. We were busy doing things—busy working, busy traveling. Basically, we felt that we weren't ready to quit being selfish. We wanted to go and play and do the things we'd been doing. When we were talking, just the two of us, and being honest, we'd admit we didn't feel like we wanted to take the responsibility for someone else's life."

"I'm the one who is not sure I want children," says Gerry, thirty-two, a stock market analyst whose husband wants a child. "We have a very good marriage and a good life. I like things the way they are. The thought of being responsible for a child for the next eighteen years overwhelms me. I feel I would have to give up so much of what I enjoy now—travel, evening classes, and free time. I also wonder how it would affect a child being raised by baby-sitters or in day care centers. And what happens when the child reaches school age, during vacations or after school hours. What about when they turn into teenagers? Some of my friends have children in their teens and their lives are nightmares with the problems of drugs, delinquency, etc. That's certainly not something to look forward to."

Even women who are trying to get pregnant feel these emotions. "I still have ambivalent feelings even though we're trying," says Wanda, thirty-one, an accounting supervisor. "I think maybe that's why it's not happening. And I get to thinking my life is OK the way it is, and why mess with it and just complicate everything."

One of the big issues that these women speak about is the loss of freedom to come and go, travel, and vacation which comes with the child-free lifestyle of the two-income upwardly mobile couple. When they have only associated with other childless, professional couples, it's often hard to see their way to another lifestyle. Marcy, thirty-one, a sales representative, and her husband have been leading this kind of life, and it helped postpone their decision making. "We've been with other childless people—taking off for a weekend to go golfing or go skiing. We could all decide on Thursday night that we were going to leave Friday after work and nobody had to worry about baby-sitters. They were convenient relationships," she says. "I know it will change when we have children because my priorities will not be what theirs are. I'm sure that if we had been around couples who had small children, my husband would have been more open to it and I would have pressed the issue sooner."

Sometimes it's giving up the freedom to make the big changes in life that bothers the clock-watchers. Mary says, "Occasionally I think, let's bag it all and move to Mexico. And I think how much fun that would be and then I think if you have a kid, you can't do that because you have to have a better environment for your kid, and you have to get your kid into good schools. You can't win."

Mothers who had children late were not exempt from these same feelings before they got pregnant. "We were having so much fun and we didn't want to have to change friends and change our lifestyle," says Tessie, twenty-eight, a software engineer who now has one-year-old twins. "I knew that no matter how serious you are about keeping your same lifestyle, it's different after having children. Everyone of our friends who had had babies had drifted away from those who hadn't. I was very worried about that."

Dana, thirty, a corporate lawyer who gave up her private practice before having her two children, was also concerned about how children would change her life, and she and her husband discussed it a lot. "We had a certain lifestyle we didn't want to give up," she says, looking back. "We entertained an awful lot. We loved big parties and we'd throw one three or four times a year. We'd raise the roof a lot. We went skiing and on vacation and I'd sleep till noon on Saturday. Those were the days. We were both avid readers. We had bought an older house that we were restoring. We felt that if we had children, all of that would come to a crashing halt. And to be truthful it did. But we knew that we did not want to be old without children and we did not want to be old and have young children. So even if we were going to give up a lot of things, there was no other alternative."

For a fifth of the clock-watchers, worries about carving out time for a child, and having enough energy for mothering, are among their top four reasons for postponing. "I know having a child would take a lot of time, and I know that between my job and my extracurricular activities I don't have much time now," says Kim, thirty-five, a head medical librarian. "I'm an amateur cello player; I took that up about six years ago. I play chamber music with my friends and I play in a community orchestra. Practice takes about an hour a day. We moved this summer to a larger house and there is painting and decorating to be done and we're both gardeners. We have some involvement with church activities and try to do a few community activities. I feel that I'm probably trying to do too much, and I hardly have time for the things I enjoy now."

Cheryl is exhausted from her career—consulting and teaching in addition to a full-time job—and that holds her back. "Having a child would totally change my whole life," she says. "And I don't ever want to resent a child; that's so unfair. That scares me. Sometimes it seems like a horrendous drain even to make dinner for myself; my husband does most of the cooking. But with a kid you've got to produce the meal. Not being able to rest, that's a big one."

Some of this concern about time and energy is indeed warranted. Having a child in the house results in a dramatic increase in the number of hours spent on chores. Jessie Bernard estimates in *The Future of Motherhood* that in a house with no children, chores take up 2.74 hours a day. When there are no children under six, 4.11 hours are spent on chores; when there are children under six, it jumps to 5.48 hours a day. And this doesn't include quality time.

Money, Money, Money

These clock-watchers for the most part live in affluent households: almost 60 percent of the couples make over $50,000 a year. Yet 36 percent of these women are so concerned about money that it is causing them to postpone children. Their husbands' feelings are also affected by family income level: 35 percent of those with household incomes under $35,000 are not ready for fatherhood, compared to only 18 percent of those with household incomes greater than $50,000. "My husband tends to worry a lot more about financial matters than I do and I thought that would be one thing that might prevent us from going ahead," says Augusta, thirty-four, the case manager in a social service agency, whose husband works for a newspaper, and whose household income is under $35,000. "The financial worries still kind of overwhelm him once in a while. He's not where he wants to be in his job and of course he's not making enough money, but I think that's going to be eternal with him."

For some people, actual income level has less of an influence on their thinking than the amount of money their family had when they were young, and the way they were brought up to think about money. "My husband wants to wait to be sure there is financial security for the child," says Nancy, twenty-seven, a software editor whose family income is over $50,000. "He's in some ways very old-fashioned. When he was small, his father was in graduate school and they were very poor. His mother had three babies in four years. He knows what effect it can have on a child when there is not enough to go around. We're saving and we own a house. We're trying to get as much of the financial network in place as we can."

One of the reasons these men and women worry is that they have probably read about the cost of raising a child today. Thomas J. Espenshade of the

Urban Institute estimated that a child born in 1981 would cost $232,000 to raise to adulthood. This figure reflected the average amount that a two-parent, one-child family, in which both parents have college educations, might spend during a period of 5 percent inflation with the child in public school. It includes food, clothing, housing, medical care, and transportation, but not college. Yet over the past two decades, the median income for couples has increased much faster than the rate of inflation, so cost should not be a major consideration. The problem is that couples have often committed themselves to a budget which includes a hefty mortgage, monthly payments on one or two cars, and travel and entertainment costs. Sometimes it's hard to see how they can cut back to have money to spend on a child, especially in today's hyped-up spending environment, where nothing but the best will do. Then, of course, if the woman wants to continue with her career even part-time, there is child care, which is the biggest expense in the early years. The mothers surveyed are shelling out just under $120 a week on average, for a total of over $6,000 a year of their after-tax income.

When a woman's salary makes up a sizable part of the household budget, she worries more about the financial drain. This makes sense because if she chooses to cut back or quit work, it will have a definite negative affect on the family's lifestyle. Marcy has been in exactly this situation for most of her married life. "One of the issues that kept us from having kids earlier was the fact that I was making excellent money, more than my husband," she says. "We both got really secure in that. I was kind of penalized for being successful—because my husband felt if we had kids I might not want to work, and what would we do without my money. So, I started to really resent my job because I thought it put off childbearing."

For Fran, thirty-six, an early childhood educator, the money problem is real in a way it is not for these other clock-watchers, and it may cause her to postpone motherhood indefinitely. She makes less than $20,000 a year, and together she and her husband make well under $35,000. For Fran, it isn't a question of being unable to afford luxuries, if she quit work to be a full-time mother, but even the basic things—like decent food, medical care, and a place to live. "If I had a child I would want to spend a great deal of time with that child, to observe, and share, in a special way," she says. "I would be willing to quit work to do it, or work part-time, but I can't afford to quit work, and part-time work at above the minimum wage is almost nonexistent. My husband has an inconsistent salary which is very low. In addition, he feels the same way—he wants to be with the child. So if we could figure out a way to work part-time, each of us, and share child care, and still see each other once in a while, and afford to live, I would do it like a shot. It seems impossible now, unlikely in the near future.

"Having children is the most important thing most of us can ever do. To have such a profound effect on another person, on their descendants, on society, is a responsibility one cannot take lightly. It must be done well, or not at all. Children are our investment in the future. They are our privilege and our joy and our responsibility. As much as I want a child, I want to do the best job I possibly can, and I will not begin without minimizing the handicaps. I must weigh the risk of having a child with Down's syndrome against the problems that I know are certain—the effects of poverty. If I were to have a child now, it would make me frustrated and would probably make my husband dysfunctional. Under those conditions, we could not do our best during the critical early years which we know are most important in determining the outcome in a child's life—social, emotional, intellectual, and physical. I would rather start out with a small risk than a certain and serious handicap."

Gut Feelings

For 14 percent of the clock-watchers, the idea of pregnancy and childbirth is upsetting; they would really rather not go through either of them. Yet oddly enough, most of the women who have these feelings do want a child. "Some of my friends have had an awful time being pregnant; one almost died," says Mary. "I wonder how they can do it. We talk about the physical things. One of my friends said it was terrible, the baby takes over your body. My mother was sick during pregnancy, so that may have some influence on me. I think, 'God, is it worth it?' It's like playing with dynamite."

For Abigail, thirty, an assistant manager with a regional office of a federal agency, pregnancy and childbirth mean a loss of control, and that bothers her: "I always feel that I want to be in total control of every situation, myself, the way I feel. I'm that sort of person. With pregnancy, you are totally out of control of your body. You don't have control over what happens to you; what will come, will come; it's irreversible. I'd do a lot of homework to relieve my own anxiety about pregnancy. I'm also kind of sick of hearing about all the childbirth techniques that keep you in control, and what a wonderful experience it is. I'd rather be totally unconscious, and just get it over with and not know what's going on."

Sometimes women have a visceral feeling about pregnancy which they find hard to explain. This is true of Kim. "I'm not sure why pregnancy bothers me," she says. "I really can't put my finger on it. It's not the danger; my husband is a physician; I work in a hospital; I deal with health care stuff all the time. We certainly live in a city where there is superb medical care available. I'm sure I'd be the kind of person who would get sick, but I don't think that's it. It's not the personal, beauty-image thing; that's never been important to me. But when I see pregnant women, I think, 'There but for the grace of God . . .' It's interesting, but it's not something I would seek out. There was a program a couple of winters ago sponsored by the pediatric hospital about choosing when to have children. I went to that, and I bet half the women were pregnant; it was spooky and I almost got up and left. It was like: it's catching. It was a very nonintellectual, gut level kind of feeling. I'm not used to having those sort of feelings."

The whole question of motherhood—whether or not a woman will be good at this incredibly important endeavor—brings out all sorts of other gut level feelings in the clock-watchers. Never before in their lives have they faced a job for which they have little or no experience, no résumé, and an undetermined amount of ability to handle the demands and responsibilities it entails. No one is hiring them over a list of other applicants, giving an automatic boost to their level of confidence. And it's not a job they can walk away from if they don't like it. Once they take on the responsibility for a child, it's theirs for at least the next eighteen years. No wonder a third of the clock-watchers do not feel particularly confident of their abilities. For 17 percent, these fears are so strong that they are one of the top four reasons they are postponing getting pregnant.

"I worry about having the patience," says Renee, thirty-six, a regional administrator for a computer company, who has had the experience of helping to raise a stepchild. "I don't like to see children hurt; they seem to bruise easily and it's hard to make a point without hurting their feelings. You have to watch your temper. And I worry about getting everything done on time. I'm learning not to get so uptight about things going the way you think they are going to. A glass of milk spilling can change a whole schedule."

Hannah, twenty-eight, who is leaving the corporate world to sell real estate, is gradually working out her concerns about taking on this additional job. "Everything worries me about being a good mother," she says. "It's scary. But I'm glad there's so much information now on parenting. There used to be only two ways: the right way and the wrong way. I'm feeling a little more comfortable that the kids will probably turn out OK no matter what we do."

Childhood's Long Shadow

For a number of the clock-watchers, their fears about their ability to do a good job as a mother derive from childhood experiences which are still reverberating in their psyches. This is true for Sally, who has been married for fifteen years and who grew up in a closely spaced family. "Having a child is the biggest decision anybody could make and my feelings are that I'm not sure I could live up to being a good mother," she says. "I know the way I am and where I came from. I always said I'd never have a lot of kids because there was never enough to go around in my family. My mother had the first four of us a year or two apart. I never got the attention from my parents; it really does have an impact. I think, as a result, I would probably have a tendency to go overboard. I have two dogs and I spoil them rotten. I worry about them constantly. I think I'd either be too permissive or too strict."

Sophia, thirty-two, a ballet teacher, didn't feel neglected by her parents, but she worries about replicating in her children negative feelings about herself which were handed down to her. "I have a lot of insecurities that have worked to my advantage in getting me to where I am but I don't want to pass them on, and it's hard not to," she says. "I've always felt the pretty girls got ahead; that I always had to work twice as hard academically and in every way. Even though by many people's standards I am not unattractive at all, I don't quite feel that way. I don't want my kids to go through that. My husband believes you can raise your children to be good whole people, to feel good about themselves and what they want to do. He is a living example of that and I admire him so much for it. But I'm still struggling with it. When my kids see me getting ready to go somewhere with tears in my eyes because I want to look better and feel better, it's going to be passed on to them in a secondary way. It's been an awful struggle for me my whole life, and I think how much more I could have accomplished if I could have overcome that. My father made me feel unattractive and my mother herself was insecure. She didn't make me feel insecure directly; she's my best friend—she was my matron of honor. But I hear myself saying the same things she did. It was passed on to me seeing her go through it."

Some of these clock-watchers lived through childhood situations that were truly destructive, and that gave them no basis on which to build images of themselves as mothers. That they have become successful adults who desire to have children speaks of great inner strength. "My parents were both alcoholics," says Nancy. "Every few months my father would just go nuts. He didn't drink every day. He was a very responsible worker, a responsible provider and father, but every once in a while he would go off on a toot and make a damn fool of himself. It's inherently destabilizing. He was also an extravagant guy, which meant that money was always a problem, which is why I'm such a bug about financial security. My husband says I'm allergic to spending money.

"My mother was the daily kind of drinker, and she was also a mean drunk —in a pattern that is classic to women who are alcoholics. They tend to push off their emotional problems on their kids. She is now in AA and doesn't drink. But it's not something we discuss, so I probably have a lot of unresolved emotional baggage about it. Being the child of alcoholics has made me less confident about everything. The demands I place on myself are disproportional in every respect. It's going to be a real challenge, keeping my perspective as a parent. I know what I'm not going to do as a mother, but I have no idea how to do it right."

Charlotte, thirty-four, a part-time counselor of graduate students, also lived with parental alcoholism, in her mother and her stepmother. "My mother was not an alcoholic when my father married her," she says. "Apparently, everything was fine with my parents for twelve years and then she had me when she was about forty and everything went down the tubes overnight —alcoholism, and violence, and locking me in a room. They had her in shock treatments; it was very tragic and very extreme. My father got custody of me because of the alcoholism, and then my mother died in a hotel fire. He married again, and my stepmother, also late in life, had a child and became an alcoholic. As she drank more and more, she became very unpleasant. She used me as a scapegoat. She could be very controlled and behaved in public situations, but at home she was really different.

"My father was a good parent, by any standards: he was a good listener; he was nurturing, attentive. But the second time around he didn't admit what damage was being done to me; he thought I was older and I could put up with it. But there were a lot of years from ages seven to eighteen when I wasn't old enough. He would tell me I'd have to understand she was sick.

"One of the things about being the child of an alcoholic is that you tend to be fairly self-critical and perfectionistic. Because I'm self-critical I want to be a really good parent. It isn't enough for me to say I'd probably be better than half the parents in the world. It's that perfectionism. And it's also not having any clear role model. I'm nervous; I don't have a lot of peers with children and no good female role model I can watch parenting. Yet if I look rationally at my own past, it's obvious a parent can make a lot of mistakes and kids can weather all of that and come through. God knows I won't be that bad."

For a number of the clock-watchers, their childhood experiences and family's structure have not affected their confidence in their ability to mother, but rather turned them against having children. In a few cases, their own mother's life, and the strictures placed on it by motherhood, have set a very negative example. "My mother had four kids. My father was a professional jazz musician and he also owned an insurance agency so he was an absentee father," says Cheryl. "I remember even before I entered kindergarten hearing my mother cry at night and say, 'If it wasn't for you kids . . .' I remember her telling me many times, 'Don't have kids; it ruins your life.' That was such a powerful deterrent for me. I think she still feels the same way. She loves us kids very much, but she told me she likes us more now that we are adults. The three girls got that message: none of us have kids."

Another influence on these women's feelings about having children is their place in the family pecking order. Women who were the oldest children in their families—especially when the families were large—want children less than their younger siblings do, and only children want them least of all. Only 50 percent of the only children, and only 55 percent of the oldest children, want a child very much, compared to 67 percent of those who were the middle or youngest children.

Women who were the oldest children in large families experienced in an intimate way all the hard work and responsibility that motherhood entails, and that has often influenced them against it. This is true of Patricia, forty, a congressional investigator who only in the last year has come to want a child. "I'm the oldest of seven. It's an Irish Catholic family, needless to say," she adds. "We were not poor. We lived in a huge house with seven bedrooms and seven bathrooms and a three-car garage; we belonged to a country club and had a summer house and went to Catholic school.

"My poor mother worked so hard all the time. My father never changed a diaper, never carried out a dish, would step out of his clothes and leave them on the floor. He was the role model for everyone else—dumping on my poor mother. Part of my thinking was that this was how having children had to be. Having a family was very chaotic and my mother looked so old and so tired and I thought, Why would you ever want to do this? She didn't have much help; someone came to do the ironing and to clean, but as soon as the woman got done, it started all over. I pitched in and helped a lot and took the kids places because my mother was too tired to go. I was the only one of us who wanted to travel. And I felt that a family and travel were mutually exclusive."

Only children have the opposite problem: they can't envision themselves as mothers because they were never around babies and children, and they don't know how to react to them. They just don't get that rush of maternal feeling other women do. "I'm not your typical mother, your typical maternity patient," says Augusta, who is pregnant with her first (and, she says, only) child. "If a woman brings a baby into the office, all the other women jump up and go, 'Oooh!' I don't have those feelings. I've never been around babies; I don't have any siblings; I don't have any cousins; there are no relatives with babies. I don't consciously feel uncomfortable, I just have no interest. But I'm looking forward to mine. Now that I'm pregnant, I find myself smiling and nodding at a baby and I say to myself, 'Oh God, I hate women who do that!' "

Meredith, thirty-nine and a bookkeeper, another only child, who had her first and only child when she was thirty-seven, had much the same feelings: "When I was younger I didn't know anything about children, or ever have anything to do with them. I suppose I must have done a little bit of baby-sitting in college, but that doesn't necessarily predispose you to wanting them. They seemed basically boring and uninteresting."

A woman's own family history is not the only influence on her mind-set about babies and children. Those that she comes in contact with as an adult also exert a pull—one way or the other. Ten percent of the clock-watchers indicate that they turn away or ignore the babies of other women. But 54 percent report that they are feeling more tenderness, wanting to touch or even hold them. Dean, thirty-one, a foundation program officer, finds this is true of herself. "I was never fond of babies; I'm still not," she says. "But I am a little bit better about liking babies than I used to be. Up to age twenty-six, I wasn't interested; I am more interested now and enjoy holding them a bit more, but I'm still glad to give them back to their mothers. I never have the feeling that I want to take a baby home with me. I think it's coming, but very slowly. I want to touch a little more, hold a little more. My husband is much better with kids than I am; he has a crew of neighborhood kids who follow him around."

Even women who very much want a child don't like all children. Helene, thirty-two, a secretary, feels very much this way. "I have very little patience," she says, "and after two hours with friends' kids I feel like hanging them up. Everyone says it's different when it's yours, but what if it's not? We went to

London on vacation recently. In stores and restaurants over there there are signs that say, Parents Must Control Their Children, not like over here where they only say, Children Must Be Accompanied by a Responsible Adult. The children in Europe are so well behaved. I like that. I've always thought of a child as a little person, not as a goo-goo, ga-ga."

Those Important Husbands

Two people do, after all, come together to make a child, and when the relationship seems uncertain, or the female half of the duo thinks that if she gets pregnant it might harm her marriage, she doesn't want to risk it. One or the other of these conditions holds true for 16 percent of the clock-watchers.

On the other hand, the longer a woman has been with her partner, the more she worries that having a child will harm their well-established relationship, and the more ambivalent she becomes. Over 30 percent of the women who have been married more than ten years feel this way, compared to only 8 percent of those who have been married less than two years. Ellen, thirty-one, an artist and illustrator, says, "Our ten-year relationship has been a wondrous experience which continues only to improve with time. A great deal of effort and love has been invested to make it work. We marvel at our happiness. This leads us to wonder whether having children is a good idea. Will they enhance our marriage or interfere with a very secure partnership/friendship?"

Even when a woman definitely wants to have a child, she can still worry about what it will do to her marriage. This is true for Evonne, twenty-eight, a division manager of an interior design department, who has been married for four years and has seen some bad effects of parenthood on the marriages of her friends. "We've worked really hard; we're getting ready to build a house; we've really set everything in order. But that's the scariest thing. Everyone we know is doing that—working it out just the way they want to do it. And then the time comes to have the kids, and either it turns out you can't, or if you do, it's the biggest shock what it does to the marriage. Here you were, these coordinated, precise individuals, and the kid throws you haywire. The biggest thing I've noticed with some of my friends is that they wait five to ten years to have a child, and up to that point their husbands have done 50 percent of everything. They think they know how it's going to be once the child comes. The husbands even claim they'll still do 50 percent. But the women keep working full-time or part-time, and suddenly the husband turns into a husband who cuts the grass on the weekend and reads the paper at night, and the wife reverts to 'the wife.' Boom, it's back to tradition.

"I asked my husband, 'Are you going to do that to me?' We like to get things out in the open. He said if I am working full-time, he'll help just like he does now. If I'm working part-time, he expects I'll take more responsibility. And if I stay home full-time, then he feels my job is the home and the child."

Miranda, twenty-nine, an advertising and sales promotion director, has convinced her husband that she can try to get pregnant in the next year, but she worries about having time together once they do. "We've got a really neat relationship; we're good together, and I'm concerned. I understand that having a kid throws you into hyperspace. I'm afraid we're going to lose the only time we have together. We both work upwards of twelve hours a day. Obviously, something is going to have to give. Sunday mornings are our very good time together; I understand Sunday mornings go away. Since there is so little quality time for us now, I'm nervous. How does it fit in? It totally changes the way you relate to one another."

One note of comfort to these women is that 84 percent of all the mothers who had their children once the clock started ticking are still with their husbands—parenthood did not steer the ship of marriage onto the proverbial rocks.

When their husbands aren't ready for fatherhood—a situation facing 24 percent of the clock-watchers—they have not taken matters into their own hands, but instead have waited for their spouses to resolve their ambivalence. These women need to have the solid support of their mates in this extremely complex life venture. In order to be able to offer that support and feel comfortable about becoming fathers, some of these men simply want more time within the marriage. As men are married longer, they gather the strength to overcome their fears.

What is so frightening about fatherhood? Tim Page in an "About Men" column in the New York *Times Magazine* beautifully delineates some of the psychological ramifications for this generation.

For a man, the decision to become a father is, in some ways a *memento mori.* It is an admission of our own mortality. We resign our supremacy in the vanguard, and take up the good fight for someone even newer, even more helpless than ourselves. Yet it is also a supreme affirmation. I have heard it said that all young men believe in their primacy, but it sometimes seems that the members of my age group came to maturity believing—silently but profoundly—that these were the final days; that we were to have no sequel. Our fear of immediate extinction has caused many of us to pass through life as though it were an endless Sunday brunch, grasping out halfheartedly at trends and textures. I have spent my share of time mouthing the platitudes of nihilism, while secretly frightened of caring too deeply. If you hold on to nothing, little can be taken from you.

Many of the men married to clock-watchers have not probed so deeply into their psyches for the cause of their reluctance. They have instead found good reasons for waiting staring them in the face. Finances are a big one—a sort of traditional impulse from the days when men were the providers. Another is the place a man finds himself in his career. If he doesn't feel he's made it yet, he wants to postpone fatherhood. Sandy, twenty-seven, a management associate at a New York bank, is facing this kind of reluctance in her husband. "It has to do with his success," she says. "It's not that having kids will curtail what he wants to do, but he's a writer, and he's also working full-time. He took a year and a half off to write a novel which hasn't been published. He's now a copywriter for one of the networks in advertising. He wants to write a book, he wants to be a novelist, he wants to write a TV show, he wants to be a sitcom staff writer, or whatever. Once he feels like his real career is well on its way, I think he'll feel more settled and be able to say, 'Now my life is doing what I want it to do. Now I can add a child.' He also feels too young. He's told me that he should have married a younger woman; he's a few months younger than I am. And my biological clock is screaming."

Marcy has been married eight years to a man who presented her with a multitude of reasons why they should wait—all of which turned out not to be the real reason at all. "For me it was never an issue of if I would have kids, but a question of when I would have them. My husband used a lot of excuses to postpone it: I smoked, and I quit smoking. Let's buy a house, let's pay some bills, let's save some money. And we did all these things on schedule, but we got no closer to being ready. And every time I'd bring it up, there was always something else on the agenda. He had this endless list. He didn't want to have to tell me, 'I don't want to have kids.' "

Another big issue that causes husbands to delay is children from a prior marriage, especially if he has a difficult relationship with them, or problems with his ex-wife about seeing them. "At thirty-one I met and married my husband and am thinking much more about getting pregnant," says Louisa, thirty-two, a teacher. "My husband married young and has two children from that marriage. He really seems to have mixed feelings about another child, especially since he's enjoying his present 'newlywed' freedom, and his relationship with his children is really strained. I wonder if because he has children it will take away from the excitement of our 'firstborn.' I also worry that I'm forcing him into another child he really doesn't want. And the biological clock ticks on . . ."

Hillary, twenty-eight, the proprietor of a store, is facing the same kind of reluctance on her husband's part. "Marrying a man with children from a previous marriage is a large deterrent to planning more children," she says. "My husband has had great problems regarding visitation with his children since our marriage. This conflict with his ex-wife and the frustration he feels at not being able to see his children brings on anxiety that the same thing could happen again. This leads to reluctance on my part to push him into having a child of our own, and my philosophy of 'Oh, well, maybe I can wait a few years.' "

The clock-watchers faced with reluctant husbands seem to take one of two tacks in dealing with them. Some women, like Louisa and Hillary, seem to fear pushing their mates at all. They let the subject slide. Others bring it up for discussion on a regular basis in hopes of some resolution. Lana, thirty, a computer sales representative, has worried about being pushy, but she also didn't want to table the discussion just because it made her husband uncomfortable. "In the beginning we didn't talk about it too much," she says. "He was under a combination of career and personal pressures. He'd gotten into sales just three years ago and switched companies nine months ago, and he had problems at work. He was also feeling a weight of responsibility because I wanted to start our family. One night he woke up with an anxiety attack, and we went to one of these emergency units. That's when he started counseling. I pretty much left it up to him to work it out with the counselor. I felt if I pushed him and he wasn't ready, he'd resent me and we'd end up even farther apart," she says. "So I'd bring up the subject every couple of months. At one point he said to me, 'Why do you keep bringing this up?' I said, 'Hey, I'm in sales. If you don't ask for the order, you don't get it. If you want me to go away for a month, I'll go away for a month, but then I'll come back and ask you again.' "

Sandy thinks she brings up the subject too much for her husband's liking, but she can't help herself. "I don't think it runs cyclical with my period, but I talk about it too often," she says. "He doesn't get mad. But he has said, 'I'm not ready; we're not having kids yet; I can't deal with something two years off.' We just had this discussion at breakfast this morning. We were talking about money and savings, and I said that in a year and a half I wanted to get pregnant and he pushed his chair back from the table and crossed his arms and said, 'Do you know what you just did?' He just can't deal with it right now. In a year and a half he'll have to deal with it."

Talk, Talk, Talk

When both members of a couple are indecisive about the issue of children, more often than not they avoid having serious discussions about whether or not they are going to become parents, and if so, when. They don't truly air their hopes and fears about parenthood, the new relationship it will forge between them, and how they see the new roles they will play. Instead, they skirt the issue, talking in circles, getting no nearer to the center of their dilemma. "I find myself shouting for my husband to come in and look at this commercial with a little baby on TV. 'Oh, isn't he darling,' " Cheryl confesses. "My husband is gagging. He's just about as hung up on the subject as I am, but I think he's less ready. He's a teacher and he coaches the high school tennis team and he runs children's art camps. He'd be an excellent father. But he says he'd have trouble coming back from school refreshed and ready to give his energy to children at home after being with kids all day. There'd be no escape.

"We go on these long walks sometimes and we'll be flipping stones into the water, and laughing and telling jokes and singing a song, and one of us will look at the other and say, 'Wouldn't a child enjoy this?' So there seems to be a real missing element. We talk about it a lot, most of the time laughing at each other about how hung up we are on the subject. But we do a really fine job of avoiding any real deliberation. I don't want to put any pressure on him. But the more we talk, the clearer it is to me that we should have a serious discussion instead of just teasing each other."

Sometimes the clock-watchers know a point in their lives is coming when a serious discussion will naturally have to occur. Until then, their mutual ambivalence keeps the subject from getting the full treatment. This is true for Sally, who has been married since she was twenty-one, and her husband. "I think my husband does want a child at times. He'll say, 'Wouldn't it be nice?' and we have been thinking about it," she says. "That has really been in the past two or three years. We went through a separation almost five years ago. We got back together after nine months and since then I guess our marriage has become stronger. I look at things differently now. He'll see a little kid and he'll say, 'Isn't he cute; wouldn't it be nice for us to have one?' and I'll say, 'Yes, in some respects it would, but think about this: number one, number two, number three . . .' I can name reasons not to. So we're kind of both ambivalent about it, probably me more than him. I think that if something happened and I did get pregnant, he would be very happy, whereas I honestly don't know how I'd react. At this point nothing has made me change my inclination not to have one.

"I have to make a decision next June. My doctor is stopping the pill because of my age. Am I going to have a tubal ligation? Should my husband have a vasectomy? That's a decision we're going to have to make. It's kind of scary because it's so final. We'll probably use some other form of birth control because I don't think I could make the decision to have a tubal ligation and I don't think I can ask my husband to have a vasectomy. I know what happened before when we were separated and if something should happen and things didn't work out, he'd be stuck. Suppose he found someone else? This decision point is going to make us sit down and discuss it in a way we haven't before. If he wanted it more than he has, it might influence me to go ahead. But I'd have to let him know what my thoughts are, my concerns. I'd have to bring all of them to his attention, and then we'd have to make a decision."

Mary has set her financial goal for 1988 and doesn't feel a pressing need to have a serious discussion with her husband until then. "Once in a while I bring it up," she says. "My husband never brings it up—but maybe once a week or so I'll say, 'Do you think we'll ever have kids?' And sometimes he'll say, 'Nah, I don't think so,' and I'll say, 'I don't think we will either.' And that's it. Other times, we'll discuss it more. When we've been with relatives or friends who have kids, it's brought to our attention and we talk about it a little bit more. It's kind of funny, because I always thought he was more positive about it than I was. But it almost seems as if he's getting more ambivalent as I am getting more interested. I don't know. I asked him recently if he was perhaps getting less interested in having kids, and he said, 'Oh no, I'm about the same.' He's more of a family person than I am with all my activities; he's more of a home person. I'm hardly ever here. But he's not an emotionally expressive person, so it's hard to know what he thinks. You can't get much out of him.

"I think that if I made up my mind a definite yes, he'd be comfortable. I'm not sure I would be if he made up his mind a definite yes. I think both of us could live with a definite no coming from either of us. I've gotten to the point where I feel that if I'm supposed to have kids, I'll know it, intuitively. I sort of feel like I'm warming up to it, but if I got pregnant right now, I'd seriously consider an abortion. I go to a psychologist once in a while and hash over what is going on in my life. She asks if we're going to have kids and I say we talk about it but we're just not ready. I told her about my financial goal for 1988 and that then kids would be up for discussion."

Some clock-watchers have had serious discussions, but they have emerged from them with the issue unresolved.

"We talked about a year ago and there are a number of excellent books I found, some that were very nonjudgmental and good at getting out all the aspects of the way we felt," says Kim. "I think my husband grew up always assuming he would be a father without thinking about it very much. If I said that I couldn't do it, that there was no way, I think he'd support me in that. But I think he kind of really would like children. For a while after those discussions, I'd sit at work at the computers, when I didn't have to think but I had to be there, and I'd find myself drifting away and being terrified because there was this issue hanging over me. That has kind of gone away because there have been other more immediate decisions connected to moving into our new house which have taken over a bit. But it's still there. And we talk about it off and on."

When time is running out for a couple, it obviously forces the issue into the open—but knowing they have to decide doesn't mean that it makes it easier. Penelope, forty, a full professor who teaches technical writing, is about to get married to her high school boyfriend who has come back into her life in the last year. He is the father of two daughters, aged eight and thirteen, but her first marriage, which ended eleven years ago, was childless. "One of my regrets about getting divorced at age twenty-nine was that I thought I'd probably never have kids," she says. "But then I just didn't think about it for a long time because I was busy, and I was never the kind of person who wanted to have a baby badly enough to do it by myself. Forty seems really old to have kids, but one of my fiancé's charms is that he doesn't think of our marriage as starting over. He just thinks we're going back to where we should have been years ago, and why not give it a try. If we're going to do it, we better start trying right away. We need to make up our minds. I don't know. It would be a big step. I can't decide. We've just gone through a lot of that 'are we going to do this or not?' stuff. I talked to my doctor who doesn't think there is any physical problem, except that I'm crazy.

"I never baby-sat; I've never been around babies except my brother. I've changed one diaper in my whole life. That doesn't worry me particularly. The whole thing is so scary anyway, it can't get any scarier. Yet I've known people who aren't as competent as I am and they did it and the kids lived. You really can't do too much damage not knowing anything."

Pros and Cons

Throughout their twenties, and sometimes early thirties, this kid, this baby they might someday have, seemed to be waiting for these women across a great distance. Now, as the clock ticks louder, the distance has shortened, and with every month that passes, it grows shorter still. The journey is coming to an end. Now the baby is right in front of them. Do they reach out to touch it and gather it into their arms? Or do they fear the burden of responsibility, and the changes it will bring, and therefore pass it by? With the baby right in front of them, their conflict is much greater than it was when they saw it only from a distance. The closeness makes their desire for the baby, and their desire to avoid it, that much stronger. The conflict of emotions can be so intense that it can tie them in knots.

What are the payoffs of motherhood? they ask themselves. They know the risks: the imposition on time, energy, money, and space; the chores, the noise, the hassle; the sleepless nights; the end of privacy in their marriages. . . . Will nurturing a child, giving and receiving love, fulfilling their biological potential, be worth all that? How can a woman make a balance sheet of pros and cons out of such dissimilar items? Mary puts it succinctly when she says: "I can't see any logical reasons for having kids. But if you think like that you'll probably never have them because it isn't a logical thing. It's more an irrational emotional thing."

Martha, twenty-seven, an insurance agent, echoes these thoughts: "Right now my husband and I can't think of one good reason why we should have a child," she says. "We are not ruling it out for the future, but we don't see one in the near future. We don't feel it would be a good financial decision at the moment. We also enjoy being able to go on a moment's notice and would feel confined by a child. The strange thing about my hesitation is that I have always loved children and they seem very attracted to me. I practically raised my brother and I have enjoyed coaching youth sports. I'm even thinking of going back to college for my teaching credential. But there is something about the day-to-day routine and responsibility that frightens me. I just don't know if I'd be a good mother."

Some women postpone having a child month to month, and year to year, hoping the pros or the cons will tip the scale one way or the other. "I was thinking when I was twenty-five that I didn't want kids then but maybe later . . . and I've been thinking that way every single year since," says Dina, thirty-two, a lieutenant in the Navy. "I wish I would just accidentally get pregnant, and I had no decision to make, but that's impossible—my husband has had a vasectomy. We've been to an artificial insemination doctor, and my husband has signed all the forms. I could do it anytime I want to, but I haven't. I'm turned off by the method. I'm going through the military and they use the sperm bank at Silver Springs. The way they do it is only to match for blood type and race and if you are inseminated six different times, it could be by six different men. And then it's not frozen sperm; it's fresh hot sperm from that morning. Yuch. I want more remove.

"At the moment I'm leaning toward not doing it. But when I get bored with my job I think that what I ought to do is quit and have a baby. But then summer comes, when I get to travel—last year I went to Japan and Italy—it goes the other way. I've been seeing a therapist in a group situation in order to deal with this issue of whether to have a baby or not have a baby. I talked about it in my group and they said if I was turned off by the method I probably didn't want to go through with it. But then I see that all these people my age are having children and I feel like they are all getting a new toy and I'm not going to get one. But as one of the women in my group pointed out, I could have one, I'm choosing not to."

Diana, twenty-nine, an executive director of a human services agency, who lives with her boyfriend, has more positive feelings about having a baby, but not enough to put her firmly in one camp. "In my twenties I didn't want to care for anyone else, I just wanted to do my own thing, and a baby seemed to be an intrusion in my life," she says. "I also had an existential feeling: Why bring kids into this horrible world? What good is that going to do? Sometimes I still feel that way—hearing about all the things that can go wrong with kids, seeing people who are having problems with their kids, or whose child is sick and their whole life ruined. I have a lot of love to give, but I'm not sure if I want to love someone quite that much.

"I go through periods when I really want a child, and I want one *now*, and I go through periods when I think—maybe, but not right now. I don't know why I change back and forth. I guess I want them when I'm around them a lot. Sometimes it seems to just wash over me. Then, again, one of my staff people just had a baby and she brought it to a meeting, and I didn't get that 'God, I have to have one' feeling I sometimes do. I think it's something that I want, but not right now.

"Even in my high periods when I really want one, the rationalist tends to come in. Sometimes I get lax about birth control, and then afterward I think, 'What the hell did you just do? You don't want this.' It's like there's something outside of me making me do these things. It's really strange when that kind of thing comes over me and I have to get myself back in control again."

PART II

BABY TIME

4

The Alarm Goes Off

This is the story of changing perspectives. For half of the clock-watchers babies were not a part of the picture they drew of their future selves. Although they didn't have a strong vision of themselves as mothers, almost 80 percent of them report that their feelings have changed radically in the last few years. Their clocks, which have been ticking quietly since puberty and for years have been easily ignored, are now deafening. They feel something significant is missing from their lives; there is an emptiness, a lack of purpose, a sense of their own mortality, a need to nurture—and they feel driven, sometimes physically as well as emotionally, to have a child before it's too late.

They may not be ready to go ahead tomorrow—career and personal issues may still stand in their way—but many are anxious to have a baby as soon as circumstances allow. In this change of heart they are very similar to the women who became mothers later in life: almost two thirds of them also found themselves doing an about-face in the years before they gave birth.

Some of the clock-watchers can't pinpoint their change in feeling because it has been so gradual. Often it is still in progress—a woman is not yet ready for motherhood, but she feels herself moving in that direction. "I'm a little more relaxed now, thinking that it would be OK," says Kim, thirty-five, a head medical librarian. "My husband and I have been married for two and a half years, a second marriage for both of us. He has no children either. The longer I'm in this relationship, the more I see that it's very solid and supportive, and I think it might work. It would probably be all right. The house we moved to this summer is, as far as we're concerned, our forever house, and so now I have a visual picture of where I am physically, and we have plenty of room. Realistically, I could do it with my career. I think my career would be all right. I have a number of friends who are also medical librarians who have worked out things like being a part-time department head. Every other mother has had to work through this; my mother had to do it.

"When I moved back here in 1977 after my divorce and I changed jobs, I thought that other people had been through this too; this wasn't any big deal. And I suspect I should remember that when I think about having a child. Sometimes I think a couple more years will resolve it. But I'm thirty-four, and how many more "couple years" do I have? My mother was thirty-five when I was born, and so I know what it's like to be the child of older parents and that part doesn't bother me a bit. And I don't worry about the medical part; I don't have anything in my history that would make any of this a problem. So I can kind of see myself coming around. Except that I can't quite bring myself to say, 'OK, let's do it.' "

For Kim, many factors are combining to make her feel more positive. More often, however, a clock-watcher can trace her new feelings to one experience or part of her life—her relationship with her husband, her sudden awareness of time's inexorable forward march, a change in her thinking about the importance of her career, a new exposure to babies or simply a desire to love one of her own.

The Manly Influence

Sometimes an unsatisfactory relationship with a man has made a woman come to grips with how she really feels about having babies. "I don't think I ever viewed myself as one of these women who 'love' children and couldn't wait until I had them," says Anita, thirty-four, a director of community services, who now has two and is hoping for a third. "But about the time I was twenty-five or twenty-six I was living with a man who had a lot of problems and I realized that I more or less took care of him. It dawned on me that if I ever wanted to have children, I'd better get rid of this guy and find someone else. That was the first time I knew it was something I wanted in my life, that I would like to have a family."

Even more often, a strong, positive, loving relationship with the right man has caused a woman to change. Janis, thirty-six, a sales planning manager who now has a three-year-old daughter says, "When I was twenty-eight, I got a huge attack of baby fever. About a year and a half before that I had hooked up with the guy I eventually married. I think once I was in that kind of relationship, and could see it as genuine, long-term, and fulfilling, that started the change."

Like a number of other women Sarah, thirty-five, a manager of information systems, went through a bad first marriage before finding the right man who wanted to have a family and changed her feelings. "With my first husband, a lot of my negative feelings about motherhood stemmed from his lack of desire for children, the type of person he was, and the competitive nature of our relationship," she says. "Because of those factors, I placed my career first and foremost. Probably compounding that situation was the fact that none of our close friends had any children. When I remarried, I was thirty-three, and by then I had undergone many changes, or maybe I had just found myself again. My second husband is a very understanding, sensitive, patient man and it was not difficult for me to see that he would be a wonderful father. Knowing that, knowing the biological clock was fast ticking away, and experiencing the joys that many of our friends (and my only brother) were now having with their children, I underwent a total and complete change in desire and attitude."

The Hands of Time

Sarah's concerns about time running out are voiced by almost half of the clock-watchers, particularly those who very much want a child. For some of these women, having a cutoff may indeed, in and of itself, cause a change of heart. Seventy percent of the women who are very anxious about time running out report that their feelings have changed for the positive, compared to 42 percent of those with only a mild concern about the months, and years, passing by.

Jack Brehm, a professor of psychology at Duke University, defined such a change with his Reactance Theory. Basically, it states that people attempt to maintain their freedom to act, and when this freedom is threatened, they do whatever they can to retain it. In the case of the clock-watchers, time itself is threatening their freedom to have a baby, and forcing them to make a decision. As they get closer and closer to the cutoff, the pressure to make a choice increases: it's now or never. Instead of choosing not to have a child, as they have all along, the pressure can cause them to change their minds, because only in this way are they able to maintain their freedom. Wanda, thirty-one, an accounting supervisor, says, "I think I've gotten less ambivalent because of age. It's true what you hear about the clock ticking, and I think age really does affect a woman. It's something you shouldn't do because everyone else is doing it. You've got to do it for the right reason, but age does enter into it—knowing you have to make a decision, that there's a cutoff."

Time pressure also changed the feelings of Meredith, thirty-nine, a book-keeper who recently had her first child nine months after getting married. "There certainly wasn't any single incident—a blinding flash that changed me," she says. "But I began thinking about children more. The chances are very good that it had something to do with my age. My friends were all talking about it. As all of us got into our mid-thirties, it was a constant topic of conversation. Going from a strong position against it, a lot of us began to shift slowly. I guess whenever you're faced with something that's an absolute finality—you either do it or you don't—you begin to really weigh your alternatives a lot more carefully and figure, 'Well, if I miss out on this, I'll be missing out on something I'll never know about or experience.' You can't just put it aside and then change your mind later."

Many of the clock-watchers speak about this new sense, which has come as they have gotten older, that if they don't have a child they will be "missing something." "Our decision to have a child was similar to any couple's in the post–birth control era. It was like any decision you make where you are giving up something forever," says Deborah, thirty-seven, a vice president and marketing director who had her son at thirty-five. "There was the question, Do I really want to do this? I did a lot of testing of my feelings to see if I was doing it because I somehow felt I had to. After a lot of self-examination, I realized I couldn't ever envision looking back on my life and picturing a scenario that did not include a child. I think that's what convinced me."

Cheryl, thirty-one, an assistant director of an industry council, whose mother spoke so negatively about the limits children put on her life, was astounded by this recognition that she might be missing something if she remained childless. "At age twenty-three, I approached doctors asking them to sterilize me and they refused; they said they wouldn't do it to someone so young who hadn't had a child. I'm glad now they didn't listen to me. All of a sudden, around age twenty-eight or twenty-nine I got zingy about kids. I began wanting to kiss every baby I saw on the back of the neck. The other day a woman drove by in a car with a little baby on her lap and she was holding the baby close to her face and kissing it and I just melted. Two women in my support group are therapists and they've told me I light up when I talk about children. My eyes get starry. I think part of it is that as I get older I'm more cognizant of what I might miss in my life. I realize I may be missing one of life's most worthwhile, most meaningful experiences. I'm more aware of my mortality than I was in my early twenties."

One barometer of Cheryl's change in feeling about motherhood is her parallel change in feeling about having an abortion: "I've always been very prochoice, and I always thought having an abortion would be a very clinical decision," she says. "But then before we were married we had a pregnancy scare. I grieved for the baby. It amazed me; I was heartbroken. It turned out that I wasn't pregnant, but if I had been, I doubt that I would have had that abortion."

The passage of time has also changed many of these women's feelings about motherhood by altering the way they view themselves. Once a woman feels she has accomplished what she set out to do in her life and sees herself as a mature adult who is comfortable with herself, having a child can come to be viewed as a positive act instead of a negative one. Motherhood no longer seems like a trap because the clock-watchers have been independent and successful. The role they've discarded can now be added to their lives.

"It took about ten years after I left home for me to have a change of heart about having children," says Mindy, thirty, a pilot with a major airline. "I had pretty much raised my little brother, and I felt that that kept me from doing a lot of things. I guess, after I had my career well established, and I was doing what I wanted to do, it didn't seem as if it would hamper me at all. What changed is that instead of thinking about what kids could keep me from doing, I started to think of what I could do with them."

The same was true for Connie, thirty-six, a sales representative, who is pregnant for the first time. "I was finally ready and desiring motherhood," she says. "I needed to resolve the educational, career, and personal portions of my life first. I really believe that many women my age finally want children because they reach the 'ready' stage in their own personal development. They have fulfilled their own lives to the point that they are ready to give to a child."

Sometimes, these changed feelings about motherhood are related more to a new sense of maturity than to feelings of accomplishment. After her recent divorce, Rachel, thirty-five, an M.B.A. supervisor, found her "thinking had undergone a metamorphosis. Until recently, I did not want children. However, as I've gotten more confidence in myself, I feel a desire to share what I've learned and experienced with the next generation. As I've been growing and expanding, going from being very introverted and shy, to being more outgoing, more sure of myself, my perception of children and parenthood has changed."

Anne, thirty, a director of marketing, says, "I expected to be in the Never-Want-a-Child camp. I was surprised how much I wanted one. I wasn't thinking about children when I got married; I wasn't thinking about marriage when I got married. Having children was something that adults did. I waited not so much to get settled in my job as to get settled in myself. I wasn't ready to tackle both. I'm not waiting anymore. I'm ready now, and we're trying. I think you're either ready to do it or you're not. It's not a staged process."

Pam, twenty-eight, whose mother gave up any life outside the home for her children and her marriage, has come to the same sense of herself. "When I was in my early twenties I felt very strongly that I never wanted to have children," she says. "I think it was because I felt I would never be able to express myself, or pursue my own dreams if I did. It started changing four or five years ago. Toward the end of graduate school, I really grew up in a lot of ways. I started to teach, and I started to feel that I wasn't so much at the whim of forces beyond my control, that I could control my own life, and I had more confidence in myself. It didn't seem as if having a child would make me lose control the way it had before."

For Patricia, forty, a congressional investigator who is the oldest of seven children, the change was triggered by her mother's death, which made her take a new look at herself and what was important in life. She had always wanted to travel and be free, and she had rebelled against her mother's belief that it was her destiny to become a mother. "It was really my mother's only expectation for me, and that was a major reason I was not eager for children," she says. "It wasn't until she died last year that I even began to think about the option. When I was younger I only saw the responsibility. Now I see the possibilities—that you're giving up less than you are getting in return. It just doesn't look like it would be that awful prospect it once was. I've had a great deal of freedom, and freedom is boring to some extent. Also, getting older, and knowing how final that is, and that the possibility will not exist, and may not now, has affected me. It's been very interesting how my mind has gone full circle."

Mid-life Crisis

The clock-watchers have made a commitment to their careers that has been every bit as strong as a man's. Does that mean they are subject to the same kind of mid-life career crisis that many men go through? The answer is yes—

with a twist. A fair amount is known about men's mid-life crisis. As they approach forty and realize they will not be among the 5 percent to make it to the top, they often experience a drop in their commitment to work. Jobs simply do not hold the same significance in their lives that they once did. In order to renew their feeling that their endeavors are important, many men make a career switch—typically around age thirty-eight.

For baby boomers this promotion squeeze is tighter than for other generations simply because there are so many of us. It means that more of us will end up in jobs that don't satisfy us. In *Great Expectations,* Landon Jones reports that 68 percent of those who want to express themselves in their work, and 77 percent of those who want to be challenged, will be disappointed. S. P. Hersh, M.D., a practicing psychiatrist and former director of the National Institutes of Mental Health, has described this state of mind in *The Executive Parent.* "Despite all the rituals, awards, and incentives with which we surround ourselves, [we realize that] rarely will our work have any lasting significance. This factor may partly explain why many of us existing in the modern technocracy have a deeply felt need for some sense of continuity. We need to feel involved with something that frees us from our . . . relative insignificance."

When career women come up against these feelings, they have a whole other unexplored area of life in which to find continuity and significance: motherhood. Suddenly what was viewed as a negative that could wreak havoc on a career may be seen as an important life experience. A number of the clock-watchers, married and single, have undergone a shift of feelings about the significance of their careers, which has in turn made them reconsider what is important in their lives, opening them up to the possibility that children would be a positive addition. "I sometimes feel, 'So what that I have this career and I have this education.' That stuff is not enough for me now," says Laura, thirty-one, a family therapist and marketing director whose mother urged her away from early marriage and motherhood. "Five years ago it was enough. But when women have been actively pursuing a career, they find themselves in the same place men were, only we called it a mid-life crisis when men had it. Now it's called the biological clock. You feel, 'This is it?' After you bump around in the world for a few years, you feel, 'This is what I wanted so badly?' It's interesting, and I wouldn't change what I've done for anything in the world, but I'm at a turning point and I see that I don't necessarily need for the next ten years to be like the last ten years. I've had a lot of fun and accomplished all my goals, the big ones anyway, and now I can see my life changing to accommodate a child within the next three years."

A similar set of feelings rose up in Jessie, thirty-six, who has a Ph.D. and is teaching at the college level. For her, they were triggered by having finally accomplished what she set out to do in her career. "For the first five years of our marriage we wanted my husband to get a vasectomy," she says. "Then in about 1982, after being promoted to middle management and completing course work for my doctorate, I began to ask myself if that was all there was in life. Within a few weeks, we were both very excited about the prospect of raising a family." Unfortunately for her and her husband, this was no easy task. They are an "undetermined case" of mid-life infertility, and three years later are still childless.

Single women may suddenly feel that the parts of their lives they have put on the back burner—marriage and motherhood—are more important than the careers they have built their lives around. When asked if they would track their lives along the same course, less than half of them said they would, whereas two thirds of the married clock-watchers would follow the same life path. Carrie, thirty-eight, the managing editor of an industry magazine, is one who would have done it differently. She believes her concentration on her career has cost her marriage and motherhood, and at this point in her life, that career doesn't seem so all important anymore. "I see myself as a typical product of my times—putting career first, being career-minded," she says. "I tell the young women at work to get married and have their children and then have their career. Women in their mid-forties write to Anne Landers and cry about having given up so many years to raise a family and be married, and now they have the empty nest and they haven't been trained for anything and they don't know what to do. I say, "BS, don't cry to me. At forty-five, you still have twenty years to put in and have a wonderful career. At forty-five, you can't be sure of having two or four children. I've given up all that for a career.

"I've put a lot of time into my profession, and I love it. But I've finally reached a point where I realize it's just a job. I have fame to some extent, but so what. If I left this industry for a year, I'd go back and people would say, 'Carrie who?' But a child is a permanent thing, a part of your life. I look at my great-aunt who is seventy-nine and I see her as a victim of her times—back in the days when she was young, one daughter stayed home to take care of the invalid parents. As a result she never married. I grew up in the sixties and seventies and I'm a victim of mine—what has happened to me is the typical thing that happened to women."

Baby Lust

Many of these clock-watchers have found that at least part of the reason for their change of heart is the end of the isolation of their youth—when they didn't know people with children or even see many children. Being around babies and toddlers has made them want to be mothers themselves. Almost half of them report that they have a strong physical desire to touch and hold babies. They also find themselves thinking a lot about having a baby of their own—over 80 percent of the women who have experienced this change of heart think about having a baby more than once a week.

"Lots of my friends and relatives have children, and that's played a large role in my new thinking because children are much less foreign to me now," says Anne. "When I mention having a baby it's a little more real—I've held lots of them and hung out with lots of them for hours at a time. It was hard for me to imagine wanting a baby three or four years ago when I wasn't hanging out with them. Now I see them two or three times a week. I have an actual relationship with these children."

Sometimes it's one particular child who has caused the change. Dorothy, twenty-nine, a joint data base coordinator, says she always thought she'd have children someday, but her boyfriend wasn't interested. "When we were involved, there were so many things we wanted, and I thought maybe I wasn't cut out to have children," she says. "He had always been sort of cool on the subject. So it was something I put to the back of my mind—saying, 'Well, maybe I won't have children. I don't know.' Then my brother and sister-in-law had a baby and that changed everything. From the moment I saw that baby I knew that was something I wanted to experience myself. My sister-in-law went into labor and my parents and I went to the hospital so we could be there when the baby was born. I was so charged up about it because we got to see him right away. They brought him in to be cleaned up and suctioned and weighed and we saw all that. It was really exciting." Her boyfriend had a negative reaction to her excitement—"he didn't even want to hear about it"—which made Dorothy realize there was something fundamentally wrong between them. She broke up with him two months later, after a six-and-a-half-year relationship. Now, she says, "I'm at a point in my life where being able to experience my friends' children or my nephew is fulfilling something in me. When I'm around women who are pregnant, I find I feel I'm missing out on something—all the changes and experiences of being pregnant, anticipating the birth and getting excited. And I find myself thinking that it is something I want."

When she was young, Barbara, twenty-nine, a dean of students at a small Midwestern college, didn't want a child. But then, five years ago, she met the baby who changed her mind. "I was working as a hall director and one of my colleagues who lived in the residence hall in the apartment right next to mine had a little baby named Joshua, whom I met when he was two months old. For two years we lived right next door to one another and worked together and ate all our meals together. So for two years I was with Joshua every day and I watched him grow up and witnessed his development. The whole thing made me realize what a miracle it was, and it made me want one of my own."

Getting to know her husband's five-year-old nephew changed Stephanie, thirty-five, who now has two small children. "When we got married, I was the one saying I didn't know if I ever wanted to have kids," she says. "My husband said, 'We'll just see what happens.' He never pushed it one way or the other. Then one summer we had a week's visit from his nephew. It did something to me. Of course, whenever we went places, people thought I was his mother. I was a teacher, and I'd taken care of kids in that capacity. But this was a child who was related to my husband, and it was different. It was interesting to think about the genetics. And it was interesting to take care of him, to realize he had to be refueled every few hours, and if you didn't do that, he'd fall apart. One night he fell asleep at the table and his face went right into the food. It was a whole new ball game. He was fun, and I had a good time with him. I took him to the library, and we went to the beach together as a family. That visit was in August and I got pregnant in October."

The Nurturing Need

In 1979 Betty Friedan wrote in the New York *Times Magazine,* "Motherhood, the profound human impulse to have children, is more than a mystique." Some of these women have discovered this is surprisingly true for them. They have been overcome by an unexpected, and overwhelming, need to create and care for a baby. "I expected to have children, but I didn't anticipate the emotional need to have children," says Hannah, twenty-eight, who is three months pregnant and changing careers to real estate. "I thought having children was something that came with being a woman, but I didn't anticipate that it would be something I would enjoy doing. The nurturing need was something I couldn't ignore. When these new feelings of wanting to be a mother first surfaced, it was killing me because my husband wasn't ready. It tore me apart."

These same feelings caught Caitlin, thirty-two, a video program coordinator, by surprise. "At about age twenty-six, while a relationship with a man was developing into a very good one, or so I thought, I was overcome with feelings of motherhood," she remembers. "I would intently watch mothers and their babies; I would stare at pregnant women, watching them breathe, watching their every move. I would read everything I could about having a baby and would spend hours looking at baby clothing in department stores. I had such an urge to have a baby then, probably because I believed that this relationship would lead to marriage and eventually to having children. When it suddenly ended, those thoughts and feelings did not, and I literally had to beat them back to get them out of my mind, to stop them from tormenting me so!"

Like Caitlin, most clock-watchers who talk about their need to have a baby are very emotional about it. Helene, thirty-two, a secretary, says, "I've wanted to be a mommy since I was a baby. But damn if I can describe the urge I feel now. It's not physical, but it's an overwhelming desire. If I'm with my husband and he's acting like a little boy, I'm overwhelmed with love. I want to hold part of him that we made together."

Gail, thirty-three, finishing her doctorate in psychology, speaks in the same way. "Once I realized I would finish my doctorate, I wanted to get pregnant. I was physically and emotionally tormented until we decided to have a baby. My husband actually decided the date we could start to try. I was crazy about the whole thing. I conceived my first ovulation. My immediate feeling was one of relief."

Accidents Can Happen

Sometimes a woman doesn't have the luxury of waiting for a change of heart but finds herself accidentally pregnant. This unexpected state of affairs can cause her to change her mind. This happened to Natalie, thirty-one, a consultant with her own marketing services company. She ended up miscarrying at four and a half months, but she says that "the pregnancy turned us around completely, and I think it was the only thing that could have. We had had long discussions about whether to have children or not. We knew we didn't want any until we were both settled in our careers. That happened when we were about twenty-four. Then, from about ages twenty-five to thirty, we'd have discussions about whether to start a family. As far as my husband was concerned, he liked things the way they were. He couldn't see any reason to bring children into it. I wasn't so sure. I just felt that there was more to life, and that I would be missing out on something if I was sixty years old and hadn't had a child. I love children. I'm a Brownie leader. I act like a big kid around kids. In a way, I was afraid that being a mother would change all that. All the neighborhood kids know I don't have any so I'm a pushover.

"When I took that little home pregnancy test, I was lying on the kitchen floor in hysterics crying. And my husband was saying, 'What's the matter? What's the matter?' He thought I had cancer or something. But it was just because I was so shocked. Then we debated an abortion for about a day because we plan everything and this didn't go according to plan. It only took that long to say, 'Why not now? We're thirty-one, we're old enough.'

"It wasn't too long before ecstasy set in. We were so excited, so happy, that the times we had discussed parenting as just a 'possibility' seemed light-years behind, and so insignificant. It was amazing, the doors that opened to us when people found out we were going to be parents. They had a new link to us, and they could share experiences." Since the miscarriage, Natalie and her husband have been trying to have a child again—so far without success.

Cynthia, thirty, a regional sales manager of her company, wasn't any more ready than Natalie when she got pregnant; in fact, things could not have been at a worse juncture at work because she had just undertaken a difficult new job. "I always knew I wanted kids," she says, "but who knows how long we would have put it off? There never seemed to be a good time. I had been using a diaphragm and then my sister-in-law, who had been using foam for quite a few years, convinced me it was just as good so I switched. I used it successfully for about a year and a half and then suddenly it didn't work. In my gut I knew I was pregnant before the test. I went to the doctor when I was about six weeks along and found out I definitely was. It was a terrific shock; I broke down in tears. I considered an abortion, but only briefly. I found out on a Friday and by Monday I knew I wanted to keep it. My husband and I talked a lot and considered all the different options. For years he was always making jokes that if I got pregnant I could always have an abortion. So when I found out I was, I feared that would be what he wanted. He felt quite the opposite when reality hit. We're both very happy someone made the decision for us."

Fear almost paralyzed Margaret, thirty-one, a director of marketing for a hotel chain, and her husband, and an accidental pregnancy was probably the only thing that could have gotten them off square one. "Motherhood . . .

how that scared me! For four years I had put that possibility as my lowest of priorities," she confesses. "Eventually, my husband came to accept that he would just have to wait to be a father. Naturally, when I did find out I was three months pregnant, it was a shock to everyone, but especially to him. I can still remember his words: 'Who gave you permission to get pregnant?' By then I was too ill with afternoon/evening sickness to remind him he was with me at the time. My husband was fearful of whether I could handle my new condition and still continue to work at a demanding job and still be wife to him. We suffered through many an argument, and at one point I went so far as to state that in order to save our marriage I would have an abortion. My statement frightened him as well as me. I really wanted to have this baby. From then on he was very supportive. We both came to realize we were scared at becoming parents."

Beatrice, thirty-five, a recreation therapist who has a three-year-old daughter, still doesn't know if she would ever have been ready to become a parent except by accident. "My husband and I had decided we weren't going to have any children, but we were not to the point where we were going to do something permanent about it," she says. "Neither of us was quite able to do that. But I was almost there when he said he thought he was bailing out on me, that he wanted to have a child. He said he was getting older and settling down and he felt more mature. He had done things he wanted to do, and he thought he needed a child to feel fulfilled. He sort of took on the female role. He began to try to talk me into it. He used really emotional ways, like, 'Can you imagine what a child of ours would look like?' And he'd start describing a little girl to me, and a little boy to me. I was partially drawn to it, but part of me was saying, 'You bastard. You changed on me and I can't handle this.'

"I was trying to buy time. I was very ambivalent. Part of me said, 'He wants this and I love him and I want to give him what he wants,' and part of me was saying, 'I just can't do this.' I was really trying not to face it. He was still trying to talk me into it and I was still holding out but I was beginning to feel more favorable toward the idea. We were trying to make some decisions, and I was trying to put it off when I magically became pregnant. I had just had an IUD put in. It was my third one and we knew we needed to use some other form of contraception along with that. We're not sure what happened, but maybe we made love in the night, which we have done, sort of dreaming it—but it was real.

"I began to suspect I was pregnant when I was on an outing and began to feel sick. I thought it was very strange. Someone said, 'You're probably pregnant,' and I said, 'No way.' But I was. I only went in for the test after a couple of other people said the same thing and I noticed that my breasts were sore. When the test was positive, I thought about an abortion for maybe five minutes. My spiritual beliefs, my values, just said I couldn't do that. 'I'm still ambivalent,' I said, 'but I'd rather deal with the child than deal with the abortion.' My husband was really afraid that I might want to abort, and he was trying to be understanding, but underneath, he was saying, 'Oh, please don't. Don't put me through this.' And I'd look into those pitiful eyes.

"I had to go through the whole thing of having my IUD taken out which could have caused me to miscarry. I had to stay in bed for forty-eight hours after they took it out. And I did stay practically flat on my back for that whole time. The embryo was attached very high in the uterus and the IUD was below it, so it didn't tear anything."

Time Is of the Essence

Many of the clock-watchers have not changed their feelings about motherhood because of the pressure of time, but the clock has propelled them into a state of readiness—into making a decision now. "We've just recently decided to start a family soon," says Nina, thirty-one, a secretary. "It's been on our minds for a while, but I had to make up my mind as to whether I was ready for it. I knew that I wanted to have children, but there always seemed to be time, later, in the future. Then one day I realized I'm thirty-one, and time goes by so quickly and the future is now."

Although Nina and her compatriots have a decade or more before the clock actually runs out, many of them have set the alarm to go off much earlier. They have two main reasons for doing so—not wanting to be "old" parents, and worries about the potential difficulty of getting pregnant or having a defective child as they grow older. Miranda, twenty-nine, an advertising and sales promotion director, feels a sense of urgency for both these reasons. "I'll be thirty in a couple of months and I've always looked forward to it and thought that everything is starting to come together. But I'm going into this pre-thirty depression—that I'm nowhere yet," she says. "The excitement has turned into disbelief that I'm really going to be thirty. Most of the women in my social circle are pregnant—two are due in March, one in April, and three in May. It's everywhere. I can't believe this thirty bull is really hitting me so strongly. I've always felt that I had a lot of time, and now I don't seem to. It's little things: I can't stay up as late as I used to be able to; I can't drink, and I used to be able to. I just really feel that I want to be a young parent; I don't want to feel that I won't have much time left with my husband after our kids are grown. I don't want us to be old parents. My father was an old father. He was fifty when I was born. My kids probably won't have grandparents for much of their lives.

"Also, my mother conceived once in her life when she was thirty-six, and although my gynecologist says her fertility has nothing to do with mine, it makes me very uneasy. I've never had an accident; I've never been pregnant and my husband has never gotten anyone pregnant. So I worry. It may take us a little longer. My friends say that everyone worries—that it's a normal fear. But you hear more and more about people who are having trouble."

Anne echoes these sentiments. "I'd like to have two kids, two or three years apart, and I don't want to have kids late in my thirties if I can avoid it," she says. "I'm getting more tired every year. I just don't think I want to fight those battles then. And I'd like to be less than sixty when my kids go to college. That's really the issue. And I'm afraid of the increased risk beyond a certain age. It would be ideal to have two kids by the time I'm thirty-five."

A number of the clock-watchers—all of whom want to have children— seem to want them now so that they won't have them around later. They talk about getting back to a prechild lifestyle while they have the money and the health to enjoy it. Martha, twenty-seven, an insurance agent, says, "My parents had us so spread apart that they are in their early fifties with two teenagers. I sense their fatigue and lack of patience and they seem so old and boring compared to the parents I was able to enjoy. On the other hand, my in-laws also had four children, but closer together, so they have none at home now and can enjoy early retirement, peace and quiet, vacations, etc. This is why I hear the clock so early. I don't want teenagers when I'm fifty."

Although she is desperate to have a child, and is smitten by all babies, Sandy, twenty-seven, a management associate at a bank, even speaks of "getting rid" of her kids while she is still young. "For me, having children when you are younger is the ideal thing to do. My parents had us when my mother was in her early twenties, and now they are fifty and forty-nine and they have three children out of the house. To me that's smart. I obviously am not going to be able to do that. But I want to have two and if I don't have one by thirty, I'll be having the second when I'm getting old physically. I don't want to be an old parent. When I'm in my fifties, I will have a lot more money and be able to do a lot more things, and I don't want to have kids to drag around."

Often these women's fears of infertility or birth defects are triggered by their friends' experiences, or the attention the world at large is paying to such issues. Sandy says, "Biologically, it's easier to carry a child with a younger body, and it's easier to get pregnant. A friend of mine who is thirty-four just had a Down's syndrome child, and that freaks me out. There are more problems with pregnancy. A friend who was twenty-eight had her baby die inside at six months. I have been pregnant once, so I assume I'm OK. Six months before I even want to try, I'll see my doctor and have my IUD out."

"I've seen so many of my friends get to thirty and say, 'OK, let's have a kid.' And they're really having problems getting pregnant, or they're experiencing miscarriages and stillbirths," says Evonne, twenty-eight, a division manager of an interior design department. "It does raise the question in my mind: Is it the environment? Is it waiting too long? I grew up near a nuclear plant, I'm on the pill, I tend to miss a balanced diet because of my work schedule, I am under a fair amount of stress, and Michigan's beef and fish are tainted with pollutants. I'd just really like to start my family before I'm thirty if I can."

Mindy, who had her son when she was twenty-nine, had those same fears. "The reason I had my IUD out was that most of my friends were taking six months to three years to get pregnant," she says. "They were having a terrible time because of being on birth control for so long. So I thought, 'Good grief, three years from now I can't even have two kids because I'll be so old when I have the first one I'll have to have them right after each other.' " Her fears were unfounded. She got pregnant right away.

While she was in graduate school in economics, Elizabeth, thirty, a financial economist who has a one-year-old daughter, was working for the ob/gyn department of George Washington University Medical Center. "I saw all the infertility patients coming in, and I was sure I had endometriosis. I had also heard that multiple partners along the way could cause problems, and I worried about that. It provided pressure to begin to at least try to see if I was going to have those problems or not."

Unlike most of these younger clock-watchers, Gillian, twenty-eight, an office administrator who has been married for nine years, has a medical reason for being pressured. She is a severe asthmatic, and the choices she faces are pretty grim. "My allergist and my gynecologist agree that my chances of dying from having a baby are high," she says. "I have been on cortisone steroids for a year and a half. In February, my ob/gyn commented that I may be sterile from this drug. My husband and I haven't used birth control in a year. We lost a baby seven years ago. I was only three and a half months along, but the doctors felt it wasn't getting enough oxygen. Our families have waited for years for a baby. We're both the oldest, and the first to get married. We still haven't told them about the miscarriage. They'd be heartbroken.

"Both of my doctors told me five years ago that I shouldn't have children in my thirties. My allergist says he needs a year's warning to help me get in physical condition and to wean me off some medications as much as possible. The deadline is now! And if I do try I may die. My husband says he really doesn't want children, but he's fabulous with them. I feel such pressure. For years I said no children, but now that my options are dwindling I can't think of anything else. What do I do? Decide not to have children and always wish I had? Become pregnant and maybe not live? Or just maybe have my health so damaged I may never recover? Yet I daydream, and I lie awake at night trying to decide. I'm still not sure what my decision will be. Knowing the dangers, why are my feelings toward having a child so intense?"

But even though they feel the pressure of time, less than half of the clock-watchers intend to get pregnant in the next year, and less than 20 percent of those who are ambivalent will take the plunge.

Ready . . . Get Set . . . Go

Much has been written by psychologists such as Erik Erikson about what it means to be ready for motherhood. He feels that when a woman reaches that point, she is ready for a stage of life in which the focus shifts from herself as number one to another human being, her child, for whom she accepts responsibility and who moves front and center in her life drama. It also means that she shifts her focus from the present, and her own immediate gratification, to the future, in which she has staked a new claim. Pamela Daniels and Kathy Weingarten in their book *Sooner or Later: The Timing of Parenthood in Adult Lives* talk about "a shift that is both a developmental moment in itself and a setting for subsequent growth and change."

Many of the clock-watchers have obviously hashed through issues such as the added responsibility for another person, but even when the decision is a difficult one to make, one they have been grappling with for a long time, they don't speak about their readiness in these terms. They don't see this step to motherhood as representing a shift of focus from themselves—although it may indeed be one. Instead, they feel ready because they have come to believe that what a child will add to their lives will be significant enough to be worth the sacrifices, and they are also willing to accept that they are entering a realm with no guarantees.

Jennifer, thirty, a public relations writer with her own business, passed through all the checkpoints in reaching her recent decision. She didn't want children at all through her early adulthood, and although her position had softened, she was still going back and forth in her mind whether to make the leap into motherhood when she answered the survey. Six months later she had more or less resolved her feelings. "In my first marriage I never wanted children," she says. "In fact, I used that as a way of getting out of the marriage because he wanted them and I said I never would and he'd be happier with someone else. When I was twenty-two or twenty-three I had a physician offer to sterilize me because I said I felt so strongly about it. I thank God now that I didn't.

"When I met my current husband, he said clearly he'd always felt he wanted children. I said I was sorry I didn't. We established a relationship knowing that. He resolved not having one. He loved me more. He would have made any compromises necessary. But as time went on, the idea of a family appealed to me more and more. He comes from a wonderful Jewish family in New York City, which is totally different from mine. Family is very important, and the values of family are really stressed. Having children is a wonderful joyous event. I know he would make a wonderful father. Nearly all our close friends have had children and we live in a wonderful neighborhood for children. I've also started my own business doing public relations writing at home, creating the perfect, flexible, career situation. I even got the travel bug out of my system with a big trip to France, from which we just returned. All the barriers have been removed.

"We're actually trying. It's been a general building feeling toward having a child, but I specifically chose the trip as a trigger to go ahead. There was no reason to put it off beyond that. Still I have ambiguity. I grew up as a loner and place great value on privacy and freedom. I fled from a small town, filled with the urge to travel and compensate for a noneventful youth. I'm afraid of the imposition a child will make on my time and energy, afraid there won't be enough to go around. I can't picture myself as a mother although that is waning gradually. I'm aware of the financial drain it will be and worry that I will miss my old freedom once it is too late.

"But something inside tells me these are needless fears (so does my husband). My life won't be restricted, but it should instead be fuller with a component I can't begin to envision but suspect will have its own rewards. I'm still scared to death. I'm just closing my eyes and jumping out of the plane and hoping my parachute opens. I'm just trying to have the confidence that it will be OK."

Unlike Jennifer, Renee, thirty-six, a regional administrator for a computer company, always pictured herself as a mother, but she also finds herself with unresolved ambivalence, even as she tries to get pregnant. "The decision whether or not to have a child has gone back and forth since I got married at age thirty, and I've been thinking about it since my early twenties," she says. "I always wondered when the time would be that I'd have children. When I got married and had my stepchild, I felt my husband needed time to get into a marriage again, and not suddenly have another child too. So we put it off. We talked about it and wondered if we were getting too old. He's going to be forty-three. Time goes by.

"Two years ago we decided not to have children and my husband was just about to have a vasectomy, but before he did he went to a sperm bank and made a couple of deposits in case we changed our minds. He didn't go through with the vasectomy, and we decided a year ago to try and it worked, but I had a very early miscarriage. And all of a sudden we were panicking again: should we, shouldn't we. I finally decided I was going to miss it. It's something I want. But I still worry that I'm making the right decision. As much as I've gone back and forth, and as much as I'm trying to have one now and want to do it, I do wonder if it's the right thing. I have a very happy marriage, and we enjoy the little free time we have. I enjoy just doing things alone with my husband. Maybe I have only 5 percent doubt, but when you're happy, you wonder: Is it going to make me happier? Am I toying with my happiness? But I do think it will add something to my life."

For many clock-watchers the decision has not been so agonizing. Circumstances, more than conviction or indecision, have kept a couple from heading in the baby direction. Naomi, thirty-one, a marketing research consultant with her own business, who is two months pregnant, recalls her journey: "My husband doesn't express his feelings very much, so when he does say something, then I know he really means it," she says. "I remember back when I proposed to him, I wasn't that interested in having babies. I was twenty-five; we were just finishing graduate school. And I sort of thought he wasn't into having babies either. But he asked me how I felt about it and said he'd like to have one. However, until very recently his career has not really been in place, so we hadn't given it much more thought. Now his position is financially secure.

"He is going to be forty next year and it was really more his biological clock than mine. We wanted to have a child before he was forty. I'm almost thirty-two and I've been reading all this stuff that a lot of women are waiting longer than that. If he'd been thirty-three, let's say, then I possibly might have thought about waiting longer. I might have given myself another couple of years. Yet everyone I know in my age range was having a baby, and I thought, 'Gee whiz, maybe I ought to do it too.' So earlier this year we talked about having babies again, and about four months ago we stopped using birth control."

Seeing the way other women are handling motherhood—the impact it is having on their lives—can also have a significant influence on a clock-watcher's feelings of readiness to join them. Naomi's decision was made easier not only because a lot of her friends were having babies, but because they were handling it in ways that looked appealing to her. "Until recently my only role models were my brothers and sisters who had kids. They were in traditional marriages where the mother stayed home full-time through the first ten years," she says. "But then I started getting new role models—friends who would take their babies to the movies and camping and everywhere, and it put very little crimp in their lives. And I started to really evaluate our social life. Most of it is kind of going over to someone's house and if you've got a baby and they've got a baby then it's really not a big deal. So in a sense, that's made it easier.

"Also, my friends with babies have pointed out a lot of the positive aspects. In comparison with all these women who had been through the experience and were raising children, I felt sort of young and naïve and I'd reconciled that we wanted to have some at some point, so I thought, 'Why not now?' "

Having a lot of friends with children also helped Jennifer make up her mind. "I see a lot of babies, and talk to friends who have just had them, and pregnant friends," she says. "It all serves to remind me that I'll have a network of friends going through it with me. And it's helped me see myself as a mother, now that I've decided to go ahead. I hold friends' babies and feel very maternal. We recently spent a whole weekend with friends who have a twenty-month-old. It was a revelation to me. He was a delight and he took to me, and I took to him. It was interesting to see the positive impact he had on their lives.

"I haven't seen any negative aspects to it yet. One couple with a month-old baby took him to a party on Saturday night. They're very portable. We have friends who handle it in different ways. Some totally restrict their lives because of children, but I'm able to see that it needn't be that way. It's what you make it. It doesn't have to restrict you. It's interesting; when you make up your mind about something, you try to support that decision. I think I seek out ways to support my new feelings rather than to refute them. It's obviously selective perception."

Taking the Plunge Together

Many of these women and their husbands are hand in hand out on the cliff and ready to jump. The water looks inviting—but hidden rocks may lurk below the surface. The sun is hot on their backs. They sidle up to the edge. They look at each other. "Are we going to step off?" They vacillate, they talk, they worry. Yes, no, maybe, not yet. Sometimes they just leave it to "fate."

Myra, thirty-four, a marketing consultant with her own business, now the mother of an eight-month-old son, and her husband were teetering on the edge for a long time. Their discussions lasted three years. "When we were first married, my husband was dead set against having children," she says. "It was primarily the responsibility that turned him off. He didn't see himself in that role, even though he's always been great with kids. In fact, a lot of friends of his were even surprised that he got married when he did. A lot of people saw him as a free spirit who would never settle down. The first years of the marriage were a big adjustment for him.

"We didn't talk about it too often until I became thirty and then I became more obsessed with it. By thirty-two, I wanted to make the decision. But he was the one who would say very seriously, at least once a month: 'What are we going to do?' He's four years older than I am and when he hit thirty-five and was approaching forty, he changed his mind. The impetus to do it came from him. He said, 'I think we should think about having a kid, and if we're going to, we should do it soon.' It didn't come as a great shock to me, because it wasn't all of a sudden. We'd been talking about it regularly. But we never got to the point where we made a conscious decision: 'Let's have a child; let's try.' We decided to stop using birth control and take our chances. And I became pregnant right away. I said, 'Gee, I could have done with a couple of months of trying.' "

Sometimes this do-si-do with the big decision bothers one partner or the other so much that they jump off the cliff pulling the other along with them. Even after Mindy and her husband agreed they wanted a child, he couldn't take the step. "We both wanted it but we were too afraid to admit we were changing our minds," she says. "In fact we just about split up because we both decided about the same time that we wanted families but we knew the

other one didn't. We didn't open up to each other about it because it seemed
like a closed subject. Even when we did admit it, he'd say, 'Let's wait a little
longer.' I'd say, 'Let's not wait too long.' I'm finally the one who went off
birth control and said, 'Well, I'm not on birth control anymore. What do you
want to do about it?' I got pregnant within a month—much faster than I
thought I would."

Tessie, twenty-eight, a software engineer who is now the mother of twins,
and her husband made their decision to leap together, but his desire for
parenthood was definitely a big influence on her willingness to do so. "I didn't
get over my concerns about our lifestyle until I had the babies. But we did
plan to have them," she says. "At first we thought, 'We don't want to have
children because we'll lose all of our friends.' Then we learned that our
current set of best friends, Bill and Carol, were going to have a baby, so we'd
be losing them anyway. We sat down and had a heart-to-heart and decided
that if we were going to have them, now was probably the best time. But we
still worried about the changes. My husband definitely wanted children more
than I did. If I hadn't had a partner who felt that way, I never would have
considered it."

For Pat, thirty-seven, a copywriter who had her daughter eight months
ago, her husband was the one who made the decision to leap. "We talked
about children before we got married and he said he really wanted to have
kids and I said I did too, but it wasn't a real emotional commitment. It was
sort of, 'Everybody does that. Yeah, I want to do that too,' " she says. "In
fact, I kept putting my husband off: 'Wait, wait, wait . . . Let's get used to
each other first . . .' Finally he asked, 'Are we ever going to do this?' We had
planned this trip to Disney World, and I said I didn't want to be pregnant on
our trip because I figured either I wouldn't look good or I wouldn't feel good.
So I said, 'Let's have our vacation and we can start trying when we come
back.' We had hardly walked in the front door, when he wanted to start. He
said, 'You promised. . . .' I always do what I say I will, and forty-five minutes later I was pregnant."

But sometimes husbands who have wanted to be fathers from the beginning
and finally convince their wives that this is a good idea, find themselves
taking a step back and questioning whether they really want to dive in after
all. Patricia, who decided after her mother died that she wanted to have a
child, found herself having to talk her husband back into it. "It's ironic that
he always wanted them from the beginning, but when I changed my mind, he
wasn't so sure," she says. "As he got older, he liked having all his time and
energy and money for himself. He has mixed feelings, and he's saying OK

partly because there is just a limited chance now. I also think he feels some anger that I waited so long to change my mind."

Convincing That Man

Usually the clock-watcher finds she is the one who is poised on the edge, ready to leap, and her husband is hanging back with excuses for waiting, or refusing to even discuss it. Most women faced with such reluctant husbands have gotten them to agree eventually. For some of them, the task has been relatively easy—their strong commitment has been enough to convince their partner. Denise, thirty-nine, a full-time mother starting her own business from home, got married at thirty-seven for the first time and had a child nine months later. "I suppose we started talking about children after dating for six to eight months. He was pretty neutral on the idea," she says. "But by the time we got engaged, he definitely wanted to have children. And now that we've had one, he's dying to have another. He changed because I think he knew how much I cared about having children, and I was extremely confident about how wonderful it would be."

Deborah is married to a man who was initially very ambivalent because he has three grown children. "Then, as our friends started having children and he started seeing me around children, he saw how much it meant to me and he changed," she says. "Even before our son was born two years ago, he came to consider this experience a very different one because his three children were born in an era when fathers didn't participate as much as they do now. He was very young, traveling three nights a week, and on the way up the ladder; he never saw his kids. And he was married to a woman who said, 'Daddies don't do that; Mommies do.' "

For Marcy, thirty-one, a sales representative whose husband kept adding to the agenda of what they had to accomplish before they had children, it was a much longer haul before he turned around and headed toward the edge. Her first step was to convince him that they should have counseling. "I didn't want to end up forty and bitter and have the relationship end that way. And I didn't want to force him into it and wreck our marriage," she says. "The counseling was very helpful. It was the two of us together with a married couple who are both ordained ministers. The man had done his doctorate on a special program for couples. It consisted of twenty-five questions that we answered in writing individually while they observed our body language.

Then the counseling session consisted of going through the questions—my husband reading his answers and me reading mine. It started out with pretty general things like, 'What's something I always wanted to do but know I'll never have the chance to?' It got into 'Who's been the most influential person in my life?' and 'What do I like best about my spouse and what do I like best about myself?'

"When we started the counseling, the counselors told us they knew we were going to be a special couple because our communication and our relationship was already at a place where they try to bring couples during counseling. We just had this one major issue that was troubling us and that's why it was so difficult. My husband's feelings about having a child came out in counseling. He was afraid that if I didn't want to go back to work, he wouldn't be able to provide us with the kind of lifestyle we'd become used to with me working and no children. He was afraid he'd feel like a failure as a provider. He was also afraid of losing me, of changing our relationship, and that was a fear I shared, because we do have an excellent relationship. We've been married for eight years and we've been together for twelve, and we're used to just having each other. Also, both our families are back in the Midwest, so basically it's just the two of us.

"One of the questions was 'Ten years from now I see myself as————.' I said, 'John, why don't you go first.' And he said, 'In ten years I see myself as a father.' It was the first time he had admitted it. There was a lot of crying and hugging and everything. Then the counselors asked me how I felt about it and I said, 'Gee, it kind of puts the ball back in my court.' I had to realize that I was trying to make John the heavy: if he didn't want them, it was easy for me to want them because it wasn't going to happen. I also felt that I was getting my way again. I felt confused. I felt like I was a Cheshire cat. But my husband is not one to bow to pressure. Once we talked about it, I realized he does want it. He's gotten kind of used to the idea. He was really afraid of tiny newborn babies; he said if he could go down to the store and get a three-year-old, he'd have no problem being a father. He's an only child, and he was married before when he was nineteen and she was seventeen and they had a baby and lost it; it was premature and hydrocephalic. He says it doesn't affect him, but I can't imagine that it doesn't.

"Since the counseling, he's talked about it with some of the people he works with—he's the boss—and his secretary comes in every day with some tip on how to get pregnant. I was being pretty secretive about it because it was a real emotional issue. I only told these two close friends. But then we'd talk to people and they'd say, 'Are you pregnant yet?' and I found out he was talking about it. Now people are saying, 'You'll be a wonderful father,' and he's worried about that. But I think he's father material. That's one of the reasons I've wanted to have a child with him—he's a really strong figure.

"We're now getting in position financially so when the time comes I don't feel I have to go back to work in six weeks but can take three or six months off. We're going to start trying in six months. By then we'll be thirty-two and thirty-six. I guess more than anything, we'd put off the issue of children for so long that something had to be done. We needed to find out if that was where we were going. I'm real glad it turned out this way because I wouldn't want to leave my husband. I'm not sure I would have, and I'm glad I don't have to find out."

When her husband didn't want to talk about the subject, Lana, thirty, a computer sales representative, brought it up monthly anyway, and finally, after he went for counseling on his own, he started to slowly approach the edge. "At first he didn't want me to go off the pill; we had agreed on January, and he wanted me to wait longer," she says. "Then a month later he said it was OK, I could go off it. Then we used the alternative methods and at the end of the three months he still wasn't ready to make the commitment, but he would start taking chances. I would be the one saying, 'Wait a minute, let me go upstairs and get the foam,' and he'd say, 'Nah, let's not worry about it.' I'd kid him about it: 'I think you just want it to happen so you don't have to take the responsibility of saying, "Yes, I made a conscious decision."' Then the following month, the day I thought I ovulated, I casually mentioned it and he said, 'Well, let's go for it.' It's not something we ended up talking about in detail."

Emma, thirty-four, an advertising executive, never had thought she would want a child, and she and her husband had not even broached the subject for years. When her feelings began to change, it took her husband completely by surprise. "One night I mentioned to my husband that I was thinking along these lines," she says, "and he wouldn't even discuss it with me for the first three or four days I tried to bring it up. He'd say, 'You know how I feel about it,' and I'd say, 'No. I really don't know how you feel about it. You have to tell me.' He said, 'We haven't discussed this for years and all of a sudden you're talking about having a family and what if I get all enthused about this and a week from now you say you really don't want to.' He had to get used to the idea too. I think he'd always felt, much more than I did, that someday he would end up having a child because that's sort of what one did. When I was twenty-five, I would have sworn I would never have kids, but he never felt that way. It was getting him used to the idea that I was actually considering it that way was hard."

Let's Make a Deal

Some of the clock-watchers have gotten their husbands to agree to having a family by establishing an agenda of things that must be done before they dive in, and then checking them off, one by one. But if the husband is looking for "the perfect time," that agenda can expand relentlessly. This happened to Augusta, thirty-four, a case manager in a social service agency. "I got married when I was thirty, and then I started thinking about having kids," she says. "I had had so much fun before that and moved around and traveled and I didn't really take the time to think about it. But then you get older and your parents get older and they start asking, and you start thinking about it a little more. That's when we started throwing the idea around. My husband is four years younger than I am, so for him there was more time to play with, and it's easier to sit back when it's not your body. But he understood my time pressure. We were both cooperating. I always get my way and I've learned that I get it faster by not saying anything, but bringing up the subject now and again, and very calmly and very rationally talking about it and then letting it go. He thinks about it and he stews and stews and then eventually I get my way.

"But having a baby was one of those things that was really easy to keep putting off: it wasn't the right time, the jobs weren't right financially, or blah, blah, blah. It was one thing after the other. We bought our first house last February and that was sort of the last thing. We're going to buy a house and then we're going to try. Everything had to be just right. We've always planned and followed through on it; our lives have always gone according to plan. But I finally convinced him that there is always going to be a problem, there is always going to be something wrong—we'd always find an excuse, so we might as well start trying."

For Helene getting her husband to agree also took a lot of quiet perseverance, mainly because he is already the father of two daughters from his previous marriage. "When my husband asked me to marry him, we talked about having children of our own. I wouldn't have gone ahead if he'd been totally opposed. But it was put on the back burner," she says. "The guilt he feels over having left his children 'without a father' has made it difficult to adjust to my wanting a child. He hasn't seen them in about three years. When he got divorced, the eldest was five and he explained to her what divorce was. He spent weekends with her and took her on trips until she was about ten. She could never understand why he was leaving her at the end of a trip. She'd say, 'You don't love me. You don't have fun with me.' And that just ripped him apart because he'd raised her entirely. His wife worked days and he worked nights. His daughter is very precocious and smart and looks exactly like him. He couldn't stand to make her unhappy, so he stopped seeing her. We're working now on reestablishing a relationship. She's going to be thirteen next month. I told him she'll probably only have two words for him and they're not going to be nice. But he's going to have to keep working at it; he knows it's something he has to do.

"Recently, I've started talking about having a baby again. He said, 'You really want one, huh? I don't want to be changing diapers at forty-one.' And I said that men in their fifties and sixties were having them. Now, when we go on vacation, or we have dinner and a few drinks, we talk. He'll say, 'When we have this baby that you keep talking about, I want you to teach it a second language.' Or, 'I'm fed up with work and I want to come home and pat my wife on the ass and play with my kid.'

"He's coming around. But we're still paying for our wedding. We're waiting until a few more things are paid for, and his job is a little more secure. He's trying to get promoted or transferred. He works for the airlines and we've had it with New York. I don't want to raise a baby here. So we're trying to get transferred out west or down south—one of the newer cities that are opening up like Atlanta, where the child will have benefits of theater and museums but won't be afraid to play outside. It's rough. He's been told to just sit tight. He might even go back to being an agent because they can put in for transfers easily, but he is in management and the airlines freeze you in one place.

"I haven't ovulated in four years because I'm on the pill. I'm going to get off it in May, and then try in July or August. It gives us eight or nine months to get the other stuff straightened out. If I can get pregnant right away, I'd have the baby when I'm still thirty-four."

As mentioned earlier, the partners of many of these women have had families already, and that's the major reason they don't want more children. It may be the hardest objection to overcome, but many of the clock-watchers, like Helene, have done so—through one means or another. Janet, thirty-nine, a writer and professor living in Australia, almost quit seeing the father of her son, now two, because he originally felt just this way. "After my divorce, the first stable relationship I was in broke up over the issue of having a child," she says. "What that did for me was to clarify the type of man I wanted, and it made me decide to be honest with anyone with whom I subsequently became closely involved. I was not going to live with, or marry someone who didn't want a child.

"When I met Bill at the local folk music club—we both play guitar—he had his twelve-year-old son living with him and an eight-year-old daughter living with his ex-wife. His own life was in flux and he was trying to change careers. I could see to some extent that he wasn't going to be a possibility for a permanent relationship, but we went out all the same because we liked each other. We got along so well that I became worried about where the relationship was leading. It was clear he wasn't interested in having any more children. His son was giving him some trouble and he had his own life to sort out.

"After a few months I got up the courage to spell out what I wanted. We talked at length and the upshot was that I said I thought we shouldn't see each other anymore. We were both unhappy, but that seemed to be what we should do. Love intervened. The next day we decided to give it a month and just see how we got on without thinking about children. So we did. By that time we both realized we had something too good to lose. Bill then reversed his thinking and decided he'd like to have a child with me. I was scared, but the risk of actually telling someone what I wanted, which of course made me vulnerable, resulted in getting what I wanted."

Some of the deals these women with stepchildren have cut are more obvious than others. Eleanor, forty-six, a psychotherapist and writer, became a mother at forty-one after she negotiated a baby care contract with her husband who has three grown daughters from his first marriage. "At first my husband wasn't keen on the idea at all and didn't see how he could go through it again, and that was the reason I waited three years after we were married, so we could talk ourselves into it," she says. "The deal we made, which was perfectly acceptable to both of us because he'd been through it three times and I hadn't and love taking care of babies, was that I would do the basic baby care, and between the housekeeper, myself, and my mother-in-law, he wouldn't have to do baby care unless he wanted to. I let him off the hook, and I think it was fair because he was making a concession in agreeing to do it at all.

"Once he'd agreed, I felt I needed to make some ultimatum to myself that I was going to seriously begin to have a family. So I combined it with a trip to China when I was forty, which I felt was a momentous occasion in my life. I told my sister in Chicago that I would send her a picture of me on the Great

Wall with my diaphragm cut up in a thousand pieces, and that I would be throwing it off the wall. To be absolutely certain, I left China and went to Japan and searched out a shrine that was especially known for fertility and I got a little red bag filled with special herbs that I'm sure also helped. Within six months I was pregnant."

Of Chores and All That

In this postliberation decade, when most two-career couples are sharing the housework, it is interesting that the division of baby care has not been hashed over in most of these women's households. Perhaps it doesn't become a compelling issue for most of them until they are faced with the imminent arrival of their infant. Erica, thirty, an architectural designer and personnel consultant, did discuss this subject with her husband before she got pregnant, an unusual move it seems. "My husband was noncommittal about having children," she says. "If I wanted them, it would be fine with him. But I wanted to make sure it wouldn't be that I wanted them, therefore I'd have to take care of them. And it's not like that at all. He agreed he'd be involved beforehand, and he's very supportive and very loving and very attached to them."

Anne is one of the few other women interviewed who brought up the subject with her husband before trying to conceive. "One virtue of waiting is that you get to talk while you wait and you get to watch other people and you get to work out vicariously what you would do in that situation," she says. "We're not making assumptions that any particular area is any one person's responsibility. So, I don't assume if the school closes because of snow that I'm necessarily the one staying home. That wasn't true two years ago; that took some conversation. I'm glad that we had it without a screaming kid in the background. We know that it's a shared responsibility. No one is more responsible for the child than the other. There isn't the assumption that if Daddy is tired it will be Mommy's responsibility even if she is tired too.

"My husband probably does more around the house than I do. He likes it. That always gives me a lot of hope. He had a classic upbringing and didn't do anything to help, but he watched his father being very responsible. He's very unusual. If we make lists, it's together. I don't know of any other couples like us. With most couples who share, the husband helps out, but it's still the wife's responsibility to think up the chores."

Most couples, if they've thought about it at all, have not arrived at such a mutual vision of "life with child." "My husband has a male sense of things that need to be done," says Nancy, twenty-seven, a software editor. "He's good about doing stuff when reminded, or if he notices. But he doesn't see things the same way I do. He doesn't initiate. And he really expects you to praise him lavishly when he does anything. It's not proportionate, and I can see that might be a problem down the line. But he is good with kids. His youngest sister is eight years younger and he was very involved with her infancy. He knows how to handle babies and he's not under the illusion that they don't smell."

Naomi, who is ten weeks pregnant, has just recently begun to realize how little her husband understands about what is going to happen in seven months: "We work well together when we kind of lay things out. That's the only way we can do it. We schedule the major stuff that bugs us. We've talked about putting some of the baby chores on some kind of schedule so we know who's to do what. My husband tends to not anticipate things that will have to be done. So we still have to talk about that. We've been doing our own cleaning: an hour on Saturday. He does downstairs and I do upstairs. And I said that when the baby came we were getting help. And he said, 'What do we need help with?' I don't think he really fathoms what's going to happen."

This is exactly what worries Polly, thirty, an educational program manager who was one of six children and has been trying to get pregnant for a year. As a consequence, she is trying to educate her husband now, before they are both on the hot seat. "I borrow friends' kids and have them at home so my husband gets some experience with them," she says. "He's the middle child of three and had no experience with small children. He likes them, once they are walking and communicating, but he doesn't go out of his way to be with them. I've had babies home overnight and he helps. But he doesn't understand how much caretaking they need, and sometimes he wants me to help him at the same time the baby is crying. When I go to the baby, it pisses him off. I'd rather he find out about it with someone else's child."

Some women have no illusions of equality in these matters mainly because of their husband's schedules. "My husband's hours are really erratic with the police department," says Patricia. "He's a homicide detective. Yesterday, he went to work at 4:45 A.M. and got home at 7:30 P.M. I think he would be supportive, but even among my most feminist friends and their most feminist husbands, equal is a long way off, just because attitudes are so deep-seated.

"But maybe after waiting this long, he'll be very interested. Some men come out of this much better than you would think, maybe because they did wait longer. My brother who is thirty-six changes diapers and gets up in the middle of the night for feedings—and this is a boy who had never done any of these tasks. But he's just thrilled with his child."

5

The Single-Mother Option

For single clock-watchers smitten with baby lust, there is an alternative to waiting for the right man to show up. They can become mothers on their own. Women are doing it all around them—not only Hollywood stars such as Farrah Fawcett and Jessica Lange, but ordinary middle-class women too. The media is hot to capitalize on this new trend—the stories of single mothers have been featured in *People, New York Magazine, Ms., Esquire,* etc. An interesting conception scenario pleased millions in *The Big Chill.*

Twenty years ago all this would have been unthinkable. Before the women's movement and the sexual revolution, the stigma attached to pregnancy out of wedlock sent women scurrying to the altar before they started to show, or off to a home for unwed mothers where they could hide out during their pregnancy before putting the baby up for adoption. Children born to women who chose to keep them were still thought of as bastards.

But single women today do not have to worry about ruining their own lives, or those of their offspring. Being born out of wedlock no longer causes an automatic social stigma and possible rejection. In fact, with divorce rates as high as they are—50 percent of the children in grade school have parents who are divorced—children of single mothers are almost indistinguishable from those who once had a father living at home. No man around the house no longer means no marriage.

Who Would Do It?

In this new, more liberal atmosphere, it's not surprising that almost two thirds of the single clock-watchers say they would consider having a baby on their own. What may be surprising is what kind of women they are. When they were growing up, their vision of themselves as mothers was no stronger than that of other single women. They don't feel particularly unhappy with their lives today. And if they were to remain childless forever, they would be no sadder than the women who would not opt for single motherhood.

But there are some major differences between these potential single mothers and those who would not go ahead on their own. For one thing, they are considerably more frustrated at still being childless. They want to be mothers, and they wish it were yesterday. Whether they are trying to get pregnant now, or are planning to wait for a few years, most are determined to have a child one way or the other—and they won't let the logistics of getting pregnant, their work, their finances, or their families swerve them off course. "I want to be pregnant so badly. I really want a baby," says Maggie, thirty, a social worker who is giving herself three years to find a husband. "I have this need for nurturing. I don't think it's selfish. It's a need to raise somebody, to have somebody I can take care of, and be able to push out of the nest, and feel all that love for. I will have one come hell or high water.

"I went through this Lamaze class this summer with a friend and I was almost having a pseudopregnancy. I was her labor coach, along with her husband, who is a fireman. It was exhausting—thirty-six hours. She ended up with a section, but it was so exciting, I had chill bumps. They let me take pictures right after the baby was born. Now, when I see her nursing her child, I want to nurse it too. I think she senses that. Anytime I pick up anyone's baby, I have an overwhelming urge. They're never afraid of me. My sister-in-law also had a baby last year and when I'm visiting I'll go in and fondle the baby clothes. I do this at my friend's house too. And when I go to a store, I'll go into the baby department and kind of dream."

If a woman hears the clock ticking and is filled with anxiety about how much time she has left, she is more likely to consider going ahead on her own. The rapid approach of her thirty-fifth birthday, and a reassessment of the probability of finding the right man, triggered the decision for Maryanne, thirty-four, a vice president of her company, who is planning to be artificially inseminated soon. "I'd actually been thinking about it for several years, but for a while I figured that if I didn't meet someone and get married, I'd probably adopt," she says. "But I also felt, 'Hell, if there is no man around,

I'll just do it myself.' When I started to think more seriously about it in the last year, it was because of my biological clock. About six to nine months ago, my period was a little erratic and I suddenly became aware that I was getting older, and maybe if I waited a couple of years it would be too late. Also, and this was the hardest thing, I finally faced up to the fact that I don't think there's a man out there for me. I freely admit that I'd much rather fall in love and have a man fall in love with me and get married and have babies together. But I finally accepted that this probably wasn't going to happen. I'm almost thirty-five and I haven't come close to finding someone I want to spend the rest of my life with."

Single women who have experienced a recent change of heart about having a baby can find that their desire for motherhood is so strong that it may push them over the edge. Rita, thirty-eight, a clerk-typist, who has chosen the father for her child and is waiting for him to get over sudden cold feet, expresses such feelings. "When I was married from age eighteen to twenty-one, I didn't want to have a child because I wasn't old enough. In my early thirties, I thought it would be something I'd do when I was older. Well, I'm older. I see babies on the street now and I smile. When I'm near one, I want to pick it up. I don't think it's normal behavior for me. My brother's kids used to give me headaches. Now I get depressed when I get my period."

Colleen, forty-two, who owns her own graphic design business, has experienced much of the same change of feelings as she's gotten older and unsuccessfully tried to get pregnant with her married lover. "I enjoy children," she says, "and I'm at a time in my life when I can appreciate children. Before I was too busy for them. I had too much that I needed to do, and wanted to do —that I *had* to do, and with children I didn't think I'd ever get to it. And yet that time went too fast . . . and here I am. I don't fantasize about it now, but when I'm holding a baby I think, 'Yes, I would like to have a child.' My feelings have intensified over the last ten years. Now I see a child as an addition to my life, as a plus."

Women who say they would go ahead on their own also express somewhat different reasons for having a child than those who would not do so. More of them feel their lives are empty and worry about being alone in old age. Joyce, thirty-six, a sales representative who recently experienced a big change of heart about having a child, finds her feelings are so strong she has even moved out of the home she owns with her long-term boyfriend because he is so opposed to becoming a father. "I don't want to turn around as an older woman and feel a sense of emptiness in my life," she says. "I feel I would have really missed a tremendous giving of love that I'm just dying to give."

Caitlin, thirty-two, a video program coordinator, who moved away from her fiancé in order to further her career, says, "I want to have a kid, I know I do. I know I'd be a good mother, and I just want to experience it. Just seeing babies and women with babies and that whole lifestyle, I just don't want to miss it. It makes me sad to think about not having one. It really does. I see my folks, who I think have done a pretty damn good job with four kids, and I want to be able to do the same. To see a child grow and give it opportunities and let it see the world. Boy, without that I'd be really disappointed and probably a little bitter."

Women who can't imagine not having a child are also more likely to consider becoming single mothers. Theresa, forty, a project consultant who is involved with a thirty-two-year-old man, is one of them. "I feel that it's so important to be part of a family. It feels so odd to me to come home to my own condominium, lock the door, and be all by myself," she says. "It's so different from the way I was raised, in a big family, with lots of cousins, lots of family occasions.

"I'm a member of a summer house where for the first few years the members were all single, but over the ten years we've had it, people have gotten married and had children. And rather than keep looking for childless adults, we started to introduce the children into the house. It's made it an extended family. I look forward to those weekends, even though the cocktails on the porch are not as relaxing as they were because you've got to keep the little fingers out of the food. But it's real life, and I yearn for it. One family has three little girls and I'm so reminded of my own childhood, I ache for it. I really relate to that mother—she's from a family of all girls too."

Many of the potential single mothers have been pregnant as adults and for various reasons they've chosen to have an abortion—a choice they would not make if they became pregnant again.

For Evelyn, thirty-nine, a divorced program analyst, her three abortions have increased her desire for a child. "I think I know who I am, where I'm going, and what I can do on my own," she says. "I would like to have a child. While I would prefer to share that experience with a man I love, I feel that I may not be able to find the ideal circumstances—I never have before. Consequently, I plan to try to get pregnant. I'm getting too old to wait for Mr. Right and I feel I need to proceed as if he won't come along. I don't feel guilty about using a man to get pregnant. I've always been a giver, which is why I think I'll be a good mother, and just once I want to be a taker. I'm not looking for a husband, financial support, etc.—just the seed for a child. I believe that if I'm willing and able to be responsible for a child, that choice should be mine."

Boyfriends as Fathers

A clock-watcher's obvious first choice for a father for her child is a man with whom she already has a relationship—her boyfriend; over two thirds of the potential single mothers would pick him. When they are living with a man, they are even more likely to consider single motherhood as a possibility.

But at the same time, women who are happily involved in a good relationship are very concerned about messing things up by getting pregnant on purpose, and without prior consultation with the father-to-be. Almost 90 percent of them would discuss it with their boyfriend in advance. In fact, the only way many of them can imagine having a child while single is by accident. If it happened, almost two thirds of them would expect their boyfriend to be involved with his child and with themselves (35 percent are even hoping that a child will help these men to make the commitment so many seem to dread: marriage).

Four years ago, Diana, twenty-nine, an executive director of a human services agency, was faced with such an accidental pregnancy, and she decided on an abortion—a choice she would not make if it happened now. "For a while, I thought I might have the child," she says. "But my parents were totally opposed because my boyfriend is black. My mother's feeling is that children have enough problems growing up without racial problems too. I think that's bull. You have to deal with what life doles out to you. But I find it is hard to act like an adult around my parents. I revert to being a child.

"Also, my boyfriend wasn't ready, and I would have had to do it alone. He remembers that we'd decided to have the baby and I went home and my parents screwed me up. I remember that I had sort of made the decision to go ahead, but he wouldn't commit. His big line at the time was, 'Life has no guarantees. I could walk out tomorrow and get hit by a car.' I told him I wasn't asking him to live forever—I just wanted him to tell me that he would be there as much as he was able. He couldn't do that. My parents were giving me absolutely no support. I felt that I was out there pretty much alone. It was more than I could handle."

Although Diana thinks she could handle it better now, she still wouldn't get pregnant on purpose. "If I inadvertently became pregnant, and he still couldn't commit, I think I'd have the child," she says. "And I think that now he would be there. He's a lot more settled about a lot of things. He used to drink heavily and he doesn't drink at all anymore. He's got some goals. He may not have a career, but I think he's got a lot more maturity. We talk about marriage more now than we did before. But I don't want to get married because I'm pregnant. I'd much rather we made a conscious decision that we would get married, and then I'd get pregnant."

Joyce's feelings are completely the opposite. Although her boyfriend vehemently opposes becoming a father in the conventional sense, she thinks he might be willing to father a child for her as a single mother. "John and I are both kind of open to alternatives to living in the same house and being married and having children. When I moved out, we thought we'd like to carry on our relationship living separately," she says. "I can see that if it remains strong in a year or two that I could have a child with him. That would really be perfect if I was going to do it alone. John is not adverse to that idea."

Colleen has also been open to alternatives. Over the span of a few years she tried, unsuccessfully, to have a child with the married man she was involved with for eleven years—without any real expectation that he would make major adjustments in his life.

Before going ahead, she was honest with him about it—in a circuitous sort of way. "At age thirty-seven," she says, "I realized I was getting no younger, and Wes was getting no younger, and that it seemed to be time for us to have a child," she says. "I stopped taking the pill. I never really fully told him that I'd done it, but he was aware of it. One time he said, 'Where are your pills?' and I told him I'd stopped. I had a diaphragm and I used it a few times and then said, 'I'm getting tired of all this birth control nonsense,' and he knew the diaphragm was no longer there. One day we were driving back to New York from our weekend away and I said that I'd like to have a child, and he said, 'Uh, do what you want.' He was a very undemonstrative person. It meant, 'It's OK, I'll be there.' But he never liked to say let *us* do anything. It was, 'You can if you want to' or 'I will if I want to.'

"If I'd ever told Wes that we had to make love because I was ovulating, he'd have said, 'No, we don't.' He was a spontaneous person. He'd rather say, 'No I don't want a kid,' than to have to deal with the pressure to having to perform right now. So I'd seduce him and not tell him why. I can't imagine why he didn't figure it out. I remember walking into his country house and taking off my top and he said, 'What the f—— are you doing?' and I said, 'I want to play,' and he said, 'Jesus Christ, you are crazy,' and then he got into it. I teased him into it. But I'm sure he had no idea what it was about. Then, there were times I'd think that I had better fool around when I really didn't want to so it wouldn't become too obvious. I'd seduce him just so I wouldn't set up a pattern. The whole thing was with his approval—'Yes, we can have a child if you want it'—but it was an applied approval. Discussion would have ruined it.

"I never did conceive. I have no idea why. I think the problem was Wes. It took him and his wife ten years to have a child. If I had gotten pregnant I don't know whether he would have finally left his wife. It didn't enter my mind. But it might have done a lot of good for the relationship. The only time it was really awful was the last three months. If I'd gotten pregnant then, he never would have known about it and I would still have walked out and had the baby on my own. If he had asked, I would have told him, and he could have done what he wanted to."

Wanted: Good Father Material

The problem for many women who want to have a child is that they don't have a man in their lives. The ones who want to get pregnant now are put in the position of examining each man they come in contact with as a potential father. Most of them would like to find a solid relationship for themselves as well, but some are willing to get pregnant by a man they admire or, if all else fails, by any suitable guy they might meet up with. Some have given up on men and are heading to a sperm bank. What sets these women apart is that their determination to pursue this course of action now has made them resolve their worries about logistics—money and careers—and about the aftermath—what to tell the child about their father, and how to raise a child alone.

Now that Colleen has split up for good with Wes, she is looking for another man with whom to have a child. She doesn't expect marriage or even a long-term romantic relationship, but she thinks it should be someone she likes and could have a solid friendship with—and someone who would be a responsible father. "There are one or two men I might consider, but I haven't gotten around to honestly telling them that—maybe I'm not so convinced they'd be the right father. They are both divorced and are fathers already who have good working relationships with one or two of their children; that's important. I'd also like our relationship to get to a certain point before I'd think about getting pregnant. One fellow I've been seeing for three weeks, and I know that if it goes further, I probably will open up and say this is what I would like and see what he would like. If he's willing to father the child, but doesn't know what involvement he'd want, that's OK. It's more important that I feel comfortable in the relationship now than to know it's going to go on for a long time, or sustain itself forever. I want to be honest, but I'm willing to get pregnant and go on my way. I don't care about getting married. If the father wants to be involved on a full-time basis and I feel drawn to him, maybe we'd get married, but we might just live together. It might only get important as the child is growing up."

Because she has always been a planner, Colleen is naturally trying to plan out every aspect of choosing a father and having a child. "Part of me is saying I want to find the right father, plan the whole thing. The other part is saying that the best things that happen to me are spontaneous," she says. "For instance, I didn't plan to start my business. I just got fed up doing things for other people and finding no recompense for it. I knew I could be doing something for myself.

"The dichotomy in my thinking is making me crazy. In the last week I slept with a man and didn't use any birth control. I didn't organize it or plan it. Our lovemaking was very spontaneous and I didn't have any birth control with me. I didn't have any intention of making love to him, but I enjoyed it. He asked what would happen if I got pregnant. I said I'd know the 'what if' later. I felt, 'Whatever happens, happens.' When I ovulate, I have a discharge, so I know. This was a fringe time of the month.

"If I'm pregnant, I'd be entirely on my own. This relationship could never work. I don't know whether I'd even tell him because he wants children. He'd feel used and somewhat less than human. He'd want a relationship with the child. If I have conceived, I will wrestle a lot with my conscience to know what to do. I don't know whether this man could make the transition into friendship with me so he could be a father to the child and not want any relationship with me. It's very difficult for me to think about. I did something that could have ramifications for the rest of my life. I'm half happy and half terrified. I guess if I'm pregnant, I'll cope."

The finances and logistics of being a single mother don't overly concern Colleen because her family is behind her and she is very willing to be flexible about her career—to make whatever adjustments are necessary. "I've talked with my family about having a baby off and on for probably the last twelve to fifteen years," she says. "I'd get any support they could give. That's how they are. Going to live at home for a year would be fine. My sister has said that if I ever had a baby and couldn't take care of it for the first couple of months, she would do so. If I didn't want to involve the child's father, I would turn to my family. My father was a terrific father. He's sixty-six, but very young at heart. My mother is sixty-five going on forty. I have a brother-in-law who has been terrific with his family. My nephew is sixteen and we've always been very close. Because my family is warm and supportive, a child would have male role models.

"My business would work out fine with a child. I have no work agenda I want to accomplish before getting pregnant, although I'd like to have a little more money coming in—to have a nest egg against the old rainy day. If I were living with someone who made a big enough income, I'd slow down my business, keep only one or two of my clients, and bring in free-lancers to do it so I could spend all my time with my child, and then gradually build it back up again. But if I were all on my own and found I needed more money to provide for the child, I'd also be willing to change—to take an advertising agency job if that made more sense. Whether I did that, or moved home with my parents to save money, would depend on the situation at the time."

Some of the clock-watchers seem to be a good deal more frantic about finding a father-cum-boyfriend than Colleen is. Beverly, thirty-seven, an orthopedic surgeon, is even keeping a diary of her search: "Who is to be the father? I want it to be someone that I care enough about and trust enough that I would want him to be a part of my own life. I want it to be someone that I could unreservedly tell my children about when and as they want to know. I don't know what I will say to a child except that I feel I must be able to speak of love, or at least the beginnings of love, in a person that I admire, trust, and wish to be in my life as much of forever as is available these days. This kind of man is relatively infrequent in my acquaintance—especially when I add in the other requirements that make up the physical attraction necessary for me to want to make love to him. How should I pick? Of the people I am currently dating, is there one I would be proud to have as part of my life?"

Because she's received a negative response from some of the men she's spoken with, Beverly is beginning to think that she is best off not speaking honestly about her intentions. "Most men have quite strong feelings about having children, not knowing whether they could handle abandoning their offspring, and being unsure of whether I would make claims on their time, estate, etc.," she writes. "I'm to the point of deciding that I won't tell the men anymore that I might become pregnant (these days they never seem to ask about birth control anyway). Anyway, telling them makes having a relationship with them much more complicated since they seem to feel that I'm only interested in their sperm."

After some deliberation, Beverly decided that one of her lovers, whom she calls Q to preserve his anonymity, is the right man to father her child. In diary entries ranging over a month she describes their negotiations: "Q is willing and even at times wants to make babies with me as long as no one knows and as long as I would make no claim against his estate. At the same time he feels he would want to stay involved as an uncle. I can promise to make no claims, but I can't promise that no one will know. I am so poor at hiding my feelings about people that I think anyone that really knows me will guess and to keep them from guessing I must barrage them with false Adams. So I spend less time with Q—the person I want to be with.

"I'm getting a little lost in interpreting Q's feelings about me. He said earlier this week he wanted to wait a couple of months to actually try conceiving. Now he says for me not to use my diaphragm. So the birth control rests with him. He is suggesting investments for me to allow for the future of the baby we will make. That he would spontaneously think about this credits his sincerity about actually doing it. I have desire and lust and loneliness that I feel comfortable asking him to satisfy, and I also feel a growing affection for him. I see that as my trust grows, my involvement is stronger. This week I will have dates with two other men and stay out the night afterward with Q so that we can confuse everyone else about who the father might be if I am fortunate enough to become pregnant. I feel this will all work out. It's a very happy feeling."

A few days later she wrote: "Q has decided to go for it. Wore me out last night. It's hard to say exactly how I feel that I might be pregnant. Secure. Like a small soft, hot spot in my stomach. Mona Lisa. I'm so glad that it's him. Release of love within me. That I would feel his spirit with me, in a child, and it feels passionately supportive and protective." But within days, Beverly finds Q is backing off, that he "feels a little taken advantage of. I think it's emotional backlash, in part, with an increasing involvement." She in turn began to get fed up with "all the secrecy and not being able to stay with him at night. I don't want to hide my feelings. This plan with Q is just too complicated, too confusing. . . . After spending Friday night with him I was told I would have to leave because his grown daughter might be coming over later. I felt extremely angry and hurt, and I decided that I wasn't handling the dynamics of the relationship very well and that I should withdraw. I told him so, that it was my decision and that I shouldn't spend my time thinking about him."

Two days later Beverly drew a pregnancy blood test on herself. "I figured if a junkie can do it, so can I. Put the tourniquet on a little too tight and when I put the needle in, squirted blood all over the place. Then didn't have a free hand to let the tourniquet loose and hadn't put it in position to use my teeth well." The test came back negative. And the questions began.

"Now what?" she asked. "Another man? Sperm donation by one of my friends? Give up? Artificial insemination? Put on hold for a while? How does someone even know that they 'should have' children, that they are ready, that they can handle it once they have made the commitment to go ahead? It seems to me that motherhood would be fun, enjoyable, and satisfying. I don't ignore the many problems, but I feel that on balance being a mother is something that I want for myself. I like to be around children. I'm very interested in the babies, pregnancies, and growing children of my friends and family. But after being up all night in surgery, I wonder about whether I would be able to take care of another person. I would definitely have to have help, of the live-in variety. Right now I would like someone to take care of me, to hold me. I feel so tired."

Fifteen percent of the potential single mothers are not looking for a boyfriend to father their child, but instead would choose a man they admire. Rita has picked the prospective father of her child from this pool. He is someone she thinks would make a good father and whom she feels attracted to and yet comfortable with. "I chose him because I think he'll be there for the long haul for our child. His father was an absent father and I think he's compensating for that with his own children and would with ours. My relationship to him is both close and distant. There's an elusiveness there that is probably part of the attraction. If we do have a child together, it might have a negative effect on the relationship because he'd relate to me only as the mother of his child. But I think we'd be able to maintain a good working friendship."

Unlike Beverly's Q, who did not want to make any financial commitment to his child-to-be, Rita's friend feels obligated to make one—even though she did not ask him to do so. Because he is having some financial problems, he is now getting cold feet about going ahead. This worries her. "I know for a fact that he is having financial difficulties, but I'm not sure if his recent concerns are strictly as a result of that or if he has had second thoughts and just doesn't want to tell me," she says. "I worry that I'm getting more and more gray and I have health problems and the clock is ticking, but I am willing to let him have a little more time."

In case this man doesn't come through for her, Rita has considered other alternatives. "I haven't gotten as far as the sperm bank," she says. "But I've thought about a number of men who are friends or people that I date and I've eliminated just about all of them. There are three who have the wife at home and the kids in the suburbs and they are looking forward to an end to their responsibilities and they are also very conventional, so if they were to father a child they would feel they had to assume the responsibility. I don't think it would be fair to them; it would make them resentful of me, or the child. They might do it and then afterward feel, 'Oh my God, what did I just do?' I've had a few volunteers, but I think they are more interested in the immediate rewards—hopping into bed, the idea of being the proud papa, the bouncing baby routine—and not in the long term. They're very carefree and don't like responsibility. And they don't have a track record. I don't know what kind of father they would be."

Although many single women are worried about the financial responsibility of having a child on their own, more women who are earning less than $20,000 a year are considering single motherhood than those in higher-income brackets. Rita is one of them, and the finances do not particularly concern her. "When I changed jobs last spring, I took a fairly large cut in salary and by next August or September I should be making quite a bit more. If I were not to become pregnant until after the pay increase, or if I weren't to deliver until after it, it would be much more practical financially, though even then it will be tight, I'm sure. But I don't spend a lot and I'm used to pinching pennies. I know how to enjoy life and still be poor. So I think that somehow it's going to work out. I don't think I'll need help from the father even though he feels he'd be obliged to give it. I'm intending to have some serious conversations with him in the near future about this.

"I'm also not worried about being single and pregnant at my job. It might have been a big deal at my old job because it was very rigid and corporate and old school and more especially because I'm white and the intended father is minority. The job I have now is with the federal government and I don't think they'll make a fuss. What I worry about most is good child care. I don't know what I'll do. His mother has said she'll help as much as she can, and his grandmother can help, but I'm not sure if she could handle five days a week. There seem to be good sources around Washington for child care, and one of my friends just became pregnant so she's going to have to deal with all these problems before I do."

When a woman has decided that she definitely wants to become a single mother, but she has not found the right man to father her child and doesn't have a selection of candidates to choose among, it can make her extremely upset. Heather, thirty-five, a senior marketing representative, who has found it very hard to get men to make a commitment, finds herself in this position, and talking about the subject reduces her to tears. She has just accepted a promotion which is moving her from Jackson, Mississippi, back East to her corporation's home office, where perhaps she will meet new men who will qualify. At the moment the only guy she'd consider is saying no. "My situation is kind of like the woman in *The Big Chill* who has some really sharp, intelligent, attractive friends around her," she says. "The one I'd really like to be the father is kind of like the man in that movie. He has all the qualifications of someone I'd be looking for. But he doesn't want to know he has a child somewhere he's not involved with. He says that he doesn't see how he could be the father of a child that he didn't participate in raising. And he's not committed to me enough to get married and raise a child. And yet he probably sleeps with four to five women a month—there's no telling how many children he's fathered."

What she really wants from a man is not just his sperm, but some continuum for the child. "There are problems if you just pick up someone and sleep with him," she says. "It would be nice if the child could find out who the father was and pursue that side of his or her life. If the father were someone I chose, especially a friend, he would be there for the child to know those kinds of things." But if Heather isn't able to find that kind of man, it won't stop her from going ahead and becoming a mother. She'll find alternative father figures. "Whatever the situation turns out to be, what I feel I have to get across to the child is how important it was for me to have him or her. I'm going to try not to have a son. I'll do the acidic douche and try for a girl. If I do have a boy, I'll try to fill as much of that role as I can, and I'll get him involved with Big Brother, or something like that."

Because having a baby is the most important thing in her life, Heather does not fret over how single motherhood might affect her career, or how she'll handle it financially. "I think it will come as a surprise to those at work who don't know me well that I'm doing this, and I'm sure there will be some eyebrows raised, but I'm also sure I won't get fired," she says. "I've already got the timing down. If I get pregnant in May, I'd deliver in the winter and I can wear big clothes. I think my salary will be sufficient even though my new house is more expensive. I've got $25,000 in a thrift fund, for college. It's hard to think about planning for retirement with all this money around and thinking of myself alone."

The less a relationship with a man matters to a woman—whether for herself or for her unborn child—the less likely she is to tell him that she wants to get pregnant. Under a third of these women would keep their intentions secret from a man they admire, whereas 80 percent who would settle for any suitable—attractive, healthy, intelligent—man would keep their mouths shut. Take Regina, thirty-two, a free-lance writer, who says she has "given up on finding a husband or even a reliable lover. For the last two or three years, I've simply been trying to get pregnant," she says. "I've found that mentioning my desire to have a child terminates any sexual relationship, and I've therefore quit saying anything about it. However, an unstable, intermittent partner situation is not as yet conducive to impregnation. I refuse to be indiscriminate in a choice of partners. I want to know who the father is—to say whose eyes, nose, etc., the child has—to know something about him since the child will ask eventually."

But even when a relationship does matter, if a woman has been turned down by one prospective father, she may decide not to tell the others. This may smack of callousness, but, often, if a woman wants a baby badly enough, she doesn't care. "I've always been very ethical and honest with people in my life and I can't imagine tricking someone that I care for," says Joyce. "But there is a part of me that says I'm going to do what I want to do. I have this little nasty feeling in there that it's very selfish, but I will do whatever seems right for me at the time."

Clara, thirty-eight, a public health adviser who expected to be married and have a family long ago, has been "actively investigating, then pursuing pregnancy as a single woman for four years. I did a great deal of reading, discussed it with two very close friends, enrolled in foster parent/adoption classes the county sponsors, tentatively approached a 'fatherless grandchild' scenario with my mother, and finally took the plunge, asking a favorite lover to be the father. He procrastinated, finally declined, and broke my heart since I consider artificial insemination a definite second-best option.

"His refusal sent me to a women's health center, which is enrolled in an artificial insemination (AI) program. I was charting ovulation periods in preparation for my baby when I got a job offer to return to a city where the man I love lives—not the lover mentioned before. So I'm now looking positively at two options: possible pregnancy by Mr. Right (unbeknownst to him) or through AI here before I leave."

For most of these women, artificial insemination is one of the least preferred methods of achieving what they want. Only 13 percent would choose it. Many are turned off because they want to look back at an act of love. But when Maryanne made the decision that she wanted a baby, she chose AI over finding a man. "There is no man in my life and there is no one likely to come along," she says. "I've been looking for a long time. At one point I considered adopting, but seeing what couples go through, I came to the conclusion this would be easier. Plus, while I don't have a burning desire to be pregnant, I like the idea of having nine months to prepare for a very dramatic change in my life."

Her planning for this step has been quite meticulous. "I first went to my own gynecologist, and he ran all sorts of tests to make sure I ovulate. I'm taking my temperature so I know when it happens. The time between ovulation and when I start bleeding is a little shorter than normal, so my doctor did an endometrial biopsy right before my period to make sure the lining of my uterus was mature enough, and it was. Everything was normal. I've never had abdominal surgery that could have led to infections or tubal scarring. Tomorrow is my first appointment with the specialist who will do the insemination. He has the sperm bank. I think I get to pick certain physical characteristics. The very first question I'm asking is whether they do screening for AIDS. Beyond that, given some options, I'll probably look for someone who's tall because I'm very short, and someone who has similar coloring. Most of the donors, as I understand it, are medical students, which appeals to me because I'd like to pick someone who is an intelligent person. I'd also look at the donor's medical history—heart conditions, diabetes. The other choices aren't that critical to me. I don't give a whole lot of thought to genetics and that sort of stuff. Even though I'm an intelligent person and the donor is intelligent, I don't believe I'll necessarily have a child who gets straight A's."

Shortly after deciding that this was something she definitely wanted to do, Maryanne took a deep breath and told her parents. "I was very worried about how they would react because they are kind of conservative and they live in a small town in Alabama, and what would they do when they had to say their unmarried daughter was pregnant? I was treating them to a week of vacation in Bermuda with me, and I wrote a letter that I mailed so they would get it right before they joined me. It seemed like a good idea because that way if they had any immediate negative reactions or concerns, they could express them to each other privately, and by the time they would sit down to talk to me about it, they would have had a chance to work through them, and I wouldn't have to deal with it.

"My letter was manipulative. I told them how important it was for me to be a mother, and how much they mean to me, and how I realized all that they had given me, and that I in turn want to give a child. As I wrote it, I sat there and cried. They cried too as they read it. They were ecstatic. They think it's wonderful. They live in a town of 50,000 people and I swear 40,500 people have seen my letter."

The reception at work to Maryanne's decision has also been good. "The one person I talked to was my boss. He's about five years older than I am. He thinks it's wonderful, and in fact that makes a big difference to me. It's not that I wouldn't go ahead if he didn't think it was so great, but his attitude really does make me feel more comfortable about it. I know that during my pregnancy I'll have doctor appointments and maybe feel sick in the morning. After the baby is born, I'll have conflicts and feel as if I'll need to be home when I'm at the office and at the office when I'm home. To know he's supportive really helps. I told him I wondered how the senior management would feel—I'm in upper-middle management. He sort of chastised me. He said, 'Maryanne, this is something for you. Don't worry about what these people think.' He has two kids and they are so important to him. He said, 'It's the best thing my wife and I ever did, having kids.' "

The logistics of single pregnancy and motherhood also do not overly concern Maryanne. She plans to arrange through her church to have someone she can call in case of a medical emergency during her pregnancy; her mother is going to come help her in the last weeks and after the baby is born; she owns her own three-bedroom house, and she hopes to hire a live-in nanny. But she does worry a bit about what she will tell her child, and about role models if she has a son. However, she is keeping a very positive attitude. "I will tell the truth, but how I will communicate it to a small child so that he or she can understand, I don't know. When a child is old enough to ask, 'Why don't I have a daddy?' he or she isn't old enough to understand artificial insemination. I would certainly not hide anything. That is partly why I wouldn't just find some man to go to bed with and get pregnant, because I don't think I would feel comfortable explaining that. I don't want to lie. I've never been any good at lying. I'm going to ask the specialist if he will give my name and address to other single women who are having AI and see if we can form some sort of support group. I also plan to contact Single Parents by Choice. I do worry about role models for a boy. I worry more about a boy in the early years, especially since my father and brother don't live here; my parents are five hundred miles away. I'd just have to find friends around here to serve in that capacity. I'm not so concerned after age four or five because there's the Big Brother program and sports activities.

"But every time I start worrying about how I'm going to deal with this and how I'm going to deal with that, I come back to a statement I often make to myself: 'Maryanne, you've coped with a lot of things in your life. You've managed to overcome troubles and problems. You've not had an easy life. But you are strong and capable and you've got good friends and a very supportive family. It's not going to be easy, but you can handle it.' "

The Five-Year Plan

Eighty percent of the women who say they are considering single motherhood plan on waiting three to five years before going ahead. Most are hoping that the elusive right man for them will show up and they will be able to have babies under normal circumstances. But at the same time, many are trying to get their finances in better order so that once they reach their cutoff date they will feel more secure going ahead on their own if that is the only way open to them.

Although they aren't rushing to get pregnant, most of the planners seem positive that they will take on motherhood alone if that is their only alternative. Caitlin, who left her fiancé in Iowa and pursued her career to Phoenix, has set thirty-eight as the cutoff age for herself. "If I'm not married by then I could see myself going that route via a sperm bank or a good friend à la *The Big Chill.* I seriously think that at this point I would do that to have the experience of having a child because it's something I've always wanted and I'm not about to give that up. A couple of my girlfriends who are married have told me I might just be better off that way."

If she is to go ahead, having enough money is extremely important to Caitlin. "I'm getting pretty close to being financially set," she says. "I just got a fairly sizable raise that came with my last promotion and I see that as increasing, and within the next three to four years I'd be ready financially. That's one of the top considerations. I'd definitely have to have certain things in order—purchasing a house, and having some other income coming in from free-lancing, so that if the child were ill and I stayed home, I'd have that flexibility. Even then I'm sure it would be hard financially. I also wouldn't discount keeping my roommates or finding a roommate who also has a child so we could help each other out. That would give additional financial and moral support."

When some of these women talk about becoming a single mother, it seems as if the child to come will be a substitute for the husband they could not find. As Gina, thirty-two, a division secretary, says, "Without a loving marriage, I don't think I'd really feel fulfilled unless I have a child." Even though she has many doubts about going ahead, she also doesn't think she can deny herself this source of love, so she has set a cutoff date. "I just went to my gynecologist for my yearly exam and I told him, 'I've set my goal—thirty-five. That's three more years. If I haven't met someone and I'm not married, I'm having a baby anyway.' He said, 'Good for you.'

"Yet I know I'll have to do some real soul-searching. I've thought about changing my living arrangement so that I could afford to do it. I recently moved back home. I love my parents dearly and we get along well. I know I would be welcome here with a baby, but I don't want to put the burden of watching the baby on them. It wouldn't be fair. I'm making a good amount of money where I am (close to $20,000 a year), but I don't think I could afford conventional child care. However, my business has just started a day care center on the premises, and you pay a minimal amount, so that would be possible. But I didn't want to be that kind of mother—a working mother. I didn't want to have to put a tiny baby in a day care center. So I'm torn."

Since Gina hasn't been dating anyone for quite a while, she also worries about how she would get pregnant. If no one new comes into her life, she's decided to ask a former lover, and to be straight with him. "There are a couple of guys in my life whom I loved to a certain point, and we had a relationship, but they were scared off by the commitment thing. I'm still friends with them. If they would be willing, they are the kinds of men I'd consider. I know their personalities. I know there is nothing terrible in their past. If I'm going to do it, they're whose child I'd like to have. I think I'd tell them in advance. That would be the only way to do it. I'd never want to trap someone. If it happened unintentionally, that would be one thing, but I'd still want to let them know. If they didn't agree, I'd hope to find someone else."

Like two thirds of the women who are considering pregnancy by a man they admire, Gina does not expect him to undertake any of the normal responsibilities of fatherhood. "I've even thought about telling them that if they'd be willing to do this with me, I'd sign a legal document absolving them of any type of financial or other obligation. This would be my child. If they wanted to see the baby they could, but I wouldn't come to them for anything."

And if no man in her life is willing to do this for her? Gina would be stymied because she doesn't think she could handle artificial insemination. "For me, part of having a child is the actual conception, being with someone, loving someone, making love," she says. "The thought of not doing that . . . I'd probably say, 'Well, then I won't have a child.' I want that closeness, to have that type of a memory. If I were married I could handle AI by my husband's sperm, or in vitro fertilization, because I'd have his love in my life.

I even think if I were married and found out I could not have children, I could handle that because I'd still have the love I've been looking for."

Maybe Baby

Other women are not as far along the road to single motherhood as these planners but feel there's a possibility that later something will change in their lives and they will want to take such a radical step. They have set no cutoff date, and they aren't making adjustments in their lives now to accommodate a baby later. Many of them seem almost fatalistic—if it's meant to be, they will know it.

For Gwen, twenty-nine, an artists' representative with her own business, it is a question of chemistry—of a physical desire to have a child. In her early twenties Gwen went through a period of baby lust which amazed her and she thinks it could happen again. If it does, she would be willing to make a major career change so that she could afford to have a child. "I'd really want to do it right, and part of doing it right when you are single is having live-in help or access to the proper, quality child care that I had as a kid. That costs money," she says. "If that chemistry happened again, I know I could have access to the type of financial situation I would need. Someone offered me a job last week, and it was that kind of money, but I would have had to give up my own business and I don't want to do that now. The chemical reaction isn't going off anymore. I figure fate will have something to do with whether it happens or not, whether I get pregnant or adopt. There are a lot of kids out there who otherwise would not be loved. I could adopt a fourteen-year-old— that would be fine. Having a baby is not what I need. It's sharing a world with a child. If I don't do either, I'll find myself contributing somehow, being auntie to someone else, or just helping out with children."

Her commitment to her career can also make a woman hesitant about becoming a single mother—especially if she fears her career will suffer for it. "I want to make Major on my next promotion in 1988–89 and having a child while unwed would severely hurt my chances," says Amber, twenty-eight, an Air Force officer. "But there is a bright spot. At the present time two of my colleagues—black, single, and female—are pregnant. One has already opted to leave the Air Force, but the other is planning to stay in. A dozen of us are watching her to see how it goes. Her next evaluation is due in three months when she will be seven months pregnant. If everything goes well with her, many of us would seriously consider single motherhood."

As her career has rapidly progressed, Suzanne, twenty-nine, a systems engineer, has found her work becoming more and more important to her, and this new attitude has moved her further away from the possibility of having a child alone. "Until the last year, I would have said yes, there is a point at which I would seriously consider the option of changing jobs so that I could accommodate a child in my life as a single mother," she says. "But I really feel I have a career now and that any move I made down that path would probably hurt me. The next step up the ladder for me in seven years or so will probably be a position in our home office, which is in Ohio. Folks in Ohio do not do the traveling that we do. So it's very possible that I could combine my career with single motherhood then."

Some single women are further away from single motherhood now than they were earlier in their lives. As they age, they begin looking at the situation more realistically, and having a child on their own seems more remote. This is true for Melanie, thirty-five, an art director. "When I was twenty-five," she says, "I thought I would have a child on my own when I turned thirty. When I turned thirty, I thought I wasn't ready yet. Now at thirty-five, I see how hard two parents need to work to raise a child and I no longer think I have the stamina and patience to do it. But one friend said something that makes sense: 'There's so much divorce today that a lot of children end up with only one parent anyway.' And I could give a child more love than a lot of people can."

Melanie's concerns about having a child on her own also involve her career, which is not where she would like it to be. "I think the only way I could have a baby on my own is if I had a secure and growing career that would enable me to buy help—to have a housekeeper. But I'm not in that position. I feel in such turmoil over my career right now that I couldn't consider having a baby. I'm doing very well in my work, but it seems that in publishing you get to a point where you can't go any higher, and I'm in that position. There is no next level. I don't see where my career should be going. In advertising, on the art side, people keep advancing, but the stories I hear about advertising are just horrible—terrible clients, terrible pressures. I'm going to be doing a lot of thinking in the very near future about what I want to do. A fortune-teller told me that there was going to be a big change in my life, that I would be doing something entirely different. I feel pressure to make a next step, within a year. After the holidays I want to get my résumé and my portfolio together, and update it, and maybe start going to talk to people to see what other directions I could go with the skills I already have."

Solving her career quandary before seriously considering single mother-hood is so important to Melanie that she turned down an opportunity to get pregnant by a former boyfriend while on her recent vacation in Australia. "It was always a long-distance romance, and I always knew we wouldn't end up together," she says. "It was extremely tempting to think about getting preg-nant by him. It was the right time of the month. I may never see him again as long as I live. But I realized it was a fantasy."

Not for Me

The women who are saying no to single motherhood are doing so not because they don't want children, but because they don't want to bring a child into the world alone. A number believe that having two parents is very important. Others do not think they could handle the responsibility alone. "I love kids, and I think I'm good with kids," says Dorothy, twenty-nine, a joint data base coordinator who broke up with her boyfriend of six and a half years because he wouldn't commit to and didn't want children. "As I've grown older the thought of raising children doesn't scare me as much. When I was younger I really wondered if I'd do a good job, be a good parent. But at this point, I wouldn't become a single mother. My main reason for saying no is I realize all the work involved and I just wonder about having a career and raising a child and I don't think I could handle it alone financially or emotionally right now."

Camille, thirty-one, an assistant director of career services, also worries about the impact on her life and on the child's. "A woman in my apartment building had a child in her late thirties. The baby is a year old now, and I'm seeing how rough it is to raise a child by yourself. If I did it, I'm thinking I'd adopt a child who was five or six because I wouldn't be able to care for a baby by myself. I also have a hard time thinking about doing it on my own because I don't think it would be best for the child. People always have a curiosity about who their parents are, and it would be hard to raise a child without having a father to share with the child. I guess I'm a little old-fashioned."

What's best for the child is also on the mind of Valerie, thirty-four, a sales coordinator. "I'm trying to be very adult and intelligent about it," she says. "I've seen many of my women friends who were married go ahead and have children and the majority of them are now separated or divorced. It's a result of the times—the lack of responsibility, of commitment that people have to things that should be very important. I don't think it's a good time to bring a child into the world.

"I came from a separated home. My father left when I was three. I think that also has a lot to do with my feelings. I've seen what troubles arise from that situation. And because of the financial difficulties I've gone through, I've seen what a lack of money can do to a person's life. I'm very concerned about my financial security and a lot of my efforts are directed to that end. Basic things today are so damn expensive. Even though I'm making a lot of money —far more than the national average—just covering living expenses and trying to save for the future are hard. Yet I have quite a fight within myself because when you are single, you very much want to have a family, to have another person in your life, but by the same token I don't think it's possible for me."

6

Our Real Biological Clocks

What does it mean to be human? Our cerebral cortex is what makes us capable of language, of reason, of creativity. But at the base of the human brain is a collection of tissue which is also present in animal brains. It governs the body's temperature, regulates breathing, tells us when we are thirsty, and when we are hungry. It reacts to tides, gravity, seasons, the planet's position in its orbit around the sun. It regulates libido, depression, rage, sexual desire and reproductive cycles. It is a power unto itself, operating beyond the control of personality, will or intelligence. It is the hypothalamus.

The hypothalamus is part of the limbic system of the old forebrain which we share with ancient vertebrate ancestors: fish, amphibians, reptiles, birds. It communicates chemically with the large organs of the body—the heart, lungs, stomach, and digestive tract—the olfactory nerve (which governs the sense of smell), and the pituitary gland which controls the activity of the body's hormonal, endocrine system.

Through its interaction with the pituitary gland, the hypothalamus regulates the male and female sexual reproductive systems. It does so by sending a chemical messenger to the pituitary which tells it when to release a particular hormone into the body's bloodstream, or not to release it. These hormones from the pituitary, called gonadotropic hormones, control the cycles of menstruation and ovulation, and the changes of life at puberty—our biological clocks.

These real biological clocks operate in silence, and most of the time we are totally unaware of them. We menstruate each month, but the cycle that our body moves through from menses to menses is not apparent to most of us. We marveled at the dramatic transformation of our bodies at puberty, but since then we have not felt the changes in our reproductive systems that happen as we age and move toward menopause.

In order to understand the clock that controls the life cycle of our reproductive system, it is first necessary to understand the clock that controls the monthly cycle of ovulation and menstruation. Each month, the hypothalamus conducts our hormonal system so that an egg is released from one of our ovaries, the lining of our uterus is prepared to nurture a fertilized ovum, and if the egg is not fertilized, the lining is sloughed off in menstruation and the cycle begins again. The monthly concerto played by these hormones is intricate and dramatic. Let's examine the music.

The Monthly Concerto

It all actually begins while each woman is still inside her mother's womb. Within the female fetus, eggs are created at the bottom of the abdomen; from there they travel into the ovary. By the eighth month of pregnancy, each baby girl has six million eggs. Two thirds of them will disappear before she is born. At three months of age, she has only one egg left for every six she originally produced.

Until puberty each female's hypothalamus releases inhibiting factors that keep her from becoming sexually mature. But when the growth hormone switches off those inhibiting factors, girls begin breast development, their pubic hair appears, and their bodies grow rapidly, particularly in the year and a half before menstruation begins. The first menstrual period usually occurs two and a half years after the beginning of breast development.

From that menstruation on, thirteen or so times a year for the next thirty to forty years, the hypothalamus waves its baton and the female cycle begins (unless of course a woman has conceived a child). It starts by producing a chemical messenger called a gonadotropin-releasing hormone (GnRH), which directs the pituitary to send the follicle-stimulating hormone (FSH) through the bloodstream to the ovaries. There it stimulates the growth of the follicles which contain the eggs. This release of FSH occurs during the first seven days of the cycle.

As they grow, the follicles produce estrogen, which prepares the uterus for a possible pregnancy. The estrogen levels begin to rise from day seven to day fourteen of the cycle, slowly at first, and then rapidly. When the estrogen circulating in the body rises, it feeds back to the pituitary and triggers it to reduce the amount of FSH production, which in turn stops further development of the follicles.

The circulating estrogen also cues the pituitary to release another hormone called the luteinizing hormone (LH). It is this hormone that causes the final development of one of the eggs in one of the follicles and its release from the ovary. Under the influence of LH, this one follicle continues to grow, and as it does it produces fluid which bathes the maturing egg which is resting at the bottom. When the egg is fully mature, the follicle migrates up from inside the body of the ovary to the surface, which has become a thinner and thinner roof over its head. As the follicle ruptures and the fluid inside gushes forth, carrying the egg to the outside of the ovary, the estrogen levels surge to their peak. The high estrogen levels also cause the brief release of prolactin from the pituitary. Immediately following the release of the egg, the estrogens fall abruptly.

At the exact moment when the egg is about to pop out alone and loose into the abdominal cavity, some unknown force tells the fallopian tube to move over the precise area of the ovary where the ripe egg is located. The end of the fallopian tube resembles the cup of a tulip or a daffodil. The petals, or fingers, of this cup gather up the egg and carry it into the tube, where it begins its journey to the uterus, a journey in which it may meet with a sperm that will penetrate it, resulting in a pregnancy and the possible birth of a baby nine months later, or a journey it may make alone, in which case it will be sloughed off by the body with the lining of the uterus during the next menstrual period.

Once the egg is released, its follicle grows into an important new structure called the corpus luteum. The corpus luteum makes progesterone, which is responsible for changes in the breasts during each cycle. It also helps prepare the lining of the uterus to receive the egg if it has been fertilized (it will implant in the uterine lining approximately nine days after conception), and it supports the development of the fertilized egg until the placenta takes over that function during the second month of pregnancy. As the corpus luteum grows in this first week after ovulation—the luteal phase of the cycle—estrogens are also produced in increasing amounts. The LH and FSH levels are both low during this phase because the progesterone feeds back to the pituitary and in effect tells it to slow down FSH and LH production.

If the egg has not been fertilized, it does not implant in the lining of the uterus, and during the second week after ovulation the corpus luteum begins to disintegrate and stops producing progesterone, and the pituitary stops receiving the signal inhibiting FSH production. So, as the corpus luteum regresses, the level of FSH begins to gradually rise and it starts the development of a new set of follicles. Progesterone and estrogen return to baseline levels, menstruation occurs, and the whole cycle begins again.

The hypothalamus and the pituitary can be viewed as providers of the important gonadotropin hormones for the functioning of the system. Whereas, says Nanette Santoro, M.D., a clinical and research fellow in reproductive endocrinology at Massachusetts General Hospital, "The ovary can be seen as the modulator of the system. It influences the waxing and the waning level of hormones, and tells the pituitary what hormones it wants and when."

Of course, if the egg is fertilized and is carried to term, the cycle is interrupted by pregnancy. Once the fertilized ovum burrows into the lining of the uterus, the placenta starts to develop. It produces three important hormones. The first is human chorionic gonadotropin (HCG), which is what pregnancy tests measure. HCG is necessary for the fertilized ovum to develop, and it also stimulates the corpus luteum to continue to produce both progesterone and estrogen until the placenta is mature enough to assume these functions. By the middle of the second month of pregnancy, the placenta takes over estrogen and progesterone production. Estrogen levels continue to rise right up to delivery; progesterone levels increase gradually until the twenty-fourth week of pregnancy, then rise more rapidly to the thirty-second week, where the level remains stable until delivery. Proof of the placenta's role in progesterone production can be found in the cases of pregnant women who have had both ovaries removed at the end of the second month of pregnancy and have experienced no drop in their progesterone level. Their fetuses have continued to grow normally as all the necessary progesterone was produced by the placenta.

The cycle of menstruation and ovulation is also interrupted by use of the birth control pill, which basically puts into the body a level of estrogen similar to what is produced by the ovary during pregnancy. "It shuts off the pituitary so the production of the gonadotropins is low and the ovaries go to sleep," says Dr. Santoro. "LH and FSH levels drop down to nearly undetectable amounts. The follicles don't mature and the eggs aren't released. It's a sort of pregnancy-like state, with elevated progesterone levels—not as high as in pregnancy, but higher than normal."

It's been suggested that perhaps modern women may experience too many of these monthly cycles uninterrupted by pregnancy and that may be the reason that so many of us experience difficulties such as PMS and endometriosis. In *Sex and Destiny,* Germaine Greer points out that we are among the first generations to have thirteen menstruations a year for most of our adult lives because we are using effective contraception, and are not bearing many children or nursing them for extended periods of time. By contrast, our ancestors spent most of their adult lives pregnant or lactating, which usually delays the return of menstruation. Women in hunter-gatherer societies—in which all human beings lived for thousands upon thousands of years—might not have many menstruations after their first one. In these societies, young women tend to marry soon after their first menstruation and quickly become pregnant. They nurse each child for four years, delaying the return of menstruation and providing a fairly effective method of birth control.

The increased incidence of breast cancer also has been associated with our low modern birthrate, which causes the breasts to undergo stimulation by estrogen and progesterone during each monthly menstrual cycle over long uninterrupted periods of time. This theory is supported by the fact that considerable protection against breast cancer is provided by the act of nursing our children, which delays the return of menstruation after childbirth. Some researchers have shown that the risk of getting breast cancer decreases from 1 in 25 chances to 1 out of 125 when a baby is nursed for six months. Protection may also be provided by the use of the birth control pill, which in shutting down the cyclical system, stops the breasts from going through monthly hormonal stimulation. Recent research has also shown that women who were athletic when young and experienced a delay in the onset of menstruation, or whose continuing athletic endeavors cause them to stop menstruating, have a lower incidence of breast cancer, as well as other cancers of the female reproductive system.

Hormones and Sex

It should be of little surprise that the gonadotropic hormones are also involved in our sexual drive. They cause us to be more responsive to sex at one time of the reproductive cycle than at other times. Women's interest in sex and level of sexual activity increases about 25 percent in the three-day period of ovulation according to research conducted at Wesleyan University and reported in the *New England Journal of Medicine* in 1978.

Indeed, just under 25 percent of the clock-watchers report that they are aware of being more interested in sex when they are ovulating. "A long time ago a woman who was about five years older than I am said, 'You have to decide if having a child is something you truly want to do or if it's simply biological,' " says Lydia, thirty-two, a senior secretarial specialist, who is single. "I've kind of paid attention to that. When I went to Boston in May, I made love without contraception for the first time in my life. The urge was so strong that I was willing to have a child by myself. I did not get pregnant— luckily, I guess. But the urge was almost overwhelming. A lot of women in my age group, both married and single, are going through the same thing. We all seem to be in the throes of this urge to propagate the species. I try to stay in touch with my body and I've found that particularly during ovulation, my sexual urges are very strong. I'm very much aware of them."

At the time of ovulation, estrogen is building in the lining of the womb and progesterone is subtly raising the body's temperature, which gives the body color and tone. The high level of estrogen also changes the mucus in the cervix so it becomes clear and watery and is greatly increased in quantity. At other times the mucus is thick, gray, and the consistency of gelatin. The thinner, more abundant mucus allows the sperm to navigate through the cervix into the uterus. At ovulation the rise in progesterone also makes a woman more receptive to sex. This rise is accompanied by a peak in testosterone produced by the adrenal glands, which makes the clitoris more sensitive and increases the sex drive. This three-day period around ovulation is the only point in the cycle that all three of these hormones are elevated at the same time. (Testosterone levels are also high during a woman's menses, and some research has shown a high level of sexual interest and activity at this time.)

By arranging our hormone production to make us most receptive to sexual activity at the time when we are most likely to conceive a child is nature's way of ensuring the continuation of the species. It may be difficult for some of us to accept that our biology is influencing our actions in such a way, but we must remember that we are animals, and as animals, our limbic system controls us in ways we are not consciously aware. As Robert Rose, a pioneer researcher of sexual behavior at the University of Texas, wrote in an editorial accompanying the *New England Journal* article: "The rather extreme assertion that sexuality in human females has become independent of biological influences ignores our evolutionary heritage, a large number of animal studies, and the crucial role of reproductive biology in general."

In fact, according to Alice Rossi, Ph.D., the Harriet Martineau Professor of Sociology at the University of Massachusetts, one of the hormones produced by our pituitary glands provides "a clear link between sexuality and maternalism." That hormone is oxytocin, and it plays a crucial role during the sexual act, in childbirth, and in lactation—a role that shows the strong connection between sexuality and reproduction. During sex, the stimulation of a woman sends neural impulses to her hypothalamus, which in turn signals the pituitary to release oxytocin. The oxytocin causes nipple erection, but more important, it is responsible for contractions in the uterus during orgasm that push the sperm farther along on their journey up the fallopian tubes to find the egg. The sperm ride the waves the oxytocin creates in the uterus—these heralded long-distance swimmers don't make the journey entirely under their own power.

Although the whole picture of why labor begins sometime around forty weeks of pregnancy is still unclear, it is known that a drop in the level of progesterone allows an increase in the level of oxytocin—as well as the prostaglandins—and this shift in the hormonal pattern helps bring on labor. During labor our uterine contractions are caused by the high levels of oxytocin circulating in our systems (Pitocin, which is used to induce contractions, is a synthetic form of oxytocin).

Oxytocin also causes the breasts to let down their milk during nursing so that the baby can receive it easily. In the second half of pregnancy, the pituitary begins to produce prolactin, which causes milk to be stored in the breasts; it is present from the fifth or sixth month on. If a woman has a premature birth, she will lactate. After birth, as the estrogen and progesterone levels abruptly decrease because the placenta has been removed, women's breasts are no longer inhibited from secreting milk, and the milk supply comes in.

The baby's sucking on the breast continues to produce prolactin and ensures the production of milk. It also stimulates the nipple, which triggers the release of oxytocin by the pituitary and causes the milk to "let down" from the alveoli and ducts where it is stored into the main milk sinuses under the nipple, which the baby can empty by sucking. If the milk does not let down, the baby can only retrieve that which is already in the milk sinuses—about 30 percent of the supply—and none of the fat content of the milk, which is all in the milk stored in the alveoli and milk ducts. The baby may be getting adequate fluids, but if the milk is not letting down properly, he or she will be continually hungry. In other words, the release of oxytocin is essential for successful nursing.

Some nursing mothers become so hormonally attuned to their babies that thinking about them, or hearing them cry, will cause the release of oxytocin, and their milk will let down before the baby begins to suck. The oxytocin released during nursing also performs another important job: it contracts the uterus so that it is restored to prepregnancy condition. And, notes Alice

Rossi, the role of the oxytocin in stimulating the mother's nipples and uterus during nursing provides her with "erotogenic pleasure," which adds to her desire to nurse and ensures the well-being of her baby.

Hormones and Our Cycles

Obviously our hormonal system exerts a silent influence on our sexual and reproductive behavior. But does the communication run the other way? Does the hypothalamus and its subsidiary hormonal glands which govern our reproductive cycles—our biological clocks—react to our thoughts and emotions? The answer is yes.

The hypothalamus is also connected to the neocortex of the cerebrum in the new forebrain—the part of the brain with which we process information from the world outside so that we are conscious of all that is going on around us. A great deal of research in neuroendocrinology is centering on the connections between nerve cells in the neocortex and in the hypothalamus, and the biochemistry within these cells. At the present time no one knows for certain how the biochemistry works, but work it does. "Because the hypothalamus is part of the old cortex surrounding the brain stem, this also implicates the nervous system in endocrine functioning," notes Alice Rossi. "Neurons producing the releasing factors [in the hypothalamus] receive electrical signals from the rest of the brain and are subject to 'behavioral' influences and to the modulating influences of the gonadal hormones on neural circuits underlying behavior. . . . Social stimuli may thus impinge upon hormonal secretion through the nervous system."

The hormonal system seems to be particularly sensitive to stress. "The limbic system of which the hypothalamus is a part is very responsive to external stimulae—flight-or-fight type stimulae—and it does seem that that area of the brain is involved in stress responses," says Dr. Santoro. Adds Raphael Jewelewicz, M.D., chief of the Division of Reproductive Endocrinology at the College of Physicians and Surgeons of Columbia University, "There is no question that emotions affect the menstrual cycle. It works through the neuropeptides in the central nervous system."

Scientists are able to examine how our hormonal system reacts to our emotional response to stress when the response is so strong that it throws the system completely out of whack. Let's look at two opposite ways that this happens: first, in women who have stopped ovulating and menstruating because of stress, and second, in women who want to have a baby so much that their bodies mimic pregnancy although there is no baby inside.

Hypothalamic Amenorrhea

If a woman is under a great deal of stress, her menstrual periods will completely stop. Her hypothalamus will stop making GnRH, or it will make so little that there's not enough to trigger the pituitary to release FSH to get the cycle going. The stress can be physical—the kind an athlete puts on her body by rigorous and severe training, or an anorexic puts on her body by starvation. Or the stress can be emotional. "A patient may say, 'This all started ten years ago when my father died,' and boom, the system shuts off and doesn't come back on," says Dr. Santoro. She estimates that about 3 percent of women suffer from this condition.

"There are lots of fancy theories to explain why this can happen," she continues, "but we have not been able to measure the changes in the brain chemicals. The evidence we have now is that it's the result of the loss of the hypothalamus's ability to make or release GnRH. All the right neurons are there for it to be produced—but there are other regulating neurons that are preventing GnRH from being released."

At Massachusetts General Hospital, patients with hypothalamic amenorrhea are being successfully treated with GnRH therapy. Patients wear a pack containing GnRH, which is delivered to their bloodstream intravenously in pulses every hour to two hours. The frequency has to be altered constantly because pulse rates speed up and slow down. Most of the women on the therapy are outpatients—they can live their normal lives, and even jog or play tennis.

"The GnRH starts the whole system right up again, but it still won't work without the therapy," says Dr. Santoro. "We had hoped that we could prime the pump and get these women through one menstrual cycle and the body would take over. Their systems do wake right up and they have a normal cycle, just like women hitting puberty. But if we take the pump out, they go right back to where they were."

What is truly amazing about the GnRH therapy is that the women on it go from being in a state where their entire reproductive system is shut off to having a totally functional system which allows them to conceive a child and carry it to term. Eighty-six percent of the women on the therapy have become pregnant.

"The big selling point of GnRH is that it is highly specific unlike Clomid or Perganol," says Dr. Santoro. "It's correcting the defect at the level of the defect, and it seems to allow all the normal feedback that occurs between the ovary and the pituitary. The internal controls on ovulation are all there. There's no hyperstimulating—making too much estrogen and having multiple follicles mature as there is with Clomid and Perganol."

The one problem these women do experience is that after the birth of their children, they tend to have a real hormone crash. All women experience a big drop in their estrogen levels after delivery, but most women still make a small amount of estrogen. These women make none.

Pseudocyesis

Pseudocyesis—false pregnancy—demonstrates perhaps even more strongly than hypothalamic amenorrhea how our emotional state can affect the chemical and hormonal workings of our bodies. "It bridges the gap between the physical and the psychological," says Dr. Santoro.

A woman with pseudocyesis wants to be pregnant, fervently believes she is pregnant, and her emotional state causes her hormonal system to act in a way that makes her body take on the physical symptoms of pregnancy. She stops menstruating. She experiences nausea and vomiting. Her breasts swell. Her abdomen swells up and can stay that way for months. "Sometimes abdominal gas patterns can look like fetal movements," says Dr. Santoro. "Some women also have elevated prolactin levels and some of them will lactate."

A woman with pseudocyesis also stops ovulating, and thus her ovaries stop making progesterone, which means that her system is overexposed to whatever estrogen is circulating. Because there is no progesterone being made by the ovaries, the LH levels go way up and they remain fairly high. The elevated LH level can cause a pregnancy test to come out positive because it mimics what happens in a normal pregnancy where the placenta makes HCG. It's thought that the high LH level may also be biologically responsible for inducing some of the symptoms of pregnancy—although it is not nearly as high as with a normal pregnancy.

"These women are stuck in a steady hormonal state in which they do not have periods and they have fairly constant hormone levels," says Dr. Santoro.

"I had a patient who came in close to term. Her belly was huge and she proceeded to describe with terrific accuracy all the symptoms of pregnancy. Unless you examine someone and realize her uterus is small, you can be fooled." Pseudocyesis can be treated with progesterone, by injection or orally. It brings on a period and all the symptoms of the pregnancy disappear.

When a woman is trying to get pregnant, and she waits every month, hoping not to get her period, she can also experience some of the symptoms of pregnancy—what could be a sort of mild form of pseudocyesis. Her breasts may feel particularly swollen, she may have to urinate more than usual, she may even feel a little nauseous, and her menses may be very light, or late. Just under 10 percent of the clock-watchers report such symptoms. "I get cramps; I get bloating; my breasts swell," says Wanda, thirty-one, an accounting supervisor, whose husband has infertility problems. "I wait for my period. Last month it was a day late, and I got to thinking maybe I was. But it turned out I wasn't."

Even some of the women who want to have a baby but are using contraception because they don't want to be pregnant now report these symptoms. "I have an IUD and don't expect to be pregnant; I expect not to be," says Sandy, twenty-seven, a management associate at a New York bank, whose husband is not ready. "Yet when I'm about to get my period, my body begins feeling pregnant. I was pregnant years ago and had an abortion and since then my body has felt pregnant every month. Every month biology and emotion combine to make me go crazy."

Aging and the Clock

Although there is evidence that our emotions influence the action of our hormones, there is at present no proof that the loop runs the other way—that changes in our hormones can influence our emotions. Too little is known about the connections between the cerebral cortex and the hormone system for most neuroendocrinologists to even hazard a guess about how a woman's desire to have a child—the sudden baby lust many of the clock-watchers report—might be affected by the changes in our hormone system that happen as we age. As Dr. Santoro says, "It's hard to relate a system of which we are totally unaware to something we're consciously feeling." Dr. Jewelewicz adds, "There is really no evidence that there are discernible hormonal changes which you can correlate with increase in age and an increase in the desire to have children."

But scientists do know a fair amount about what does happen as our sexual and reproductive systems age. For one thing, it seems clear that women's level of sexual desire does not peak soon after they reach puberty as men's does, but later, at about age twenty-eight. It is then maintained at this level until age forty-five. Almost a quarter of the clock-watchers in fact are aware that they have a greater sexual desire at this time of their life than they did earlier. This timetable roughly corresponds to the one governing ovulation—and thus the number of chances we have to conceive when we are sexually active. When we begin to menstruate at puberty, we do not ovulate in all of our menstrual cycles. As we mature, the proportion of cycles in which we do ovulate rises until our early thirties. It then stays constant until our late thirties to early forties when it drops again.

Women's reproductive life story has three basic phases. It ascends gradually to a high plateau. It stays there for a long optimal period for reproduction, and then it gradually descends the slope again. These movements can be traced by measuring the length of the menstrual cycle itself, and how much variation in length there is between cycles, the length of the phases before and after ovulation, how often cycles occur without ovulation, how often conception occurs at different ages, and the outcome of pregnancy at different ages.

The length of the menstrual cycle declines with age up until the early forties, and then increases in the premenopausal years. From age twenty-four to forty-two, it decreases gradually from thirty days to twenty-six and a half days. As the cycle shortens, the number of days after ovulation decrease. Cycles of twenty-seven to twenty-eight days long have a fourteen-day phase after ovulation, those of twenty-one to twenty-six days long have a postovulatory phase of thirteen days. From around age forty-three, cycle length increases from twenty-seven days until it is fifty-seven days by age forty-nine or fifty. Approximately forty to fifty cycles prior to the onset of menopause, the length of the menstrual cycles increases abruptly, as does the variation between them.

What is happening here hormonally? Through our thirties, there are no noticeable hormonal changes. But as women move into the premenopausal phase at around age forty, their estrogen levels begin to drop. However, "the general hormonal pattern appears to be relatively normal, and women do appear to consistently ovulate, although for some reason their ability to get pregnant goes down," says Dr. Santoro. "Their FSH levels, which stimulate their ovaries to ovulate and to produce estrogen, tend to be higher and they get higher and higher as the ovaries get more resistant, so to speak, to the FSH stimulant," Dr. Santoro adds.

Dr. Jewelewicz paints a grimmer picture of the premenopausal period for women who are still hoping to bear children. A study just came out from the College of Physicians & Surgeons that he says shows "that about 10 years before menopause there is a tremendous drop in fertility. If the average age of menopause is 52, this drop happens at 42. All the tests are going to be normal, but the rate of pregnancy is going to be much lower. The number of eggs a 40-year-old woman has is considerably less than a 20-year-old has. She may ovulate less, and when she does get pregnant, there may be something wrong with the egg because it is an aged egg. There is a significantly higher rate of miscarriages at this time."

Menopause itself is the final stage of the process begun during the premenopausal period. Fewer and fewer of the follicles in the ovaries contain eggs and thus are capable of producing estrogen and progesterone, which would restrain the pituitary from releasing FSH and LH. So the levels of the stimulating hormones, particularly FSH, go way, way up. Women in menopause also have increased levels of GnRH, the hormonal messenger from the hypothalamus that tells the pituitary to produce FSH and LH. It stays at a high level for about twenty years after menopause and it continues to trigger the pituitary to release those two hormones in great quantities because the ovaries are so unresponsive.

"It tries to whip the ovaries into working," says Dr. Santoro. "But they can't. The ovaries fail. That's what causes menopause." And so the reproductive clock strikes its final hour.

7

Getting Pregnant
Fertility and the Clock

Waiting like a menacing cloud over every woman's horizon is the specter of infertility, because until each of us is pregnant, we never know if we can be. For years we have taken contraceptive precautions and worried each time our periods were late. Suddenly, now that we are ready to make a baby, we realize how ironic it would be if we had never needed to worry about contraception at all. We spin out again and again every tale of success after long and difficult treatment. We pass them on to friends like gold coins. Stories of failure are pushed from our minds, never to be repeated. They are not forgotten, just buried; ready to rise and haunt us. We ask ourselves: Will we be plunged into that darkest of battles, the one within our own bodies?

"It haunts me that there may be something wrong," says Cheryl, thirty-one, an assistant director of an industry council. "I've had chlamydia [a sexually transmitted disease] twice and I realize that causes infertility. After all these years of agonizing about having a baby, if I finally do make this momentous decision, I might discover that I can't."

For about one in ten of the clock-watchers, these fears have come true. For 90 percent of the couples who can't get pregnant and seek medical help, testing reveals the source of their problem. But the other 10 percent are left in the dark. No physical reason can be found for their lack of success, and no treatment can be given. They may become pregnant; they may not. For them, it might as well be the nineteenth century for all the good the medical advances against infertility will do them. When Jessie, thirty-six, an instructional assistant with a Ph.D., and her husband discovered they were in this category, at first they brooded. "Both of us were surprised and taken aback by the reality of the situation. In all likelihood we will never be parents. But as we've adjusted to that, we've decided that as long as we are child-free, we are going to enjoy ourselves. We are both challenged by our work, but we also love to travel and we are negotiating changes in our salary and vacation benefits so that we can do so for six to ten weeks each year. If I wake up to find I'm expecting sometime between now and my fortieth birthday, that's OK too."

Of those couples with an identifiable problem, 40 percent is due to male sperm production; 40 percent to female structural complications such as damaged fallopian tubes or endocrine (hormonal) deficiencies such as a lack of ovulation; and 20 percent to an incompatibility between the egg and the sperm. Over 60 percent of these problems can be treated. For these couples, it's a question of how far they will go, how much pain, expense, and emotional torment they are willing to endure before the woman gets pregnant and carries a child to term, or gives up. "Since I got married again three years ago I've had two miscarriages, major surgery for endometriosis and another operation to remove one ovary damaged by pelvic inflammatory disease," says Sybil, thirty-six, an attorney with the federal government. "My hormones went crazy so I'm now taking Clomid [a drug that causes ovulation]. I've also been in therapy for the last six months. One of the hardest things is knowing when to draw the line, admitting it's not going to happen for you. Right now I think I'll go on for another year. If I'm not pregnant by then, I'll cut my losses and get on with it. In the past year I've been on such an emotional roller coaster that I don't know from one week to the next how I'm going to be thinking or feeling. It's real hard for me to look far into the future and predict what I'm going to feel. But the longer it goes on, the more of a sense you have that it's not going to happen. Some days I feel, 'I'm going to *make* this happen to me.' Some days I don't feel that way. It's almost a fatalistic feeling: if it's going to happen, it's going to happen."

The Risk of Waiting

How much of a woman's infertility is related to her age, to her decision to postpone childbearing into her thirties? The answer is not clear. Some recent studies indicate that the decline in fertility among older women is modest, and that a woman's health and habits have almost as much to do with it as her age does. John Bongaarts, Ph.D., a senior associate at the Population Council, writes in *Family Planning Perspectives* that "age-related infertility does exist but is not nearly as much as [a recent] 'scare' report suggests." He estimates that only 9 percent of women thirty to thirty-four and 20 percent of women thirty-five to thirty-nine are infertile. And he goes further, saying that a woman twenty-five to twenty-nine would increase her risk of infertility by only four percentage points if she waited an additional five years before having children.

One of the reasons Dr. Bongaarts's data is so optimistic is that it is not based on a one-year period of trying to conceive without success. He writes that "infertility estimates based on 12 months of exposure greatly exaggerate the risk of ultimate involuntary childlessness inherent in voluntary postponement of child bearing. The true proportions [of] infertile [women] should be based not on a single year but on several years of observation."

Yet when women have been followed for three years, the picture for those thirty and over is not substantially better. Of women who had not conceived after one year, the vast majority of those thirty and over had also not conceived after three years: 68 percent of those thirty to thirty-four, 83 percent of those thirty-five to thirty-nine, and 86 percent of those forty to forty-four. "Those who had not conceived after three years probably never will conceive; that is, they are probably sterile," writes Gerry Hendershot and other researchers at the National Center for Health Statistics who dispute Dr. Bongaarts's estimates of infertility. "It is apparent," concludes Hendershot in *Family Planning Perspectives,* "that women who postpone having their first child until their 30s do face an increased risk that they will not be able to conceive. The evidence presented by Bongaarts that the increase is 'modest' may understate [that risk]."

What these statistics don't say is who is liable to risk infertility by waiting. And in fact it seems that there are two tracts of women—those without any infertility or health problems who will maintain their fertility pretty much unchanged through their thirties, as many of the clock-watchers have done, and those who have problems that will only get worse with age. For them, waiting may mean never.

What are those problems? One of the major causes of infertility in women of all ages is pelvic inflammatory disease (PID), but the older a woman is, the more years she has had to develop it. If she has been sexually active, and married late, her chances of having caught some sexually transmitted disease that causes PID are very good. One of the main culprits is chlamydia, which accounts for approximately 50 percent of all cases of PID. It's been estimated that as many as 150,000 women who currently have chlamydia will become sterile. The big problem with chlamydia is figuring out that you have it. In many women, the symptoms are so mild they go unnoticed, or they are mistaken for the symptoms of other infections. Like gonorrhea, chlamydia can cause an increase in vaginal discharge, or it may result in frequent and painful urination which is usually associated with urinary tract infection. Only a few women experience the classic symptom of PID—severe lower abdominal pain. A misdiagnosis will mean that the wrong treatment is prescribed, and the chlamydia will continue to wreak its havoc.

If not discovered and treated early, PID can cause structural damage to the ovaries, the uterus, and the fallopian tubes. Ovarian scarring can stop ovulation; scars in the uterus can prevent implantation of a fertilized egg. If the tubes are scarred by PID, the egg cannot make its journey toward the uterus, nor can the sperm reach the egg.

But sometimes the damage to the tubes is only partial and the sperm are able to travel up the tubes to fertilize the egg. The result is an ectopic pregnancy, where the ovum implants in the wall of the tube (or very occasionally in other sites such as the abdominal cavity or the ovary) because it is blocked from reaching the uterus. As the ovum burrows into the tube, it causes it to rupture and hemorrhage into the abdominal cavity. This is a life-threatening condition unless discovered promptly so that the pregnancy and usually the tube can be removed. The numbers of ectopic pregnancies have increased so rapidly in recent years that the Centers for Disease Control have called the disease an epidemic.

Another cause of PID is the IUD. When it is inserted, bacteria enter the uterus with it and can cause an infection. Women using the IUD have four times the number of pelvic abscesses and infections and three times the numbers of cases of salpingitis, which is inflammation of the fallopian tubes. In addition, it is thought by some researchers that sexually transmitted diseases ride the backs of the sperm during intercourse and that because the IUD lets the sperm into the uterus—as barrier methods do not—it allows the diseases access to the tubes.

With each episode of PID, the likelihood of tubal scarring increases: 12 percent with the first, 30 percent with the second, and 75 percent with the third. Charlotte, thirty-four, a part-time counselor of graduate students, says she has had so many pelvic infections that she doesn't even have an internist —she just sees a gynecologist. Her worst bout with PID was almost six years ago. "I could have had it for several months," she says. "By the time I went to the doctor I was running a fever. The doctor did a pelvic and I went up to the ceiling it hurt so much. I saw two different doctors, first one in a little town outside Omaha, and then one in Omaha. The second wanted to do a laparoscopy [a simple hospital procedure in which the tubes are examined through two long instruments inserted through a tiny slit in the abdomen] to see the damage, but I chickened out. I just stayed home and nursed myself and took my antibiotics faithfully, all the way to the last one. There is definitely damage there. I can even feel the scarring. You know when you have a cut and it has a scab on it—you can feel the pull of the skin. It's a slight feeling, but it's there. I can tell when I ovulate on one side because I have a pain right there."

Women who wait to have children also increase their risk of developing endometriosis, which has been estimated to cause 30 percent of the cases of female infertility. It is so common in women in their thirties who have never had children that it's been called the working woman's disease. In endometriosis, which is also known as the chocolate cyst disease, cells that normally line the uterus and are sloughed off in menstruation instead migrate up the fallopian tubes and out into the pelvic cavity, where they implant and grow. In the process, they scar the tubes or grow up over the ovaries. The classic symptoms of endometriosis are painful menstrual periods and painful intercourse. But 50 percent of the women with endometriosis experience none of these symptoms. They only discover they are victims of the disease during a laparoscopy in connection with a fertility workup.

Most of the clock-watchers who have discovered that they have endometriosis realize that their postponement of childbearing, for career or private goals, is what has brought it on, and they would live their lives differently if only they could. "Given my present physical condition, and the mental anguish my infertility has caused me and is causing me, I would not do this all over for anything," says Sybil. "Having a child early may be the most viable solution after all. At least that's the way I see it now as I face the very real possibility of a future with no children, only a career. In my twenties, it was a foregone conclusion that I could have a family when I wanted it. Who ever heard of infertility in those days? What a hassle being in the generation on the cutting edge of women's rights. I sure hope our children and grandchildren get to make better-informed choices. Then maybe all of the grief will seem worth it. Right now it hardly seems so to me."

As seen in the last chapter, there is also a relationship between age and ovulation, especially as women approach and enter their forties. Some statistics show that women in their thirties may ovulate only eight to ten times a year versus thirteen times a year for those in their twenties. It's also been demonstrated through *in vitro* fertilization that women in their thirties and forties may have eggs that are not as easily fertilized as younger women's.

And as Dr. Jewelewicz, the chief of the Division of Reproductive Endocrinology at the College of Physicians & Surgeons of Columbia University, stated, the eggs that are left in the ovaries are old eggs, which means that more of them may be imperfect and if fertilized will be miscarried.

As the postovulatory phase of the menstrual cycle shortens in the late thirties, it can also result in hormonal problems associated with the corpus luteum called luteal phase defects. Once the egg is fertilized, it is the job of the corpus luteum to produce enough progesterone to adequately build up the endometrium, the lining of the uterus, so that the egg can implant and grow for approximately the first two months of pregnancy until the placenta takes over progesterone production. If the corpus luteum is not doing its job properly because of inadequate stimulation by the hormones from the pituitary LH and FSH, the result is infertility or a first trimester miscarriage.

Like other immunological diseases such as arthritis, sperm antibody problems tend to get worse with age. Thirty percent of infertile people have been estimated to have some antibody problem, with women being affected twice as often as men. What happens is that the woman, or the man, produces antibodies that destroy the sperm before they can fertilize the egg. The woman may have antibodies only in her cervical mucus, but it is more likely that her entire system produces them. The man's antibodies are in his seminal fluid.

Fibroid tumors are another problem associated with advancing age. Approximately a quarter of all women aged thirty to fifty have fibroids, but the number in whom they cause infertility is smaller. They can also grow so thickly in the uterus they can keep an egg from implanting, or cause repeated miscarriages because the growing placenta cannot get sufficient purchase on the uterine wall.

One of the most serious effects of aging on having a successful pregnancy is an increased risk of miscarriage in the first trimester. It's been estimated that 40 to 60 percent of miscarriages at this stage of pregnancy can be attributed to chromosomal abnormalities, and these have been shown to occur more frequently among older women. One study that tracked miscarriages (or as doctors call them, spontaneous abortions) in pregnancies under twelve weeks found that they rose from 40 per 1,000 women in their twenties to 75 per 1,000 women aged thirty to thirty-four to 150 per 1,000 women thirty-five and older —a doubling of risk from the early to the late thirties.

Women who are waiting to have a child are obviously putting themselves in a race against the clock if they do have a problem—there are simply fewer months and years left for the complicated testing and treatment necessary to determine the cause of the problem and try to correct it.

Testing Ahead of Time

Since time can literally pass a woman by if she waits too long to begin trying to have a child, the question arises: Is it possible to determine one's fertility prognosis earlier so a more informed decision can be made about waiting? In this way, if a problem is found treatment can begin. Yes, but it requires a fair degree of motivation.

First of all, a woman can improve her chances of conceiving by changing her habits. There is already a great deal of evidence that smoking during pregnancy adversely affects the growth, and health, of the baby, but now it seems it can even impede a woman's chances of having a baby. A recent article in the *Journal of the American Medical Association* reported that smokers have a 3.4 times greater chance of not conceiving for a year than do nonsmokers. The same is true of alcohol and drug use. It is known that they can harm the fetus, and now evidence is coming in that eliminating or restricting their use before attempting to conceive improves a woman's chance of getting pregnant.

Women should also examine the form of contraception they have been using all these years. If a woman has been taking birth control pills, she should certainly plan to go off them three or more months before trying to conceive. If a woman has been on the pill for a long time, she might do well to switch her contraception so her fertility can be restored even if she does not want to have a child for a few years. Twenty percent of users do not ovulate for two to three months after going off the pill, and another 20 percent do not conceive in a year—their ovulation may still not be back to normal.

The IUD, with its risk of causing infection, is another form of contraception that childless women should avoid. Even if a woman is having no obvious problem with her IUD, it should probably be removed if she wants to have a child in the future, and she should use a diaphragm or have her partner use a condom instead. Both of these methods have the additional advantage of preventing any sexually transmitted diseases from reaching the uterus.

A woman should also have yearly checkups with her gynecologist, which will usually catch things such as fibroids, endometriosis, kidney disorders, venereal disease, high blood pressure, and diabetes, which can affect an ability either to conceive or to carry a pregnancy to term.

In addition, all women, but especially those who are sexually active, should be tested for chlamydia every six months. A newly available test gives a diagnosis in under four hours. It is only in this way that chlamydia can be sorted out from the other sexually transmitted diseases that it mimics, so the right antibiotic can be prescribed. Penicillin, the normal treatment for gonorrhea, or sulfa drugs, which are used against a urinary infection, will not touch chlamydia. The correct treatment is tetracycline. Another genital infection that has virtually no symptoms and has been implicated both in infertility and in first trimester miscarriage is T-mycoplasma. Tetracycline will also eradicate T-mycoplasma.

A woman can find out if she ovulates by taking her temperature with a basal thermometer before she gets out of bed each morning. Charting ovulation for at least three months is usually required for a gynecologist to be able to get an accurate reading. The temperature should rise and stay up for thirteen to fourteen days after ovulation. No increase in temperature means possible ovulatory problems. A costly, but more accurate, alternative to the temperature chart is the ovulation stick, newly on the market, which quickly tells the precise time of ovulation each month by measuring the LH surge which occurs twenty-four to thirty-six hours ahead of ovulation. When the stick turns blue, ovulation is imminent. Some women don't need to do this self-testing; they have obvious difficulties with ovulation—the number of days between their menstrual periods is very irregular, or they don't menstruate at all—and for them, an early trip to an infertility specialist is definitely a good idea.

A simple blood test will be able to determine why a woman doesn't ovulate, so the correct treatment can be prescribed when she wants to get pregnant. Most failure to ovulate is the result of a failure of the pituitary to produce enough LH or FSH, or of the hypothalamus to produce the releasing hormone GnRH. But some is caused by polycystic ovary disease; by a condition called hyperprolactinemia, in which there is too much prolactin in the blood, which suppresses ovulation; by endometriosis which has damaged the ovaries; or by the use of the birth control pill for too extended a period of time.

If the blood test shows that FSH and LH are circulating, the hypothalamus is at fault, and the treatment is usually Clomid, or Seraphene, which stimulate the hypothalamus. It is taken for five days, and ovulation occurs five to ten later. The dosage can range from 50 to 200 milligrams a day, depending on how responsive (or unresponsive) a woman's ovaries are. Clomid may take six to eight months to work; women should not give up on it too early. It does cause ovulation in 80 percent of the women treated, and 66 percent of those who ovulate conceive.

When the pituitary fails to produce the surge of FSH and LH necessary to stimulate the growth of an egg and trigger its release, the drug that is used is Pergonal—the brand name for human menopausal gonadotropin, which is extracted from urine of women going through menopause. If Clomid fails to induce ovulation, a woman is often put on Pergonal. It is a much more complicated treatment than Clomid, which is taken orally. Pergonal is actually two different drugs. One is injected daily in the beginning of the cycle; the other injected once at midcycle. A woman also has to have her blood tested daily and have several pelvic examinations and ultrasonograms to monitor the enlargement of her ovaries.

If a woman's cycle is shorter than it has been in the past, it may mean that her postovulatory phase is shorter, which could indicate luteal phase problems. An endometrial biopsy can be performed shortly before menstruation to determine if the hormone levels in the endometrium are sufficient to sustain a pregnancy, and to confirm that a woman does ovulate. The cervix is slightly dilated and the uterine lining is scraped with a curette. It is usually done with a local anesthesia in the office. Dolores, thirty-eight, a nurse-midwife, has been through three or four of them and she says, "I do complain. I'm not nice. I know what instruments they use. I tell the doctor he has to put a local anesthetic in because I can't tolerate it. Sometimes I take a mild tranquilizer beforehand, and also a Motrin or a mild prostaglandin to keep the uterus from contracting."

Since the quantity or quality of the man's sperm is at fault in 40 percent of all infertility cases, the husband's sperm should be counted at the time a woman's ovulation is being tested. A normal ejaculation should contain more than twenty million vigorous sperm. The percentage with motility—the ability to swim in a straight line—should be 60 percent at a minimum. If the numbers of sperm are low, further counts should be done over a six-month period to verify this finding. Then testing by a urologist who specializes in infertility will be required to find out why sperm production is inadequate. The possibilities include abnormal tissue in the testicles which may impede circulation, varicocele—varicose veins in the scrotum, which are believed to be responsible for 40 percent of male infertility—prostate gland troubles, genetic flaws, and hormonal trouble. Treatment for male infertility is less advanced than for female infertility, but knowing there is a problem early still buys time.

But in one area, treatment is extremely advanced: vasectomy reversals. Even for men who have had previously unsuccessful reversals, or vasectomies done years ago, the rate of success is extremely high. For over 90 percent of the twenty-five hundred patients who have had reversals done by Sherman J. Silber, M.D., a reproductive microsurgeon at St. Luke's Hospital in St. Louis, Missouri, and author of *How to Get Pregnant,* the operation has been a success, meaning normal sperm counts, motility, and fertility.

If ovulation and sperm counts are normal, couples can rule out another source of infertility problems by having a postcoital test during the time of ovulation to examine the quantity and quality of cervical mucus and to count the number and condition of sperm close to the cervix. It's a simple procedure which should reassure all concerned if the results are normal. The couple has intercourse two to eight hours before the appointment, during which the doctor aspirates mucus from the woman's cervix and examines it. The mucus should be thin and spin out into a thread. When it dries on a slide, it should crystalize so that it resembles the shape of a fern when viewed under a microscope. Thick mucus at the time of ovulation can prevent the sperm from getting through the cervix, a problem that can usually be solved with drug therapy.

The number and activity of the sperm in the fluid is also examined with a microscope. If few active sperm are present, the woman may have antibodies that are attacking and destroying the sperm, or the man may be producing antibodies in his seminal fluid that attack his sperm. According to Sidney Shulman, Ph.D., director of the Sperm Antibody Laboratory in New York, 60 to 80 percent of patients with poor postcoital tests have antibodies, but 20 percent of those who have a good postcoital test also have antibodies.

To determine if there is an antibody problem, a woman's cervical mucus and her blood plasma must be tested separately to see if her problem is localized or throughout her system. A man's seminal plasma must also be tested for clumping of the sperm. The test should be repeated three to four times to assure accuracy.

When pregnancy is desired, a short course of high-dose cortisone therapy, which will suppress the immune system, can be given to whichever partner has the problem. It is successful in 30 percent of the cases. If the man is producing antibodies in his seminal fluid, his sperm can also be washed three times using a method called SWIM and then artificially inseminated into his wife.

A new treatment for such "allergy" cases, as well as low sperm counts, has been found to have a 30 percent success rate. It is called gamete intrafallopian transfer (GIFT). It was developed by Ricardo Asch, M.D., of the University of Texas Health Science Center in San Antonio. A woman's ovaries are stimulated hormonally so that eggs are developed and matured. Then a laparoscope extracts the ripe eggs. They are mixed with about a hundred thousand of her husband's washed sperm and are immediately reinserted at the end of the fallopian tube near the ovary. The egg (or eggs) are thus fertilized in the fallopian tube as they would be naturally, begin their division there, and travel to the uterus in the normal manner.

None of these procedures is particularly invasive or expensive, and there is no need to undergo such testing unless symptoms warrant it. If a woman knows she has had even one episode of PID, or if she is having any irregular menstrual bleeding or abdominal cramping (signals of endometriosis), it might be wise to request further testing, which requires anesthesia and a brief hospitalization. Damage from PID can be assessed by a hysterosalpingogram, which X-rays the tubes. Dye is injected up through the cervix into the uterus. It flows up each of the fallopian tubes in turn. If it spills out into the abdominal cavity, all is well. It is often done in conjunction with a laparoscopy, which will allow a doctor to see if there is scarring of the fallopian tubes or ovaries, uterine abnormalities, or endometriosis.

If scarring does show up, the adhesions can often be corrected with laser surgery. But this operation should be done only at the time a woman wants to conceive. The rate of conception is highest in the six months following tubal surgery. In cases where the tubes cannot be unblocked, the only hope for a pregnancy is in vitro fertilization, which has a success rate ranging from 10 to 35 percent, depending on the center in which it is being performed.

Endometriosis can be treated with a number of hormonal prescriptions, including the birth control pill, which prevents ovulation and thus simulates pregnancy—the best-known method to keep endometriosis from occurring. But many gynecologists think that the only permanent cure is surgery to remove the cysts, followed by hormone therapy to control new growths. The operation can be relatively simple if the endometriosis is small and concentrated in just a few areas. But if it is extensive, it will require major abdominal surgery to remove it and yet spare as much as possible of the ovaries, at least one tube, and the uterus.

Success rates of women with endometriosis depend on the mildness of the case, and the age of the woman. Seventy-five percent of the women with mild cases get pregnant, fifty percent of those with moderate cases, and a third of those who had severe cases. Yet among women over thirty-five, only 25 percent have been able to conceive. The faster a woman can conceive the better:

35 percent of the women who conceive do so in the first year; 15 to 20 percent more do so in the next year.

If these tests show no problems, a couple should feel fairly confident that postponing pregnancy a few more years will not mean that they are inadvertently choosing childlessness. And if problems do show up, they can begin treatment for them now—giving themselves a gift of time that they would innocently have wasted. It should be noted, however, that gynecologists may be reluctant to perform hysterosalpingograms or laparoscopies because of the risks involved, unless a couple has already tried to conceive for a year without success.

Counting the Days

Once a woman begins trying to have a baby, of course, she becomes acutely aware of her monthly cycle in a way she never has been before. Anne, thirty, a director of marketing, has been trying for only a few months and she already feels the pressure. "It's sort of manic: When is this going to happen? Every month it makes things very important. I'm trying to avoid taking my temperature, but I am probably putting off the inevitable. I did do it for one month a while ago and it seemed to be sort of normal. I went through a few cycles where I said, 'Oh my God, this must be it, I'm pregnant. It's a new feeling.' And I wasn't. So I've decided my judgment is just not trustworthy. But as the due date for my period gets closer and closer, my hopes start to rise even though I'm trying not to let them."

After a woman starts infertility treatment, or has a miscarriage, all these feelings are accentuated. "[Women] may become preoccupied with searching for signs of pregnancy," notes Miriam D. Mazor, M.D., a clinical instructor in the Department of Psychiatry at Harvard Medical School in an article in *Psychology Today.* "When the flow actually begins, many women are plunged into a depression verging on despair." Some of the clock-watchers have successfully handled these feelings by staying busy. Dolores, who is in treatment, says, "For a few months I changed my habits in the second half of my cycle, but it was the pits. You figure the egg is multiplying, but it's not implanted in the uterus for the first five or more days, so I'll drink a couple of glasses of wine. I've just decided that I'm going to take life as it comes. I'm terribly busy and I just keep going and going all the time and a lot of time I don't even think about it—I don't even know where I am in my cycle. Yet the last forty-eight hours before I'm going to start my period I do get depressed, saying, 'This is the pits.' But for the most part I'm optimistic it's going to work."

Sybil, since her two miscarriages, has not been able to stay so calm. "Two weeks out of the month I can drink and do bizarre things," she says. "The other two weeks I don't drink. I don't go in Jacuzzis. The first half, I'm always very optimistic. The second half, I'm on edge. The worst time is the few days before I get my period and I feel it coming. I try to think about what the symptoms of those two pregnancies were: When did my breasts start feeling tender? When did I have to urinate more? And I can't remember. All I know is that cycle after cycle goes by and I don't feel any different. When I start to bleed, it's really a relief because it means I am moving into the next cycle."

Although she is not yet involved in infertility treatment, Natalie, thirty-one, a self-employed marketing consultant, also finds herself constantly on edge. She got pregnant accidentally a year ago and miscarried at four months. Since then, she has been trying to get pregnant again and is scheduled to start testing for infertility in two more months if she has not succeeded. "Every month it hits home that another month has passed," she says. "It's hard because I have an ulcer and a lot of mornings I do wake up kind of nauseous, but it's because we had some wine the night before, or I've been worried about something, or I have a client coming. But I'll think, 'Is this the ulcer or am I pregnant? Remember last month you thought you were pregnant.' It's hard not to think about it; it pervades everything you do."

Women wait not only for their periods, but also for ovulation, and they schedule sex to fall on the right days. Natalie, thirty-one, a marketing consultant with her own business who has been trying to get pregnant since her miscarriage, manages this somewhat surreptitiously. "I kind of set it up, I don't really tell him," she says. "He knows I'm trying to get pregnant, but we don't really talk about it. At about the fourteenth day I do special things like make a terrific dinner, or wear something sexy. If it doesn't work, I don't push it, but it usually does. He knows what I'm doing, but since I don't come right out and say, 'We have to do it now,' it's not like performing on schedule. It's performing because I want him, instead of because I want to get pregnant."

When Patricia, forty, a congressional investigator, finally decided she wanted a child, she discovered that she didn't ovulate. She has been in treatment with Clomid for a year now with scheduled sex as part of the deal—a part she finds amusing. "Before we started all this, when people would say they were trying to have a baby, I'd say, 'What could it take?' Now I under-stand. Now my husband is the one who has the headache—having to perform on demand. Once I decided I'd wear something erotic. I have this one lace negligee, and he said, 'This is not you. When was the last time you wore that?' It was the night we got married—ten years ago."

Because her schedule and her husband's are so hectic, Sybil is using the ovulation stick to perfect her sexual timing. "The stick is supposed to turn blue, and when it is the brightest, you are supposed to take action," she says. "I just decided that timing is everything. My husband and I are both lawyers and we have incredibly stressful jobs; it is just out of the question for us to have sex during the week unless there is a good reason. When you are in this situation and you've been in it as long as I have, your mind plays all sort of incredible games on you. I know when I ovulate, and I know that every other day in the middle of the cycle is all you need to do to cover yourself. We've done that for months, but this method provides just a little bit of reassurance that I won't be twelve hours off and worry, 'Gee, should we do it tonight or in the morning?' I'm not sure it's going to make all that much difference. But you just keep trying to think there is something you can do. You want to retain control."

Out of Their Hands

Control is one of the main issues for these couples throughout their treat-ment. It helps them keep some emotional balance during the stressful months, or years, ahead. Control begins with finding the right doctor or university-affiliated infertility program.

Holly, thirty-one, a production scheduling supervisor, didn't go directly to a specialist. "I waited eight months before thinking something was wrong because I hadn't gotten pregnant," she says. "Then I spent a year and a half having haphazard, frustrating treatments with my regular gynecologist. She had some good ideas, but there was no plan. I decided I'd had enough of that. We live near the University of Virginia and they have a team specializing in infertility. I waited three to four months to get in."

Just because a doctor is a specialist, it doesn't mean he's the right person for a particular couple, as Harriet, thirty-five, an artist, and her husband discovered. "The first doctor we went to claimed to be an infertility specialist and wasn't," she says. "Then I saw a specialist in Buffalo, where we lived for eight months while my mother was dying. Then when we got home, we were with a team of experts the Buffalo doctor recommended. They dealt with me as a number, a piece of meat, a test case, not as a human being. I needed a bedside person. I was just a guinea pig to them. I was put on Clomid for about sixteen cycles, and the doctors we are with now asked me why I was on Clomid for so long. I have temperature charts to paper my house with, all showing that my temperature drops and then rises again, that I ovulate. That isn't our problem. We're sort of allergic to each other. My body believes that Edward's sperm are invaders and fights them off.

"The most frustrating part is the waste of time, doing all this when it wasn't the problem. I wrote the doctors a five-page letter, documenting all the treatment. I never heard from them. I sent a copy to the doctor in Buffalo and he called me here at home and told me he was so distressed that I was treated that way.

"We are now with another team and I'm happy. They are the best. Edward is now seeing a urologist, which no one had ever suggested. Our doctor on the team is the only doctor who's ever said to us, 'We don't know why pregnancy happens. It's a miracle. There's no good explanation for it—the sperm being able to enter the egg. Scientifically, it should be rejected.' I really respect him a lot. To get answers from someone who is direct and businesslike but shows a little bit of caring about who I am, it makes a big difference and it helps emotionally. It makes me feel more positive."

Harriet and her husband have been on this merry-go-round for five years, and she sometimes thinks she's ready to get off. "After a while, you wish someone would say to you, 'No, you can't have kids,' or 'Keep trying, you'll make it.' Then we could decide where to go from there—adopt, not adopt. I suppose I'll give myself a couple more years, but I can't go on and on medically. It gets more frustrating as time goes by, having to deal with the letdowns, with the emotional highs and lows.

"Edward and I haven't talked a lot about the next step. It's never consumed us the way it has consumed friends of ours. They think and talk about absolutely nothing else. But there is so much else going on in our lives—interests and friends and things that we enjoy doing that it's not the most important thing. Yes, we'd like to have kids, and yes, we're having medical difficulties, but there are other things occupying our lives. My career is just rounding a corner. There are days when I think our life is fine—there is nothing wrong with it. And then I'm with a kid and someone says, 'Gosh, do you have kids? You're great with kids.' And I think I do want one, I get back in the mood. On a scale of one to ten for wanting a child, I'm probably a five right now. Edward is an eight. But there was a time when he thought our life wasn't so bad. It's so easy to pick up and do things—go on vacations, on trips.

"In the last four months we haven't been on the documentation road, or doing anything scientific. We've just enjoyed having sex whenever we wanted to do it. The infertility hasn't been a big issue, but it's becoming one again. We've got to decide what we're going to do. We'll probably go the next step and try sperm washing and artificial insemination. If that doesn't work, we have to decide whether we want to do in vitro. That's pretty much the last thing left to try because we're not going to do the surrogate mother stuff."

Couples faced with male sperm production problems have less sophisticated treatment to resort to, and thus can feel even more hopeless about their situation than those who can tap into the higher technology available for solving female problems. Wanda, thirty-one, an accounting supervisor, even wishes the infertility were hers instead of her husband's because it might be more easily corrected. Her worst moments involve hearing that friends are pregnant. "Last week I found out that another friend was expecting and it upset me terribly. I bring it home and it affects my relationship with my husband. I think, 'Oh, why can't I have one.' He told me that I can't go through this each time I find out someone is pregnant, but I was upset all weekend, and we ended up having a fight."

One solution that has been presented to Wanda and her husband is artificial insemination by donor (AID). But they both have problems with it. Her husband thinks it would be hard for him to love a child who wasn't really his own. Wanda is more concerned about the pregnancy: "The idea of carrying a child around inside me which wasn't his is really foreign to me," she says. "I told my doctor that and he said the only reason we won't have a child is because I decide not to, and there's no reason to deny my husband being a father. It's something I guess I would consider if all else fails, but it would take a lot of counseling to get me to that point." Yet Dr. Mazor reports that most couples who have taken this route are happy with it. Their biggest worry is what to tell the child about his or her conception—indeed, whether to tell at all.

Time, that ticking of the clock, is the biggest enemy of infertility patients and that is particularly true for those in their late thirties or forties. Patricia feels this acutely. "I don't ovulate at all—even with massive doses of Clomid," she says. "The thing that's frustrating is wondering if it's related to age or if I was always this way. My own gynecologist never suggested simple tests I could have had. He said, 'Give it time. Give it time.' And now there's such a limited time left." Even though she has some grave doubts, she is about to start treatment with Pergonal. "If this doesn't work, there are no alternatives. I have hormonal deficiencies and a lack of full thyroid function. I'm worried about it. Double or nothing I could handle, but seven babies I don't know. The emotional strain the Frustacis went through of having all those children die would be terrible. I'm going to be forty-one in a few months and I also worry about the risk to the child, but a woman who works upstairs from me took Pergonal and she's had her amniocentesis and everything is fine, and she's forty-one already."

Time puts a different kind of pressure on women who are treated for endometriosis or tubal adhesions because they are told to try to get pregnant immediately as the odds for success are most in their favor the first year after surgery. This instruction has put Alexis, twenty-nine, a pricing manager, in a real bind. "I've just made a career change within my company," she says, "and I feel that this is probably not the best time to get pregnant. But the clock is ticking. I don't feel in control of my life. My company, which is very progressive about women and their careers, still exhibits a fair degree of resentment when women managers get pregnant and take maternity leave—despite the fact that all except one have come back before their leaves ended and actively managed their operations during their leaves." Faced with this conflict, Alexis intends to follow her ob/gyn's advice. "It should be an interesting year," she concludes.

When this allotted year runs out without success, it can be extremely debilitating emotionally. This has happened to Sybil. Her infertility saga began when she miscarried at six weeks. Her doctor did a laparoscopy and discovered adhesions on her tubes, one ovary that had been damaged by PID, plus a mild case of endometriosis. She had surgery to remove her ovary, clear up the adhesions, and cauterize the endometriosis. Because her menstrual cycles were only twenty-six days long and she ovulated about day thirteen, her doctor also did an endometrial biopsy, which she says checked out. But he told her he would put her on progesterone suppositories as soon as he knew she was pregnant. She got pregnant again the first month after the surgery, but the suppositories didn't make a difference—she promptly miscarried anyway at five weeks.

"After the surgery and the second miscarriage, I had this artificial goal to get pregnant again within a year because the doctor said the odds are cut down," she says. "So I set the goal, and I was convinced I would get pregnant again because it happened so fast that second time. But now the year has passed, so the artificial goal has been removed and I think I can relax and take it one month at a time. But I'm also very concerned that my endometriosis may have returned though I have no symptoms. I didn't have the classic symptoms before. I had no pain at all—just some irregular bleeding in connection with my periods. They got longer and weirder just before I had my surgery. So if I don't get pregnant in the next four months, I'll probably have the doctor take another look.

"I just started going to an infertility support group last night. There are six other couples in it and a leader. Of the seven women, six have endometriosis. It was such a downer. I know a lot of people who have had infertility problems and overcome them and had kids. But not one of them had endometriosis, and I suddenly began to think that I didn't know anyone who had it and had gotten pregnant and had a baby. The last twelve months have been the worst of my life. I've probably sunk to the lowest lows of my existence. We went on vacation a month or so ago. It was much needed and too long postponed. It helped me a lot. I was feeling pretty good when we got back, until I went to this group. It made me slip a little. I'm not down in the depths by any means, but hearing all these people with the same kind of problem was pretty discouraging."

Many women experience a multitude of infertility problems. Sybil is one of them. She has also been on Clomid for a year now to correct erratic ovulation, which began after her second miscarriage. "I went totally in the tank and my body freaked out on me," she says. "I had three cycles where there was no question that the second half was screwed up—I was either not ovulating, or ovulating late. Once I had a seventeen-day cycle. That convinced the doctor he should do something and he gave me Clomid even though I was ovulating, because he knew it would give me a twenty-eight day cycle. It worked like a champ.

"But I still haven't gotten pregnant again. Before I started using the ovulation sticks, we did sonograms to determine the precise time of ovulation and then artificial insemination with my husband's sperm. I did it because I thought I might get pregnant faster and it would reduce the pressure on our sexual relationship. We could have sex for pleasure. But the frustrations I was alleviating were replaced by a whole new set of frustrations—visits to the doctor's office, sonograms, hassles with scheduling.

"A few months ago I finally threw up my hands and said enough. We're taking a rest from what I consider to be high tech. I'm still taking Clomid, and my doctor just increased my dosage. And we're trying on our own. We got pregnant twice on our own. And we never have the other way. Now that we're not doing inseminations, I've kind of gotten myself back on top of things at work. I've also switched my exercise program so that I'm doing something different that I enjoy. I've read that it's good to refocus and get other things going in your life, and then things fall into place. It may be a variation on the theme of 'Just relax, and it will happen.' "

Dolores also has a multitude of infertility problems, and as part of her treatment she, too, is on Clomid. But unlike Sybil, she is gung-ho high tech. "Six months ago I had a laparoscopy, which confirmed that I had adhesions from my ruptured appendix, which occurred when I was twelve. They were everywhere. Then three months ago I had a laparotomy, which freed up the adhesions to my tubes and ovaries. They did a hysterosalpingogram afterward and found the tubes were clear. The dye spilled out into the abdomen really well. I also have hormonal problems, so I'm taking Clomid in the first part of the cycle and progesterone suppositories in the second half. I've heard that some doctors are giving estrogen at midcycle to increase the cervical mucus, which Clomid really screws up.

"I'm using ovulation sticks to time my ovulation. And then we're doing artificial insemination with my husband's sperm. My husband had a vasectomy reversal that was very successful. And he's tremendously optimistic and supportive. He has to get his sperm sample every month. He calls it LDS, long-distance sex. He calls his collection cup Bertha, and he says they should paint big lips on the specimen cups. He makes it very humorous.

"As soon as the ovulation stick says I've ovulated, I go in with a sample of my husband's sperm in Bertha. Because they insert it right into the uterus, they have to wash it to get off this protein substance covering it which will give me a reaction. So I take it to one office to be washed and then to another office to do the insemination. Then I stay lying down for about twenty minutes. I don't have any problem thinking about getting pregnant this way. It's just another procedure."

Part of the reason Dolores is so level-headed about her treatment is that her work as a midwife with pregnant women and infertility patients keeps her very busy and gives her a different perspective. "I don't have time for it to spill over," she says. "It's just one other thing in my life. I'm optimistic that it's going to work. I just feel it's going to. I know I'll be mad as hell if it doesn't, and I'm going to work like hell to make it work. But I'm not angry like most infertility patients. Most women have difficulty coping with their bodies not being normal. But ever since I knew what a ruptured appendix could do to the tubes and ovaries, I knew I would have a problem. I know some women who don't have the history I do, and the doctor does a laparoscopy and they are full of adhesions and there is no known reason for it. I'm sure that must be much more difficult to handle."

The Edge of Success

From the moment a woman who wants a baby knows she is pregnant, she starts forming a relationship with that tiny being inside her. If she miscarries, it is a devastating loss, and one that is particularly hard to deal with because there is no burial, no official mourning, and indeed, nothing to mourn. When well-meaning friends and relations say it was for the best because the baby probably had major defects, and that she can always try again, they offer no solace. A woman who has miscarried experiences an emptiness that takes months to go away (and often does not until she is pregnant again), and she can be overcome with guilt, feeling that it was something she did that killed her baby.

Even when she already has children, a miscarriage can affect a woman to the core of her being. "I didn't know the meaning of the word 'miscarriage' until it happened to me," says Anita, thirty-four, a director of community services, who has two boys, three and a half and two. "I was eight weeks along, and I had just told my family. On Labor Day weekend I started bleeding and bled for three days and finally the baby came out, which was awfully gut-wrenching, holding it in my hands. I have these books that show that at six weeks they have fingers and toes. I thought, What should I do? Name it? Bury it in my backyard? I heard the standard things from everyone —60 percent of the time there is something wrong with the baby; you have a couple of normal kids, no big deal. I didn't want to push it any further. I didn't ask for a pathology report. I didn't want to know if the baby was somehow disfigured or a mutant. Ignorance is bliss. I tried not to dwell on it. But I'll never forget it."

Ginger, thirty-seven, a director of personnel and the mother of a seven-year-old son from her first marriage, had a miscarriage shortly after she got married the second time. "It was an awful experience, really devastating," she remembers. "I hope it never happens again. Looking back, I guess I knew something was wrong from the beginning. I had some spotting early. I started to get morning sickness and then it stopped. I said, 'If I'm going to get morning sickness, I know I'm going to have it longer than this.' When I was about ten weeks along, I started bleeding. I bled for about a week, and then it got worse over the weekend. On top of that I had a high fever which had nothing to do with the miscarriage—my son had it too. On Monday the bleeding was pretty bad so I went to see the doctor and he asked me to come back that evening for an ultrasound and as they were doing it I started hemorrhaging and I ended up in the emergency room. Since I had eaten that day, they wouldn't give me an anesthetic and I had a D&C without one." Ginger is now eight months pregnant with a second son.

Sometimes a miscarriage is the first indication that a woman has an infertility problem. This is what happened to Kristin, twenty-eight, who recently lost her job as a juvenile court officer and is thinking of going back to school for a Ph.D. in marriage and family therapy. In her early twenties, she had not wanted to have children, and it was a point of negotiation with her husband for three years before they got married. She finally decided that she did want a child, and she started trying to get pregnant shortly after the wedding. "I had a really terrible pregnancy from the very beginning with lots of spotting and bleeding," she says. "I had a sonogram and they found that the baby had died at about fourteen weeks. I went through that feeling that it was all my fault—I shouldn't have gone to that bar where it was so smoky even though I didn't have a drink; I shouldn't have had that full glass of wine. Then I kind of let go of that. I had told a lot of people. We were very excited. I wouldn't do that again—absolutely not.

"The miscarriage has made both of us want to have a child more, but I haven't been able to conceive again. I waited for about four months and then I started taking my temperature, and I found out I have not been ovulating. We went the Clomid route for a while, but since then we've worried about our finances because I lost my job and whether this is the right time to have a baby. So I've stopped the Clomid for a while because it's so expensive—six dollars a pill. My gynecologist thinks I may be one of those women who ovulates sporadically. I know when I do when I'm not on Clomid because I have PMS like no tomorrow. I was on the pill for years, and I don't know whether that has anything to do with it. I get a regular period.

"We're not using contraception. I haven't used any for a year. It depends on what kind of mood I'm in whether I want to get my period or I don't want to get it. Sometimes I think it might as well come because this isn't a good time. And then it will come and I'll feel kind of bad. If I see new babies or hear that one of our friends is going to have a baby, it makes me think about my situation. I sometimes feel cheated by God."

For Natalie and her husband, pregnancy was an accident. But the miscarriage she suffered at four months was the worst experience either of them had ever gone through, and like Kristin, she has not been able to get pregnant again. "I had taken birth control pills since I was seventeen and I stopped taking them because my doctor said I'd been on them long enough," she remembers. "The first month after stopping I got pregnant. That was last September. There was something wrong from the beginning, but my doctor didn't want to tell me. But I knew that something was weird. He never gave that A-OK sign. Part of me thought it was just my imagination, but somewhere inside I said, 'He's not quite telling you everything.' He kept saying, 'Let's give it another two weeks. Maybe you've missed on your dates.'

"The last visit was a week or so before Christmas. I had a sonogram, and it wasn't growing at all. It was obvious it had started disintegrating. There was nothing in there. You say, 'Why? What did I do? What can I do in the future?' I'd skied, but not very hard and I hadn't fallen. But what if it was the altitude? And the doctor said that it was nothing I could have done. But they don't know why these things happen, and doctors are supposed to know. I went into shock, and I was put in the hospital and put to sleep and had a D&C.

"I couldn't believe this was happening to me because I've always gotten everything I wanted. I've never had any health problems. I wanted to go to college and get my degree, and I did that. I wanted to start my business, and I did that. I said, 'Wait a minute. These things don't happen to me!' I kept a journal during that time and it was the only thing that pulled me through. It's hard, working at home; I didn't have a lot to keep my mind off it. It was like the whole world had ended. People treat it like losing a puppy or something. There's no funeral; it's just gone, but you didn't see it go. People feel sorry for you, but they don't understand it hurts just as much as losing a baby, no matter how early on you lost it. It also makes you tougher. You realize that it is not like a storybook: you are pregnant, therefore you are going to have a baby. I learned you never tell your family.

"But we had told people and we had all kinds of little baby presents around. I knew I had passed a big hurdle when, five or six months later, I hadn't gotten pregnant again and I gave away all the baby things. That seemed to be a big turning point. I couldn't have done it before. But I let that part go, and I moved on.

"After the miscarriage, the doctor told me that the sooner I could start trying to get pregnant, the better it would be for my psyche. And then, of course, I heard from a lot of friends and relatives that they had had miscarriages but gotten pregnant right away again. It didn't happen with me. We're still trying, and it's almost a year. My doctor first said to give it six months. I went back after six months and said, 'What's wrong?' I'd been taking my temperature and everything. He said, 'I'll tell you what to do. Don't take your temperature; don't do anything. Just relax and don't think about it and if you aren't pregnant in six months, come back in and we'll do tests. But I bet you don't have to come back.' Well, I have one more month left, and it looks like I'm going to go back.

"It's kind of a hard situation. Now that it's been a year, my husband kind of feels that it should be a roll of the dice—if we are meant to be parents, we will be; if we aren't, we won't. That's not as easy for me. I feel determined to make it work. I got a taste of what it's like, and it's something I definitely want. It would be very hard for me to give it up, and it's also very hard for me to relax and say, 'Oh, leave it up to nature.' If that was the way it should be, then I wouldn't have been taking the pill for all those years. And the more determined I get, the harder it is.

"If it turns out I can't have a child, I would feel a little bitter. We are the first generation that has had the option of not having children, and the problems I've had are things my mother couldn't have told me because they didn't have such reliable methods of birth control. I feel someone should have told me at twenty-five that things might not be as easy as I thought they'd be at thirty. My mother was twenty-nine when she had me, and she had my youngest sister when she was thirty-seven, so I never had any misgivings about starting my family in my late twenties, or early thirties. That was the master plan. I knew that my husband, who really didn't want kids when he was twenty-five, who said, 'Maybe later,' would come around. But now I hear about women who take six years to get pregnant. Now I hear my clock ticking a lot.

"The other day my husband asked, 'When are we going to cut it off? How old do you want to be and have a little baby around?' At first we picked thirty-five, and then we said that wasn't fair, that we'd give it ten years, and if by the time we're in our early forties we haven't been able to have children, we'd just have to accept it. That's life. I've got a lot of little nieces and nephews. But I don't want to wait that long. I want a baby now. Now is the perfect time. I have a free-lance business built up. Everything is running fine. The money is fine. It's the perfect time, but my stupid body won't cooperate. And it's ruining my concentration. I just wish I could get this uncertainty out of my life. I'm so used to having everything planned."

Yet with all this, Natalie says she still feels optimistic. "You know how you can have a profound revelation, and it usually comes in a dream? I had a dream recently that woke me up in the middle of the night. I heard my own voice saying, 'Why are you worried? You are going to get pregnant next year. There's no problem. Why are you putting yourself through this hell?' And I thought, 'Maybe my inner regulating mechanism knows more about me than I do.' "

For someone like Sybil, miscarriage is even more terrible—a giant step backward after the leap forward of conceiving. It's been over a year since her second miscarriage, and she still thinks about it. "My miscarriages raised a whole other set of problems because I worry if I do get pregnant will I be able to hold on to it. For the first couple of months after the last one, that was uppermost in my mind. If I do get pregnant again, I'm going to be paranoid. Now, I don't think about that so much because I'm having no success getting pregnant. How can you go on to step two if you can't get past step one? It's a special frustration to think that I was that much closer and I didn't get what I want.

"One of the things we talked about last night in our group was a reunion our group leader had attended of formerly infertile people who had gotten pregnant and had children. The stories of the pregnancy experiences of those people were horrible. It doesn't stop when you are pregnant. You spend the whole nine months on edge. These women didn't enjoy their pregnancies. And even after the babies were born, they couldn't return to their normal selves.

"It's really true that infertility is a major life crisis that people don't get over, kids or no kids. I think about what scars this has left on me forever, whether I have a baby or not. What has it done to my relationship with my husband? To my feelings about myself? I'm a classic overachiever. This is the first thing in my life that I have not been able to get if I just worked hard for it. And there's not a damn thing I can do and I've never felt so helpless in my life. It's a really humbling experience. It's like aging. You really come to grips with your own mortality."

Settling for Adoption

Experts say that infertility patients are surpassed only by terminal cancer patients in their willingness to undergo procedures. And with new treatments and technology becoming available all the time, it makes it even harder to know when to throw in the towel. But as the process winds along through the months and years without a successful conception, couples are brought to think more and more about the other alternative. Do they only want their own biological child? Or do they want to be parents, to have a family and nurture a child even if it is not biologically theirs? If they decide that they definitely want a family, one way or the other, it is easier for them to set a date by which they will give up on the treatments and begin to pursue this course of action.

Tammy, twenty-eight, formerly an administrative manager for a major corporation, and her husband set that date, but they continued treatment right up to it. Tammy's problem was that she almost never ovulated. "We'd been trying for some time to have a child and we were pretty much at the point of giving up. We'd been through intensive infertility treatments and it didn't look like anything was working. Structurally, I'm fine, but I have multiple and severe hormone deficiencies, which mean that I don't get periods and I don't ovulate. I get maybe one period a year, which is great if you don't want to have a baby. We'd been married maybe four or five years when I started on active infertility treatments with drugs. The doctor figured that during those five years I'd ovulated maybe twice. It was always a joke between my husband and me that when I'd ovulate I'd be in Atlanta and he'd be in Phoenix and I'd call him and tell him to meet me in the No Tell Motel in Kansas City.

"I was on a triple dosage of Clomid by the time they were done with me and even with that it didn't look as if I was ovulating. They were about to start me on Pergonal, which was a last resort. They also had me on progesterone for the second half of my cycle. We had set January as a time to begin adoption procedures if it didn't look like there was going to be any hope I'd get pregnant. I succeeded the week before that deadline. I knew right away. At ten days I was convinced and I hadn't even missed a period yet. I remember telling my mother and a couple of friends and my husband and they all thought I was crazy and that I was setting myself up for a disappointment. But I just knew. I felt so different. Classic symptoms—I felt like I hadn't slept in a week and I was sleeping twelve hours a night. My stomach felt funny and my breasts were really sore. I remember lifting my arm to wave to someone at work and it hurt. It was confirmed with a pregnancy test at sixteen days. I told the world." Tammy is now the mother of an eighteen-month-old son and is expecting a second baby, conceived without recourse to any drugs. Pregnancy itself straightened out her hormonal system.

Doreen, twenty-nine, a staff accountant with a CPA firm, and her husband had a similar attitude to Tammy's about the importance of children in their lives. "I come from a very traditional family, as does my husband," says

Doreen. "We just assumed children would be a natural part of our life together. Eight years ago the scenario was for me to have children and work
part-time as a bookkeeper. But it didn't work out that way. A pregnancy
never happened in spite of lengthy and stressful testing and treatment.

"So for the past three years we have been pursuing adoption of an infant
and expect to at least have to wait two more years before a child comes to us.
We'll have a day's notice and then we'll be parents. I just have to believe in
myself and my husband and those close to us who will lend support that we'll
be able to handle it.

"But in the meantime, I'm not one to just sit at home waiting for my
dreams to come true. Life is something you have to go out and grab, so I
returned to school while working as a paraprofessional with a C.P.A. and
now have my B.S. in business and a very promising career."

For most couples faced with infertility, the journey toward adoption is
more difficult than it was for Doreen. Not only do they have to be convinced
that there is nothing more that can be done medically, but husband and wife
have to arrive at the same viewpoint about the importance of children in their
lives, and they have to get over negative feelings about the intrusion into their
lives that the adoption process requires. This is one of the worries for Natalie.
"We have a kind of underground lifestyle," she says. "We wouldn't really
want to involve a lot of legal authorities in our lives. My husband says he
doesn't want to have kids that much, if that's what you have to go through to
get them. With pregnancy, we both made it happen, and we're both responsible and in the bad times we can't say, 'This was your stupid idea.' Adopting, I
would have to push the whole thing through, and in bad times it would be
harder. He even criticizes the way I handle the animals, letting them run all
over the place—a cockatiel who doesn't live in a cage. But maybe we'll
change if we get more desperate."

Harriet is the one holding back from adoption in her marriage. "I think
Edward would want to adopt a kid if we went through all the medical stuff
and didn't have our own," she says. "But I have a problem with it. I haven't
gotten to that point. Yet I sometimes see people with kids and I think, What
difference does it make if they aren't biologically yours? In our support group
we talk about this a lot. One couple is ready to adopt. One husband is close
but the wife isn't because she still wants to have her own. The social worker
has adopted a little girl. I'm not there yet."

Some women realize they may never get there. Barbara Eck Menning, the
founder of RESOLVE, the support network for infertile couples, has said that
there are some people for whom pregnancy and the childbirth experience, as

well as genetic continuity, are very important, and if these are denied them they don't want a child in any other way. Sybil is probably among them. Despite all her problems, Sybil and her husband have not yet looked into adoption. "I've talked to friends who are doing it," she says, "and it takes three years. By then I'll be forty and my husband will be forty-eight. Can I wait that long? I think if I don't get on the list now, it will only get worse, but I'm in a quandary. I have this incredible biological need to have a baby of my own. I had a baby when I was eighteen and I gave it up for adoption. I had just started college and I came from a very strict authoritarian Catholic home. There was no question in my mind that I wasn't going to have an abortion and no question in my parents' mind that I wasn't going to get married. I have never regretted that decision for a minute, but it only makes this situation that much worse—'My God, I had one chance, and look at me.' I have a very strong need to replace that child. I don't fully understand it, but I realize that physical, emotional drive is there. Adoption doesn't hold a candle to it. You talk about 'the empty womb,' 'biology as destiny,' and all that stuff we liberated women thought was a bunch of nonsense, and you get to this age, and you have these sorts of problems, and you realize it's not."

8

The Elderly Primagravida

It used to be that a married woman who reached thirty without having children was out of step with the times. Motherhood was the occupation of glowing, newly married young women who had barely untied their mother's apron strings before knotting their own. If women with gray hair were seen pushing baby carriages, they were usually assumed to be grandmothers, not mothers. In those not too distant days, the idea that a woman should do her childbearing while she was young was reinforced by the medical profession, which believed that the risks of pregnancy went up dramatically in a woman's thirties.

But as more and more women have postponed childbearing, this medical and social picture has begun to change. The rate of first births among women aged thirty to forty-four increased a whopping 116 percent in the 1970s. In 1976, when Pamela Daniels and Kathy Weingarten began their study, *Sooner or Later: The Timing of Parenthood in Adult Lives,* they found that the "late-timing" parent was thirty. But by 1979 when they finished their interviews, "the boundaries had shifted dramatically"—to an age range of thirty-seven to forty-four. With the improved economic conditions of the 1980s, these trends have accelerated. From 1980 to 1983 first births for women thirty to forty-four jumped 14.3 percent.

These new mothers are better educated and many are professionally employed—which is, in fact, a large part of the reason they have delayed having children. In the 1970s the proportion of first-time mothers age thirty to thirty-four who had completed at least four years of college rose from 28 percent to 48 percent. By 1980 almost half of the women having their first baby in their thirties were professionals.

the face) and proteinuria (excretion of protein in the urine because the kidneys are not functioning adequately). Some of the early warning signs are headaches, sudden weight gain, swelling of the fingers or face, and blurring or dimming of vision.

Pre-eclampsia is more likely to develop in women over thirty-five who are pregnant for the first time, or who have chronic hypertension, kidney disease, or diabetes. Women are often hospitalized and given complete bed rest, as well as meals that are high in protein to make up for that lost in the urine. With mild cases, three to four days of treatment will usually do the trick and a woman can return home, although she will be closely monitored. But with a more severe case, a woman may have to remain hospitalized until delivery. If a woman is near term and the baby is mature enough, an early delivery may be safer for both mother and child, and labor may be induced.

This is what happened to Eleanor, forty-six, a psychotherapist and author, who was forty-one when she gave birth to her first and only child. Her pregnancy was easy except for a problem with her vision—and high blood pressure, which developed into pre-eclampsia near the end of her pregnancy. "I was put into the hospital seven days before Heather was born because my blood pressure went higher. A week later, in the evening I began to feel silly and the doctor came in and I told him I felt as high as a kite. That was his clue. He took my blood pressure and it had soared up. Immediately I was taken into the labor room and given pitocin to induce me. Heather was born seven and a half hours later."

When pre-eclampsia is extremely severe, it can produce convulsions. This is called eclampsia. Three to five percent of women with eclampsia die, and it increases the risk of death for the baby by 20 percent. However, it is a rare occurrence for women who eat properly and receive good prenatal care.

Gestational diabetes—diabetes that begins during pregnancy and disappears once a woman has delivered—is the other problem that women over thirty-five are at greater risk of developing during pregnancy. It is a result of the greater metabolic demands on the body during pregnancy. The baby receives most of its "food" in the form of glucose (sugar), just as the mother's body does. Insulin, produced by the pancreas, regulates the processing (metabolism) and storage of the glucose. As the baby grows, it demands more glucose, which can deplete the mother's supply if she does not have proper nutrition.

The baby's increasing demand for glucose also means an increased demand for its regulator: insulin. But at the same time, the action of insulin can be interfered with by hormones produced by the placenta which feed back into the maternal bloodstream. The pancreas must therefore produce larger amounts of insulin to control the metabolism and storage of the glucose so essential for both the mother and the baby. This stress on the metabolic system and the pancreas can bring on gestational diabetes.

Often the first sign of it is sugar in the urine sample collected at each prenatal visit. But some ob/gyns believe in screening all pregnant women, especially those over thirty-five, for abnormal blood sugar levels. Two simple tests are a fasting blood sugar test, in which a woman does not eat after 10 P.M. the night before, and has her blood drawn before her first meal of the next day, and a postprandial test in which blood is tested two hours after a meal. If more precise measurements are required, a glucose tolerance test will be done. It begins with a fasting blood sugar test, after which a woman swallows a glucose solution. Her blood is then drawn every hour for three to six hours to test how she has metabolized the glucose.

Treatment for gestational diabetes usually involves careful regulation of the diet to control metabolism. Six small meals a day, instead of three big ones, are recommended to prevent drops in blood sugar levels. Meals should be made up of 45 to 50 percent carbohydrates, 30 percent fats, and 20 to 25 percent protein. Fasting blood sugar levels are taken at every visit. If they are too high, a woman may have to have insulin therapy—15 percent of patients with gestational diabetes require this treatment.

If a woman's metabolism is not under control, the risk is increased that her baby will die before delivery. Poor metabolic control increases other complications such as pre-eclampsia; an excessively large baby (over ten pounds), and pyelonephritis (a bacterial infection of the kidneys). Occurring less often is a condition known as ketoacidosis. This happens when insufficient glucose is available for energy; the body then uses stored fats, producing acids called ketones. When too many ketones build up (ketoacidosis) it can cause nausea, vomiting, abdominal pain, and lack of energy.

Complication-free Pregnancies

Only a few of the "late" mothers interviewed experienced these dangerous complications. Instead, their pregnancies fit the pattern of the healthy, professional, older mother-to-be: problem free. That does not mean however, that they escaped all the discomforts. Some suffered a lot. Stephanie, thirty-five, a former teacher who had her children at thirty-one and thirty-four, was afflicted with a particularly bizarre disorder—"a liver enzyme imbalance [called cholestasis of pregnancy], which happened in the latter part of my pregnancies and made me itch all over. There's no treatment for it but delivery. My doctor the first time didn't know what it was and he told me it was all in my mind. I thought I was going to flip out. I couldn't sleep and it went on for weeks and weeks. The second time it only lasted a week. I also had tendonitis the first time; I couldn't shift my car, I couldn't write, and I was working and had the school principal breathing down my neck to finish my reports."

Just like mothers-to-be of all ages, many of these women endured first trimester nausea, sometimes accompanied by severe headaches. Pat, thirty-seven, a copywriter who gave birth to her daughter when she was thirty-six, had night sickness for four months. Her obstetrician told her "it was quite common among women who work because they know they have to be somewhere and be responsible and hold together in the morning. But as soon as they can relax, they get sick. I also had headaches that were so horrible at one point I told my ob/gyn I wanted him to send me to a neurosurgeon because I was sure I had a brain tumor, and in fact I was hoping I did because at least they could take it out. That's how bad the headaches were. I'd come home and cry it hurt so much. But once that was over, it was fine."

Older mothers-to-be may not feel as energetic as younger ones—and not just in the first months when tiredness can overcome even women in their prime childbearing years. Ginger, thirty-seven, a director of personnel and eight months pregnant with her second son, looks back at her first pregnancy when she was twenty-nine and sees a difference. "My recollection is that the first time didn't make me as tired," she says. "I just don't have the energy I had before. My job is also more demanding now, and perhaps that has something to do with it. Yet I'm in better shape this time, working out and trying to stay fit. But it just seems that it's been physically more demanding."

Pregnancy is, of course, a time not only of immense physical change, but of mental upheaval as a woman ponders the world that awaits her as a mother. How she feels about having a child is naturally reflected in how she feels about her pregnancy. Beatrice, a recreation therapist who is now thirty-five and the mother of a three-year-old daughter, didn't want to have children and found herself accidentally pregnant. Although she decided to have the child because her husband wanted one and because her spiritual beliefs would not let her have an abortion, she didn't enjoy it. "I felt really ugly and really fat," she says. "I swam a lot because I didn't feel pregnant when I swam. I worked clear up until five days before her birth because I didn't want to sit around. That made me feel uglier and fatter."

The feelings of Gail, thirty-three, a psychologist and mother of a one-year-old son, were exactly the opposite. She was "tormented" until she and her husband decided to have a baby. "I had planned to do my dissertation research during my pregnancy," she remembers, "but the hormonal changes took away *all* my ambition—I just wanted to daydream and look out the window. I am very glad that I gave myself the opportunity to do that and really experience my pregnancy and make it the number one part of my life."

Pregnancy also can bring to the fore issues of autonomy and self-determination—issues women have been grappling with in one way or another throughout their adult lives. For Samantha, thirty-five, a weaver, who had her son when she was thirty-three, these feelings kept her from enjoying her pregnancy. "I felt my body was betraying me in all these ways," she says. "I guess I've always felt I could control my life, control what happens to me. But this was something I couldn't control very well. When I'd feel sick, I'd be upset because I didn't want to feel that way, I wanted to be active. But I couldn't do anything about it."

It was her own sudden vulnerability, both physical and emotional, that made Deborah, thirty-seven, a vice president at a multinational bank when she had her son at age thirty-three, feel a lessening of control. "The sense of this baby growing in my body made me realize I didn't have as many options," she says. "I needed to stay in the job I was in; I couldn't make a change. And I had a strong sense that I was first taking care of this other life, so I needed to be taken care of."

The vulnerability of the life inside her can also make pregnant women extremely anxious. During her first pregnancy, Stephanie kept worrying about having a handicapped child. "I was teaching handicapped kids," she remembers, "and I had two friends, one whose baby died of meconium aspiration [it inhaled meconium, its own waste product, which can be released into the amniotic fluid] and another one who delivered at twenty-eight weeks and the baby had Trisomy-18, which is a chromosome abnormality. He died five days later. Both these deaths happened during my pregnancy. Then, the people I worked with were full of these wives' tales. In my mind I knew they were crazy, but I was constantly surrounded by them. The woman who shared my classroom was a real old-fashioned lady from North Carolina who had all these ideas about pregnancy: I was going to mark my child if I raised my voice. If I stood on a chair, I could have a miscarriage. Spooky stuff."

Then there were the "late" mothers who had pregnancies which were almost totally free of discomfort—physical or mental. They conceived quickly and were healthy and happy throughout, working and exercising—aerobics, tennis, even Nautilus—right to the end. Meredith, thirty-nine, a self-employed bookkeeper who had her son at thirty-seven, says, "I got pregnant the second month we tried after our marriage; the first month I was devastated when I didn't. The pregnancy was wonderful. I have never been healthier in my life. I used to have back problems and they have disappeared. I used to have terrible cramps, and they have disappeared. I think I might have gotten one cold that whole year. Other than total exhaustion in the beginning, I really enjoyed it."

Denise, thirty-nine, a former nurse, who also started trying to get pregnant right after she got married at thirty-seven, succeeded instantly. "When we found out, we were still in shock from having just gotten married. We didn't know which end was up, but we were really happy. I've always been very active and healthy and I didn't have any problems. I was uncomfortable the last couple of weeks because I was so big, but other than that I was fine."

Pregnancy was also an exciting, healthy time for Emma, thirty-four, an advertising director, who had her son at thirty-two after years of not wanting a child at all. "My pregnancy was planned like the invasion of Normandy," she remembers. "I had been on the pill forever, and we had to go through the whole routine of how long I should be off it before we could start to try. I stayed off for six months just to play it safe. We started watching what we were eating and I tried to get into better shape. I went to the doctor and made sure I'd had various and sundry diseases like German measles beforehand. We figured out when we would start trying and that it would take us three to six months to get pregnant. We were wrong there. We got pregnant immediately. It was the only thing that threw off our schedule. We were planning a spring baby and he showed up in January.

"I had no problems with the pregnancy—not even a single day of morning sickness, even though I have a funny stomach. I felt fabulous. I was really excited about it. I was enormous, but I never felt strange about that, maybe because I've never had a weight problem so it was just exciting. I started wearing maternity clothes at three months. I was ravenous too. I probably gained three to five pounds before I even knew I was pregnant. I'd look at those charts for ideal weight gain and think if I kept on the curve I was on I'd weigh three hundred pounds."

Pregnancy and Work

Orchestrating work and pregnancy may be more taxing for many women than the pregnancy itself. It starts with when and how to present it to the boss —a big question especially when a woman is in a demanding job to which she wants to return after her leave. Some women found, to their surprise, that their bosses were very nice about this major change in status. When Cynthia, thirty, a national accounts manager who traveled 90 percent of the time for her job, got pregnant unexpectedly, she was able to work things out in a way that was beneficial to her boss as well as to her. "I did a lot of thinking about how I would handle it and how I could keep all the pieces together and come back to the job," she says. "Then I told my boss. He's quite an understanding guy. I'd been with the company long enough, and he knows I'm a hard worker, so we worked it out.

"I had to travel pretty extensively throughout the country until my fifth month. But then we made a change. There was a possibility at that time that the owner was going to sell the company. My boss was the vice president and he didn't want to have that title; he wanted a lower one so he wouldn't be fired. So he decided to become national sales manager and I went back to being regional sales manager—my old job. I did a lot of work by phone and just covered my territory. Truthfully, I didn't work very hard."

Lana, thirty, a sales representative for a computer company, suffered from nausea and headaches the first three months of her pregnancy, which drove her to tell her boss earlier than she might have. She found he was supportive —up to a point; then it was business as usual. "I told at six weeks," she says. "I was starting to get really tired and I was coming in late in the mornings. I wasn't feeling well, so I'd sneak off for little twenty-minute naps in the afternoon. He was really good about it. I was surprised. He said it was great, but then he asked me if I had thought about my plans. They were setting our quotas for the next year and I thought if I told him that I'd be out for two months before he set mine, he might not set it so high. But he did anyway."

Deborah, who became pregnant at thirty-three, was surprised by her boss's reaction because it was the opposite of Lana's—he didn't want to know anything about her plans. At the time, she had already started interviewing for a job within her department which would have meant a lot of travel to South America. "These things take a while," she says. "When I got to be three months pregnant, I was still being considered. But even if I was going to be Hercules, I realized that the kinds of shots I would need made it impossible. So I went to tell my boss. He said, 'That's great for you. Great.' I said, 'Now here's my plan . . .' And he cut me off, 'No, you don't have to tell me any of that.' I said, 'I want to tell you.' If I were going on vacation, I'd tell him about the dates and the timing. But he wouldn't discuss it with me. It was a sign of his fear about discrimination suits. He just said to let personnel know."

Because her boss had had a bad experience with other pregnant employees, Kathleen, twenty-nine, then a junior-level officer of a large commercial bank, was afraid to tell him before her promotion to vice president came through. "I just didn't know how the bank would react," she remembers. Before my pregnancy, a number of women had left after having their babies. My particular boss, who was a senior vice president, had the experience of two women in his division saying they *were* coming back, right up until the last minute. Then he got a call and they said they weren't after all. Even though I was certain I was coming back, he couldn't be sure, because that is what the others had said. So I was hesitant to tell him before my promotion went through.

"The problem was that I have to travel a lot for work and my doctor said not to travel during the first trimester. I kept trying to postpone trips without letting the real reason be known. But, I finally had to tell him because we had an important trip coming up. The promotion still hadn't gone through. When I told him, he blanched. I reassured him and reassured him that I was coming back. He said, 'Fine.' Companies are a little bit hamstrung because they can't say, 'Are you sure?' He said he believed me, and later he told me he had been 80 percent sure. But it didn't have any effect on my promotion."

The second time around, things went more smoothly at work for Kathleen. "I went and told my boss I was pregnant, and he said, " 'Oh, I know.' I said, 'What do you mean, you know?' He said he'd seen the signs: I'd given up coffee and I wasn't drinking. He said he'd known for weeks. This time he's very nonchalant. It's just: 'How much time do you need?' Once you've established yourself, that you're not going to be running off, they are much more relaxed about it."

The increased hormonal levels of pregnancy can slow a woman down, and her increasing bulk can make it hard for her to get around toward the end, but most of these women managed quite well with their jobs—often working up to the day before delivery. One of them called this "the new female macho"—a sort of stand against the paternalistic attitudes of male superiors.

Daphne, thirty-two, an account supervisor who had her son when she was thirty-one, found her pregnancy made her more productive. "I'd been working at the company for four years. It's a fairly small company, and not very family oriented. There were some things going on there that had made me toy with the idea of making a job change. But with the pregnancy to focus on, I seemed to relax at work and enjoy myself. Physically I felt great and I ended up working through Friday and went into labor that night. I didn't have any intentions of being a superwoman, but you do want to show that pregnancy is not an illness. Since I felt great and was enjoying my work, there was no reason to leave.

"I did sense a change in attitude toward me at work when I was pregnant —I got a lot of sympathy from some men. I was a little disturbed when the president of the company was talking about my job and the maternity leave and coming back and he was saying he assumed I wouldn't want to travel after I had the baby—making assumptions about what I would want to do or how I would spend my time. But most of this was in a friendly and caring way and I never felt they were deliberately denying me responsibilities because of my pregnancy."

The corporate environment at her multinational bank had come to be more accepting of pregnant women executives when Deborah was expecting, and that made it easier on her. "There was some accommodation to me during the pregnancy," she remembers. "In meetings, there was this sense I couldn't move as quickly. But they became pretty blind to it after a while, partly because it was an environment with a number of pregnant women executives. So they weren't saying, 'Oh God, now that woman who works here is pregnant!'

"One of the vice-presidents who had gone through a pregnancy five or six years before me said that she had once gone to lunch in the executive dining room, and overheard a man say, 'It's bad enough that they let them eat here now, but do they have to come here when they are like *that?*' "

Deborah's pregnancy went past term and she went on working, but more as a favor to her boss than anything else. "He kept saying, 'Can't you stay one more week? Just one more week?' I told him it was out of my hands. I did stay a week beyond my due date. But then one day I had to go for my second sonogram and my husband and I had lunch. He walked me back to my office to get some things and said to my boss, 'John, this is goodbye.' "

Margie was charting new ground when she had her son at thirty-two and therefore felt some pressure to work as long as she could to prove she could do it, despite her chronic high blood pressure. "There are not that many women with Ph.D.s at my company and a lesser proportion in middle management, and, suddenly, one was pregnant. It does affect people's perceptions of you. Although no one treated me as though I was less serious about my work, I think they expected me to take leave a lot sooner than I did. I managed to stay by coming in late and leaving early. The big problem was getting myself there. Once I was there it wasn't so bad. I just made people come to me. I worked until two weeks before my due date."

Sometimes being a pioneer is far more difficult. It was for Margaret, thirty-one, a low-level manager in hotel sales who got pregnant accidentally at twenty-eight. "I was the first woman manager to become pregnant," she says. "Because I realized my position was precarious, I did not ask for any special treatment despite the fact I suffered from afternoon/evening sickness. I continued my normal work routine, making outside sales calls, sales trips, and putting in the required ten hours a day five days a week plus five hours one Saturday a month. I made sure I reported to work on time and not once did I call in 'sick.' I only excused myself for my monthly visits with my obstetrician. I knew the director of sales and the general manager were watching my performance. Once the general manager (a parent himself) saw my dedication, he was very supportive. However, I cannot say the same for the director of sales, a woman, who was my immediate supervisor. She tried every way she could think of to force me to take an early pregnancy leave. How at times I wanted to oblige her! But I worked up to my last day, which was a Friday, and on Monday afternoon I checked into the hospital to have the baby."

For Victoria, thirty-two, an anesthesiologist who works 40 percent of the time in obstetrics, her recent pregnancy was a snap, but it certainly stirred the waters at work. "I've read that the higher the level of responsibility you have, the easier your pregnancy is," she says. "I don't know if that's true, but it was in my case. I wasn't tired. I didn't have morning sickness. I didn't have anything. I continued to do aerobics all the time and I lifted Nautilus until the day I delivered. That made it easier to wait to tell them at work. I didn't say anything until I was five months. With scrubs you can hide things pretty well. When I started to wear maternity clothes I thought I should tell them. And it caused a real uproar—more than I thought it would. It was a very stressful time for me because we were working really long hours and all of a sudden they were thinking, 'Maybe she won't want to work because she's tired.' Yet the day before I was on the same hundred-hour-a-week schedule they were.

"It really irked me that they were so paternalistic. It was the talk of the operating room for days. No physician had ever had a baby there before. Some thought it was the most irresponsible thing they'd ever heard of. So I finally had to sit down and write a letter to everyone detailing my plans for my pregnancy, detailing what I was going to do about child care, how long I was going to be off, etc. That finally put an end to all the carrying on."

Testing the Baby

One of the reasons older mothers can remain serene during their pregnancies is the availability of genetic testing which can assure them that their baby has no chromosomal abnormalities. What is most to be feared is Down's syndrome (Mongolism), a genetic disorder which causes some degree of mental retardation, ranging from moderate to severe. There is also a distinctive appearance: short stature, small hands with short stubby fingers, flabby arms and legs, a tongue too large for the mouth so that it protrudes, a skin fold at the inner corner of the eye, and a flat face with a low bridge over the nose. Forty to sixty percent of all Down's syndrome children have heart defects; many also suffer from defects of the eyes and ears.

Down's is caused by a chromosomal malformation. Normally, during conception twenty-three chromosomes from the mother bond with twenty-three chromosomes from the father. These chromosomes are repeated over and over in each cell in the body. But a Down's syndrome child receives an extra number twenty-one chromosome from the mother's egg so that it has forty-seven instead of forty-six chromosomes.

The incidence of Down's increases rapidly as women age, going from 1 in 885 births at age thirty to 1 in 32 at age forty-five. The exact year-by-year progression is shown in this table.

Maternal Age	Fractional Rate
30	1/885
31	1/826
32	1/725
33	1/592
34	1/465
35	1/365
36	1/287
37	1/225
38	1/177
39	1/139

Maternal Age	Fractional Rate
40	1/109
41	1/85
42	1/67
43	1/53
44	1/41
45	1/32

Yet age may be only part of the picture. No one has examined factors such as nutrition, general health, drug or alcohol abuse, exposure to toxic chemicals or X-rays, which might also influence the chances of having a Down's syndrome child.

Amniocentesis is recommended for all women over thirty-five years of age. It can detect all known chromosomal disorders such as: Down's syndrome, a single-gene defect such as cystic fibrosis or Tay-Sachs, and sex-linked hereditary disorders such as hemophilia. Malformations caused by defects of the neural tube such as spina bifida and anencephaly, show up because they create high levels of alpha-fetoprotein in the amniotic fluid.

Amniocentesis is performed at the fifteenth to seventeenth week of pregnancy in the doctor's office or on an outpatient basis at a hospital. The position of the fetus and the placenta is determined first by ultrasound so that the procedure will not disturb the pregnancy. The abdomen is coated with an antiseptic solution to prevent infection, and a local anesthetic is usually given first. A long thin needle is then inserted through the woman's abdomen into the amniotic fluid surrounding the fetus, and a small amount of fluid is withdrawn. It is a simple, relatively painless procedure that takes all of ten minutes. The risk of miscarriage after amniocentesis is less than 1 percent.

The geneticists grow the fetal cells that are present in the amniotic fluid in a nutrient broth. Then they photograph the chromosomes and arrange them into the twenty-three pairs according to size and structure. They can determine if there the correct number is present and note if any are broken or have missing segments. Since the chromosomes indicating sex (xX for a girl and xY for a boy) are studied, the sex of the baby can also be determined. The cells need several weeks to multiply and be examined so the results from amniocentesis are usually not available for three to four weeks. If the baby is found to be abnormal, the pregnancy can still be terminated at twenty weeks.

With amniocentesis, the normal psychological timetable of pregnancy is altered, write Virginia Apgar and Joan Beck in *Is My Baby All Right? A*

Guide to Birth Defects. There is an "overriding sense of two distinct segments —the one before, the other after, the amniocentesis report. The mood of early pregnancy . . . is one of anxious suspense and withholding of belief until prospective parents know that it is a 'pregnancy they can keep.' The first trimester's psychological task of accepting the pregnancy must be postponed until after the results of the amniocentesis are known; fears of miscarriage are obscured by the knowledge of the reason for the amniocentesis."

This long wait with its accompanying worry may soon be avoided. A genetic test called chorionic villi sampling (CVS) is currently being studied in many medical centers across the country. It can be done between the eighth and twelfth weeks of pregnancy (the ninth and tenth weeks are best) with complete chromosome analysis available in two weeks. The great advantage is that if something is wrong, an abortion can be performed in the first trimester when it is least dangerous. CVS can detect all the genetic abnormalities that amniocentesis does, but it cannot find neural tube defects such as spina bifida. But they can be detected by measuring the alfa-fetoprotein level in the mother's blood, at sixteen weeks of pregnancy.

In very early pregnancy the chorion, a membrane surrounding the fetal gestational sac just outside the amniotic membrane, is covered by fingerlike projections (villi), which grow into the wall of the uterus to eventually become the placenta. When the cells of the embryo are dividing, the outer portion of them develops the supporting structures such as the amnion and chorion, while the inner portion becomes the fetus. Because the chorion originally starts from the same cell as the fetus, it contains the same genetic material as the fetus. Its rapid growth at this stage of pregnancy means that the laboratory study of its chromosomes and biochemistry can be completed much more quickly. To collect pieces of chorion, a thin plastic catheter is gently inserted through the cervix. Suction is applied while the catheter is withdrawn. The entire procedure is monitored by ultrasound. No anesthesia is required.

The risk of miscarriage from CVS appears to be slightly greater than from amniocentesis (1.8 percent versus .5 percent to .75 percent). "The experience to date (only 3,200) has shown that the potential complications of infection and cramping post-procedure are very small," notes the Division of Medical Genetics at Mt. Sinai School of Medicine in New York, one of the medical centers studying CVS. "Bleeding following the procedure may occur in about one third of the patients and is usually only spotting. Some women have heavy bleeding but in our experience this has not led directly to loss of the pregnancy." Further data will indicate what proportion of the miscarriages may have occurred anyway because of chromosomal abnormalities, which are considered to be the cause of 50 percent of all first trimester miscarriages.

Delivery

As noted earlier, older women have a greater risk of a number of complications at the time of delivery. One of these is premature rupture of membranes (the water breaking) anytime before labor begins. The further along in pregnancy a woman is, the greater the chance her baby has to survive. If the pregnancy is less than thirty-two weeks, doctors may try to prevent the onset of labor with drugs called beta-adrenergics (the most common brand name is Ritodrine), which cause the uterus to relax and stop contracting. This is important since any additional time in the womb will improve the baby's chances of survival. However, these drugs work best before the membranes have ruptured and before the cervix thins out completely (effaces) or opens to three to four centimeters. The risk to the baby of being born too soon must also be weighed against the risk of waiting. After the amniotic sac is broken, the baby and the mother may be at risk for developing an infection. Between thirty-two and thirty-seven weeks of pregnancy, this risk of infection becomes the main worry for the obstetrician. Tests performed on the amniotic fluid, usually obtained by amniocentesis, can document the maturity of the baby's lungs. Once the baby is felt to be mature, labor can be induced. After thirty-seven weeks of pregnancy, labor usually will begin on its own within twenty-four hours after rupture of the amniotic membranes, although in some women it does not start for forty-eight to seventy-two hours.

When the membranes rupture, it is important to go to the hospital to be closely monitored for infection. The mother's temperature is taken and a white blood cell count may also be done twice a day. The baby's heart rate is counted at least every four hours, or it may be continually monitored. An increase in either the baby's heart rate, the mother's temperature or white blood cell count may indicate infection. Amniocentesis can also be used to assess the amniotic fluid for infection. If infection is suspected, labor will be induced with pitocin, a drug that stimulates contractions, or a C-section will be performed. If they remain normal, the doctor often waits for labor to set in normally.

Another related problem older women face more often is premature labor, which is labor beginning after the twentieth week and before the thirty-seventh week of pregnancy. It can be heralded by premature rupture of the membranes, or contractions can just start on their own. Women are at risk for premature labor if: they have had previous premature babies, smoke more than half a pack of cigarettes a day, have hypertension, poor nutrition, and use drugs (including alcohol). Fibroid tumors and previous cervical surgery such as a D&C places one at an increased risk of having a premature baby. Other situations, such as a commute of more than one and a half hours a day, and stress may also increase the risk.

If the membranes have not ruptured, bed rest, and lots of it, is universally recommended for premature labor. Physical activity—exercise, lifting, house-cleaning, commuting, and sexual intercourse—is often restricted. If contractions persist they can often be halted with beta-adrenergics.

Germaine, thirty-seven, a documentary filmmaker, went through the terrifying experience of premature labor and delivery with her second child. "I was thirty-three weeks pregnant when it happened. A week or so earlier I had had some staining, which I realized much later was my mucus plug going, but at the time I didn't think of that. I had had a cough during my whole pregnancy, and a broken rib, and my doctor thought maybe I stained because of all the coughing. But then, one night my waters broke. I didn't know that is what it was at first. It was more like dripping. I thought it might be a urinary infection. But in the morning, when it kept on, I began to think maybe they had ruptured. I was having really mild and very irregular contractions.

"By then, there was a terrible blizzard raging outside, and I didn't know if we could get into New York to the hospital. All the roads were supposed to be closed, but we made it by noon. I still wasn't having any contractions to speak of. It took an hour or so to get settled in a labor room and to be examined. I was three centimeters dilated. The doctors wanted to give me Ritodrine to stop the labor, but I didn't know much about it and I wasn't sure I wanted it because they said it had only a 50 percent chance of working and it might only buy a few hours. I have a real thing about drugs. Think of DES and all the damage it's done which didn't show up until years later. While we were arguing about this, my temperature was taken and it had gone up. So, they wanted to do an amniocentesis to check on the baby. I wasn't sure I wanted them to do this either. Meanwhile, my contractions had intensified. I went to the bathroom and while I was in there I got this fantastic urge to push. I realized the baby was coming now. During those twenty minutes I had dilated to ten centimeters. All the discussion was moot.

"I only pushed about ten times and she was out. She weighed five pounds three ounces and she did well on her Apgar scores, but after letting me see her for a moment, they whisked her away to the intensive care nursery. I didn't realize then that anything serious was wrong. She was such a good size it didn't occur to me. But she had Haline membrane disease, which means her lungs were immature, and she had to have oxygen and be hooked up to IVs and a respirator.

"There aren't words to describe how frightened I was, how scary it all was, seeing her with tubes all over her like that. For the first three days nobody had an optimistic word for me. I went up to take her picture, so I'd have something to remember her by and a nurse said to me, 'We don't know if she'll be here tomorrow.' If she survived, no one knew if she'd be retarded, or blind from the oxygen, which can happen if the dosage has to be extremely high.

"I went home after three days and immediately developed a fever of 105 so I couldn't even go see her in the hospital. It was terrible. I pumped my milk and threw it away. They wouldn't let her have milk. She got her food through IVs. She was there two and a half weeks before she could come home. It all seems so long ago now—two and a half years—and it turns out she's just fine. We are very lucky."

During delivery older mothers also have a greater chance of bleeding excessively. This is what happened the first time to Stephanie, who worried throughout her pregnancy at thirty-one about having a handicapped child. "I was an emotional and physical wreck when I went into labor," she remembers. "I had pre-eclampsia. They broke the bag of waters and put me on Pitocin. There was shoulder dystocia where his shoulders got stuck coming out, which is dangerous because it cuts off the oxygen. The rectal wall tore through with third-degree lacerations. I hemorrhaged and lost three pints of blood. It was a twenty-nine-hour labor. I had two IVs, one in each arm."

The flip side of this nightmare was the delivery of Stephanie's second child. "I was absolutely terrified to have another baby," she says. "But I was an only child and I didn't want to do that to anybody. The second time was a dream. What I did was to educate myself about childbirth. I wanted a home birth and the midwife I chose wasn't in favor of it. She said she'd do it only if I could get a doctor who would approve it. The doctor who backed her up on her cases didn't want to allow it because of my hemorrhaging, which could repeat itself.

"So then I was back to finding the kind of birth I wanted in a hospital setting. I hired a woman who was a part-time nurse in the hospital where I was going to deliver. She was a childbirth educator, a wonderful human being. She became my labor coach, and my go-between with the medical establishment so I wouldn't have all the intervention I'd had the first time. My husband was working out of town at the time and she gave us private childbirth classes. She stayed with me through the labor, along with my husband, and I had a lot of emotional support. It was a very straightforward four-hour labor. It was so joyful and so different, and so easy. I can't even say it was awfully painful—it was just uncomfortable at most. The doctor was right that I did have some bleeding at the end, and the staff was concerned enough that it might increase that they gave me some sort of suppository, and that was more uncomfortable than the birth, but it did slow it down. The doctor was also concerned that I was going to have another big baby because my son weighed nine pounds ten ounces, but she was a pound lighter."

Older mothers also more often face the possibility that the baby will be in an abnormal position. Some of the more common ones are breech presentation (foot first) and transverse (lying across the uterus). Obstetricians will often try to turn a baby around in the last weeks before term, but more often than not the baby returns to the original position. In that case, most doctors will perform a C-section. Tessie, twenty-eight, a software engineer who had been reluctant to have a baby, had a C-section when she recently delivered because the baby was breech—and out came surprise twins. "We only found out there were two when one was born," she remembers. "They checked for two heartbeats, but one baby was completely on top of the other so they never heard two. And since they never suspected anything, I never had an ultrasound done. I wasn't enormous. I only gained thirty-five pounds. I have one sister who never looked pregnant the whole time, so I guess it's something that runs in our family. I was big, but no bigger than anyone else gets.

When I went into labor, the baby was still breech, so they did a C-section. They pulled the boy out and my doctor said, "Wait a minute. I see another foot in there," and of course my husband said, 'OK, Doc, cut the jokes,' because he really is a funny doctor. And then he pulled out another baby, a little girl. It was really exciting. I was awake and my husband was there and my first words were, 'Wes, we are done.' They were pretty good size for twins. The boy was six pounds one ounce and the girl was four pounds twelve ounces. They didn't have to stay any extra time in the hospital. But between her being a little light and my having a section, we all stayed a full week."

Perhaps the most common problem for older mothers is a longer, more difficult labor, with slower dilation. This may occur because the uterine muscles lose their tone as women age. A number of the older mothers went through this kind of experience, with many of them also having a great deal of trouble pushing their babies out. Some of them made it through with a vaginal delivery; others ended up with a C-section. Myra, thirty-four, a marketing consultant who just had her son, says, "We went through the classes and I somehow got this impression that once you are through transition the pushing is the easiest part. But I had three and a half hours of pushing and I thought I'd die. All together it was a seventeen-hour labor. I also thought I would recover quickly, but I was completely zonked, just wiped out. I wasn't prepared for that, I guess no one is."

Transition was where Janis, thirty-six, the sales planning manager who had her daughter at thirty-four, got stuck. "I woke up in heavy labor," she recalls. "The problem was that I hadn't eaten anything and I hadn't gotten any sleep because I went to bed at 1:30 and woke up at 2:30. It proceeded very nicely until I got into transition and then my contractions weakened terribly. I didn't get any Pitocin for about an hour and then they were very careful about the dosage so it took about another hour for it to take. So I was in transition for two hours. It was the part I most dreaded. They were very close to giving me a C-section when suddenly the Pitocin seemed to grab hold and then the rest went in minutes.

"I never saw her being born because I was so exhausted and wanted so much to squeeze her out that I never even opened my eyes. I wanted out of the whole thing. Also I had this huge hemorrhoid that I had been developing and nobody understood that I was scared to push too hard because I felt something was going to burst. They all said it was my imagination, but then when they went to stitch me up after the episiotomy, the doctor said, 'Oh, so this is why you were feeling that way.' "

For Cynthia, who recently gave birth to her daughter, pushing was only part of the problem with her lengthy labor. "I had an eighteen-hour-plus labor with three-minute contractions from the beginning, but I could talk through them. It was nice and easy. But then it kept on for all those hours and it got hard. They gave me a real mild relaxant because my doctor knew I wanted natural childbirth. It didn't do diddly squat for me. What happened was that I developed pre-eclampsia during labor and my blood pressure shot up to 190 over 150. So I had to have an IV and oxygen during my entire labor. That was kind of a bummer. I came one millimeter away from a section because once I was dilated to ten centimeters after fourteen hours, it took four and a half hours to push her out. She was eight pounds ten ounces so she wasn't giant, but she wasn't small either. She was that one inch too big to get through, so the doctor finally used forceps, and once he did that it was real smooth and she was all the way out. And once it's done, you know, you are in heaven."

One of the main reasons for a C-section is labor that is not progressing normally. The membranes may rupture prematurely, labor may stop and start, or a woman may not dilate past a certain point. The other major cause is dystocia, which can be the result of an overly large or out-of-position baby, or a problem with the structure of the mother; either of these conditions means the baby cannot exit the uterus the normal way. These two reasons account for 43 percent of the cesarean sections performed. Why older mothers have more sections is not completely clear. It is thought that it may result from their longer, more difficult labors, and increased caution on the part of their doctors.

Emma had an extremely easy pregnancy at thirty-two, but when she was a week overdue, her membranes ruptured, and that was the beginning of a long, difficult labor which ended in a section. "I went into labor with an hour's sleep," she remembers. "We'd gone out to celebrate my birthday. The baby was due December 30 and it was January 6. As we were getting ready to go to bed, I told my husband I just didn't think it was going to be much longer. He said, 'Do you feel anything?' I said, 'No.' It was just instinct. An hour later I woke up, wide awake. I couldn't figure out what was going on. Then there was the proverbial champagne cork: I jumped, the baby jumped, and the water went. I woke Frank up and he was totally disoriented. In fifteen minutes I was in fairly strong labor. The hospital staff said that since the waters had broken I had to go in.

"I was in labor forever. It started petering out and they started Pitocin and I had nurse-midwives and I had my husband. We were in labor for over thirty hours. It's true that you fall asleep between contractions, even when they are that close. It's terrible, you are so disoriented. I guess after about twenty hours or so they did an epidural because I was at four centimeters and I just said, 'I can't do this anymore.' So that gave me a chance to nap a little.

"I kept progressing just enough that they kept going. They were watching my temperature really carefully and if there was any elevation, they said they'd have to do a section because of the risk of infection. At midnight we'd been in labor for twenty-four hours. I started pushing at one A.M. I pushed for three hours and he just was not going to come out. After all of this he said, 'No way.' So after three hours the temperature was starting to go up a little bit and they said I'd given it a real good shot and they asked me how I felt about a section. At that point, anything was OK. I said, 'That sounds super. Take the Pitocin out. Put something more in the epidural and let's go.'

"The recovery was fine. I didn't have problems with gas pains. I didn't even have any problem sitting up in recovery and getting onto the little cart to go up to my room. He was born early Saturday morning and I went home Wednesday morning. The doctor said if she'd known I was going to be in such good shape, she'd have let me go home Tuesday."

C-sections are also done for other kinds of emergencies. One of those is placenta abruptia, where the placenta pulls away from the wall of the uterus before delivery. It happens in one out of every fifty to eighty pregnancies, and is more likely in women with hypertension, and those who smoke heavily. If the placenta separates completely, the oxygen supply to the baby is cut off. Unless delivered within minutes, the baby will die. With partial separation, the condition is still critical, but doctors have a little more time. This is what happened to Deborah, who was thirty-three at the time. "I went to my doctor on a Monday," she recalls. "He gave me a pelvic and he said it would be another week at least and I came home. I went to lie down and take a nap and I hemorrhaged. My father drove me crosstown to New York Hospital and I had general anesthesia and an emergency C-section. It was crazy, with the bells whistling, and the elevators shutting down regular service to get me up to OR. For someone who had never had surgery before, this was something." Her baby boy was fine.

These stories may read like a series of bad, bad dreams. But some of the older mothers had the kinds of labor and delivery that could be advertisements for natural childbirth.

"I had a long labor, eighteen hours, but a totally natural childbirth," says Janet, thirty-nine, a writer and teacher. "The doctor said he thought I had a remarkable tolerance to pain. I was up and walking half an hour later, and Alex was alert and healthy."

Some had labors that were so short they seem more like those of seasoned mothers having their fourth or fifth child. "We did the Bradley method which is natural, and it went very well," remembers Beatrice, who thought she was fat and ugly throughout her pregnancy. "I was in labor for only six hours. Once they started, the pains were coming real fast, like three minutes apart, no letting up, and my husband was right there the whole time. When I needed help making some decisions, he was the one with the ideas. At one point, he couldn't figure out what to do, so he called our childbirth teacher. He helped me breathe while he was on the phone. When they said that they could see her head and to relax, I burst into tears. I felt tearful for days. It was an incredible experience."

Wendy, thirty-four, a customer communications specialist who had her daughter when she was thirty-two, also labored for only six hours. "I delivered two and a half weeks early so I missed those last uncomfortable weeks," she says. "I think I had it easy for a first pregnancy. I only pushed about ten times. There was just one hour that was really painful. We were really excited when she was born. I think deep in my heart I was hoping for a girl, but it never even occurred to me to ask what sex she was until the doctor said it was a girl. Emotionally, it was such a high. It's a baby, it's breathing. OK."

And then there is Meredith, who at thirty-seven had the kind of delivery every woman wishes for. "We went to a birthing center. We left the house and he was born forty-five minutes after we got there. We had wanted a home birth but because of my age and for a first baby people thought we should be a bit more conservative. The birthing center was a wonderful alternative. I'm an absolute convert."

A midwife birth in a hospital setting or at a birthing center, instead of at home, probably is safer for an older mother and her baby. This is especially true if it's her first, or if she had a difficult delivery before. Gretchen, thirty-one, a former librarian and writer, discovered the truth of this at her home birth. "We got a midwife up in the Berkeley area because it was easier for me to see her during the day after work, so we had to have the birth at a friend's house in Oakland because she wouldn't come to Martinez. But, of course, I went into labor at home. I cleaned the house, even the bathroom ceiling. I swam half a mile. I did all the grocery shopping. I was standing in line at the grocery store when I started to get contractions a minute apart. I thought maybe I was already in transition, and 'Oh, my God, we have to get to Oakland.' I rushed home and called the midwife and she asked me if I'd had a bloody show yet, and I hadn't so she told me not to worry, I wasn't in transition. Then ten minutes later I had a bloody show and I called her back and she said I probably had twelve hours left. I called Jim and he came home. We had to load up the car with everything we wanted for a week at my friend's house. Then we drove up there.

"Jim probably spent an hour and a half putting the plastic covering on the bed. I think he was frazzled. The only comfortable position during the contractions was kneeling leaning forward. The midwife sent over an assistant who was still learning, who examined me and told me she thought I was totally dilated, but when she checked again she found I was only two centimeters. I had a whole night of these strange contractions.

"In the morning the midwife came over and made me get up out of that position and take a shower. I was seven centimeters dilated. The shower sped everything up. I went into transition almost immediately—that was the best part. I finally felt the contractions were doing something. They went from these strange little things which were keeping me up all night to ones that felt like waves, that felt great.

"But once I got completely dilated the baby's head started to come down and that felt real strange. And the pushing part was hard because she weighed nine pounds. Her head went through without my getting torn but then when they saw her head, she wasn't breathing right so they made me push her out really quick. It turned out her shoulders got a little squished and it made her not breathe as deeply, and she wasn't crying, and her color wasn't as good as they want. So—this was the bad part—three minutes after she was born they took her to the hospital and kept her in an isolet for eight hours of observation. I was lying there being stitched up, and crying. I had a baby and she wasn't there."

What It's All About: The Baby

As noted earlier, if they carry to term and do not deliver prematurely, women over thirty-five run an increased risk of having a baby who is smaller than it should be because its growth has been impaired while in the womb. These babies are called smaller than gestational age (SGA) babies. One reason for this is that older mothers are more likely to have hypertension or other medical problems, such as kidney or vascular disorders, that affect the supply of blood—and nutrients—that the growing baby receives. Hypertension is thought to be responsible for 20 to 30 percent or more of all impaired growth. Other preventable causes of growth impairment are heavy cigarette smoking, alcoholism, drug addiction, and poor nutrition. Eating properly in pregnancy, and gaining at least twenty-four to twenty-seven pounds, decreases the chance of having an SGA baby.

The good news is that they have the same Apgar scores as those born to younger mothers. The Apgar Scoring System, invented by Virginia Apgar, M.D., a clinical professor of pediatrics at Cornell Medical College, rates the baby on five measurements within sixty seconds after birth, and again at five minutes. APGAR is an acronym for the five measurements: appearance, pulse, grimace, activity, and respiration. The baby is scored on a scale of zero to two on each.

	2	1	0
APPEARANCE	pink all over	body pink; arms and legs bluish	entire body blue
PULSE	above 100/min	less than 100/min	no pulse
GRIMACE	cries vigorously when slapped lightly on soles	grimace or slight cry	no response
ACTIVITY	active motions	some movement arms and legs	limp, motionless
RESPIRATION	strong efforts to breathe; vigorous crying	slow, irregular breathing	no respiration

Dr. Apgar writes in *Is My Baby Alright?*:

A majority of newborn babies receive an Apgar score totaling 7 to 10 when tested 60 seconds after birth. They are breathing adequately, crying, pinkish in color and active—and ready to survive independently. Infants whose score is 4, 5 or 6 usually need some immediate help to bolster their preliminary attempts at breathing and may be quickly given oxygen to assist them in respiration. There may also be thick mucus . . . or small blood clots in the throat which must be suctioned out before they can breathe adequately. A baby with an Apgar score of less than 4 is limp, unresponsive, pale, usually not breathing and possibly even without heartbeat. His throat is quickly suctioned to open a clear airway and his lungs are artificially inflated as rapidly as possible. He may need help with breathing for several minutes until he is ready to take over the lifelong job for himself. . . .

Follow-up studies show that the scores, particularly the second [taken at five minutes], are strongly predictive of the baby's chances for survival in early infancy and indicative of possible neurological damage when it has been present at birth.

So, despite all the possible complications of pregnancy and delivery which an older mother faces, her baby has just as much of a chance at a good start in life as the baby born to a much younger woman.

PART III

BECOMING MOTHERS

9

Nurturing Comes
Naturally

Are women really born nurturers? Does maternal behavior come to us naturally while men have to learn it? The answer appears to be yes. Our separate hormonal heritage sets us apart, and helps ensure our investment in the continuation of the human species.

The human baby is born more helpless, and stays helpless for a longer period of time, than the infant of any other mammal. The reason lies in the size of the female pelvis. When humans began to walk on two legs, the pelvis did not widen because that would have led to an ungainly gait, and made us vulnerable to predators. But the small pelvis requires humans to give birth prematurely—before the infant's cranial dimension get too big for passage through the birth canal. Thus, the human infant is born with essentially a fetal brain that quadruples in size after birth. "It is this fact," wrote Loren Eiseley, "which enables the child, with proper care, to assimilate all that large world which will be forever denied to its giant relative, the gorilla."

It is also this fact that makes us so helpless in infancy, and so in need of the high-quality nutrition that will ensure the exponential growth of our brains. Thus, the care and feeding—the nurturing, in its fullest sense—provided by our mothers is imperative for our survival. "It is more critical to the survival of humans than to any other mammalian species to provide for prolonged infant care through intense attachment of mother and infant," writes Alice Rossi, Ph.D., the Harriet Martineau Professor of Sociology at the University of Massachusetts.

It has been this way since the beginning of human time, and even before. We should remember, as Dr. Rossi has noted, that "we are part of a mammalian primate heritage that has existed for more than 65 million years. Homo sapiens evolved only 40,000 years ago from our immediate ancestors, the primitive hominids, which themselves evolved only two to three million years ago." Things may seem different in today's modern technological society, but even settled farming communities are a fairly recent development in human history. Well over 90 percent of human time on earth has been spent in hunter-gatherer societies where these behaviors still hold true. In existing societies such as the Kung! bushmen, mothers and infants have close physical contact for 70 percent of the day, tapering down to 30 percent by the middle of the second year. Babies of the Kung! nurse almost continuously and lactation continues for up to four or five years. Fathers are only peripherally involved. By comparison, a baby born into our modern world has this kind of close contact for only 25 percent of the day and even that for just the first few weeks, after which it quickly drops to 5 percent.

"If we read the biological program correctly," notes Selma Fraiberg in *Every Child's Birthright: In Defense of Mothering,* "the period of breast feeding insured continuity of mothering as part of the program for the formation of human bonds. . . . [Throughout history] the breast feeding mother could not be separated from her baby for long intervals. This means, of course, that the baby rarely was cared for by a stranger, and was mainly nurtured by his mother."

The Biological Basis of Parenting

It can be argued that the more critical a behavior is to the survival of a species, the more likely it is to have components that are innate, that do not have to be learned, that have become part of the biological inheritance. "On this basis, one would expect human mother-infant attachment to involve some innate factors since the female is more directly involved in the reproductive process than the male, and there is greater need for close bonding of the human infant than for other members of the species," write Robert W. Goy, director of the Wisconsin Regional Primate center, and Bruce S. McEwen, associate professor of neurobiology at The Rockefeller University in *Sexual Differentiation of the Brain.* "There are two innate orientations to the female—one involving sexual attraction to men and the other a care-giving attachment to the child—while the male has only the innate sexual attraction to the female and learns most parenting behavior from females."

Of course, many differences between men and women are learned, the result of differences in upbringing, role assignment, societal expectations, and political climate. But scientists believe the mother-infant attachment is innate not only because it is so critical to the survival of the species but because women's biology predisposes them to sensitivities, capabilities, and behavior patterns which are particularly conducive to nurturing an infant, whereas men's biology predisposes them to be more involved once their offspring have gotten older. As Dr. Rossi notes, "The attributes of mothering and fathering are inherent parts of sex differentiation. . . . Men bring their maleness to parenting, as women bring their femaleness."

A number of studies of the behavior of mothers and fathers toward a new baby support the theory of biologically based gender differences in attachment to the infant. In one study, the fathers did not attempt to care for the new baby in a significant way. They acted clumsy in company and showed even less skill in handling than they really had. "The fathers also tended to act toward the infants as if they were 'things' rather than persons they can interact with," writes Dr. Rossi about the study's findings. "Women, by contrast, tend to embrace the mother role, submerging themselves in the role and trying to act more skillfully than they in fact feel." According to another study, even if fathers learn natural childbirth techniques and are present during labor and delivery, within a few months the mothers are more attached to the babies than the fathers are.

This pattern did not change, even with a second baby. The fathers didn't act any differently toward their newborns even though they were obviously more familiar with baby care. Instead, they were much more interested in their growing toddlers whose abilities were expanding, and they left the care of the infant to the mothers, who were happy with this arrangement because it gave them time to enjoy their new babies.

By contrast, innumerable studies of mothers show that they behave in remarkably similar ways toward their infants, both immediately after birth and in the months that follow. During their first moments with their baby, they touch the baby's fingers and toes with their own fingertips. Then they put the palm of their hand on the baby's body, enclose the baby in their arms, and move their head around to get full parallel eye contact, which is called the *en face* position. Until eye contact is made, they experience increasing tension. Even mothers looking into the incubators holding their premature babies will contort themselves to get into this position in order to achieve *en face* eye contact.

The majority of mothers hold their infants close to their bodies using their left arm; it is in this position that the baby can be soothed by the mother's heartbeat so familiar from nine months in the womb. The interesting thing is that this is the position chosen even by left-handed mothers. When talking to babies, mothers speak in similar ways which they cannot duplicate unless they are talking to a baby. They open their eyes wide, and raise their eyebrows. They hold each facial expression for a long time. And when they speak, they elongate their vowels.

These differences in the parenting behavior of men and women do not mean that men cannot become attached to their infants. New fathers who feel reluctance in partaking of the physical and emotional intimacy that a relationship with their infant requires, can overcome this and become absorbed and preoccupied with the baby. The fathers of newborns in one study felt that they could distinguish the crying of their baby in the nursery from the crying of other babies, thought their baby was perfect, were strongly attracted to their baby, and felt elation and an increase in self-esteem after the birth.

The Role of Our Hormones

There is a good deal of evidence in animal and human studies that there is a strong connection between the sex hormones, androgens in males and mainly estrogens in females, and parenting behavior. But one big question that remains about the role of hormones in women is the contribution that hormonal fluctuations during pregnancy and at birth make in "triggering" maternal behavior. Jay S. Rosenblatt, Ph.D., a professor of psychology and director of the Institute of Animal Behavior at Rutgers University, has concentrated much of his research on such hormonally induced behavior in animals, particularly rats. In the animals studied, progesterone, which is an ovarian hormone that has been at a very high level for most of pregnancy, suddenly drops down very sharply and estrogen rises very sharply shortly before birth. With rats, this happens one day before birth; with sheep, ten days before.

"The onset of maternal behavior is based on this rise in estrogen," says Dr. Rosenblatt. "In humans, the pattern of hormone secretion mainly by the ovary at the end of pregnancy is similar to that which we have in animals. The rise in estrogen is believed to happen very close to the end of pregnancy. One report says 10 days before delivery, and another says it happens almost on the day of delivery. But there are no hormonal studies on maternal behavior in humans. It's only because in animals that we find that maternal behavior is hormonal that we believe it must be in humans. In every case in animals, the onset is based on hormones."

What happens in rats and other animals is that the rise in estrogen tips the balance of responding to the young, making the mother ignore or overcome the unattractive features, such as the smell of the newborn babies. "Of all the stimuli a mother faces, she selects certain ones to attend to," says Dr. Rosenblatt. "If, before a rat gives birth, we offer her a baby and a piece of food, she chooses the food. Right after birth, she chooses the baby."

In experiments, maternal behavior in virgin female rats can be induced by manipulating their hormones. If these females, who are completely inexperienced with maternal behavior, are put in a confined space with newborn rats, called pups, they become maternal in four to seven days, and the tighter the space, the more quickly this happens. But, says Dr. Rosenblatt, "if we give progesterone to them for 16 days (a pregnancy in rats is 22 days long) and then stop the progesterone and give estrogen, maternal behavior begins within two days. The same thing happens with males—because they have similar neural systems to females that can respond to the female hormones even though they do not secret these hormones. They need to be given more progesterone and more estrogen than the virgin females, but they do respond. Conversely, if you remove the estrogen from the females by taking out their ovaries, they become almost as unresponsive as the males."

Beyond Hormones

Estrogen obviously plays an important role in triggering maternal behavior for rats, but it is not all-important. Experiments have shown that it is the presence of the pups, and stimulation from them, that keeps the maternal juices flowing. "If the pups are removed, the maternal behavior declines quite rapidly," says Dr. Rosenblatt. "If you take them away at birth, by the second day, 30 percent of the females don't respond to them when they are put back, and by day four none of them respond."

Dr. Rosenblatt believes that human mothers also go through a transition from hormonally induced maternal behavior to nonhormonal psychological maternal behavior which is brought on by contact with their babies. Although there is no proof one way or the other about hormonally induced maternal behavior, numerous studies of both humans and primates have shown the importance of contact between infant and mother to the development of the attachment between them, and to the development of the young. In one study of premature infants who are isolated from their mothers in incubators surrounded by the high-tech apparatus of modern medicine, the mothers who were allowed to touch and handle their babies, even if only briefly, showed more interest in their infants even months later than those who were not allowed to have any physical contact with their babies.

The big question in terms of contact is whether there is a critical period in which contact must occur in order for the bonds of attachment to be sewn, or even a sensitive period in which such attachment is more likely to occur. The prevalent view in recent years has been that contact in the period right after birth when the level of estrogen is still high is a sensitive one in which bonding is more likely to occur. This argument is in part based on a study by Marshall Klaus, M.D., and John Kennell, M.D., at Rainbow Babies' and Children's Hospital in Cleveland, that compared mothers who were with their babies for one hour after birth and for five hours on each of the next three days to mothers whose babies were removed soon after birth.

It found that the effects of the early contact were significant. At one month, the mothers who had had the early contact picked up their babies more often when they cried; they fondled their babies more and looked into their eyes while feeding. They were also more reluctant to leave the baby with a babysitter and said they constantly thought about the baby. One year later, they were more attentive to the baby during visits to the pediatrician. Two years later they spoke differently to their babies. "The early contact mothers presented a model of better learning. They gave more stimulation to the child's thinking. They seemed to be more aware of the needs of growing children. They could interpret the environment better to them," says Dr. Kennell in "Biology Is One Key To the Bonding of Mothers and Babies" in *Smithsonian* magazine. "To think all that is the result of just 16 hours of being together in the first three days of life. The hours after birth seem to comprise a sensitive period for maternal-infant attachment."

But this view about a sensitive period for bonding has been refuted by a number of developmental psychologists and sociologists. First of all, as Dr. Rossi points out, the findings of the Klaus-Kennell study have not been replicated. But more importantly, she writes, "It is highly unlikely that small variations in early contact could be critical to human attachment to infants. For a complex organism like a human being, fixing of an essential bond is not likely to be dependent on a brief period or specific experience following childbirth."

This should make women feel a lot better—especially those who had to have anesthesia that put them under, denying them those first moments with their baby, or whose babies had trouble at birth and were whisked away to the intensive care nursery. This maternal attachment, which is part of our biological inheritance, does not have to be instant, but can grow and thicken like the stalk of a vine over the first months of life. As Dr. Rossi says, "Nature is always 'redundant,' never dependent on just one system to assure species survival. Some adults feel strongly motivated for bearing young; others have children without high motivation and then become attached at birth; still others require exposure and daily care to become attached to their young. Experience and exposure clearly are important in human animals in a way they are not called for in lower animals."

Getting Attached

The mothers interviewed for this book certainly support Dr. Rossi's hypothesis that attachment can happen in many ways, from a sense of wonder, to instant bonding, to feelings that their baby is a stranger they have promised to take care of—a stranger they fall in love with some months later. The way these feelings play out may be related to the way these women have felt about babies earlier in their lives. A quarter of them didn't dream at all of having a baby when they grew up, and another quarter dreamt only occasionally of becoming a mother. In this they are very much like the clock-watchers who are still childless.

Many of the mothers spoke of their feeling of awe when first seeing or holding their baby. After seventeen hours on Pitocin and a forceps delivery, Emily, thirty-five, the director of patient services for a home health care agency, felt extremely relieved it was over, but there also was the sense that "a miracle had landed in my lap. To look at him blew me away. I felt very attached to him, but I don't remember this overwhelming maternal bonding. I would have killed for that child, I knew that, and maybe that's what it is. When you sense that this is my baby."

For Eleanor, forty-six, a psychotherapist and author, elation began when she found out she was pregnant at age forty-one. "It was probably one of the most exciting experiences of my life. But I remember even more the day she was born. I had this absolutely powerful sense that I had made this enormous contribution to the world. I was at the Bethesda Naval Hospital, and my impulse was to climb to the top spear and shout out the news that this incredible child had been born. I was so impressed with the whole birth process and this miracle of creation. I don't think until then I had truly appreciated it all."

These feelings soon intensified into love. "I didn't realize how involved I'd be, how much I'd like being a mother. I've often thought that if I'd known how much I like mothering, I probably would have started sooner, and had a fairly large family. Admittedly, I had wonderful circumstances: a housekeeper, a flexible schedule for my work, and the opportunity to work at home. I was mature enough not to be upset by too much, but what surprised me the most was my earlier naïve idea that the important thing after she was born was to figure out how not to let her interfere with my career. As soon as she was born, I was totally involved with her, and I realized very quickly that this wasn't just a thing one did, this was a total involvement. I fell in love with her. And I decided I wasn't going to deprive her or myself of taking advantage of these early years, so I spent a great deal of time with her."

A separation at birth did nothing to change the feeling of wonder that Emma, thirty-four, an advertising director who was then thirty-two, felt about her son. Her waters broke prematurely, and she labored for more than twenty-four hours before having a C-section, so her son was taken off to the intensive care nursery for twenty-four hours of observation because of the possibility of infection. She only got to touch him, not hold him, in the operating room. "The nurses knew I felt really strongly about breast-feeding, and one of them from intensive care sneaked him down to me at 2 P.M. the afternoon he was born. She said, 'This is obviously a healthy child. I'm not supposed to be bringing him down, but I knew you wanted to nurse and there's nothing wrong with him.' So that was when I first got to hold him. It was fabulous. I was just awed. I couldn't believe I had carried him around, and that he was out here now. I'd gotten used to him inside and all of the things he'd do there. I couldn't believe we had done this. I was very excited and felt very awkward. Fortunately, he was extremely enthusiastic about nursing from the word *go*. He knew just what he wanted, and what to do, so there was no problem about that. It was really terrific."

These feelings of wonder can wash over women who really didn't care about babies before giving birth. "I hadn't been around babies much, and I didn't even like children," says Karen, thirty-two, who was thirty-one when she gave birth to her daughter. "I was the type who, if I went into a restaurant, and someone came in with a bunch of kids, would be upset if they sat near me. I always avoided children. I hated to babysit when I was a teenager. It was amazing the change that came over me right after my daughter was born. I was in a room across from the nursery and once I saw her and all the other little babies, I thought what a miracle it was. They were all wonderful and so pretty and good. I love to see other people's children now."

But her awe at having created her daughter did not translate into an immediate bond for Karen. "When I first held her I felt really strange. There was just this little stranger there. There was no maternal instinct or true love yet. It was more like 'Wow!' I was really afraid to see her when they brought her in to my room, and I had trouble nursing her. She didn't eat for three days. At three months I stopped nursing her and put her on the bottle and she scheduled right out and slept all night and has been a wonderful baby ever since. As time has passed, my confidence level has risen; it just grows. The first two months, I didn't know how I felt. But I have confidence in myself now, and motherhood is also much more rewarding than I thought it would be."

For other women, the wonder and the bond are simultaneous. This was true for Janis, thirty-six, who two years ago had the kind of bonding with her baby right after birth that Lamaze classes show in their movies. "They put her on my belly and she was all covered in vernix, and blood and her umbilical cord was wound like a telephone cord and she was warm from my body. That was a wonderful experience. We have a picture of it and whenever I see it, I remember that sensation. Then they scooped her off. I really wish she could have stayed there for a few minutes longer because that is when I felt a tremendous sense of connection—that this is the person I had been growing inside me, that we were still connected through the umbilical cord and feeling that warmth.

"Then when she was wrapped up and put in my arms I remember thinking how beautiful she was. I was expecting a red-faced, wrinkled, not especially attractive baby that I would love because she was mine. Instead, what I got was this baby who, in spite of this lengthy birth, was virtually unmarked, had a lovely complexion and was just extraordinarily beautiful. I couldn't get over it—plus all the delicacy. I kept wishing she wasn't bundled up so I could see all of her. There was a real sense of awe at having produced anything that beautiful."

Dana, thirty, a corporate lawyer who was twenty-eight when she had her son, also felt an immediate bond with her baby. "The minute I held him I knew it was the best thing I had ever done. I was ready for another baby instantly. I bonded with him instantly. I wouldn't let the nursery take him back. They thought I should rest, but I told them they could go ahead and try, it wouldn't work."

Gretchen, thirty-one, had a home delivery by midwife only to find her baby had trouble breathing and needed to be rushed off to the hospital for eight hours of observation. But this interruption in their relationship did not prevent their instant attachment. "When I walked into the intensive care nursery for the first time to see her, she knew who I was and that made it wonderful—that it was something special, a special bond."

For some women, the attachment takes longer to form—weeks, months, even years. It is the contact, the physical caring, and the response of the baby, that seem to turn on even reluctant mothers. Tessie, twenty-eight, a software engineer who had surprise twins, was never thrilled with the prospect of motherhood, and she says, "It took a little while to fall in love with them, but not too long. I never really had many maternal instincts, and when they were born, I knew they were mine, but I didn't feel very close to them just as I didn't feel close to other babies. It wasn't until we got them home and I realized that *we* had babies. I started taking care of them and they needed me. The instinct started coming out. I would breast-feed one and bottle-feed the other for one feeding and then switch for the next feeding, but feeding them was pretty constant. My mom was out for three weeks and then my mother-in-law for two weeks, so that got us through some of the roughest stages."

Six weeks also marked the attachment point for Samantha, thirty-five, a weaver, who had her son at thirty-three. "I didn't feel a surge of love when I first held him. I was too tired at that time to even care. It was, 'God, it's finally over and he's OK.' I checked his hands and feet to make sure he was all there, and I said, 'OK, take him back, I'm tired.' Little did I know I was not to sleep for quite a while.

"The maternal feelings didn't really surface for six weeks or so. I had a hard time adjusting to having a child dependent on me, realizing that I couldn't pass him off to someone else or take a day off. Talk about loss of control! I didn't realize it would be so difficult. I did breast-feed, and it helped with the bonding. It was neat. I enjoyed that."

For Daphne, thirty-two, an account supervisor, the euphoria of the first weeks, with all the attention and excitement, bottomed out when she was left alone with her baby. But despite the fact that she found it very difficult to be with him, she extended her maternity leave from three months to six months, and it turns out that this extra time did the trick. "The maternal instinct was there, but there were times I'd think, 'Why don't I just love being with this baby all day long?' There were guilt feelings. Fortunately, we met another couple in the neighborhood who have a baby who is only a month older and she had similar kinds of feelings so I had someone to kind of share it with. By around six months, when he could start to do a few things and respond and interact, I knew that I was really hooked. This baby was mine and nobody was going to take him away."

For some women the bond has taken even longer to form. Like Samantha, Myra, thirty-four, a marketing consultant with her own business, found that the exhaustion of nighttime feedings played havoc with her. Even after her son started sleeping better, she has had trouble adjusting to motherhood. "All through the pregnancy I had been concerned that the baby would be healthy. But by the time I delivered him, I didn't care if he was healthy. I didn't care if it was a boy or a girl. I just said, 'It's over.' My husband took these pictures and I look so maternal, but I was feeling, 'Now what will I do with this little thing?' and at that point he was very quiet. He hadn't started his crying. I feel like the whole first three months were really a blur. By the end of that time I felt bonded to him and I had some warm feelings, but I was just so exhausted, and I'm the kind of person who needs a straight eight hours of sleep in order to function and I didn't get it, and it only got worse as he got older.

"By three and a half months he was awake three times a night, and I thought I couldn't take it anymore. There is such pressure to nurse and he was a large child. I'm a pretty petite person and I don't think I had enough milk. There was my mother saying I should give him cereal and the pediatrician saying, 'No, no.' I finally listened to my mother. We were on vacation on the Cape and I went back to Pennsylvania with my parents to visit for a week. I'd gotten up at 1 A.M. and 4 A.M. and 6 A.M. and nursed him each time and I was in tears. My mother said, 'Why don't we try the cereal?' and we did and he started sleeping. Now he's nine months old, and I'm just starting to feel somewhat settled, like a normal person."

What About the Fathers?

Many of these mothers described their initial feelings for their babies without mentioning their husband's reaction. It's as if they were alone in the world with their private miracle. But a few of them saw their husbands bond with the baby in the first moments after birth. "He was in love with him from the first moment he had him in his arms," says Margie, thirty-five, a Ph.D. chemist and mid-level manager, who was thirty-two at the time. "Even before that, with the Lamaze lessons, he was excited. Once we made the decision to have a child, he was fine. It was making the decision that was hard for him."

"I was a lot calmer and happier because my husband was there at the birth. But the best thing was when he saw his son and was the first to hold him," remembers Roberta, thirty-seven, an administrative assistant who had her son at age thirty-four. "The look in his eyes said it all. He glowed. He felt great. It took a few days before he came back to earth. That's how happy he was."

Men may feel this euphoria, but for many of them, life goes on as it did before, baby or no baby, and their wives are left alone to cope. This happened to Janis after the birth of her daughter. "My husband was there. He has two other children but he'd never seen it from start to finish before. He was the one looking for the head to appear, waiting to see if it was a boy or a girl. He was going to be there no matter what. He had a sales meeting to run and the deal was that if I didn't go into labor before that time, so what, he would stay. If I did, then he would go.

"So he left the next day on a business trip. When you look back at some of the decisions you make because of work pressures, you think, 'Why the hell did I do that?' I had hired someone and she couldn't be found, so when I got home there was no one there. It was kind of a mess. I was trying to get temporary help, but I wasn't willing to pay three hundred dollars a week just because I was strapped. So I'd say the first few weeks were a little tough because it was brand new for me and I couldn't get a night's sleep, and my husband was out of town for a good period of time, and I didn't have anybody. My mother came a few weeks later and by that time I had the routine down, and I'd learned to take naps whenever I could."

Karen's husband didn't leave town, but his life did continue pretty much unchanged, unlike hers. "I didn't realize how hard it would hit me when I got home. My mom didn't come until four or five days later. She thought it would be better if Philip and I were alone with the baby. But I wish she'd come sooner because by the time she got there I was totally exhausted. Philip went right back to work; I didn't think of asking him to stay home. His schedule didn't change. He still had to keep up his Nautilus program and his golfing. He's a real golfer, so he was not home on weekends, and he wasn't willing to make changes on that front. I resented it because I was exhausted and I needed him there."

Things have improved in Karen's world since the first couple of months, partly because the baby has gotten to be more fun for her husband. "I had been apprehensive about being alone a lot and I was. His life went on exactly as it had been and I was totally restricted with the baby," she remembers. "With the first, you aren't as brave about taking the baby out as maybe you would be with a second one. It was really hard. The marriage wasn't going real smoothly then. I didn't realize the baby wouldn't respond to her father as well as she would later. He was so upset with her, not knowing what to do to calm her. He just wanted to not be there. She's eight months old now and from four months on, she's responded to him, things have smoothed out, and he's been willing to spend more time."

If a woman doesn't expect much involvement from her husband, it sometimes makes it easier for her when his life goes on as before. This was true for Eleanor. In order to get her husband, a doctor who had three grown children from his first marriage, to agree to have a child, she had made a pact with him that he wouldn't have to do any baby care. However, she had plenty of help from the housekeeper and her mother-in-law, so she wasn't alone and she wasn't frazzled. She thought he would form a relationship with their daughter when she was older—a time when fathers typically get more involved. "Sarah came at a very busy time in his career, and he wasn't home a lot; he was traveling and was in and out of her life," she remembers. "Part of my feeling involved the fact that he was planning to move out of this very active phase into a more contemplative/writing phase when he was in his early sixties and that was a time when she would want to be with him more than in babyhood, and he'd have the time. So it was a decent compromise, and it's working out that way. Sarah is now five, and they are getting more involved all the time. And he'll be even more available during her adolescence than he is now."

Other fathers were around, but they didn't get that nurturing impulse. Myra had trouble getting her husband over the hurdle of seeing their son as a joint project. "It was hard in the beginning," she remembers. "After about the fifth night of the baby getting up every hour on the hour, my mother arrived and she took over and walked Peter around. Bill was going back to work and he said, 'Can't you stop that kid from crying?' as if it were just my responsibility. That was the only time that happened. As Peter's gotten older, Bill's been more and more involved. In the beginning I was breast-feeding and he felt left out. He changed diapers but there really wasn't much for him to do. Until about three months, Peter was sleeping most of the time or breast-feeding. But now we have a couple of little routines, and if I want to get out for a few hours on the weekend, Bill will take over. And every night he gives Peter his bath. I really saw a change when Peter got to be about seven months —their relationship changed and Peter became attached to Bill in a way he hadn't been before. I think Bill now feels very comfortable in the role of father."

10

Living Two Lives
Our Work

Mothers who work live divided lives which use different talents and temperaments. They rush from one world to the other in the morning, worrying about being late to work, keeping their good clothes clean while feeding their kids, and not forgetting the important papers in their briefcases—the ones that should have been looked at the night before and probably weren't. During the workday they perform their jobs with their usual competence and zeal, and pray their children don't get sick on the day of a big meeting. And then at night, they make the reverse trip, picking up children from sitters, getting dinner, doing laundry, then falling into bed exhausted.

This scenario is repeated five days a week all across America. Fifty percent of the mothers of preschool-aged children are working, including thirty-three percent of those with a child less than a year old. The numbers rise as children grow up and enter school—70 percent of their mothers are employed. And the numbers are growing. By 1990, 64 percent of all women with children under age six will be working—that's 14 million women, according to the Urban Institute.

Most of the mothers interviewed for this book are among them. Perhaps because they waited to have their children, they are doing well professionally: 30 percent are in upper- or middle-management positions, 33 percent are professionals, and a third of them earn more than $35,000 a year—numbers not very different from the childless clock-watchers.

But motherhood has *not* meant that these women's work lives have continued just as they were, even if they have come back to the same job. For a few of them (2 percent), motherhood has caused them to recast themselves in a totally new role—they have quit their jobs to stay home full-time for a few years. Others have made major changes in their careers in order to get flexibility. Almost a quarter have switched to a part-time schedule at least temporarily, and 15 percent have started their own businesses in order to better combine their two worlds.

For the 87 percent who have continued to work full-time because of economic necessity or because they love their work and would not feel whole without it, there have also been changes in their working lives—adjustments of schedules, lateral moves to gain flexibility, the tempering of ambition. Yet each day, they wake to the stress of two full-time commitments, to their children and to their careers, commitments that can be in such conflict that they may occasionally pull them apart. None other than Betty Friedan recently wrote, " 'Superwomen' who are trying to 'have it all,' combining full-time careers with 'stretch-time' motherhood are enduring such relentless pressure that their younger sisters may not even dare to think about having children."

Taking Leave

It all begins with negotiating a maternity leave, which used to be much more treacherous than it is now. Since the Pregnancy Discrimination Act, a 1978 amendment to Title VII of the Civil Rights Act, most women have had at least minimal rights. The act says that "women affected by pregnancy, childbirth or related medical conditions shall be treated the same for all employment-related purposes, including receipt of benefits under fringe-benefit programs, as other persons not so affected but similar in their ability or inability to work." This law applies to all women who work for companies with fifteen or more employees. For companies with less than fifteen employees, state, not federal, law applies.

To translate, the act says basically that a pregnant woman cannot be treated any differently than any other worker who is temporarily disabled—she cannot be fired, denied a promotion, or forced to go on leave as long as she can still work, and if other workers on disability leave are entitled to get their jobs back when they return, then so is the pregnant employee. If the company has a temporary disability insurance plan, then the pregnant woman gets whatever benefits are offered: sick leave, health insurance, and disability pay, which is usually a portion of her salary.

But if there is no disability leave policy at a company, then there is also no maternity leave policy, unless the state has one. In addition, if a woman extends her maternity leave past the company's disability leave by adding on vacation time or taking an unpaid leave, she is no longer under the protection of the law, and when she returns, it's up to the employer whether to give her back her job at the same salary.

What this all comes down to for the working mother-to-be is that there are three kinds of leaves available, which can often be packaged together: unpaid, paid, and short-term disability. Unpaid leaves are what they seem to be: time off without pay and with a guarantee of an equivalent job on return—although not necessarily the same one. With an unpaid leave, all benefits—including the medical plan—can be cut off because the woman is not on the payroll. In most companies, paid leaves can usually be had by using accrued sick leave and/or vacation time. A 1984 survey by Catalyst found that only 7 percent of the responding companies granted a paid leave in addition to accrued vacation, paid sick leave, and disability. However, 95 percent of the companies had a short-term disability policy offering full or partially paid leave, usually for five to eight weeks. It appears that the larger the company, the more likely they will offer good benefits. This is because they have a pool of employees who can cover for one another, so they can afford to be flexible and set up individual maternity plans, and they can offer firmer job guarantees. In fact, 27 percent of the companies in the Catalyst survey made policy exceptions, for managers and nonmanagers.

Among the mothers surveyed, 38 percent were allowed a leave of four to eight weeks, 20 percent could take nine to twelve weeks, and 21 percent could take three to six months. On average, six weeks of this leave was paid in part or in full, although 32 percent of the mothers had to take a leave without pay, and this forced some of them to return to work sooner than they had to. Kitty, thirty-two, a manager in data processing, faced this kind of situation: "I was only given six weeks with pay," she says. "I could have had up to a six-month leave of absence with promises of a similar position, but not necessarily the same job. However, I couldn't afford to do that."

If all things were possible, two thirds of these mothers would have liked three months or more at home with their new baby. Some got their wish. Because of their job level, they held such a strong negotiating position that they were able to work out a special leave and sometimes a special way to return to work. "I was the first woman to have a baby and take a leave of absence, and they had to put together a disability plan for me," says Daphne, thirty-two, an account supervisor in a market research firm. "I originally negotiated a three-month leave. But after the baby was born, I really felt that even though I found being with him extremely trying, I needed more time to settle into motherhood, give the baby a lot of attention, and figure out child care. Fortunately, the company is fairly small and when I suggested staying out through the summer for a total of six months, they accommodated me."

Wendy, thirty-four, a customer communications specialist, was also able to negotiate a special leave—but at some risk to her career image. "Our company has a general policy of six weeks paid—but that's unless you have a doctor's excuse. That was just not acceptable to me. So I negotiated with my boss. I took my two weeks of vacation, plus the six weeks, and then an unpaid leave of absence for a month. I am one of very few women in our company who has done that. It was not looked upon favorably."

Margie, thirty-five, a Ph.D. chemist in a middle-management position at a Fortune 500 company, also worked out a nice deal for herself when her son was born. "Everyone gets six weeks paid medical leave," she says. "I got two extra weeks because of my high blood pressure. Then I told them that I wanted six months off from the time that the baby was born, and that wasn't a problem. They will grant up to a year's leave of absence unpaid, and they will guarantee you a job at the same pay scale when you get back. It doesn't mean you will be at the same level of management, or that they will be able to give you a management position when you walk back in, but you'll still be making the same amount of money. They held my job for me. I thought that was pretty good."

Margie also negotiated a gradual return to her job—which took more effort than the maternity leave itself. "Four months after David was born, I started going back to work part-time. My biggest concern was what to do with David if I found myself suddenly returning to work full-time. But coming back sooner, part-time, was something they had to *make* work. You can't get paid for a half day if you are on salary, and you can't work more than a certain number of days a week if you are working part-time. Basically, they don't want anyone working part-time. But they figured it out somehow and I came back to work two days a week for a month, and that grew to three days a week, four days a week, etc. I was back to my old schedule six months to the day after he was born. It was very good for my son. I was still nursing him, and I was able to wean him during that time."

When she was pregnant the first time at age twenty-nine, it was before the Pregnancy Act was passed, so Ginger, thirty-seven, a director of personnel, took only a four-week unpaid leave after her son was born, and felt a lot of pressure from the company to return quickly. This time, she is doing it differently, and because she's been with the company a long time and is in a position of some power, she's written her own ticket. "I came right out and said fairly early on that I planned to take a paid disability leave for two weeks before and six weeks after, or whatever is required if there are complications. And then I'll take another month of unpaid leave and then I'm going to come back part-time. I've told people that in six months I should be back full-time. I haven't decided how I'll do the part-time. I'll probably do a few hours a day in the beginning because I'll be breast-feeding and I don't want to be away a full day. On the other hand, I know there will be times where I'll need to be at work for a whole day because of meetings, so I will, but then I won't go in the next day. Basically, people here are pretty flexible and I'm in the kind of position that I can just tell them what I'm going to do and it's hard for them to challenge it. I can also take work home. I can write memos or dictate them, and then bring them in to be typed."

Like a number of other mothers, Lorraine, thirty-one, a budget analyst for her western state, returned to her job sooner than she had to. These women didn't feel they could take full advantage of the liberal maternity leave their employers allow because of the possible repercussions at work. "I took twelve weeks," says Lorraine. "It was all paid because I had accumulated enough sick leave and vacation time. The state generally allows you three months off, but you can have more if you have sick leave and vacation built up. Some women have taken six months. Those are generally people in the clerical field. I felt that taking six months would really hamper my career. There weren't any repercussions from the three months, but I found it really difficult to go back, much more so than I ever thought it would be. I would have liked more time."

The worst situation was faced by Dana, thirty, a corporate attorney in the oil industry in Texas. With her first child, Matt, she was back after only three weeks because there was no disability leave policy and therefore no maternity leave policy. Then, her company was selling off a subsidiary to another company and she had the choice of going with the subsidiary or staying with the original parent company. She chose to be sold with the subsidiary partly because the acquiring company had much better maternity benefits—up to six months off with 70 percent salary—and she knew she wanted a second baby. But all was not to be roses. "During my interview with the head of the legal department before I took the job, he asked all sorts of questions. He said, 'I know I don't have a right to ask this and you don't have to answer it, but do you plan to have any more children? How much time are you planning on taking? Do you have day care problems? How much work do you miss because you have a problem with day care?' I was astounded. But when they put you in that position, what else are you going to do but answer?"

It was quite obvious to Dana right then and there that she couldn't take full advantage of the benefits the company advertised. "When I had Cindy," she says, "I chose very purposefully to take only three months, half of what I was entitled to, in order to prove that I'm a good and dedicated worker. But even that had really negative repercussions for me. They were really put out about it, and when I came back, it was a serious problem. I got a lot of remarks that I'd only taken three weeks with Matt and this time I'd taken three months and therefore I wasn't dedicated to my career."

Some employers have even threatened women over their leaves. This is what happened to Margaret, thirty-one, who was then twenty-eight, and in hotel sales. She now works for her husband in his business. "I had to claim disability because there was no special policy governing maternity leave three years ago," she remembers. "Under their provision I was entitled to three months off with no pay and a guarantee of my same position. But I was required to sign an agreement whereby if I did not return by three months for any reason I would then owe the company three months salary. After being with this company for three years, I felt I had been slapped in the face. The director of personnel, who was female and newly married with no children, had no tact with any employee and was very good at reciting corporate policy whenever she would hear discord from anyone. I was fearful for my job. I opted for only eight weeks leave. And during those two months, I regularly received calls from my office asking for advice on my accounts, and was requested to attend meetings at the hotel."

Having gone to a lot of trouble to negotiate time away from work in order to take care of their new babies and learn about motherhood, some women find the days at home difficult. It's not that they didn't want to be with their babies, but they were used to another kind of life. Daphne quickly realized that the skills she employed at work were not much use to her in handling a baby. "Being home and on my own was totally different than work," she says. "I was used to structuring my time. I'm generally a very organized person, and a baby demands flexibility and living with an unstructured time schedule. Those first few months with my son made me realize how much is required in terms of flexibility and patience. You must be able to tolerate an unstructured chaotic environment, and turn that into a positive healthy atmosphere for the baby. Some women are very good at that, and they make good caretakers. Others are so accustomed to the work world, they cannot do this easily. Maybe it's better for them to be working."

Quite a few of these women were bored being home, and missed the working world. "Our leave is fairly liberal," says Kathleen, twenty-nine, the vice president of a large commercial bank. "You get eight weeks disability after the birth at full pay. I could have taken an additional unpaid leave for two more months, but I was ready to go back at the end of the eight weeks. I felt isolated, and I missed my colleagues at work. Those first six months are a tough time."

"It was a big adjustment to stay home with my son," says Margaret. "Of course I was busy feeding, changing diapers, washing baby clothes, and doing the daily chores of maintaining a house. However, there were those periods of lull where I found myself just a little bored, and yearning to get out of the house. I started looking forward to going to the supermarket every week. I dressed for the occasion."

Other women planned to return and changed their minds. Emma, thirty-four, then a thirty-two-year-old account supervisor, was one of them. It wasn't that she had seen herself primarily as a mother—for a long while she never wanted to have a child—but, because she was unhappy with her job, it made her think that staying home with her baby might be more satisfying. "I had been seriously planning to find another job while I was on leave, little realizing that all I'd want to do was sleep every chance I could get," she says. "After a month of leave, my husband and I went out for dinner. I was feeling so depressed about the thought of having to go back to my job. It hadn't been good for a couple of years; there were changes going on that I didn't like. We spent dinner figuring out what our savings were and how long we could go without my paycheck and not go bankrupt. My husband then volunteered, 'Why don't you just take a break, take off through the summer. You can go out and look for a job in the fall.' He's a teacher, so we'd have the summer together. Basically, that's what I did.

"It was terrific. I never imagined I'd enjoy being at home with my baby as much as I did. I don't know how much I'd enjoy it now that he's two. He'd probably drive me crazy. But when they're little, they can't run away from you. I had a really good time. I got to be a real earth mother. There was some isolation because my friends were not really close by—they were in the metropolitan area, an hour or more away—but I did start meeting more people in the neighborhood. John was home at 3 P.M., which made things easier, and I joined a health club. Several days a week he'd walk in and I'd walk out to go work out. I took a few classes at college. I felt more isolation in the beginning when it was cold, but much less so as we got into spring. And then in the summer John was home. Suddenly I began having trouble finding time to be alone." Emma started looking for a new job in the fall and found one two months later.

Susan Lund of Catalyst recommends this kind of flexibility. "Above all," she says, "keep your options open. Pregnancy is an unknown. You may think you know what your needs and desires will be, but you won't really know until the baby arrives." The problem with this approach is the way it can be perceived by those left behind on the job. "Nothing makes me angrier than a woman who says throughout her pregnancy that she wants her career and is going to return to work and then, when the baby is three months old, wants to extend her leave to six months, and after that perhaps even quits," says Sadie, thirty-six, a financial administrator and mother of two. "She's done a real disservice to her boss, her company, and other women. If she had been honest with herself, and everyone else from the start, she'd be happier and the company could have hired someone new to replace her. An office makes a great sacrifice to keep a position open for the time a woman is going to be off on her leave, and others in that office make sacrifices—working overtime, doing double duty—to cover for her during that time. She owes it to them to be up-front about her decision. If staying home is what she believes in, then I say, 'Great! Be as good a mother as you can be, but make that decision. Don't hurt the chances of the next woman who honestly is going to combine motherhood and career.'"

Sadie would be proud of Daphne, who came back to her job even though she was ready to move on to another company. "I didn't want to leave them with the impression that I was coming back and then not come back," she says. "In some ways, I felt I owed it to the other women in the company not to cause the senior staff to distrust women when they say they are taking maternity leave. Since I've been back, I have worked hard, and had more than my share of projects. I haven't complained. I didn't want them to think that here is this new mother who can't take all the work, but I recently asked my boss if the projects were being evenly distributed among the different project managers, and he admitted that I've been doing more."

Back to Work We Go

Almost all the mothers surveyed for this book returned to some kind of work after their maternity leave. Their dedication to their careers, or their financial situation, precluded any other step. In so doing, they are still in the minority.

Only 41 percent of the women who take maternity leave are back at work within one year of their baby's birth.

The transition back to work can be a hard one. Jane Lowe and Virginia Walther, social workers at Mt. Sinai Medical Center in New York City who started after–maternity leave workshops, give this advice in an article in *Parents* magazine: "The way most [mothers returning to work] handle it is to realize that you can't have it all. If you were home full-time you'd be missing other things that are important to you. Whenever you make a choice, you give up something. The point is to be satisfied that you made the best decision you could and to make sure, if you've decided to work, that your baby is in good hands when you are away."

Because Donna, thirty-five, an attorney for the federal government, leaves her three-year-old daughter and her five-month-old baby with her husband, she is able to work without anxiety. "I think about them once in a while," she says, "but I don't worry. I'll be reading a code of federal regulations and I'll think, 'I have a sweet baby at home,' and I'll think about her hair. That lasts about three seconds, and then I'll go back to work."

But sometimes, even when a woman knows she has the best of care, she can miss her baby terribly and feel guilty about returning. "It was very hard for me to go back after my three months off," says Flora, thirty, a programmer analyst. "I knew my son was in very good hands because my mother moved in with us to care for him right after he was born. But I cried almost every day during this adjustment period and missed him very much."

Janis, thirty-six, a sales planning manager for a major corporation, who had her child at age thirty-three, says, "Initially, my guilt and the insufficient time I felt I had with my baby were choking me. I had hired a good, very affectionate caregiver, and I had some flexibility in my job. Nonetheless, in a competitive sales environment, the job pressures were very strong. My own achievement needs would not allow me to 'fall behind' and yet I felt intense conflict because I did want more time with my baby. In the very beginning, I wasn't sure my daughter knew and preferred me as her own mother. It was her growing need and love for me, my own experience with her and increased confidence, that allowed me to relax and find that 'middle' ground and reconcile my conflicts."

For the months they were home, most of these mothers formed close physical bonds with their babies by nursing them. Returning to work meant severing at least several strands of this bond, or cutting it all together. Cynthia decided to completely wean her baby before she returned from her four-month leave to her job as a regional sales manager, and she got ready for that step right away. "In the first two weeks home, I introduced her to a bottle three times a week, so that when I had to wean her, it was smooth. People were so jealous of me. I nursed through to three and a half months exclusively, pumping my milk for the bottles, and then I weaned her during the two weeks before I went back. In the end, she preferred her bottle."

Kathleen didn't prepare as well as Cynthia did. Her son was eight weeks old and she was still nursing when she returned to her job. She remembers that "in the first weeks back I was leaking all over myself in a fancy French restaurant." Two weeks later, a business trip to California put an abrupt end to her nursing career.

Weaning can go much more gradually if a woman doesn't have to travel and wants to go on nursing during the feedings when she is home. Victoria, thirty-two, an anesthesiologist with dreadful twenty-four-hour shifts, was even able to continue, for a while. "Fortunately there is a nurse in our maternity services who is a lactation specialist and we have electric breast pumps so I was able to go between cases and pump. I breast-fed for about three months, but my supply wasn't as great as it would have been if I had been home more and not on such a screwy schedule. People were supportive about it. I'd freeze what I had at work, and my son's diet was supplemented a little bit with formula."

If a woman can arrange for her baby to be cared for near her home or her place of work, she may be able to continue nursing during the day. This is what Dana did when she went back to work three weeks after her son, Matt, was born. She put him into the corporation's day care center and nursed at lunch and during both breaks until he was six months old. She was also able to nurse her daughter at lunchtime at her center.

The hiatus from work, and from their working selves, that maternity leave provides, can clarify for some mothers how important their work is to them, which makes it easier for them to reconcile their two lives. "Motherhood has made me come to grips with what the job means to me," says Dana. "Before, I worked because I had to. I came from a poor family and all the women worked out of necessity. It was never a question of if I would work but what I was going to do *when* I worked. At home those three months with Cindy, my second child, I realized I needed to work. It's a creative outlet for me. I have to use my mind. Staying home is not an answer. When I stay home, I don't use my head. It got to the point this past summer that my big concern of the day was how long Cindy's nap was going to be and how much I could get done during it.

"At some point I'm going to have to talk to the children about why I work.

It's not that I don't want to be with them. It's not that I don't enjoy their company, and it's not that I like work better. But for me, it's my solution to being me. I need to work; my mind needs it; my psyche needs it. I'm relieved that I've come to grips with this issue. Part of me is a worker and another part is a mother. They are going to have to understand that while I'm a good mother, I'm simultaneously a good lawyer."

The importance of their careers makes many mothers determined to make their double lives work—no matter how difficult it is. "I'm no superwoman," says Sadie, thirty-six, the mother of two preschool children. "I'm just not willing to give up either my career or my family—and I don't have any of the advantages that you so frequently read about with working mothers. I don't work at home—I have a thirty-minute commute, minimum. I have no relatives or in-laws who live closer than five hours away. My work schedule is not flexible. I work generally from 7 A.M. to 5 P.M. (longer when I can get my husband to pick up the children) and then I bring work home—Mommy's homework. My husband doesn't get home until 7 P.M. at the earliest on a normal day. I have no housekeeper (though I probably should). My children are cared for in different locations—one in kindergarten/day care and the other with a day care mother. Although I would not give up my career to stay at home, it has been difficult getting over the guilt and adjusting to the fact that I no longer have any time to myself, that I am frequently exhausted, and that some things are just not going to get done."

But no matter how much they love their jobs, reentry can be hard when it is abrupt—an immediate return to a full schedule in a world that kept right on truckin' without them. It can be much easier on them if it can be done gradually, with a temporary part-time arrangement for a few months, such as Ginger and Margie worked out as part of their maternity package.

When a woman works for herself, this easing back in can be spread over a considerably longer time. Gail, thirty-three, was in the middle of her dissertation research for her Ph.D. in psychology when her son was born a year ago and she didn't leave him at all for the first four months. "Then I was away at the most three to four hours a day until he was about nine months old, when I began to gradually increase the time I spent away from him until I was gone for thirty-five hours a week," she says. "I now feel he's ready for day care and that he needs to be around other children. Prior to this I believe my time with him was critical to his development—only I could give him the love and security necessary for trust and the development of solid interpersonal relationships.

"As a woman in this day and age, I feel I must slow down my professional development for a period of a few years and that that is the price I pay for my biology. I do see it as temporary and I look forward to really being able to devote myself to being a psychologist and researcher in my forties."

But there are some women who happily return to an immediate full-time schedule, dive into their work, and get right back into the swim of things. "I went back to work right after Thanksgiving and within two weeks I took a trip to the West Coast for four days," says Kathleen. "I lend money to companies in the communications business, which includes cable TV. This was a convention I'd gone to every year for the past five years, so I thought I'd jump right back in and do it."

Kathleen admits that going on the trip when her son was just over two months old was pretty traumatic, but otherwise the return to work was not particularly hard "because I was so busy getting back into the routine of work and getting updated on things that had been going on. I thought about Justin a lot but it wasn't heartrending. I don't want to sound callous either. The transition went very smoothly for me, and I didn't feel that I left my heart at home. I talked to the nanny a lot on the phone—it was more concern for the baby than feeling sorry for myself."

This kind of attitude about returning to work can also help a woman if she has a second baby. "When I showed up six weeks to the day after I left, bright and cheery and working full-time, everyone said, 'Wow!' " remembers Kitty, thirty-two, who was then twenty-eight and a data processor. "No one said a word when I got pregnant again a year later. By then I was a manager and it was assumed I would be right back to work, which I was. In fact, I came in during that maternity leave to work one day during a crisis."

The advantage of self-employment, of course, is the freedom to adjust a work schedule to fit the baby's. Eleanor, forty-six, a well-established psychologist and writer who was forty-one when her daughter was born, says, "I decided I would plan my work schedule around my child's habits since I was working at home with a full-time private practice. All I did was keep shifting my practice in accordance with her nap schedule. As a result, she became a very well-regulated child. I can only think of one or two times when she actually had any problems at all while clients were here. I was prepared to be much more flexible than she required me to be."

Erica, thirty, works for herself drawing architectural plans and doing management consulting as part of a group. When her second child was born, she continued to work around her children's schedules. "I just kept putting in my twenty hours a week when I could," she says. "If I don't answer my client's calls, I lose them. I really thrive on being busy. I put in about six hours on the

management consulting group—mainly setting agendas and doing the minutes of the board meetings—and the rest on my architectural plans. I try to
do that stuff when my toddler is sleeping. The baby is not really into a
schedule yet and I can't count on a naptime from him. It's a huge juggling
act. I assume that will calm down once he's onto a schedule. Up until a few
weeks ago, I was so exhausted that when I finally got the children into bed, I
went to sleep. But I'm starting to be able to do more work at night.

"Having a home office saves me a lot of time and it's much more efficient.
My desk is just the way I left it when I come back to work. I work there when
both of them are asleep, and when my twenty-month-old is awake I can do
some work, but I can't do it in my office. I have to do it on the first floor,
where she is. She's getting pretty good about playing. We added a playroom
addition off the kitchen in the summer. She'll play in there and occupy herself. I'll sit in the dining room so I can hear her in there, dragging her toys
around. She's learning to let me work, but it's been hard for her. She wouldn't
want any part of me until she saw I was busy and then she wanted my
attention. But she is now getting used to seeing me do other things than pay
attention to her."

But eighty-five percent of these mothers work for someone else and almost
half of them put in more than forty hours a week. Having a baby has been the
impetus some of them needed to get their schedule under control—to stop
working ten- or twelve-hour days when they returned. "I love what I do, but
when you have a baby at home, and you want to get home, I think you are
more productive at work," says Kathleen. "You don't waste a lot of time.
Both my husband and I try to leave our work at work and get home and
concentrate on the baby." They have also made adjustments between them—
early shift, late shift so that their son gets a bit more time with Mommy or
Daddy at each end of the day. "We start very early in the morning, getting up
at 5:45 A.M. Justin gets up with us. I leave quite quickly, but my husband
doesn't go until 7:30 A.M., so he has almost two hours with Justin. I'm always
on the 5:30 train at night, which gets me home at 6:15, and my husband gets
home later."

A baby at home can also make work more satisfying, according to Faye
Cosby, Ph.D., a Yale psychologist. In a study reported in *Parents* magazine
she found that "for both women and men, on most measures of job satisfaction, there was a difference between those who were parents and those who
were married or single without children. The people who were parents were
more satisfied with their jobs. . . . family not only buffers the negative aspects of work, but shares in the positive aspects."

On the Job

Waiting to get established before having a child does appear to result in less damage to a career. Far fewer women who were established found that their advancement was slowed by motherhood or that they had to take on a less demanding job. Waiting also means happiness—over 82 percent of the mothers who postponed children, or weren't interested in becoming a mother until they were older, are extremely satisfied with their lives now, compared to only 58 percent of the mothers who have tried to combine work and children from early on in their careers.

For some women, however, the repercussions of motherhood on their careers don't show up in the numbers. Their stories reveal the continuing power of entrenched attitudes about women who are mothers. In the eyes of many men in this country, they do not belong on the job. A woman may be accepted up until she has this change of status, but afterward she may find that she is suddenly suspect.

When Dana came back after her three-month maternity leave with her second child—a leave she purposefully made only half as long as was allowed in order to avoid repercussions—she discovered that the men at work all thought differently of her. "They wanted to talk baby with me instead of business," she says. "A lot of my clients who are regulars had made affiliations with other lawyers in the office, and when I came back, they didn't return to me. One boss told me he'd rather assign a guy to a project that I was already assigned to because he didn't know when I would be there. I said, 'What do you mean? I'm always here; I'm rarely sick. I'm the first one here in the morning and among the last to leave.' And he said, 'Because of the babies thing.' I said, 'Look, I only have one every eighteen months.' And he said, 'You never know.'

"It hurt me politically to have a child; it's a real old-boy network. I'm going to have to work very hard to reestablish myself as a lawyer, not a mommy. It's gotten to the point where I almost refuse to talk about the kids in the office. I don't mention them. If someone asks how they are, I say, 'Oh fine, thanks. How is your family?' to indicate I know they have a family too."

Lorraine, who had her daughter two years ago, fought this attitude then, and is fighting it again because she is expecting another baby. Her battle has finally been successful, resulting in a promotion. "It only happened because I made it very, very clear that I did not want to be treated as a parent on the job. I wanted to be treated as a professional. I didn't tell anyone at work about my pregnancy for the first four months. Last time I told people at three months. This time I put it off as long as I could—wearing clothes that disguised it, lots of sweaters so you couldn't tell my skirt was unbuttoned. The men in the office like to act very paternalistic when I'm pregnant. I don't believe they have any business doing that to begin with and I had seen during my first pregnancy that they really focused on me as a mother rather than on what I was doing on the job. I said, 'By gosh, if I'm going to work, I'm going to get the best return I can on being there. I'm not doing this to get out of the house once in a while. I get a lot of personal satisfaction out of it, but I also enjoy the economic benefits and I'm going to maximize both of those since I'm here.' I would have been willing to trim that back if they'd considered a job-sharing proposal I came up with along with another pregnant budget analyst, but they wouldn't do that. So if they want me there full-time, I want to enjoy all the benefits and opportunities and challenges of being there full-time. I told them that there were many other people in the office who were parents, and that I was just another parent."

If some men won't believe that a mother can do a responsible job, other men want to ignore the whole issue, and may not outwardly admit that a woman has had a change of status—that she is just as hard a worker but she has other responsibilities too. When Cynthia, thirty, the regional sales manager, told her boss she was pregnant, he was very nice about it—probably partly because it was to his advantage. He took over her national responsibilities, which she couldn't handle because of the travel, and thus assured himself of a job from which he would not be fired during a potential buyout. At his suggestion, she took off four months instead of the six she wanted because he told her it would be much harder for her to come back to work. And again, he covered for her. All well and good until she came back from her leave. "Once I returned, my boss felt I should be just the way I was before I was a mother. He's an extremely insensitive person when it comes to that. While I understand his way of thinking—I've been a boss—it's very difficult to have a difference of understanding between two people, one with a baby and one without. So he's back to having me do extensive travel in my territory, which is the Western states. He's asked me three or four times to become national sales manager again—now that the buyout crisis is past. I politely asked if it would require more travel than I'm doing now, which is about two weeks per month, and he said yes and I said I'm sorry I'll have to pass. It's very difficult. I leave on Monday for two weeks."

Because the change in status from working woman to working woman *and* mother is hard for some employers to deal with, it may be smart for a woman in this situation to change jobs after she becomes a mother. Even though she'll lose all the points she built up from years of hard work for her company, at her new job her position in her private life will be clear to everyone from the beginning. "I think it's easier going into a job as a parent, knowing what I need and what they expect," says Emma, who quit her job during her maternity leave and after free-lancing for a year returned to full-time employment with another company. "I didn't want to travel a lot or put in overtime hours, and I was able to spell those things out in job interviews. I think that I'm more assertive than I was before. I have a lot more self-confidence than I had."

Whatever corporate environment a mother works in, trying to satisfy all the demands on her and remain sane can be extremely draining. This is thirty-year-old Leslie's description of her regular schedule as she manages three children, the youngest two years old, and a forty-plus-hour-a-week job as a trade broker. "My real problem is exhaustion. I feel like I'm on a merry-go-round trying for the brass ring. I get close to the ring in the morning when I wake up at 5:45 A.M. I start doing laundry, getting the kids up, helping them with their clothes, making beds and breakfast, getting them to remember everything they need to do and need for school. The brass ring is almost out of sight for the next hour and a half. Then I rush to get my son to preschool and go through our goodbye ritual. Then I'm rushing to work to be there at 8:30. All it takes to make me late is for my son to have trouble going to the bathroom, which of course is something he needs to do as we walk out the door. Or he decides after the oatmeal is made that he's tired of it, can he please have something else, or he spills his juice all over himself, which means a change of outfit.

"I'm a very job-oriented person and I hate to walk in late—or very late— five or ten minutes is OK where I work if it's not abused. My bosses have always been very good about my running late. They're about my age with kids of their own and are very family-oriented. I receive the most reproaches (nonverbal) from a single person in our office with no children. She feels you should be on time no matter what. My job involves dealing with business owners on a one-to-one basis all day long. I love what I do but it can be extremely stressful. Because I take phone calls and walk-ins, I don't always have control over commitments I've made, so when I need to, I stay late or come in early.

"When I leave work, I cannot get stuck in traffic if my husband is working late or my son's nursery school will be closing. I have been close to hysteria when I've been caught behind an accident. Several times I've reached the school at closing. Whew! Then it's dinner time. The kids are starving, the house is a mess, and we have other outside activities scheduled with them. Sometimes I feel I must be a masochist because I don't have to work financially, but I do mentally. I fall into bed at 10 P.M. totally exhausted."

This merry-go-round can come to a screeching halt if a child gets sick. It's such a problem that women wish they could be "immune" from sickness, that they should get passes on having sick kids. But only 44 percent of these mothers work for companies who give them paid days off in this circumstance. If a woman has her baby or child in a day care home or center, then even a cold can throw her whole life off course. Julia, twenty-eight, a secretary with a one-year-old daughter, feels continual stress because of this. "The hardest part of working when you have a small child is that somehow you feel you have to be in two places at the same time. I have an understanding boss, but I doubt very much if he will hire a woman with children after I leave. When the baby is sick, what do you do? She needs you, but you also have a big project at work and they need you too. I choose the baby every time, so I'm not a good employment risk."

When a child gets very ill or needs an operation, a woman may need a leave of absence to be with her child, and this may not sit well with her employer. Flora has been through this kind of situation. After her son was born, her mother moved into her house to take care of him, giving her the perfect setup. But things at work were not so good, even before she needed to take time off for her child's operation. At first there was no assignment for her when she returned from maternity leave and when they found an account, it was a difficult one. "The first one was at a place with deplorable conditions, where I would be working virtually alone with very little technical support. I refused to work there, and I finally managed to get myself back on the previous account," she says. "But after a couple of months I had to take a leave of absence because my son needed an operation to correct hypospadias [a condition where the urethra opens on the underside of the penis], and his doctor said I might need to stay in the hospital with him for two weeks, plus be at home for two weeks during the recovery.

"I told my employer that I might need a month off and they gave it to me with the stipulation that I could not return unless I had an account to be assigned to. When I was ready to go back, they did not have an account and I found myself on unemployment from October through January. It was difficult to find another job because I wasn't currently working and was getting rusty. But I finally landed a good position with one of the major companies in telecommunications at what I believe to be a decent salary. My son needs another operation this summer and I'm not sure how I'll handle my job situation."

When a woman reaches a certain level in her career, flexibility comes with the territory (51 percent of these mothers say their work schedule is at least somewhat flexible). This makes the demands from the home front, sickness included, easier to manage. As children grow up, having this kind of situation becomes important for other reasons—when children want their moms to be there at school parties and other functions. Deborah, thirty-seven, changed jobs when her son was two and a half, to become director of marketing for a family-oriented company, and she made sure that she would "run my own calendar and no one would check on me. Once I had to do something with my son, and they moved a whole meeting for it."

At the moment, Deborah is negotiating with two companies about new jobs, and again she is making sure she has some control over her schedule. "I'm talking to one of the big brokerage houses and I said, 'I'm not someone who punches the clock. If I have to go to the nursery school Christmas party at 10 A.M., which it was this year, I go to it.' They said, 'Of course. At the level you are at, nobody is watching the clock.' But I think there are companies where people do."

Trade-offs

The problem for Deborah, and mothers like her who pushed for years to get ahead and now have high-powered jobs, is how to reconcile their ambition with motherhood and accept the trade-offs that motherhood requires. Women who see their work as a career are considerably less likely to be willing to make a change that would make their work more compatible with motherhood, even when their current job clearly does not have flexibility; only 36 percent of them would be willing to do so, compared to almost 80 percent of those who feel their work is just a job.

Although they may not be willing to change their career path or take a different job, they may alter their expectations of themselves within their current job, and put a rein on their ambitions. According to Susan Ginsberg, the director of work and family life seminars at the Bank Street College of Education in New York City, "The demands on a woman are never heavier than when her children are small, and many women, in practice, if not in theory, make compromises with their own ambitions during that period."

Because of her recent job interviews, Deborah is in the process of reexamining her feelings about the relative importance of her career and her child. Despite the flexibility of her current job, she finds it "very boring, and it's not moving the ball forward on my career. I'm very much wrestling with the fact that some of the things I might opt to do now could really shake up our life. For instance, I'm talking to one big bank about running a number of their branches. That means working the day after Thanksgiving and being available if there's a robbery or a snowstorm. It's really like being a store manager. That would really impact on our home life. I'd have much less flexibility. I'm not sure I want to do that.

"I think there was a time I'd have done anything to get ahead—not that I'd sell my mother. But, for instance, I once considered living in Modesto, California, because I wanted to work for Dow. That was what was important, not the quality of life I'd be leading in Modesto. Now, I think I have a lot more standards about what I would and would not do. I'm definitely going to make a job change in the next three months. A couple of these opportunities are coming to closure, and what I see happening is that I'll go to another major corporation and attempt to have a second child in that environment, and recognize that I'm probably going to be staying at the same level for a couple of years.

"During an interview someone asked me if I'd rather stay in New York or have the advantage of moving up faster, further, by moving around the country. I said I'd rather stay in New York. I'm starting to see that there are going to be limitations, but it doesn't matter so much. I've reached a point where I have a six-figure income and I have a vice presidency and the jobs which would be the next big leap forward are much more all-consuming, calls all weekend, calls at night. I've been close to some of the biggies at the bank where I used to work, and I've seen the price those guys pay, and I don't think that's something I want to do right now. Unfortunately, by the time I may want to do it, when my children have their own lives, it probably won't be an option. These are the years I should be doing it. But I think I'm going as far as I can go with the caveat that I'm putting my family first."

Deborah has seen what happens to the lives of women whose ambition has not been tempered by motherhood. "I have some women friends who work down on Wall Street and it kind of comes with the territory that they work until nine or ten at night. I wouldn't take a job like that. I think I can go another few levels in life, but I recognize I'm not willing to make some of the major sacrifices. One woman whose daughter goes to my son's nursery school has a big job on Wall Street and every time I see her she's a wreck. Her daughter never has anyone at the school parties, and she's left alone with her nanny all the time. I don't think it's fair to the children."

Janis, whose daughter is three, is not yet ready to compromise her career for her child. Although she wrestles with the issue a lot, she has upward career moves she still wants to make before she can reconcile her ambition and her desire for a more balanced life.

"There is a level I can see reaching where I'd have a more relaxed kind of job. There are people there who do work fewer hours and their jobs are a lot less visible, and more independent; and that's what I'd be looking for. I see myself in this more relaxed job in two years. That's realistic. I'd feel I'd done what I needed to do. I'd proven what I needed to prove to myself. It really is a conflict in terms of when I am going to feel comfortable controlling my ambition and settling back. I think I'm getting better at that—taking some extra time off, leaving early. But I have to make some choices—that I'm not going to strive to be number one, two, or three. The competitive edge sometimes really gets ahold of me, but other times I feel that I'm doing well enough, that there's enough money, that I don't mind being in the top 25 percent. I can live with that.

"Having Blythe has been the most wonderful thing I ever decided to do. But I'm also having to reconcile myself to the fact that this kid is going to grow up with a mom who sometimes only spends an hour with her a day, or an hour and a half in broken-up segments. I'll do the best I can, and she's doing OK. But I don't like it. It's one of those old-time attitudes that I should be doing more. I just hope I've made the right decision to work as much as I have in spite of it, and that in the years to come my daughter will say that yes I did. There aren't very good models around at work. I'm sick of seeing all these single forty-year-old hard-edged women at the top."

Margie, who has a three-year-old son, is more willing to make the trade-offs on the side of work than Janis is, and choices about her next assignment have brought that realization to the fore. "I figured that having a child would change the commitment I could make to work, but I really didn't face up to it. I wouldn't let myself admit that it really would. I don't know what day-dream I was dreaming—I tried to make believe that I would be the same person.

"By now the realization has hit. I'm waiting to get a new assignment, which will happen in the next couple of weeks. I've talked to my boss about it. I'd rather take a job I can do and do well than fail because their expectations are too high. I asked if motherhood and the next assignment were incompatible. If there is something wrong at work and with David, he takes priority. By admitting at work that there are certain jobs that might interfere with motherhood, I am saying that motherhood is equally relevant and maybe I can't take on certain high-pressure, time-consuming jobs when he is three years old. I'll have to wait until he is twelve.

"Being a mother, in my opinion, will affect my long-term achievements, but I don't know whether, with or without David, I'd want to work eighteen hours a day. As difficult as it is to admit there is an arbitrary barrier, I was the one who chose that barrier, and I'd rather have David here than not."

A Fork in the Path

For some women, adding a child into the existing equation of their lives makes the numbers add up all wrong. They find that motherhood requires trade-offs that are more significant than simple adjustments to their schedule, or a slowdown in their career climb. What is interesting is that making a career shift—even to a less demanding job—because of having a child has not made these women any less satisfied with motherhood, or with their lives. Almost 80 percent of them are very happy in both regards.

If a new mother feels she must make a change but part-time is not an option, she sometimes can negotiate an alternative full-time schedule with her employer. This seems to be far more possible today than a decade ago, and in the future it should get easier still. A General Mills Survey found that 66 percent of the corporations who responded expected to have maxiflex programs in place within five years. "My boss has been marvelous and given me a four-day work week," says Anita, thirty-four, the director of community services who has two small boys. "I work from 7 A.M. to 5 P.M. and have Wednesday off. I collapse and do the laundry. That's one of the benes of my job and I won't sacrifice it no matter how much I'd like to change jobs or careers. I must think what my priorities are. Family is number one so I'll sit tight for a few more years."

Employers are also getting more reasonable about part-time arrangements; the number of part-time employees in the work force increased 50 percent from 1972 to 1982. When finances have not been a problem, 24 percent of the women surreyed have taken advantage of such opportunities after they have become mothers. They are among the most satisfied with their lives because for the most part they have come to terms with negative side of part-time employment: lost chances for advancement, the sense of slipping off the track, seeing the best assignments go to other people, and a decrease in professional pride.

The federal government is one of the employers willing to consider part-time assignments. Elizabeth, thirty, a financial economist, interviewed for her job in the research area of the Securities and Exchange Commission when she was pregnant but didn't yet know it. She was interested in that job, versus one in the larger production-oriented office because she thought they might be more lenient about a flexible schedule if she had a child. "I felt around in the beginning about how they regarded part-time work, and my boss said they'd never had anybody do it, and he didn't have a problem with it, but he'd have to run it through the rest of the hierarchy.

"Soon after, I ran into an attorney who had gotten herself part-time employment with the government and she gave me a copy of the Pregnancy Act, and research she had done on part-time employment in the commission, and she told me how she'd gone about it. You are only allowed a six-week paid leave, but then you write at that point and request a leave without pay and the terms you want when you come back. This means you don't make any big decisions before you leave.

"So at six weeks I started writing memos. It took them about three months to act on my request for part-time, but meanwhile I was home on unpaid leave. It was very tense wondering what would happen if they didn't give it to me. I really didn't want to quit the job, but my husband didn't want me to go back full-time. Luckily, they granted it, and I work from 8:30 to 4:30 three days a week and they've hired someone to fill in the other two days."

Initially, curbing her ambitions was hard for Elizabeth. "I've had to alter my expectations about what I hope to achieve, but I think a child is much more worthwhile than being a director—at least for now. I don't exclude that as a possibility for later, but the ambition of saving the world from hunger, which I used to believe I could do when I went overseas, is over. I now worry about my own daughter's hunger."

Perhaps the best working situation is the one that Mindy, thirty, a pilot, has with her airline. "I had seniority when I got pregnant," she says. "I'd been with the company three years and I was lucky to get hired when I did. They hired six hundred people behind me and now the number is up to a thousand. Sometimes you can sit at the bottom of a list for ten years and not move up at all. Having seniority has made my combination of work and motherhood possible.

"I started out as a flight engineer on the 727, and when I had the baby I decided to stay on in that job. My classmates began to move up to copilot on

the 727, but I didn't make the move because I would have had to be on call
and I couldn't do that with a baby. So in a sense, I turned down a promotion.
But it doesn't much matter. Just by seniority I'll move up to copilot in the
spring.

"I've sacrificed a little bit of money by not making the move along with the
guys, but I've gained tons of time. I only fly ten to thirteen days a month.
That's part of the union agreement. The only way you can get that schedule is
to be at the top of the list. A lot of the guys want to move up as fast as they
can, and be copilot as quickly as they can on the biggest airplane they possibly can. Same for being a captain. They work up to twenty days a month and
they pay for that. They work Christmas and they work holidays. They work
weekends and overtime. They can have back-to-back three-day trips and be
away from their families for six days in a row. I didn't want that. This month
and next I'm flying to Ft. Lauderdale/Miami. I leave here about 7 A.M. and
I'm back at 7 P.M. that night. Last month, I was flying to Hawaii. I'd leave
here at 7 A.M. Tuesday morning and be back at 7 A.M. Thursday morning. It
wasn't too tough since we had a layover of one night in Hawaii. I don't know
why more people don't hang back to get the better schedules. I can't think of
many jobs where you just work Tuesday and Wednesday and earn the money
I do—$65,000 a year.

"I don't have any plans to change my schedule because we don't need the
money and the full-time schedule is not for me. I can fill those other seventeen to twenty days a month between my child and traveling and hobbies. I
don't think I was ever as driven as some of my classmates. Maybe it's because
I have no control over it. Promotions are keyed to expansion of the airline.
There never seemed much point to saying, 'I want to be a captain,' when
maybe I wouldn't even get to be a copilot. I don't understand that macho
drive, that ambition. But most of the guys don't understand me either."

As positive as Mindy's experience has been, the experiences of Pat thirty-
seven, have been negative. Now an advertising copywriter, she was forced to
take a demotion from account executive in order to get a part-time position at
her company when her daughter was born two years ago. Only her commitment to part-time has seen her through. "The only reason I got the part-time
job was because of a political situation in the office where I temporarily held
the trump card. It was, 'You give me part-time, or else . . .' It was an un-
equality employment situation. They wanted to put a man into a position to
which I was immediately promotable, and they had to get me out of the way.
The only way they could do that was to give me part-time because they knew
that I wanted it. But in order to get it, they said I had to take the demotion."

It was at this point that Pat's company tricked her back into full-time—in the lower-level position. "I began part-time in September and the next March they came to me and told me I had to fill in full-time for a woman who was taking maternity leave. I was being Mrs. Nice Guy and I said, 'Sure.' It seemed a reasonable thing to do and I figured it would only be eight weeks because that is all they give you. But at the end of the eight weeks, she called up and said, 'Adios.' So I was left holding the bag. They asked me if I would continue to work full-time until they found someone to fill her job. Again, it seemed a reasonable request, so I worked full-time from March to mid-July. Then I worked three days a week for the rest of July and August, and then in September they came to me and said, 'Either you are going to continue to work full-time or we are going to find someone else.' I was able to push them off to the first of the year, but then I had to go back to full-time. During this whole time they never gave me a raise."

Other women have tried to negotiate a part-time schedule, and without the kind of leverage Pat had were turned down from the word *go.* "I asked to come back at 80 percent so I could have one day a week off, and I don't even think my department head took it to the vice president," says Wendy, who had a daughter last year. "There are several women who do have that situation where they are working, but I work for a utility, and most of management is in their fifties or sixties and their wives never worked. I don't think they can relate, or care to relate, to the real need for flexibility and how it could benefit the company."

Doing Their Own Thing

Having a baby is the impetus some women need to start their own business, giving them the flexibility they could not find working for someone else. Self-employment allows women not so much to balance their lives, as to integrate the various parts—work, family, self. As noted earlier, 15 percent of these women have set out to do this after becoming mothers. In taking this approach to work, they have become part of an ever-burgeoning group—1.9 million women were self-employed in this country in 1979, up 43 percent from 1972, and half of their businesses are operated from home. These mothers have found that this career move works—they are *all* extremely satisfied with their lives—more so than any other group. By way of comparison, only two-thirds of the mothers who have taken on more challenging jobs are extremely satisfied with their lives.

The easiest way for a woman to get a business off the ground is to have a client at hand who wants to hire her services. Tessie, twenty-eight, a software engineer for a major electronics firm worked out just such an arrangement when she got pregnant. She first took a six-week leave and planned to return to her job, but when she gave birth to twins, she extended her leave to four months. "I was planning on going back to work," she says. "I knew I wouldn't enjoy being home, especially toward the end of the four months, but the more I thought about it, the more options opened up. I had never wanted to work for a big company, but I'd never had an excuse not to—to start my own business. This was the right opportunity to do so. I didn't feel comfortable about going back to work full-time because work hours are so inflexible. They have flex-time but there is a core time between 8:30 A.M. and 3:30 P.M. when you have to be there, and in general, eight or nine hours a day was too much time to be away from the babies. Part-time was not an option. Personnel wouldn't let it go through even though my boss was pushing for it. But his boss suggested that maybe I could do my job on a contract basis. That meant that I would still have the opportunity for steady work, but I wouldn't have to be there every day eight hours a day.

"I thought about that for a few days and decided that maybe this was the right time to start my own business, especially since I would have one reliable, incredible client right from the beginning. I write computer manuals— the book that comes with a computer which tells you how to run it is written by me. So I went on contract when the babies were four months old. They went into full-time day care—they still go there. There just aren't enough blocks of time to get anything done otherwise. At first I worked about five hours a day and the rest of the time I either spent by myself or I picked them up early. As the project I was given neared completion I was working seventeen hours a day—so going on contract hasn't really helped me as far as part-time, but I do have flexibility. When they are sick, I don't have to call in. I can alter my hours and work in the evenings. My former company is still my only client. They keep me busy enough. But I'm probably going to go for other clients soon. My big project is winding down to a close now, so I'm finally going to write a business plan and start looking."

Because she already had a part-time business drawing architectural plans, Erica had no startup problems when she decided to quit her job as a personnel analyst with a major city when she was pregnant with her second child. "I took a six-month maternity leave from my job when I had my daughter, and came back for four months before I quit," she says. "Pregnancy wasn't the reason. I didn't even tell them I was pregnant. I'd been in the job for four years and I was getting promotions, and it was going to require more commitment and it wasn't the kind of job I wanted to spend the rest of my life doing. I also wanted to spend more time with my daughter. And it was becoming increasingly difficult to simultaneously be pregnant, have any quality time with my child, run a household, run a part-time business, maintain my relationship with my husband, and have any free time for myself. I could afford to make the move because my architectural plans business was becoming lucrative and I felt I could combine it with some consulting work to keep my income near where it had been."

Her son was born sixteen months after her daughter, and since then, Erica has followed through with her consulting plans, joining a personnel consulting group with people she knew in graduate school. "I got my degree in psychometrics and I wanted to keep up that end of my professional life. It's not a lot of work right now, which is good because it allows me to maintain professional credentials at a time when I can't devote forty hours a week to it. My architectural plans are enough to pay the bills. We're incorporating the group and I was elected CEO so I have to deal with minutes of board meetings and setting agendas, etc. There are six of us and each of us does our own thing, and we act equally in terms of finding jobs and use each other on projects as needed. So far, I can control my time by doing the administrative stuff and leaving the seminars and the stress management stuff to other people in the group. I put in about twenty hours a week total between the consulting and the architectural plans. I've had more stressful and busier times than this. Actually, I worry more about having enough work than about having too much. I don't like voids and I manage not to have them."

Even with no child care for her infant and toddler, and work responsibilities—a situation that might drive another woman mad—Erica feels that this is "the best time of my life. I feel like I'm in control. It's my schedule to juggle and I don't answer to anybody else. I can't see letting a toddler and an infant run me. They were my choice and I do manage things. The best part is that I have these years in my life to reflect on who I am and where I am going, and to be in control of things without having a boss tell me what to do. A regular job just doesn't fit with the rest of my life. It's a real problem with our society that we can't work our family lives into our normal week. We save the best hours for someone else, and kind of see our kids and our spouses when we are all tired out. But society doesn't see it this way. When I quit my full-time job, people said to me, 'Oh, you're going to be a stay-at-home mother.' They were putting this stereotype role on me that I absolutely hated. All of a sudden I wasn't going to be taken seriously, I wasn't going to have credentials. I was going to be doing something that society says is of great value—being a mother—at the same time it says that it makes you worthless. It was this awful kind of bind. Now, when people ask me how the kids are, I feel this great need to answer them briefly and then tell them what I'm doing professionally. People also don't take it seriously when you say you are working out of your home. They think you are stuffing envelopes or something. But this attitude hasn't changed my self-esteem. I feel better about myself now than when I was answering to someone else."

Some women who work for themselves before they have a baby believe that they'll be able to continue just as before, but also have their baby with them. It's only after becoming mothers that they realize they must formulate a new working life based on a new schedule. Letty, thirty-eight, a writer and publicist who had done a lot of traveling on writing assignments before the birth of her first son almost four years ago, remembers her vision of life after a baby. "Before Ted was born, I worked night and day," she says. "I was just starting in as a writer and I felt as if I had many years to make up for and I was impassioned about it. I was brought up in a family where the work ethic was important and I thought I should be working from dawn until dawn. When I got pregnant, I had this hippy vision that was really off the wall. My idea was that I was going to resume my life—traveling and writing—but that I was going to have my baby by my side. That was my vision. For a while, I really thought I'd continue to go off to the Amazon and I'd have my baby in a backpack, and it would all be very sympatico.

"After he was born, I realized I had to rethink all of it, that I did not want to go into New York, or go on assignment. I'd been doing part publicity, placing stories in the media, and part writing, and I decided to just cut out the writing for a while and concentrate on the media stuff because it was easier to do with the baby. At the time I was doing publicity for a welfare recipients organization and all of them had tons of kids and were poor and didn't have babysitters and they all took their kids with them everywhere. They welcomed me to come back and bring Ted with me. So when he was six months old, I put Ted into a backpack and went to work at this organization. But he was absolutely miserable. He did not want to sit in a playpen in this place. So then, I realized I had to work at home. I also decided to work only part-time, and I've committed myself to that schedule while my kids are small."

As radical as all these changes were for Letty, she never felt martyred because they were her choices. "I think that when you have a baby late in life, it's different," she says. "You don't feel that if it weren't for the baby you could be doing something. Just the other day I heard about a woman who is doing a very interesting project up in the Himalayas in northeastern India and I thought how four years ago I would have called up the *Smithsonian* and gotten them to send me to the Himalayas to do that story. But not now. No way José am I ever going to go to the Himalayas to do a story. For a minute I thought, 'Could I do it in two weeks?' but then I realized no. But it's more like a momentary nostalgia, a moment of sadness. But basically, being close to forty years old with these babies, I don't have the feeling that I didn't have a chance to do that. My general feeling in life is that I have the potential to do whatever I want to do, and in moments when I feel sad for myself I realize that if I really wanted to be doing that, I would be doing it. I have the ability and I would figure it out. So there's no place I can put the blame. It's my choice.

"I think that back when I was pregnant and Ted was first born, I was crippled by my own vision of myself and my friends' vision of me. People were always saying that of course I wouldn't be slowed down by having this baby and of course I'd still be traveling to Guatemala and for a while I felt I had to do those things. I even planned a trip to take Ted to Latin America, but I eventually realized I couldn't. Yet, I didn't feel like a failure. I felt more that I was being honest and wasn't it nice that I'd discovered what I really wanted to do—be a mother and work only part-time—and was not letting an old vision of myself run my life. I had those same feelings when I gave into this idea that I wanted to get married and I wanted to have a baby.

"Being a mother is my absolute number one thing in life," Letty continues. "I feel an incredible bond and intensity and joy about my children. If it were a matter of being able to choose only one thing in my life, I would choose motherhood over work hands down because when I look at my children, I see that they are my accomplishment. But at the same time I don't think I could bear being with them seven days a week, twenty-four hours a day. I need to have another identity other than being a mother. Even if we were tremendously rich, I still would be struggling along trying to accomplish what tiny bit I accomplish with part-time work. There is no doubt in my mind that I would not quit. However, if I had to chose between working full-time and not working at all, I would not work at all."

Recently, Letty was offered of a full-time job at the UN, and being confronted with the reality of what it would do to her life strengthened her convictions about the importance of her family. "I sat on the train coming back from New York and thought about what I'd have to give up," she says. "I still have some very old-fashioned values, and I realized that it's important to me to have a meal on the table at night, to make a warm place for the family to gather, to be the supplier of the family atmosphere. The thought of having to stop giving that to the people I love was terrible. I wasn't thinking how deprived they would be. I was thinking how deprived I would be. And it was one or the other. There was no way I could do those two things. And I absolutely chose not to take the job."

Letty's husband has supported her commitment to part-time, despite having conflicted feelings about it. "On the one hand he's anxious for me to go back to a full-time schedule because it's tough to bear almost the whole financial burden," she says. "But then when I say, 'Do you want your children brought up by a nanny?' he'll say, 'Absolutely not. The commitment you've made to being there is the way I want it to be.' "

When a woman's husband is making enough money so that she does not have to worry about making a contribution to household income, it gives her considerably more flexibility to get a business off the ground. This is the situation for Denise, thirty-nine, who quit her job as a cardiovascular nurse before her daughter was born sixteen months ago. "I have been interested in getting involved in some kind of business for a number of years," she says. "I'm thinking about a newsletter concerning local health care supported by local advertising. I've put out a newsletter before; the new thing for me would be getting advertising. I did a lot of research on it while I was pregnant. I still don't know if it's marketable, but I'm working on revising my business plan. I hope to be done with that in the next six months. While Ashley is small and I've got a nanny at home I'd do it part-time. I'm also trying to get pregnant again, and if I'm successful, I'll put it on hold and give the baby six months first as I did with Ashley. Eventually I'd like to be in business full-time. But I'd like to do something small to start with, which would only require a small investment, something where I could work from home and set my own schedule, and gain a little bit of experience. I feel I could expand from there. What I've discovered since having a child is that a family, and the household responsibilities and the financial responsibilities, which I take care of, has taken much more time than I ever thought they would. If I can do my exercise classes and get out part-time on business three or four days a week, that would be all I could handle."

Becoming a mother can open up some women, giving them the opportunity and the strength to make a change in their work life which allows them to commit themselves to their creative endeavors. Janet, thirty-nine, was an academic in the United States, and when she moved to Australia to get married, she found another teaching job. The marriage didn't work out, but the career track seemed like a long unbroken road until she met her husband and had a child. "If that hadn't happened, I might easily have moved somewhere else for a job and spent my energy teaching and writing scholarly articles and books," she says. "But what I really wanted to do was to concentrate more on my own writing—poetry and prose. And since having my son, that is what I have done. He goes to child care four days a week and that break allows me to write, teach part-time, and produce radio programs at a local public radio station. In other words, the decision to make a major change in my life by having a child coincided with a loosening up of my life. I don't think I would have had the guts to allow that if I had stayed childless and in the scholarly rat race. I tend to put off doing what I want most for what is expected of me."

A Change in the Wind

Other women didn't think they would want to make a change. They marched back into their old lives and old routines, but the music they are making now sounds slightly off key, and they think they want to try to play a new tune. Daphne has been trying to figure out how to do that almost since her child was born. During her maternity leave, she wrote, "I'm sitting here with my two-month-old little boy in my arms, and realizing mothering and child care is a full-time job. Yet I also have a full-time position at my company. I've extended my three-month leave to six months and basically wish I could be two people. I think the most disturbing idea prevalent today for young professionals becoming mothers is that we can somehow 'have it all.' Wouldn't it be more encouraging to spend a bit more time focusing on how to make decisions about trade-offs and sacrifices to create a personally satisfying lifestyle? It seems 'success' is still too often defined as an executive vice president who can drive her two darling children to day care in her BMW. We should broaden our definition of a successful working mother."

Eight months later, back at her full-time job, Daphne was closer to finding a new definition that suited her. "Recently I was kind of stressed out because things at work were very demanding and Michael doesn't always sleep through the night, so I was burdened and feeling badly. My husband said, 'You have two role models. You are trying to be as good as your father at work and as good as your mother at home.' I do think that's a lot of what I feel. The easiest thing is either to say, 'My job is very important to me. I can afford good child care so I'm going to let someone else care for my baby during the day, and I'm going to put my energy into work'; or to say, 'I'm going to stay home and take care of my baby; that's the most important thing to me.' But I'd like to find a middle path—I'd like to spend more time with my little boy, but at the same time I'd like to stay somewhat involved in a working situation and career interests."

One of the reasons Daphne feels so strongly about spending more time with her son is that she and her husband have values she wants to teach him. "I guess it's a combination of guilt and ego," she says, "but in order for me to be sure that my son realizes we believe family is important, and so that I can teach him things that other people can't teach him, I have to be available to him."

Daphne has been considering various approaches to get herself on this middle road. "I'm at a market research firm and the area I've been working on is direct mail so I'm thinking that one option is to propose some kind of part-time schedule to my employer and see what they say. A second option is to make a break with this company and feel confident enough that I have the skills that I can sell on a consulting basis, or that will allow me to find part-time work with someone else. I don't think I can work on retainer for my current company because the type of projects I get involved in, as far as I can see, require being available in the office; they can't be done on my own schedule or at home."

Cynthia, whose boss expects her to act exactly as she did before she became a mother six months ago, is also taking a long look at what is important to her. "This thing of the high-powered sales position and having all these responsibilities just doesn't turn me on anymore," she says. "I just don't feel like applying myself as I did. I guess what's happening in my mind is that Katie is number one on my list and that's really different from the way it used to be. I didn't think it would happen before I had her. I thought I could handle it all—that it was all going to work out, no problem. And it's not that way. She means so much to me. I want to be the most important person in her life. I think that for the next five to seven years, until she starts school and becomes a little independent person, I'd like to have the flexibility to be here. My mom wasn't home when I was young. My parents got divorced when I was three and I was in the hands of caretakers. I really missed her. I wished she could be home. And if there is any way possible that I could be here for the better part of the day, I'd like to do that for Katie."

Like many mothers going through this kind of reassessment of their lives,

Cynthia really wants a position that would allow her some flexibility. And what immediately comes to mind is having her own business. "I've never gone out on a venture on my own, but I've thought about it. My husband has come up with a few ideas for me in the industry he's in, and I was recently checking out the secretarial and résumé services and I thought, 'God I could do that!' The hardest part is setting your mind to it. I haven't yet put my nose to the grindstone to calculate how much money I could make working out of my house. But that would be the ultimate—to have my own business at home that might someday grow big enough so that I'd open an office."

When the money a woman makes is not a luxury, but at least partly necessary to keep her family in food and clothing, it is at the heart of any decision she will make about a change in her career. This is true for Cynthia. "We could afford for me to make twenty thousand dollars, which is about half of what I'm making now. But not right away. During my maternity leave, my husband took some time off too. He was closing down his company, and he didn't like the job he had so he quit. We had Katie, and we wanted to be together, so we suffered for about two months when we didn't make any money. We're just making up for that. I'd say that in a couple of months we'll be up to speed on everything so that it wouldn't affect us too much except to cut back on impulse buying for Katie. In the back of my mind, my goal is to reduce our credit card balances because that's something that people who have two decent incomes get involved in: having an outstanding balance. When I think about taking a job with less pay, or starting my own business, I'd like to have those balances as close to zero as possible. We moved to San Juan de Capistrano a year ago. Life is different here. It's a lot more relaxed, more mellow, and there are a lot of mothers who are not working, or who work part-time at their husband's businesses—stuff like that. They do OK; they have a different lifestyle and they think before they spend money. I look at it and I say, 'Gee we have a nice life. We have lots of nice things that we managed to buy when I was making good money, so maybe I could live like that.' "

For Cynthia, and women like her, salary is only part of the financial package they will give up if they pull out of their jobs. "Since I work for a big corporation," she says, "I've got the insurance, and profit sharing. I own part of the company. I'd be leaving that security, that little nest egg, and that's a little scarey. My husband makes good money but he has no benefits. I'd like to have another baby, and now that we've gone ahead and had Katie, the insurance really comes in handy. I'm kind of forcing myself to think about staying with my company for another year or two to have another baby, but then I get depressed thinking about staying with them that long. And I think it's silly to let something like insurance coverage keep you in your job and make you unhappy for another two years. So what if it costs you three thousand dollars to have the baby? Build it into your plan. It's not worth it to be gone, to be upset, to give up that time with Katie."

Some mothers feel they can manage their lives at home and on the job with one child, but they want to have a second baby, and if they are successful, they believe they will make a change.

Pat, whose company forced her to go back to a full-time schedule, says she has come to a radical resolution of the work dilemma. "My husband and I have come to the conclusion that if I get pregnant again, two children are more than I can handle and work full-time as well. If I can find a part-time job, that would be great. But I've been looking around—not very diligently, I admit—and there doesn't seem to be anything of a professional nature in this area. That's a real problem. Fortunately, my husband makes very good money and I don't have to work. It would affect our lifestyle, but not in a major way. With two children, I would stop working while the second one is new and then look for part-time work."

Wendy has reached much the same conclusion as Pat—that she will quit work for a few years when she has a second child. One of the reasons Wendy can consider such a step without wincing is that she is not concerned with climbing the corporate ladder. "I've never had high aspirations in terms of my career," she says, "to be a manager or a VP or anything. I never have five-year plans. I've just wanted a job that was interesting and challenging. Exactly what I'm working on is more important to me than a career path. In fact, I turned down a promotion four years ago to a supervisory job just because I didn't want to do annual reports.

"Quitting is a trade-off. I really feel pressed with one child, and I'm not going to be able to devote enough time to two if I'm working. Those three hours in the evening are not going to split up between two kids. And how can you measure your children's first years in dollars when it's not that you are scraping by?"

Even though she has this positive attitude, Wendy worries about what life will be like as a full-time mother. "It's hard work being home—constantly being on, and constantly being interrupted with young children, and not being able to get anything done. And you miss that adult companionship and stimulation," she says. "I'm worried that some days I'll go stark raving mad, but then I think I'll just have to make an effort to find things that are stimulating for me, and offer me a little bit of free time so that it's not 100 percent children. I had a taste of what full-time was like after Pam was born. My husband is in the state budget office and every two years he works an awful lot of overtime for four to five months. He went into that period right after she was born and it was tough. I felt kind of like a single parent. He'd get home at 7 or 8 P.M. for dinner and be gone Saturday and Sunday, so I really didn't get much time for myself. If I were home and he went into that cycle again, I know I'd have to find a couple of hours a week of child care so I could get out on my own."

Another alternative for Wendy, one that she is seriously considering, is to try to work out a free-lance project arrangement with her company, something she thinks they might go for if they knew they were going to lose her anyway. "Free-lancing is something I've always thought about doing," she says. "I think realistically the only way I could do it is if I had something fairly regular so that I could afford to get child care. I know I would not be motivated to do it just during nap times. It's always been hard for me to work at home—there are too many distractions. What I think I'm going to propose to my boss is to work free-lance for them on a fairly regular basis, with a guarantee that it would be a certain number of hours a week. The department is fairly short of help right now, and I'm working on a proposal for a project that would require adding a half-time person. I know exactly what the budget is for that, and if anyone could build a case for doing it free-lance, I'd be the one. If I get pregnant soon, and we're trying now, and I was far enough along so that I didn't have to worry about a miscarriage, I'd propose to do it. I've been in the job for eight years, and I've always gotten really good performance reviews. There's a certain amount of knowledge in my head that would make me especially qualified to do it. If they were going to lose me anyway, they might as well have me working for them on a free-lance basis."

The Ultimate Trade-off

For some women, it hasn't taken a second child to convince them that holding down a full-time job and being a mother does not work for them. They feel they are missing too much, and their children are too important to keep on putting in eight-hour days away from them in a job that doesn't seem as significant as it once might have. In his book, *The Executive Parent,* S. P. Hersh, M.D., offers the Twenty-Year Test, which these women appear to have taken: "Reflect on the meaning and importance of the work you are doing now as you might judge it twenty years hence," he writes, "and you will discover that probably 90 percent of what you are doing has little meaning and no importance in that perspective." Mathilda, thirty-six, the mother of two, puts it another way: "Working for kids is better than working for a boss."

Some women know they'll feel like this long before they become mothers. Tammy, twenty-eight, was an administrative manager with a Fortune 100 company, earning about $40,000 a year, when she became pregnant after years of infertility treatments and gave birth to a son fifteen months ago. "Even before I got pregnant," she says, "I decided that staying home and raising my child had more long-term significance than what I could do for my company. If I collected X millions of dollars for them, so what? They would have been collected by someone else if I weren't there. How many business people do you know who get to the pinnacle of their career and look back and say, 'What did it mean? Big deal! What did I do for humanity?' I didn't want to make that mistake. And I've got to be a classic candidate for the Superwoman syndrome—forever doing a hundred different things at once. I could see myself burning out. Also, having gone through all those years of infertility treatment heightened my desire to spend time with this child who seemed like such a miracle."

A major part of the decision making for any couple considering such a step is whether they can afford it. Tammy and her husband were no different. "It doesn't feel as if we've had to make any concessions, which may sound unusual since basically we cut our income by about 45 percent. We had decided that we couldn't afford for me to stay home until Roger's salary could meet all the bills, and at this point, money is tighter than it has ever been. But we don't tend to live high on the hog. We've kept loans pretty much to the mortgage. We take out a car loan when we buy a car and always pay it off the first year. We don't live extravagantly. We don't take big-deal vacations so it doesn't feel as if there were many concessions. In reality, there were because we lost close to $40,000 a year. It means we're not saving anywhere near what we were."

One problem Tammy anticipated she might find since she quit her job was a lowering of her self-esteem, and she was right. It began with the reaction of some of the mothers she worked with. "The most vocal people were professional women who were in many cases on the defensive side about working long hours and missing their children at home," she says. "They could be very condescending toward those poor downtrodden housewives who stay home all day and watch TV. They thought my mind was going to rot. I had women say to me, 'You mean you are going to stay home and take care of your baby?' as if I had to be kidding. In other cases, they were so thrilled with their own decision to work that they couldn't see any other way.

"The basic problem is that today's culture teaches us that our worth is determined not according to who we are, but by what we accomplish," she continues. "At my job I received recognition, opportunities to travel, freedom to make important decisions regarding my staff, input to future policies, etc., and this responsibility reinforced my belief that I was worth something. I had long told myself that I would not buy into that belief system, but it is insidious. The classic image of the disheveled housewife watching soap operas and eating bonbons has not helped my self-image. I no longer have the daily reinforcement from the business world which tells me that I am important and that my efforts are worthwhile. I thought I had done a pretty good job ahead of time preparing myself for this transition, and in terms of the day-to-day routine, I probably have, but I was shocked that I found at the end of every day I had to justify my own existence to myself. It was as if I had to catalog in my mind what I had accomplished in order to justify the fact that at 8 P.M. I was sitting down to read a book. I had to convince myself that I had accomplished enough that I had earned the right to take some time off. I had never felt that at work because the mere act of getting up and getting dressed and going out into the workplace was justification in and of itself. Plus there was the paycheck, and the recognition.

"Now, when Roger comes home at night, and I'm dying to talk to another intelligent adult, and all I can tell him is that I did a load of diapers, and I baked cookies and notice how clean the rug is, sometimes I feel like saying, 'Oh, come on!' So, as much as I had told myself I was not going to buy into that mentality where my worth is measured in my accomplishments, that I was going to have an internalized self-image, that I was important because I am who I am, I found that over the years I *had* bought into it. It took me a good year to come to terms with the fact that accomplishment for accomplishment I could never compete with the workplace versus being at home, but if I was that convinced that I had made the right decision and could tell myself why—that the effects of what I'm doing now are very long-term and very difficult to measure—then I could feel I was important just for who I am."

Libby, thirty-three, a secretary-receptionist, took this same route—quitting her job and staying home with her child for two and a half years before getting back into the fray. "My husband and I waited until I was twenty-eight, we had purchased a house and two cars, and I could stop work for several years to have a child. I had a good job as a customer service supervisor for a television company, and I did briefly consider going back to my job three months after my daughter was born, but since my husband's income was adequate, I decided to stay home with Charlotte until she was at least two years old. I have never felt sorry about my decision. I'd advise other women to do the same. You will never regret the time you spend with your child. They grow up so fast.

"When I started to consider going back to work. It was a lot harder than I had imagined. I found that in order to make any money after taxes, lunch money, gas, and child care were deducted, I needed to get at least $6.00 an hour. For someone who had a gap of two and a half years in her work history, it was a challenge. I enrolled in an advanced typing class and considered taking other night classes to sharpen my skills. Finally, I obtained a position as an administrative assistant at my desired salary. Now I feel my career is just beginning. I recently changed jobs and hope I am now with a company that I can grow with. I'm seriously considering going back to school for an M.B.A."

Sometimes having a child is just the excuse a woman needs to quit her job and devote herself not just to mothering, but to other interests she had little time for. When this happens, she may plan never to go back. Gretchen, thirty-one, has done this since her daughter was born, and it has made her new situation ideal for her. "I was never thrilled with my job as a high-level clerk in a university library, and I was lucky enough that my husband made good money so that I could quit. I had always really wanted to be a singer/song writer, or actress, or writer," she says. "I knew from experience that my marriage worked best when I wasn't out at play rehearsals every night or at the local coffeehouse singing, so I decided it was the perfect time to devote my creative energies and professional ambitions to writing. I wrote 150 pages of this two-volume novel when we were living in Illinois, and when we moved here, I stopped because I was depressed. Now I've started another novel and set aside the two-volume one because it's too massive for a beginning writer. I began when I was pregnant, and for the last three months of the pregnancy I wrote a lot. Now I grab what time I can for it during her nap times, but even writing only a few hours a week for six months I have finished one third of a novel. I soon hope to be able to send Annie to a babysitter or a small day care center for a few hours a day so I can have some more time. I don't need deadlines to motivate me. If I have free time, I write. My husband doesn't see that I'll ever have to bring money in. So I can have the three children I want and write. I'm also planning on starting to sing again once we move back to the Midwest. If the writing doesn't pan out, then I'll do something else. Since I'm freed of money worries, I can follow my interests.

"I feel very fulfilled and lucky. It's an exhilarating feeling to be an 'at home' mother, with all the joy and hard work that that requires, and also to be accomplishing one of my life-long dreams. The best part is being there for Annie. She is my major project. She's thriving psychologically and emotionally. The second best thing is that all day I can think about my novel. My mind is my own."

Sometimes new babies bring their mothers a whole new picture of what is important to them, and they decide while they are pregnant or soon after their child's birth that they don't want to return to their jobs. Stephanie, thirty-five, then a thirty-two-year-old research teacher who worked with special needs children, originally thought she'd combine her career with motherhood. But because of her background in childhood development, she had some philosophical doubts about that route from the beginning. "I had worked on a kibbutz in Israel one summer," she says, "and I observed the woman who took care of the children. I really felt there was something very sterile in the children being cared for in that particular environment outside of their nuclear family. It didn't click for me. I didn't know if I would want that. I also worked in a day care center before I went into public school teaching and I had 15 three-year-olds, and one aid. Some were two-and-a-half and they experienced a great deal of separation problems. Some became very attached to me and I to them. That had an effect on me too.

"But when I got pregnant, I wasn't planning on staying home. The baby was due in July and I was going to take a year off. I was guaranteed a position when I returned. I was also up for tenure that year.

"I was feeling a lot of pressure. Here I was, big and pregnant, and having some complications with the pregnancy. Because of the tenure, people were dropping in without any warning to observe my teaching. My husband finally said, 'Why are you putting yourself through all this pressure to get tenure when you don't even want to work there anymore?' He took the pressure off. I said, 'You're right. I just don't want this.' "

Stephanie was supported in her decision by a women's group she joined around that time and by other women she met who had also made the decision to stay home, but she still sometimes has problems feeling that the outside world thinks less of her. "A neighbor of mine was a Yale University law graduate and had chosen to give it up and was home, and I had her as an example. Without this support I think I would still have done it because of the circumstances of my work but I would have felt much more devastated about it. I would have felt that my career is over and what am I now? Just a housewife?

"It's been three years now and I don't think about it too much anymore. Sometimes I'll feel a little sting, for example, at a party, people will ask, 'What do you do?' I've stopped putting down 'mother' or 'homemaker' on forms that require occupation. I put down 'parent educator,' which is true because I volunteer on a hot line for parent education and breast-feeding counseling. I also lead meetings for new moms and help them manage lactation and give them advice on childbirth issues and parenting issues."

Stephanie also has a full schedule at home with her two children, who are three years and three months old. This is a description of a recent morning during which she wrote a long letter about her life with the following interruptions: "Three-year old: 'Mommy, pour me juice. . . .' Put swimsuit on, suntan lotion on. 'Mommy, get the bugs out of my pool.' Comment on sliding into pool. Discuss not wasting water. Watch through window (while writing). Dry him off. Help him get clothes on. Discuss block building. Discuss needs of baby with big brother—why baby often takes priority. Praise big brother's patience and maturity. Admire skills. Tell big brother not to interrupt mommy while she does her work. Three-month-old: 'Hold me . . . burp me . . . change me . . . nurse me. I'm tired, help me relax.' " This is not how Stephanie thought it would be going into it. "I think if a mother-to-be could spend a day or two following around a mother of a new baby, living with her, it would give her some kind of clue as to how demanding an infant can be. But the temperament of the baby is a big factor. I thought my son was really very hard and I had a tough time with him. I'd blame myself and say if I were only better at this it wouldn't be so difficult. Now I realize that so much of it is just temperament. The second one is a totally different baby. She's outgoing and she doesn't arch her back and scream when I change her diaper. My husband also says it's easier because we are more relaxed."

Now, three years into full-time motherhood, Stephanie has no regrets about her decision. The time she has with her children is extremely important to her. "I think that attention to marriage and family life is a better investment for the long-term happiness of all family members than any other job I could be doing," she says. "I take my role as a wife and mother seriously. Mothering is a proud profession. I also think that it is a myth that quality time is as good as full-time parenting. Rather, children need quantities of quality time when they need it, which is not necessarily when parents plan it. Although children can be flexible, their demands are great. The first three years are crucial for all aspects of development. Although sometimes adequate to good substitutes can be found, children need their parents. If kids were asked, 'Who would you like to take care of you?' I would be willing to bet that babies and children would always choose their own families. I think that couples planning to have children should consider children's needs and not simply their own when they make child care decisions. I don't believe you can have it all—balance career and mothering without something or someone suffering. I prefer to look at it this way—I can have it all, just not all at once. I realize there are many ways to raise a child. But part-time parenting, especially in the early years, would simply not provide enough intimacy for my children or for me."

Other women grow into motherhood slowly. They imagine that they will set up their life in a certain way—continuing their careers, fitting their child into that life—only to find some months or years later that they aren't living the way they want to. "When you're a career person and pregnant, you feel you can have it all, you are going to make it work," says Emily, thirty-five, a former director of patient services, who was thirty-four when her son was born. These feelings continued during her maternity leave. She arranged for four months off but after three months she says she "considered calling them and saying I'd come back early. It really wasn't such great shakes taking care of this little kid. I needed more. My biggest concern was getting good child care so I could go back."

It wasn't until her son reached eight months, that she reexamined what she wanted. "My son started being so much fun and I thought, 'What am I missing?' In my reading, I had always been attracted to those articles that reinforced the working mom. Anything that talked about how mom had stopped working when her child was six months old and it was the most wonderful thing in the world—I didn't read those. It wasn't my reality. But there he was, and I thought, 'As hard as this may be, and as threatening to my career, I think I want to to stop working for a while.' "

Another factor was Emily's feelings about her performance in both her roles under the time restrictions she had put on herself. "I knew that to do justice to my work I needed to spend a lot more than a forty-hour week, and I wasn't willing to do that. Working only forty hours, I was having a hard time feeling competent at work. And I didn't feel I was doing a very good job at home. We finally got a housecleaning service and that was a big help, but it was just that sense that I didn't feel I was doing anything really well at work or at home, and someone else was raising my child. The idea of quantity time versus quality time was just a bunch of hogwash. We'd come home exhausted.

We'd coexist with this child until 7:30 or 8 P.M. We'd try to spend special time with him, but we were really tired and it wasn't fun."

After being at home as a full-time mother for four months, Emily is glad she made the decision she did. "I believe in what I'm doing, but I'm not saying it's easy," she says. "But I think in our overall scheme as a family I'm doing the right thing. I want to be the one, as opposed to a babysitter, who is spending the most time. The hardest part of it is the tedium of doing the same thing every day."

What has gotten Emily through the bad times are two friends and a trade-off of kids they've arranged to give each other some free time. "We go to the play group at the community center, and we go to the story hour at the library. I had been worried about isolation when I quit my job because I did not have a very large support group in this area since when I moved I immediately got my job and I didn't have children. But through the play group I found one woman who was in exactly the same boat I was, with a boy the same age as Mark—a professional woman who had made the switch for a few years. We've been good listeners for each other. On Monday afternoon I take care of her little boy for two to three hours and on Thursday she does the same for me. I also take him to a baby-sitter for the whole day on Tuesday."

Another thing that has been hard for Emily is the realization that the world she left behind has gone right on without her—that she could be replaced. "They don't even call me with questions anymore," she says. "That sense of being needed is gone. And I'm nervous that if I take off a few more years I'll be close to forty before I reenter the working world. I think about how to go back a lot, and I've gotten a lot of reinforcement from both men and women that I'll be able to pick up my career where I left off, and that I'm doing the most important thing I can do right now."

The quandary faced by most mothers—those who have continued with careers, and those who have quit—is stated well by Eleanor, who had her only child at forty-one. "I have come to realize how little credit women get for being mothers. You can be a superb mother and nobody gives a damn. You don't get an award—there is no Pulitzer Prize. What it's forced me to begin to do is to reexamine what is considered to be valuable in this society. I'm starting to develop a two-tiered perspective for evaluating something: one is how men usually look at it, and the other is how a truly mature person would look at it. From that perspective, I want to have a balance of work, intimacy, and development of my own gifts, and some kind of moral contribution. I don't want things so heavily weighted on the side of work, and I think things had gotten that way—probably because I concentrated on career and didn't have a family for so long.

"So one of my goals over the next few years is to move more toward a balance in my life, and I have a sneaking suspicion that I may be just as productive as I was when I put so much emphasis on work. I'd still like the laurels, but I haven't figured out how to go after them and still be a good mother. I've had to sit back and think about that. I'm not willing to make the compromises that have to be made, and I don't have someone like me taking care of the other parts of my life so that I'd have the time to devote to my career. I'd love to be married to me. Then it might all work."

11

The Child Care Conundrum

While on maternity leave, sorting through new emotions, and wending their ways through unstructured days at the command of their babies' cries, the new mothers who are planning on returning to work also have to figure out what kind of care they want for their baby, and find the best situation that they can afford. It's a subject that occupies many hours of thought. Most have had child care on their minds since they first found out they were pregnant. Even women who are still twisting and turning over whether to have a child examine this piece of the puzzle. For almost 60 percent of the mothers, finding good child care is the toughest part of their new combined lives.

The big question is: What is good child care? The mothers who responded to the survey have found different answers that they believe in, and a number have learned some lessons through bad experiences they've had along the way. Before examining their solutions, perhaps a word or two from the experts is warranted.

Almost universally, child psychologists such as Selma Fraiberg, Dr. Burton White, Dr. Lee Salk, and Dr. Benjamin Spock believe that the very best caregiver is the baby's mother or father—someone who has the most invested in this new person. They express strong opinions which can seem extremely harsh to women planning on returning to work. Here's just a little of what they have to say:

DR. BURTON WHITE: "During this critical formative period, the child has a
    need to form a close attachment with a particular parent, and this is
    achieved through frequent physical contact, verbal and nonverbal inter-
    action, and the development of a sense of trust. The parent must consis-

tently and reliably respond to the child's demand for attention, or this sense of trust will not be established. The parent's contacts with the child must be frequent and sustained in the first years if the relationship is to have depth and a special meaning for the child. The amount of contact time needed is less and less as the child matures. . . . Half-day contact is quite adequate by the time the child reaches three" (from *The First Three Years of Life*).

DR. LEE SALK: "I've spent close to twenty years treating adults and I've discovered that all of the most common problems of people in therapy—the inability to form meaningful relationships, difficulties in being able to love and be loved, problems of hostility or dependency—stemmed from a lack of fulfillment of their needs in the early stages of development. It's really very simple—children desperately need to feel loved. I'm convinced that many of these kids are walking time bombs. It just might be that people who can't organize their lives to provide sufficient time for their children would be better off if they didn't have any. . . .

"All I can say is that I'm an advocate for children, not mothers and fathers. [If women want to work full-time and have a child] that's like saying they'd like to be a full-time skier and a full-time professor. They can't do both effectively. I can't tell you how many disturbed children result from that situation" (as quoted in "The Case for Staying Home," *Esquire* magazine).

DR. BENJAMIN SPOCK: "I used to say that if parents realized how important they are to their children, especially during the first two or three years, maybe they'd revise their economic goals, so one of them could stay home with the child. . . . I'm all for women's equality. I just think it's too bad, when the women's liberation movement surfaced about 1970, that so many women had to define equality in terms of pay and jobs. . . . I don't ever want to make mothers feel guilty. Now, in our book, we're telling parents that the success of substitute care depends on the quality of the care. Unfortunately, the number of good day care facilities in this country is grossly insufficient. But I have to remind myself, too, that a lot of parental care is no damn good either" (from an interview in *People Weekly*).

One circumstance that may make parental care 'no damn good' is when mothers stay home even though it drives them crazy, frustrates them, and makes them blame their baby for what they are giving up. The only long-term study of the effects of maternal employment has shown that when those kind of feelings surface, being at home not only is bad for the parent, but can have a negative impact on the child as well. Dr. Jacqueline Lerner, a mother and psychologist at Pennsylvania State University, studied the children of one hundred women over a twenty-eight-year period to see how their mother's choice to work or not to work affected their lives, as children and later as adults. Thirty-eight of the mothers worked; sixty-two stayed home with their children. "We went looking for a direct connection between adjustment in a child and a mother's employment status," says Dr. Lerner in an article in *McCall's*, "and there wasn't one to be found." What she did find was a connection between difficult children and mothers who weren't doing what they wanted to be doing. "The most poorly adjusted children were those with mothers who wanted to work but were staying home and those with working mothers who felt they really should be at home."

When the Lerner study was being done, mothers had considerably fewer choices for alternative caregivers. Thus it did not look at specifically the care received by the children whose mothers worked and what part that played in their adjustment—which brings us right back to the question of what is a good substitute for a parent. According to the Princeton Center for Infancy, in their book *The First Twelve Months of Life*, "A baby is less likely to form a strong, close bond with another human being if no one has ever had one with him. . . . Nothing is worse than a series of caretakers. A child needs one person to identify with as the mothering figure."

There is ample evidence to support this view. Most of it comes from studies of children growing up in institutions, or shuffled from one foster home to another. They are not able to form attachments, or the attachments they do form are disrupted. This can mean that their cognitive development is retarded, and that they suffer from emotional deficits. Because they lack the primary attachment to a mothering figure, they are unable to form lasting, loving relationships as a child, or an adult. The relationships they do form are from need—they take, but do not give. Obviously, the situation of children who have a mother and father who come home each night is different than these children who have no one to call their own.

The Day Care Center

But the most popular form of child care today, the day care center, unfortunately mimics institutional care for the ten to twelve hours that babies and toddlers are left there. Day care centers often have a considerable turnover of staff because the pay is low. Staff members may rotate their schedules so that infants and toddlers do not have the same caregiver every day, and each staff member is responsible for a number of babies—often too many to be able to fill the needs of each. Thus, some of the effects of day care may be the same as full-time institutional care—even if the program is full of quality educational activities and materials and is run by loving, intelligent people.

William and Wendy Dreskin ran a preschool and day care center for two years in California, and wrote a book, *The Day Care Decision,* about why they decided to close down their school because of the detrimental effects they saw in the children who were there on a full-day program. They were aggressive, both physically and verbally. They didn't cooperate as well as other children, and their tolerance for frustration was also lower.

A similar kind of program which meshed full-time day care for infants and toddlers with a Montessori nursery school in Montclair, New Jersey, eventually decided to eliminate the infant and toddler care program—one which provided care appropriate for the children's developmental level from six months up to age two—for much the same reasons. The head teacher of the Montessori program, Maureen Grady, a mother of twelve who has fifteen years of experience teaching in Montessori nursery schools and was involved in setting up the program, explains why. "I thought it was all going very well for the first three years. But then the children who had been in the day care program from the time they were six months old, or a bit older, most of them from 7 A.M. to 5:30 P.M. five days a week, fifty weeks a year, started coming upstairs for the nursery school program. They were different from the children arriving at school for the first time at age three. I was used to bright-eyed children coming to nursery school saying, 'Teach me.' But these children came into nursery school rather reluctant to relate to adults. They didn't want too much to do with us. They loved to roll around on the floor together. They interacted with each other as a group. We had to pry them away to involve them in the activities and exercises, and they didn't seem interested. We set up the environment to invite youngsters to exercise their normal curiosity, but they weren't curious. They didn't seem to care. They almost seemed shut down. There were other symptoms—they seemed more aggressive than the other children, and mad, angry, not happy to come and play in a productive way. They also seemed almost bereft of emotions—they were sort of dull. It took us several months to get these children to behave as much as possible like the curious nursery school youngsters we were used to. But two of them we could not help; they were not getting anything from being here."

The head teacher of the infant and toddler care program was also seeing the beginnings of these symptoms in the children under her care who had been there for a year or more. After considerable examination of the programs themselves, Mrs. Grady and her fellow teachers finally concluded that they weren't *doing* anything wrong—it was simply the length of the day, and the length of the day care program itself—ten hours a day, five days a week, fifty weeks a year—which was at the root of the trouble. The only solution they could see was to shut it down, and that is what they did.

"It was obvious that there was a problem inherent in day care itself, a problem that hung like a dark storm over 'good' and 'bad' day care centers alike," the Dreskins wrote concerning their similar decision to shut down their school. "The children were too young to be spending so much time away from their parents. They were like young birds being forced out of the nest and abandoned by their parents before they could fly, their wings undeveloped, unready to carry them out into the world. . . .

"For two years we watched day care children in our pre-school/day care center respond to the stresses of eight to ten hours a day of separation from their parents with tears, anger, withdrawal, or profound sadness, and we found, to our dismay, that nothing in our own affection and caring for these children could erase the sense of loss and abandonment. We came to realize that the amount of separation—the number of hours a day spent away from the parents—is a critical factor." This opinion jives with that of the child experts quoted above. But there are other experts, such as Jerome Kagan, Ph.D., who disagree, who think day care provides a good substitute for parents who work.

There is no way to resolve this issue because day care is so new there have been few studies done of its immediate impact, and there has been no time to track the long-term effects on the emotional development of the children who are attending. After reviewing forty studies of day care, Jay Belsky and Laurence Steinberg wrote in *Child Development:* "When considered from a broader perspective on human development we know shockingly little about the impact of day care on children, on their parents, and on the society in which the children and parents live. . . . To even say that the jury is still out on day care would be in our view both premature and naively optimistic. The fact of the matter is, quite frankly, that the majority of the evidence has yet to be presented, much less subpoenaed."

The experts also disagree on whether there are advantages in terms of cognitive development to children going to group day care. The Dreskins point out that "the studies strongly suggest that full-time day care has absolutely no educational benefits over the much more limited separation of half-day preschool," and indeed that by the first grades of elementary school the advantages children with a preschool background have over those reared only at home have evened out. This has been shown to be particularly true for low-risk children from relatively advantaged families.

It is even thought that full-time group day care can stifle creativity and independent thinking and have a negative educational impact. Studies by Bruno Bettleheim, Erik Erickson, and others have compared kibbutz children who are raised in group care situations with Israeli children raised in families and found a lack of individuality in the kibbutz children; they showed a sameness in personality and an absence of the elements that result in independent and creative thinking. Observations in this country of full-time day care children, particularly those "with above average intelligence or special creative abilities," has shown that "full-time day care can have an adverse effect, stifling creativity and discouraging independent thinking," write the Dreskins.

Day care centers can also be places that breed disease. Research presented in the *New England Journal of Medicine,* the *Journal of Pediatrics,* the *Journal of the American Medical Association,* and the *Journal of Infectious Diseases* shows that children and babies attending day care centers run a considerably greater risk of catching a number of serious, sometimes life-threatening diseases, which they can pass on to family members. And this happens not only in centers located in urban ghettos, but also in those used by suburban middle- to upper-income families. One of the main reasons for the increased risk of disease transmission is the nature of children, which, according to the Child Day Care Infectious Disease Study Group of the Centers for Disease Control, includes "close, repeated person-to-person contact; lack of fecal continence prior to toilet training; frequent exploration of the environment with their mouths, offering opportunity for fecal-oral transmission [of disease] as well as for the spread of respiratory secretions; and requirement for frequent hands-on contact by staff."

The diseases are of two kinds, those spread by the fecal-oral route, which children who are not yet toilet-trained are at greatest risk of acquiring, and those transmitted by the respiratory route. Hepatitis A, a liver disease, is one of the most common infections spread by the fecal-oral route. Children usually do not show symptoms, but adults do—fever, diarrhea, headache, anorexia and jaundice. In a study in Phoenix, 66 percent of the day care centers enrolling infants younger than a year had at least one outbreak. It is estimated that centers which enroll children under age two have a greater than 50 percent chance of spreading the disease.

A number of highly contagious bacterial infections of the digestive tract which cause severe diarrhea and are very serious in children under two years old have been linked to day care centers, and are also passed through the fecal-oral route. Outbreaks of shigellosis in day care centers have been reported since the early 1970s. In a study in Atlanta, giardiasis has been shown to afflict 29 to 54 percent of the children six months to three years old who attended day care centers, compared to only 2 percent of the children cared for elsewhere.

The most serious respiratory infection associated with day care centers is hemophilus influenzae, Type B. It typically attacks children four months to five years old, and it is the leading cause of bacterial meningitis. Infants with meningitis have fever, weakness, and a high-pitched cry, and the soft spot on their heads, the fontanel, may be tight or bulging. It can also attack joints, skin, underlying tissues, the middle ear, the epiglottis, the lungs, and the sac surrounding the heart. Most cases require hospitalization with antibiotics given intravenously. Five to ten percent of the very young infants infected will not survive.

Another disease connected to day care centers is cytomegalovirus, which is symptomless in children but can have disastrous consequences if contracted by a pregnant woman. In a recent study of children aged three months to five years from middle to upper socioeconomic classes, attending day care centers in Alabama, 51 percent of them were found to be excreting the virus; of the toddlers aged one to two, 83 percent were doing so. These children can carry the disease home with them, and if they infect their mother when she is pregnant, she can give the disease to her unborn child. Five to ten percent of all pregnant women who get cytomegalovirus during their pregnancies give birth to infants with the disease. It causes brain damage, retardation, liver disease, cerebral palsy, defects of the heart and hearing, and other abnormalities. There is no treatment available for the mother or the child before, or after, birth.

Other Alternatives

Of course, there are choices available other than a day care center. The most preferable is a substitute mother—the father, a relative, or a sitter who lives with the family or comes each day to the home, a person with whom the child can form an attachment to supplement the attachment to the mother which is interrupted when the mother goes back to work. "If this person becomes the object of the child's attachment," says Ben J. Susswein, Ph.D., a psychologist specializing in childhood development and family therapy, "she can help the child experience a stable emotional climate in which to make some sense of the world." Obviously, changing sitters or housekeepers every few months does not help the child develop an attachment or feel that the world is a very reliable place. Keeping one person until the child is three years old is the ideal to be strived for. "Consistency of a woman's schedule at work, and of the care giver is important—consistency of the pattern," says Dr. Susswein.

If a mother is returning to work after six to eight weeks of maternity leave, she is leaving before the time when her baby has started to get selective about people, including her. A gradual return to her job benefits her more than it does the child. What is more important to him is the quality of the substitute. By three to four months, babies respond very selectively to people, and recognize faces of people they know. By eight months they experience stranger anxiety, which is the flip side of their heightened awareness of the people they are attached to. After three months of maternity leave, it makes sense to return to work gradually or to have a mother substitute start a few weeks before a woman goes back full-time so that the baby gets used to her while Mother is still around.

The reason why child development experts are so concerned about the first three years of a child's life is that in the first half of this brief period, the child needs to form an attachment to the mother or the caregiver, and then once that is established, usually by eighteen months, the child begins the process of separating herself from the mother figure, and seeing herself as an individual. "Separation, moving away the person the child is attached to, requires that that person be there to move away from," says Dr. Susswein. "Mother, or her substitute, is used as a base of operation from which the child can travel out and travel back, and he or she will play and explore, totally ignoring the mother, as long as she's there. Although the mother is not in any obvious concrete way the object of the child's attention, her presence is background to the child's world.

"Sometimes children seem to be regressing, growing more attached," says Dr. Susswein, "which is just part of the process of making sure their person is still there for them, the attachment is still strong. They go back and forth, needing the attachment and then pulling away to explore, testing the attachment, experiencing themselves as separate from the parent. This is why three seems to be a very suitable age for school to start."

Because children are all on different schedules within this larger timetable, deciding when to put a child into group care outside the home in a pre-school or day care program or home day care situation before age three should depend on where the child is in this process. Putting a child into any kind of group program can be hard if he is going through the period of regression. Making the transition gradually can ease separation anxiety—starting a few mornings a week instead of every day and keeping the regular sitter for the other hours the mother will be gone. If a sitter to whom the child is attached leaves, a gradual transition to a new sitter—taking a few days or a week off when the sitter first starts—will also make the toddler more comfortable.

If the family cannot afford to have their baby or toddler cared for at home, on a one-to-one basis, then a day care home, say the Dreskins, is preferable to an infant center for health reasons alone. And if the ratio of babies to adults is the same in both home and center, a good day care home with one or two caregivers and only a few babies and toddlers is better emotionally for a baby than a center with many children and many caregivers.

Babies will give out clues to their feelings about their caregiver and their daily world, which parents can interpret if they are willing, says Dr. Susswein, "to slow down enough to look carefully and critically. Parents have to see beyond what they want to see. The hard part is being honest and admitting you see a change in your baby, and being willing to acknowledge that there may be an association between the care giver and your child's emotions. There are no specific signs and symptoms all children exhibit. Each child will express him or herself differently. But if you look at what is going on and are not vested in the current arrangement, you can see your child and interpret his or her feelings."

One mother of two small boys who are cared for by a babysitter four days a week while she puts in her thirty-five hours has taken a hard look beyond her current arrangement to ask a very poignant question about the future: "My husband was in Vietnam, and he said that after a battle when the soldiers were lying wounded and dying they would ask for two things: one was God, and the other was Mom. They would call for their mothers. I wonder who this generation of boys, who have been reared in day care centers and by babysitters, will be calling for. If these kids are being watched from three weeks old by someone else, or by a series of people—have we lost something entirely?"

Real Choices

A FAMILY MEMBER

If a mother goes back to work, the very best substitute for her is the father. Who else would provide the love he can to his own child? A number of the pregnant women interviewed thought that their husbands could provide at least part of the child care to their new baby because they had a schedule that was different from their own—they worked weekends and were off for two days during the week, or they worked at night—or they worked at home. However, a mere 4 percent of the mothers say that the father is the one splitting child care with them. One of these is the husband of Donna, thirty-five, who has recently retired from the Navy and had gone back to school to get a Ph.D. in anthropology and now cares for their two daughters, five months old and three years old, while she continues her career as an associate general counsel for the federal government. This has made her life exceptionally easy, and guilt-free. "He sort of slid into taking care of the baby," she says. "Our second daughter was due in the summer, so we agreed very early that he wasn't going to take any summer classes. I drive an hour each way to work, so the deal was that within a couple of weeks of the due date, he'd start driving me to work and driving me home, which he did for about ten days. I worked up until the last second. Then when time came to register for this semester, he said he wasn't going to and I said fine. He loves the material he's learning, but I sense a growing disillusion with the academic world. So it wasn't anything I asked him to do, but I was happy about it. If he registers for next semester, it will be a part-time schedule. I think he's happy with the compromise. He seems to like staying home. When I call him in the afternoon, he tells me what the kids are doing. He likes to let the baby sleep on his chest. So he doesn't get much done during the day. When she's ready to take a nap, he puts her down on his chest, and lets her sleep there. She is five months old now." Not only does Donna have her husband providing child care, but her parents are nearby and they take the baby one day a week and provide occasional afternoon care for her older daughter after her morning nursery school program.

Grandparents also make wonderful parent substitutes. Mindy, thirty, a pilot, started out with her husband providing the care to their new daughter and now has her father-in-law doing it. "John really wanted to be a househusband; he really thought that could work if he stayed home with the baby, but it wasn't enough for him. Now he's flying 727s for a charter airline, so he's happier than he's been in years. Luckily, my father-in-law came up for two weeks when I had the baby. He was just going to stay for a visit, see the baby, and leave. But he couldn't stand to leave; he liked her so much. So he decided to stay and he takes care of the baby if our schedules conflict. At first he didn't even know how to change a diaper, but now I come home and he tells me to watch out for her diaper rash.

"At first he was living with us but I'm not one who ever wanted someone that close all the time. So we ended up buying this trailer for him because it wasn't working with all of us under the same roof. It's parked on our property. He decided that if he wants to see the baby enough, he'll bend too. When he was raising his kids, there wasn't enough money and it wasn't much fun. But now we're comfortable and he doesn't have to worry about that.

"In January and February he goes south, which makes it harder for us if our schedules conflict. So I took my vacation in February this year. My husband and I won't see a lot of each other for a while, but there is only one day when one of us won't be home, and a girlfriend of mine is going to take our daughter. Sometimes I can't believe how well it's worked out."

LIVE-IN HELP

The next best thing to Daddy or a grandparent is a full-time, live-in housekeeper who becomes a member of the family. Eleanor, forty-six, a psychotherapist and writer who was forty-one when she had her daughter, already had such a housekeeper, who had worked for her husband for years and helped raise his three grown daughters. Her mother-in-law was also close at hand, and despite being in her mid-seventies, she got involved as well. "My daughter has three mothers," says Eleanor, "the housekeeper, my mother-in-law, and me. I'm the central mother; they are side mothers. That's the way she looks at it. Sometimes the two side mothers forget that they are side mothers and try to work themselves into the central mother position, and she very strongly reminds them that there is already a central mother. I let her handle that on her own."

Eighteen percent of the mothers surveyed have live-in housekeepers because that is the only way they can keep up with their demanding full-time schedule. The housekeeper is the one who not only makes it all possible but, if she's the right person, even makes it a pleasure. "Besides looking after our child," says Faith, twenty-nine, a management consultant with an international CPA firm, "our nanny also does light housekeeping, which is wonderful. When we come home, we eat dinner and relax with our baby."

For Kathleen, twenty-nine, the vice-president of a commercial bank, the housekeeper has become that substitute mommy the experts think is important, but she also doesn't believe her work has affected her son's attachment to her. "He's sixteen months old, and I'm still his favorite. He's very attached to his nanny, but I think he knows who I am and who Bill is. I think he looks at us all as three people who are a part of his family. I think he loves all three of us and enjoys being with all three of us. His nanny obviously spends more time with him during the week, but she's off all weekend and it's just Bill and me. We have a lot of fun on the weekend.

"He's always been a tremendously healthy and happy baby and I think that has contributed to my easy experience. I have friends who have babies who cry a lot or have colic, who are not that happy. But this child of mine never cries. He's always happy. When I come home from work he's smiling and giggling and when I leave in the morning he's smiling and giggling. He's an enormously well-adjusted baby. That makes it a lot easier. The hardest thing would be if he cried in the morning when I left.

"When I get home, I open the door and he hears me and comes running with this massive smile on his face. It's really easy to forget about work. It's also good for me because I'm able to release myself totally from work because I have this human being to play with at night."

The only time Kathleen noticed a change in her son was when she would return from her monthly trips for business, which took her away for three to four days. "I saw a difference in him the first few times I went away. He'd just want to sit in my lap when I came home, which was a lot of fun for both of us. That's stopped. Now I don't see a difference between when I come home from work and when I come home from a trip. He's all excited either way. Between the nanny and my husband, I don't think he suffers."

Janis, thirty-six, a sales planning manager, works fifty-five hours a week, and her husband travels a lot, so she also found that a live-in housekeeper was a necessity, so that there would be a firm structure to rely on and she could have peace of mind. But she has had some uncomfortable relationships with her housekeepers and one extremely bad experience in the three years since her daughter was born. "The first housekeeper was an older woman and she was perfect when Blythe was an infant. They were nuts about each other, but by the time she was two, Blythe was outgrowing her. When she quit, I hired a woman who gave a reference who lied for her. I interview people all the time in my work and I was really flipped out. She turned out to be a druggy and she was arrested with Blythe. The charges: under the influence of a powerful drug on a train platform and endangering the life of our child. This happened just a year after my husband's only son from his first marriage was killed in a car accident. It made us tremble even more at the possibilities of what could have been. We questioned if one of us shouldn't be home. But we couldn't afford that alternative.

"So I hired another housekeeper, who was the paradigm of stability, security, common sense, and competence. However, she lacked a sense of humor and flexibility. I hired her more as a reaction to the bad experience, and I never should have. It was not that she did anything bad with Blythe. Blythe liked her, but I just couldn't get along with her. She resented everything I said; it was all perceived as criticism. She was so defensive, and so difficult that I started avoiding her and I realized I wasn't keeping in contact with my child's routine. I was about to fire her when she found out and left."

At that point Janis was stuck with extending Blythe's preschool day care day to full-time for a month while she looked for a new housekeeper, and she saw how this affected Blythe in a number of bad ways. "That was tough on Blythe; she didn't like it. She was real tired and she worried about not being picked up. She was OK with her teachers, and a little distant with me when I picked her up, but as soon as we hit the car, she would start to scream and it would last forty-five minutes. She was very angry with me and very frightened because she wasn't used to being picked up so late. She wasn't the last one, but that didn't matter. It was also hard on me because I had to do all the cleaning and cooking and laundry and shopping. Preparing supper with a screaming kid around is a pain."

Janis now thinks she's found the right woman to live in, and her daughter is happier. "She is very playful. We wanted someone mature, but someone who had more playfulness, and this woman absolutely has it. She's easygoing. We're sponsoring her so she'll be with us for a while. Blythe is getting better. She's not crying anymore when she's picked up from school. We're keeping her in a full day, so as not to disrupt her schedule again, but as soon as snack time is over at 3:40 P.M., she's home."

However, when Mommy comes home, all is not hugs and kisses at Janis's house as it is at Kathleen's. "When I get there, sometimes I'm bone-tired and not as patient as I'd like to be, and she's getting into a lot of testing. It's a stage and there isn't much I can do about it. She's much better behaved at school, or with friends or the housekeeper. But with me, she tests. She can be as mad at me as she wants to, and as whiny and as changeable as the weather."

The importance of the parents' homecoming each night is stressed by S. P. Hersh, M.D., in *The Executive Parent:* "Returning home . . . is a significant enough transition to deserve the label of 'reentry.' . . . If we fail to recognize reentry as a real issue or fail to deal with it despite our awareness of it, our return home becomes a setup for misunderstandings, resentment, anger, and even for hurtful behavior on everyone's part. . . . Accept that returning home at night is a 'big deal.' Though quiet and often repeated, it still represents one of the day's major shifts within the daily cycle of families. . . . Knowing the importance of reentry, you should make efforts consciously to begin the shift of interest to family as soon as you leave the office."

AN OLD-FASHIONED BABY-SITTER

Many women don't have the space for a housekeeper to live in, or their schedules are so regular that there is no necessity, so they opt for a baby-sitter to come to their house each day to care for their child. Twenty-one percent of these mothers are using this form of care. Deborah, thirty-seven, a director of marketing, went through only one sitter before finding her current one. "I had no standards for hiring and in retrospect I realize I was just grateful that anyone would come work for us. I didn't realize what the gamut of quality was. She never wanted to go out of the house or do anything. She was very intimidated by being asked to go to the store. It didn't matter so much for the first six months, but at that point I realized Jeremy should get out of the house and be doing things." This experience taught Deborah what to look for, and the second time around she chose a woman who has now been with her for four and a half years and gives her the flexibility that a live-in nanny would. She can stay overnight when Deborah or her husband travels. She does housekeeping while Jeremy is in nursery school, then picks him up and takes him to birthday parties and other events.

Anita, thirty-four, a director of community services who has two small boys, has not had such consistency in a caregiver. Her situation is much more typical—she has gone through four people in three and a half years and she still doesn't feel settled. She started out the best way possible: her father-in-law took care of her older son for a year. "It was a wonderful experience; they had a ball. But then he got too old for it and there was the second one to take care of, too, and we got into the baby-sitter routine."

The second sitter she hired turned out to be completely irresponsible. "She was a young girl and she left my kids alone in the house for several hours. The second one was less than a year old and my first was almost two. Quite by coincidence, I happened to come home early because one of them had a cold and I thought I'd knock off and see how he was doing. And she wasn't there. I went through such terror until I found them. They were upstairs in their room, the back bedroom. She had shut the door on them and left them there. When she got back she said, 'Well, they take naps and they stay in there and I had a sick friend I wanted to go see.' The potentially disastrous consequences of this were really brought home to me two weeks ago when we had an electrical fire which started in their room. We happened to be home at the time, but that could have happened when she was out of the house. It makes me shudder.

"Now I have someone I trust. She's an older woman so there is some maturity there, but she has not been as reliable in terms of showing up. When that happens, I have a brother who lives three blocks away and has been unemployed for a year and a half and he comes in. I can also manipulate my four-day schedule and take a different day off, but it's not an area I have any sense of security about right now. My brother should get a job any day, we don't have good backups, and this woman may not work out."

Like a number of women, Margie, thirty-five, a Ph.D. chemist, has made the move from care in her home to an outside baby-sitter as her child has grown older. "First, I had a woman come in who I had advertised for. She was going to arrive at 7:30 A.M. and leave at 6 P.M. That lasted less than two months. My first choice before I hired her was the woman who was doing cleaning for me. She was the local grandmother. She owned a condominium and had two kids in college. She said she didn't feel she wanted to work full-time, but right after I hired this baby-sitter, she changed her mind. So when the baby-sitter quit, I asked the grandmother again and she said yes. In two weeks we switched over and she took care of David until he was two when we moved. The only problem was that right from the beginning she only worked four days a week, so on the fifth day I had someone come into the house. I had all sorts of backups for that person."

Once Margie and her husband moved, the search was on again and this time they chose a different kind of situation because David was older. "The woman who takes care of him now is certified by the state. She has a mini-farm with geese and rabbits, and most important she has another woman who comes in three or four days a week so it's not one harried mother with six kids. She also has a thirteen-year-old son, who baby-sits if I'm late. David has learned to play with other kids and he's learned his letters. You don't get the stimulation when they are there alone with a baby-sitter."

THE DAY CARE HOME

Stimulation for their children is not the only reason that 20 percent of these mothers are choosing day care homes for their children. The good ones are also reliable—a woman doesn't have to wait with baited breath for the arrival of the sitter each morning—and less expensive than an in-home baby-sitter cum housekeeper. Since 34 percent of these women can afford less than $100 a week, they are often limited to such arrangements.

As Margie found out, many states license day care homes, and that can be a good starting point for finding someone to trust. Tessie, twenty-eight, a software engineer and mother of twins, was starting her own business from home when her babies were four months old and she decided to put them into full-time day care. "We always wanted to go to a day care mom rather than a center, especially with babies. Luckily, our first choice was just going back into business and she had both infant positions open and we took them. In Colorado, licensed day care can only have two children under the age of two. She has only one other preschooler, but before and after school she has a lot of kids. My husband drops them off on his way to work and I pick them up. I've had to work a full eight hours the last two or three months, but before that a couple of afternoons a week I would pick up one or the other and spend time with just one baby."

The increasing need for child care has spawned networks of day care homes in some areas of the country, which can help a woman locate a place she thinks will fit her child. When Emma, thirty-four, an advertising executive who quit her job to spend nine months with her son, found a new job, she also found such an organization, which made her child care search a lot easier. "I was very concerned about being able to check out references for day care homes," she says. "I found a group in northern Virginia called Infant Toddler Family Day Care, which finds providers and makes sure they are trained and checks out their references and their homes and drops by periodically. They did all my footwork for me. We interviewed a couple of providers and Daniel started with one when he was eleven months old."

Because this was a time in her child's life when he was still strongly attached to his mother, he had a hard time adjusting at first. "We did a part-time arrangement the first couple of weeks to work Daniel into it," says Emma, "and he was terribly distraught. Our provider said he might well find it easier when it was full-time instead of a day there and a day off. That's what happened. When we started full-time he was upset about it and cried for the first two or three days but after that it was OK."

Other mothers haven't worried about state certification or whether the day care mother is a member of a network. They've looked locally and trusted their instincts. Pat, thirty-seven, a copywriter who until recently worked twenty-five hours a week, found her day care mom by answering her ad in the newspaper. "She's the only one I talked to. My husband took a day off from work and we spoke to her together at her house. We both really like her. She seemed to handle the baby really well. She only lives a mile away and she's the neighborhood day care lady. She has two children of her own who are eleven and thirteen and she's divorced. This is how she supports her family, so she's really reliable. Beth has been there since she was six weeks old; she is now two. There are two smaller children, but none Beth's age. She also takes revolving children, who come when their mothers go out to lunch or for an afternoon of shopping. It's worked really well for me."

Elizabeth, thirty, a financial economist who was able to negotiate a part-time job, found her day care mother on the next block when she went back after her five-month leave. "She is a marvelous woman from South America whom I have a lot of confidence in," says Elizabeth. "The first time I left my daughter there was when I went in to discuss part-time work. Once I got there I felt she was in such good hands I forgot her completely, and now at work I am guilt-free. She's seven months now and I am still breast-feeding her in the mornings and at night so the bond is really strong. She is showing some separation anxiety but I think she is forming a bond with the baby-sitter too. The baby feels very comfortable with her—she smiles all the time.

"She takes care of about four other children, some part-time and some full-time, so the number varies. She also has a daughter who helps her, and a cleaning lady. I've visited and it's very well organized. She has lots of activities and exercises she does with them. She has nicer equipment than I do. I think she's got it down to a science."

DAY CARE CENTERS

Over a third of these mothers have put their babies in private day care centers from the time they went back to work. They usually have not done so as a last resort, but rather, they thought this solution would work for them, and in most cases they believe it has. Dana, thirty, a corporate lawyer, got no maternity leave after her son was born, so three weeks after her C-section she went back to her job and put him in the center her corporation owned, which was two or three buildings from where she worked. This allowed her to nurse him during her breaks and at lunch time. "It was wonderful—the best program in town. The director has computers for three-year-olds. She has gymnastics, ballet, swimming instruction, art—an honest-to-God program. Unfortunately, the company was in the process of selling off its assets to avoid a takeover and soon there were not enough employees to make use of the center, so they got rid of it. But she kept it going and moved elsewhere and we stayed with her until I could find somewhere else close by.

"I found a new center right downtown, fifteen or sixteen blocks from my new office. The program isn't as good, but the food is good quality, everything is fresh. They are adamant on no sugar. The people who run it are Christian and they are very committed to day care, and most important, the day care worker Matt had had since he was about six months old moved with us. That really helped the transition. It would have been very difficult for him to leave her."

This continuity of care, plus the fact that Dana was able to visit the center to nurse her son three times a day when he was an infant, certainly makes her son's situation different from one faced by many babies left in day care for ten to twelve hours. The ratio of caregivers is also excellent: one to six for toddlers and one to five for babies up to eighteen months. Dana has also put her daughter in the center, and she goes at lunch to nurse her. She says, "She's getting wonderful care."

Dana has considered getting a full-time housekeeper, but she has decided against it, not only because it's expensive—$900 a month—but because her son "has flourished in day care. We think one of the reasons he's so gifted is because of the stimulation he has received. He's always been in a class with older children. He crawled at five months and he walked at nine months. He spoke in complete sentences at eighteen months. I think he'd be punished if we took him out because he loves it."

The one thing that worried Dana was Matt's health during the first year. "He got all these ear infections and colds and I went through the guilts: 'Oh my God, what am I doing?' The year he was born six close friends who are lawyers also got pregnant and we all had babies within six months. I was the only one who chose day care and Matt was sicker than the other children. I was in tears at the pediatrician because we were there all the time—at least twice a month. He said that all children have to get sick to build up immunities and that we could either let him get sick now, in day care, or wait until he's in first grade and let him get sick in school, take your pick. He was very supportive, and he was right. Matt is now healthy and rarely goes to the doctor. I firmly believe in day care and honestly I couldn't be happier."

Unlike a live-in housekeeper, day care didn't solve the problems of getting a good meal on the table at night and keeping the house clean. But Dana figured out an ingenious way to take care of that. "I've become pretty creative at finding solutions, and we're in a position to afford to have some things done for us that others can't and that is one of the reason's I'm coping," she says. "During my three-month maternity leave for Cindy, Matt got in the habit of eating a good meal each night and when I went back, I was going wild trying to make dinner when I got home. You know how toddlers are—they can't wait. So for a month, after I nursed the baby at the day care center during my lunch hour, I would rush home and get dinner in the oven with a timer so that it would be ready when we walked in the door. I was going crazy and I realized there must be another solution. What I did was to hire someone to come in once a week to clean and cook and two days a week just to cook. We found a woman we liked and she said it would be no big deal, she was in our neighborhood cleaning anyway. She comes around noon on Tuesday and Wednesday and prepares the recipe I leave and puts it in the oven and sets the timer and it's ready when we get home. On Friday, she cleans and prepares dinner too. By now, she's familiar enough with the kitchen that I don't have to leave the food out. It's as close to heaven as I can come. On the two other days we have leftovers, or I prepare something in advance or use a Crockpot."

Kitty, thirty-two, a data processing manager, has a similar situation to Dana's—with two small boys in day care—and she says, "We joke at work that I really need a wife—a third adult person who stays home and does everything that I have to do: cleans my house, and has dinner on the table when I get home, and puts my slippers on for me. I come home now and look around and say, 'Gee I wish the house were cleaner,' but I don't have the energy to do it. Everyone is screaming, and I give the kids a carrot or a piece of fruit to hold them while I make dinner. We're good at macaroni and cheese and opening a can and to hell with the beef Wellington."

Like Dana, Kitty is very happy with her current day care situation. But the center she originally enrolled her older son in was not at all to her liking. "I started out with a private sitter for Nathan, a lady who lives across our driveway. He went to her from six weeks to seven months when she decided she didn't want to do that anymore. Then we put him in a center, which I found to be a very unhappy place. It was really weird. They would make you drop off the children in the office, and they would never allow you to go back where the children were. When you came at night, you'd have to wait in the office and they'd go get your kid. I couldn't take it. I don't think anything horrible was happening but the couple of times I came at an off hour and no one was there to stop me and I went back, the babies were lying in cribs and the caretakers were reading. I thought it was really horrid. We got him out of there after a month or so and put him where he is now, which is a really good center.

"The only problem is that they don't take babies under ten months, so when Scott was born I had to put him in another center until he was old enough. I didn't want to take Nathan out of the center he was in because he was so used to it and I thought that would make the whole thing worse, so for a while we did a lot of running.

"Now they are together. Both of them are very gregarious and friendly and have adapted well to the day care situation. They seem to thrive on it. The center is in an old ranch house with a basement and they've taken out some walls. They divide the children by age and they spend time playing and learning. They do have a curriculum, even for the little ones. They work on feeding themselves and dressing themselves, and as they get older they start on colors and shapes and ABCs. The center opens at 6:30 A.M. and sometimes they get there that early. It depends on what my day is like—if I have a breakfast meeting or a big project or if I'm out of town and my husband goes to work early. They can stay until 6 P.M. and most of the time it's pretty close to that by the time they get picked up."

These children all started at day care centers as babies. Those who have begun later, after being cared for at home by their mothers or one caregiver, have not reacted nearly as well. Samantha, thirty-five, a weaver with her own business, cared for her son on her own for almost the first year, and after six months with a neighborhood baby-sitter only five hours a day two days a week, she switched to a day care center for two full days a week when he was eighteen months. "He cried every time I left, and I'd think, 'Oh, my God, what am I doing to this child?' I felt really guilty. I think that was more difficult than actually leaving him. I had those same feelings a little bit with the baby-sitter, but they weren't as bad, maybe because he was in a house and he was the only one there besides her son. After a few months, it got better and it's been great for my work. It's also really flexible so if I need extra time before a show or when I'm doing workshops, they will take him for more days during the week. He'll be able to go there until he starts kindergarten."

Ella, thirty-two, a part-time actress and formerly a medical technician, got a divorce when her son was only fifteen months and moved back to Albuquerque where her mother lived. She found a new job and her mother kept her son until he was eighteen months old, when she put him in day care. "It really affected him," she says. "He would just sit on his cot all day and stare ahead. He wouldn't even nap. It sounds like he was almost autistic. He wouldn't talk to them although he was talking sentences to me at home. He was a real early talker. It took him a long time to adjust to that change."

After day care/nursery school comes kindergarten, and the entry of children into the school system is fraught with a whole new set of problems—especially what to do after school.

Milly, thirty-five, a supervisor of municipal finance, has already been through this problem with her eight-year-old daughter, and is going to face it again with her four-year-old son. "The school my daughter is in just started a latchkey child program of gymnastics and arts and crafts, which runs from 3:15 P.M. to 6 P.M. She just stays at school and I pick her up. My son is in nursery school until 11:30 A.M. and I have a baby-sitter who picks him up from school and takes him to her home. I enrolled him in the nursery school because her daughter, who is the same age, is in that school. She moved recently from right near me to a few miles away, but my son is extremely attached to her and her family and the hassle of finding another baby-sitter is so difficult that I stuck with her. My husband picks him up, and we try to meet in the kitchen at 6 P.M.

"It's fine now, but a couple of years were a disaster. After school, we had somebody watching my daughter in our home a couple of afternoons a week, and then she went to a friend's house a couple of days a week. There were days when someone canceled out and then I'd be calling everyone I know. But this latchkey program is wonderful—it takes away so much worry.

"But next fall, I'm going to go through it all a second time. My son will start kindergarten then, but it only runs a half day and the latchkey program doesn't start until 3:15, so I'll have to find a baby-sitter. The one he is with now is in a different town so her daughter won't be in his school. Here it is only November, and I'm worrying about next September. It's something that is always on my mind."

Those Important Backups

Perhaps more than any other circumstance, sickness requires a mother to have backups for child care—especially if their children go to a day care home or center.

Lorraine, thirty-one, the budget analyst for her state, sends her daughter to two sitters with small children of their own, is also married to a man who sees their child as a fifty-fifty proposition when it comes to who stays home. "We alternate days home when she is sick," says Lorraine. "One week she had flu, and one day we both needed to be at work, so what we ended up being able to do was to send her across the street to a neighbor after her school-aged children left, and I got home to pick her up before the children returned. So I ended up taking only half a day off."

When a woman has live-in help or a sitter who comes each day, backups are not needed as often, and usually a husband and wife can manage to cover those times between them. Kathleen and her husband have a live-in nanny and they divide the responsibility for their son equally. "My husband has always helped out, probably more than 50 percent," she says. "There's a reason for it. His mother always worked. She has a Ph.D. in biology and is a deputy director of one of the Institutes of Health in Washington—a big-shot career woman. When he was Justin's age, his mother and father were getting their Ph.D.s and they were poor as church mice. They didn't have a nanny; they had the woman who lived upstairs. So he was raised in that sort of environment where mommy doesn't have to be there all day long and I think it's made a big difference. He doesn't think I'm a bad person. He'd be surprised if I did anything else but work.

"In our house, it's not automatic who stays home if Justin is sick—it's 'What's your schedule today?' and 'What's my schedule today?' We don't stay home all day. One of us takes him to the doctor and then goes in late. He's never been that sick that we felt one of us had to stay home the whole day. It's been ear infections. The first time I did stay home because I didn't know what it was and it was sort of scary, but now I recognize the symptoms and I trust the nanny to take care of him."

Deborah and her husband have an extremely reliable sitter who has been with them for four and a half years, but there are still times when they have to think on their feet because she can't come. "She was on jury duty for two weeks, and once she was ill for eight days," Deborah says. "Now that he's in nursery school, it's a little easier because I have a network of mothers and if I can get a different mother to take him each day after school, I'm covered. I've done the same thing for them."

Before Jeremy started school, covering for the sitter was tougher. "My husband and I know pretty much on an ongoing basis whose schedule is what. Whoever had the most flexibility would move their meetings. I've stayed home and so has he. On those rare occasions where we were both absolutely stuck, we've called the Babysitters Guild, who can have someone in your home in half an hour. I also know people in our apartment building I could call in an emergency to come down and sit for him."

When a woman doesn't have a husband to rely on, she has to have some other fallback arrangement in case she can't stay home, or is stuck in a meeting and can't pick her child up from day care. When Ginger's son was two and a half and she was thirty-one and assistant director of personnel, she separated from her husband and moved out of the house. Her son was in day care which ran until 6 P.M. so she could normally pick him up from work. She and her husband alternated weeks and set up a joint child care arrangement, which is still in operation six years later. But she didn't want to have to call on her ex-husband if she had a problem at work. "The one thing I did very quickly was to hire someone who would not only help me in the house but be available to pick up my son if I had an emergency," she says. "I felt I had to do that, even though spending the money was a bit of a strain. She came every afternoon to do housework for a couple of hours and if I couldn't get away from work, she could pick him up from day care and bring him home and stay with him. That was the kind of safety net I needed. Actually, I rarely had to call on her, but I needed to know she was there. I needed her not only for work, but also to feel independent from my ex-husband. I didn't want to have to call him up and ask him to pick up Charlie because I couldn't get there."

Working at Home

Just like women who work for someone else, most women who run businesses out of their homes hire a sitter or send their child to day care. If they start out without any help, many find that they can't put in enough hours at their business. This was true for Samantha. She was working forty hours a week before the birth of her son, and at first she cut her hours in half and "wove just during his naps and then as his naps got fewer and fewer, I was very frustrated. So I found a woman who would take him two days a week."

Samantha never tried to work at home while her child was cared for by a baby-sitter under the same roof. This mixture can be very difficult for all concerned. Few children seem to be able to tolerate having Mommy there, but not there for them. If they can, it may be because they have gotten used to it from very early on. Denise, thirty-nine, who is in the process of starting a medical care newsletter, puts in six or so hours a day at home while her child is cared for by her nanny. "She's been with baby-sitters once or twice a week ever since she was a few weeks old, and we've had the nanny since she was six months old," says Denise. "She's sixteen months old now, and she doesn't try to get me. She might whine a little bit as I walk back to the back bedroom, but I think that's because I spend so much time with her, and she's so happy with her nanny, she doesn't mind. I'll come out after I've been working for a while, and she's having a great time."

When mothers find it is difficult to operate their businesses out of the same space inhabited by their children, they have two solutions: either the child has to be cared for out of the house, or the business has to move out. Meredith, thirty-nine, a bookkeeper with an eighteen-month-old son, chose to send her son to a sitter in her apartment building. "I had assumed that I could have my son gently playing in his playpen at my knee and everyone told me I was nuts, and of course, they all were right," she says. "It's difficult to realize, I think, how impossible it is to work with a baby in the same room with you. I don't even try to work at home while someone else is taking care of him here.

"He's usually gone for only part of all five weekdays, generally mornings. I know how bad it can be when he is here because I once had a substitute sitter who didn't have a place to take him to and I literally had to crawl behind a counter from one room to the other in order to get to the bathroom so he wouldn't see me. Or I'd ring a little bell and she'd take him out into the hall while I zoomed from one room to another. We have the apartment literally divided in half, with gates and doors and locks between two sections, and my work is in one half. It's physically barricaded most of the time. If he's in the other section with his father, he's OK, but not with a sitter."

Myra, thirty-four, a marketing consultant, also found that coexistence was difficult, but she took the other tack and moved her business out of the house for the four days a week that she works. "Our place was really a bit too small and I'm distracted if I hear him cry, so when he was six months old, I managed to find some space that I'm subletting from a friend that is literally right around the corner. Some of the time I'm home working, but I do make it a point to get to my office a few hours a day. I was able to work it out with the phone company so that I have the same line in both places.

"I was coming home for lunch a lot, but now that he's nine months old, I'm finding that it's somewhat disruptive once I've gone in the morning to come back. It can screw up his whole afternoon. It's almost as if he's waiting for me to come back in the door after I've been gone for a couple of hours.

The sitter says he cries a little bit when I leave and some days he's a little cranky and he keeps looking at the door. So right now, my schedule can't be too flexible. But I don't feel any guilt as I might if I had to drag him to a day care center. He's home and I know he's in good hands."

12

Living Two Lives
Our Home

One moment a woman is pregnant and the next she is a mother, an instant novitiate in that secret society whose membership roll is as long as time itself. Once a member, her life will never be the same again. She may have talked to other mothers and observed friends with their new babies; she may have read books on child development and how to care for an infant, but no one can really tell her how she will feel or what her new life will be like. "I don't think either my husband or I knew what we were getting into when we had children," says Dana, thirty, a corporate attorney. "I don't think you can. People who are already parents will tell you that you won't believe what it will do to your life. And you sort of nod and go, 'Uh, huh.' But you don't know."

One of the main things having a child does to a woman's life is shift her priorities. If she is also working, her life suddenly has little room in it for anything but her child and her job. "I have a good friend who has two young children and I'd seen how her life had moved to center around her kids," says Wendy, thirty-four, a customer communications specialist. "But she was home with them and since I would be working I thought that I would be different. Neither my husband nor I were prepared for how demanding parenting is; how much work it is, how we don't do the things we used to. I think my husband, a little bit more than I, regrets giving up some of that stuff, especially the skiing. I think because I'm working I want to spend every spare moment I have with my daughter. I really guard that time preciously. I think that's one thing that women who are contemplating a career and parenting have to really consider. I've found that just about everything else in my life that was expendable has been expended. I go to work, and I spend as much time as I can with my daughter. The thing which has suffered is time for myself. I don't exercise at all anymore, which I feel really badly about. But I can't justify leaving for an hour in the evening to exercise when I only have three hours. I also don't have the time to spend with friends that I used to—there are only so many hours in the day."

This constant battle with the clock, wishing they could cram more into the hours they have free from work, seems to come with the working mother's territory. Half of the mothers said that having no free time for themselves was one of the toughest aspects of combining motherhood with a career. "Free time for myself?" Meredith, thirty-nine, a bookkeeper with her own business asks incredulously. "I think you'd have to spell each of those words very carefully and give me a dictionary before I could find them. It's very frustrating. I feel so guilty if everyone is out of the house and I have these desperate cravings to sit down and pick up a book. I used to be an enormous reader— I'd go through a book or two a day. And for six months after the baby was born I didn't finish one book. I have no time for it anymore. I'm either working or with him. The day he was old enough to let me close the bathroom door behind me was pure bliss."

The flip side of how little free time a woman has is the number of demands made on her in the time she is home. In *Sooner or Later: The Timing of Parenthood in Adult Lives,* Pamela Daniels and Kathy Weingarten write: "The price of holding down two demanding occupations, one at home and the other away, is high: constant fatigue and overloaded circuits." Janis, thirty-six, a sales planning manager, couldn't agree more. "It's hard to imagine before becoming a parent, the unrelenting demands—no letup, little rest, no moments just to be with myself. As exciting and loving as it was, my first year as a mother seemed like a long treadmill."

"No letup" is also exactly the way Anita, thirty-four, a director of community services, describes her life with two young children. "I may have one or two hours a week—at the most—to do what I want to do, and that is often to take a nap. That's because I'm bone-tired. From 6 A.M. until 9 P.M. when I get my boys to bed I am 'on'—either for my job or as a mom. In many ways, the children are more demanding than my work because of the seemingly ceaseless nature of their needs. I also believe that their demands for caring and attention are heightened because their time with me is limited to three hours a day during my four-day workweek."

The reason these mothers are so exhausted—40 percent say it is one of their major problems—is that, like Wendy and Anita, they are dedicated to spending what time they have left over from work with their children, engaged in quality activities. "We're both really committed to being good parents," says Dana, who has a two-year-old son and a six-month-old daughter. "We spend a lot of time with our children. There's never a moment when we're home that one of us is not with the children. We don't put them in a room and say, 'Go play.' One of us goes in there and plays with them, whatever they want to do.

"The toughest time for us was back when Matt was seven or eight months old and he went through a stage where he woke up at 5:30 A.M. every day. On weekends it was horrible. He'd have only a one-and-a-half-hour nap all day. It was very draining. We were so exhausted we went to bed at 8 P.M. at night. There were other things we wanted to do: we wanted to go skiing, we wanted to goof off, read a book, lay around, ignore him. But we were committed to not doing that. It was very stressful. We finally developed a system where I'd take the morning and my husband would take the afternoon. We still do it with the two of them. So I'll get up, get breakfast, watch 'Sesame Street,' read books, play, whatever. . . . And then come noon it's Daddy's turn, and then at 5 P.M. we both do it. It's meant juggling aspects of our lives that we did not know existed."

Lifestyle = Family Style

Obviously, the commitment to spend time with children instead of running off for skiing weekends, or going out for romantic French dinners à deux, means a radical change in lifestyle. Now that they are parents, these new mothers and fathers do things as a family with their children instead of as a couple. Although nonparents might perceive this change as a sacrifice, mother after mother indicated that she didn't feel this way at all. "Ask me the last time I was out to dinner or a movie," says Pat, thirty-seven, a copywriter and mother of one. "We do go out, but it's once every four or five months. Lots of times we take her with us when we go out to dinner. But frankly, I don't miss the old life. We just have a good time, all of us being together."

This new version of a full life has been embraced by many mothers. One of them is Maude, thirty-four, a manager of marketing and the mother of two. "Having children simply means that one does different things. Instead of going to Paris, we go to Yellowstone. Instead of spending evenings at art galleries, we play our piano in our living room decorated with original artwork by our children. In the continuum of life, twenty years spent living with children is a small percentage, yet children enrich the entire lifetime. What better excuse does an adult have for going to Disney World, reading *Charlotte's Web,* or making model decoys and dollhouses than having to do it 'because of the children'? I do not find raising children to be self-sacrificing. I do it by choice and reap many undefinable and unmeasurable rewards."

Deborah, thirty-seven, a director of marketing, feels much the same way. "Jeremy is very involved in our lifestyle," she says. "Going out to restaurants, on trips. I can't think of a time when we felt we were making a sacrifice because he's here now. We've wanted to go on vacations where he could come with us. I've never had the feeling, 'If it weren't for Jeremy, we could be doing this and this.' "

Obviously, these children have fit nicely into their parents' lives. But if they had come along sooner, that might have not been the case. Mindy, thirty, an airline pilot who works part-time, says this was definitely true for her and her husband. "The first five years of our marriage we spent running around the country," she says. "We flew rock groups to concerts. We took every job we wanted to. We moved ten times. We got a lot of the gypsy out of our systems. By the time our daughter came along, we had settled in. We weren't drinking tequila and dancing all night and getting drunk and going to parties anymore. But she doesn't tie us down. If we want to travel, we hop on the airplane with her and go to Portland or Florida or Phoenix. We don't want to go out very much. We are doing more things at home. I just enjoy being with her, watching her change and learn, playing with her, taking her places. I never had this much fun when I was baby-sitting or taking care of my little brother. My husband feels the same way. It's been so much more fun than we thought it would."

Although she had been worried that having a child would end her social life, Tessie, twenty-eight, a software engineer who had surprise twins, has found that keeping up relationships isn't all that difficult because most of their friends are also new parents operating under the same time restraints she and her husband are. "I thought that once we had babies, we would never socialize anymore," she says. "That's not true. Especially when they were tiny infants, we took them with us to all our parties. We never left them at home. Now that they are a year old, it's more difficult to take them anywhere because they don't sleep except in their own beds, and we also have to get home early because they are awake at 6 A.M. It has ended up that we go out a lot more often with the people who have children."

The feelings of many new mothers about their lifestyle as parents are nicely summed up by Janis: "It's very hard for women who are considering motherhood to understand that mothers don't perceive the trade-offs as a sacrifice.

When parents take their children with them, or say they can't do something because they have to stay with their child, it's not saying that they don't want to be with their child. They are choosing to spend time with their child because it makes them feel good, because the child is a person, and they like being around that person. Women who aren't mothers can't begin to appreciate the reward because they don't know what it feels like. All they can see is what they are losing; they can't see what they are getting instead. For mothers, the trade-offs don't seem like real trade-offs." The truth of this analysis is borne out by the numbers—mothers feel no more frustration in their personal lives than do women without children.

Supportive Husbands

One of the reasons these mothers are happy with their complicated lives is that most of their husbands are extremely involved fathers, and they are often almost equal partners in terms of housework. This equality can make the marriage even stronger. "Having a child has altered my husband's and my relationship for the better," says Wendy, whose daughter is one. "He's a very enthusiastic father and, with both of us working, that is so important—having his concern and his willingness to share the household tasks and the parenting tasks. I feel closer to him for having made a child together."

Many of these women have figured out what household task their husbands like to do—grocery shopping, cooking, laundry, vacuuming—and have ceded it over to their mates on a permanent basis. Anita is married to this type of man, which is a good thing since she hates cleaning and has basically refused to do it. "I'm as lucky as a woman can be when it comes to this kid thing," she says. "My husband is terrifically family-oriented. He loves spending time with the kids; he has changed just as many diapers as I have. He's also pretty good about chores. I think you find a rare one who is doing 50 percent, and he isn't. But he vacuums our nine-room house. I don't even know how the vacuum cleaner works and I don't want to know. Even if the house looks terrible and needs to be vacuumed, I'm not going to do it. That's his thing. Mine is cooking the meals and cleaning up the kitchen. I hate housework, and working at a job is my great excuse for not doing it."

Both child care and chores get divided in half at the home of Milly, thirty-five, the supervisor of municipal finance who has two children, three and eight. "My husband does exactly what I would do," she says. "I don't know how women do it whose husbands don't help. Generally, he thinks of dinner before I do—he's more food-oriented. There are certain things I have to ask him to do—like clean the bathroom. But with most of the household stuff, he is as likely as I am to think of what needs to be done. He'd never dare to say he was out of underwear. When we were first together, I was washing and ironing his shirts and I thought, 'Why doesn't he take these to the cleaner?' I asked him and he said, 'I used to do that before you lived here,' and I said, 'Well you can do it again. I'm not going to wash and iron your shirts.' He picked up on that and realized it pertained to everything. He gets our son, who's three, dressed in the morning. He does whatever a mother would do for a child. I don't know how I would maintain any sanity, or not be even more exhausted than I am if he didn't contribute."

The one area in which Milly feels she is totally responsible is acting as the "psychological parent. I'm the one who's always thinking 'They are due for their shots. Did Sean put an extra sweater on? Sean has the sniffles, I'll have to put on the vaporizer.' If I say to my husband, 'We need the vaporizer,' he will immediately go and get it. But it's draining in itself to have to do all the thinking."

According to these wives, many of their husbands who are helpful now exhibited this kind of behavior long before they became fathers. Some of them grew up this way. Stephanie, thirty-five, who is home with her two children, is married to one of them. "Right now he's folding laundry and putting the baby's clothes away," she says. "Many men in our particular situation would say, 'You are home. You do the house stuff.' But he still shares work with me in the home, more than many men whose wives work outside the home do. He was always like that. He had a mother who when he'd say, 'What's for dinner?' she'd say, 'Whatever you fix.' And he was president of his fraternity and cooked for a hundred people. He was very independent and self-sufficient. Our first date, he made me a duck dinner."

Another reason that many of these mothers keep their sanity is that they have changed their expectations about how clean their house should be, or simply don't take on chores that they might have gotten involved in before they had kids. "Whether or not the brass coat rack gets polished is not a big deal, but at one point it was," says Dana. "We used to haul out the good china and crystal twice a month to eat on because I thought it was obscene to have it and not use it. We'd have a formal dinner in the dining room with candles. Now the stuff sits in the china cabinet and I don't care."

For Kitty, thirty-two, the data processing manager and mother of two, changing her expectations about cleanliness has helped keep her marriage working because her husband is not an egalitarian partner when it comes to housework. "He's wonderful with the children," she says. "He's just a terrific father and he'll do anything with the kids. I think he really believes that he helps around the house, but I don't agree, and it's a source of contention. He probably does as much or more than most men I hear about, but the laundry basket could sit there for a week with dirty clothes in it and he just doesn't see it. I think if there were no clean clothes in his drawer he'd find some dirty ones and put them on. I certainly have relaxed my standards over the years. I've never been the happy homemaker, but I do like to know that the health department wouldn't shut me down."

How helpful husbands are about chores is obviously an issue apart from how much responsibility they are willing to take in the care and nurturing of their children. Most of these fathers have been very involved right from infancy. When a mother is home with a baby, on duty twenty-four hours a day, having her husband take over at the end of the day can be the difference between sanity and the asylum. It was for Denise, thirty-nine. "During the first six months when I was here alone," she says, "I felt the responsibility so intensely, and when my husband would come home, we'd always joke that he'd been to the beach all day and now it was time for him to go to work. And I'd go out and go over to Burger King and read in peace for an hour and totally relax. He has a really good attitude, and he's so helpful."

Quite a number of these men had children in previous marriages and the experience of fathering that time around was not a very satisfying one. They are making up for it with their new offspring. The husband of Victoria, thirty-two, the anesthesiologist, is in the process of starting his own business from home—something which is possible only because she is making enough money. He thus has more time with his son, now eleven months, than she does. "He does a lot with the baby, and he's really involved," says Victoria. "His first child was an unsatisfying relationship, and he's had to redeem himself in a lot of ways. He's enjoying it very much. On the weekends when the nanny is off, he has the baby all the time when I'm working. When I'm working during the week, particularly on a thirty-six-hour shift, he'll bring the baby down at night to visit and have dinner. He's been really supportive."

When they met, the mate of Janet, thirty-nine, a professor and writer, had two children from his first marriage, and his teenaged son was living with him. At that point, he didn't want to have any more children because the two he had were causing him enough trouble. But, she says, "He has never regretted the decision to have another child. Our son is very bright and very strong-willed, which makes him a trial often enough. But he is also loving and delightful. I marvel at him daily, as does David. He has much more to do with him than he had with his two older children—the opportunity of being a different kind of father. I love watching them together, and David is thankful for this new experience he couldn't have predicted."

Fatherhood is a process of adjustment just as motherhood is, and some men grow into their new role more slowly than others. But, as babies become children with whom fathers forge a relationship, giving up favorite activities in order to spend time with their offspring comes more easily to many of them. "It's sort of evolved that my husband takes Jeremy to school," says Deborah, whose son is four. "Even though the housekeeper could do it, he likes that time with his son. They do lots of activities together, and when I'm on the road, they go out to dinner, just the two of them. My husband really enjoys it. He loves the camaraderie and the things they do together. I think he would be absolutely lost without Jeremy. He is in his fifties and I know he's feeling as if there is going to be a time in his life where he's going to want to spend more time on the golf course, but he's conscientious enough that right now he'd have a hard time doing that at the expense of time with Jeremy."

On the other side are a few husbands who have gone right on with their lives, at work or at play, as if they had never become fathers at all and it doesn't make their wives one bit happy. That is the situation Samantha, thirty-five, a weaver, is facing because her husband's business is so time-consuming. "He's at work twelve hours a day six or seven days a week," she says. "It's awful. We hardly ever see him. When it's your own business, you have to devote more time to it, I know that. But I'm still really resentful. I'm having a difficult time. I will put aside my work to do family things, and he won't. Ethan really misses his father. There are times when he'll just sit and cry and say, 'I want my pop pop.' I'll tell him that he's at work and there are times he can sort of understand that, but there are other times when it doesn't help. And it's bad for Tom too because he's missing out on so much of his son growing up and really knowing him."

Karen, thirty-two, who has an eight-month-old daughter and is home full-time, has suffered not because of her husband's work but because of all his other activities, which he has not been willing to curtail. "My husband is a very active person, not a homebody," she says. "Getting him to calm down his nonwork activities so he's home more has been a real problem. Maybe I'm not feeling it so much right now because it's not golf season. He's a real golfer, and during the season he's usually not home on the weekends. He's not willing to make changes on that front. When the season starts again, he'll be right back to it. I don't know how I'll handle that. Maybe we'll go along with him."

Marriage Consequences

When these mothers look at the state of their marriages after motherhood, they often feel badly on behalf of their husbands because they aren't devoting the attention to them that they once did. Over a third of them regret having so little time for their husbands. Meredith, thirty-nine, a bookkeeper with her own business, says, "All the mothers I've spoken to have the same problem. There's not enough of us to go around. My husband is having more trouble figuring out his career moves because I can't be as supportive. I don't catch the signals as fast. I'm so distracted by everything else that is going on in the house. It's both the time and the emotional energy. There are times when I absolutely resent sitting still and watching a TV program together because I know that if I could only get that load of laundry done I wouldn't have to do it tomorrow. I know that's not fair to him."

Even when a woman is not working, she can feel this way. Tammy, twenty-eight, who quit her administrative job with a Fortune 500 company to stay home with her son, says, "It took a while for Roger and me to adjust to marriage with a baby. In the very early months, the baby took a higher priority than I thought he would. Mentally, I spent so much time paying attention to the baby that I felt badly I didn't give attention to Roger."

Some husbands are quite open in letting their wives know that they still need attention. Eleanor, forty-six, a psychologist, is married to one of them. "Things have definitely changed in our marriage," she says now, five years after her daughter was born. "She definitely takes up time I had alone with my husband, and he complained about that, especially during the first year or two. He said, 'You're not the same anymore.' I think what changed was that I used to mother him a lot, pouring all my mothering into thinking about his comfort, and when I had a baby, I had another outlet for those feelings, and I expected him to grow up, and he didn't like that idea. We talked this over many times, and he finally understood that I'd gone through a phase of mothering him, but it wasn't in my lifetime contract. He sort of moved out of that phase, and into an extraordinarily busy work phase, with overstress. So I took on a sort of counselor role. But we didn't have time to do that in the evenings with our daughter, so what we'd do is sleep for a few hours and then wake up in the middle of the night and talk. That's when we really settle most of our problems. We also schedule time together. We make dates for dinner regularly. We plan surprises for each other, with one of us taking the other one out for a whole evening with interesting things to do."

When a woman works full-time in an office and has a baby or a toddler at home, the stress on a marriage is probably at its highest, and time off as a couple is extremely important. "The marriage is the most vulnerable in terms of being shortchanged," says Anita, who has two boys, ages two and three and a half. "If I am too tired from work and the kids, I don't want to stay up to talk with my husband. I don't have the energy. And though I may feel like making love, I'll get the urge at 10:30 A.M. when I am at work and by 10:30 P.M. a team of charging horses couldn't wake me. As soon as my head hits the pillow, I'm out. The year I had my second, it was the worst. I was a walking zombie. I really felt that we weren't doing right by each other, and I longed to get away and just be with my husband. But because we saw our children so little during the week, it was hard to 'abandon' them so we could go to a show or dinner. Also, I didn't even have the energy to go out. I wanted him to watch the kids for me so I could have a nap. Now that they are older, we've gotten out more and it's been terrific. What a difference to have a couple of dates now and then. You have to make a commitment to do that."

Many of these women have found that getting away together—even just for a weekend or an overnight—can act as a restorative tonic for a marriage that isn't getting the attention it deserves. Margie, thirty-five, the Ph.D. chemist and midlevel manager at a major corporation, just went away for her first overnight with her husband, leaving their three-year-old son with his baby-sitter. They had been through a rough year. Their son had constant ear infections and a burst eardrum and they built their own house and moved. "In trying to do all of this, my relationship with my husband often took lowest priority. I have to plan every hour and make time for him, and I'm not always successful. If we didn't have a good marriage, we wouldn't be together —not after this last year. The overnight was great for both of us. He said he thought it was a really good idea and that we should do it three or four times a year. I said, 'Bravo.' "

Janis and her husband are also trying to schedule time away but recently it has been difficult. "My husband is vital to me, but the constant stress and fatigue have had an impact on my role as a wife. My sexual desires are very low. Disappointing as it is to me, I try to respond to my husband. I just keep thinking that we have to keep in contact and get through the next year or two. I don't see anything coming up soon to improve things—not until his work schedule changes. But it's a very strong marriage. I know that is true when I think of the stress we've had to live with—the death of his twenty-year-old son from his first marriage in an auto accident, my father in the hospital for six weeks, his father with open heart surgery, and my mother with cancer—and see that we've been able to work through all of it and stay strong."

When a Marriage Doesn't Make It

Only 15 percent of the mothers who had children late have been involved in marriages that didn't work out, leaving them to cope with motherhood as single parents. But having children under even these conditions has not made them any less happy being mothers. It's not an easy road to travel, but their caravans have moved forward on pretty solid wheels. And in many cases, they have hooked up with another man and made a new life as a family.

Of all the divorces described by the women interviewed, Melissa, thirty-two, a secretary, has been through the most devastating, and even she is happy she has her little boy. "My husband left before my son was born," she says. "We'd only been married for a short time although I'd known him a long time. He lost his job and then I became pregnant and everything was going fine for a while—Philip was very excited about it. But then he slowly started withdrawing. A couple of months before the baby came, he left. He was a very violent person, and he became more so the longer the pregnancy went. I don't think he could handle the fact that he was having a child. He has no contact with us at all. He sends financial support through the courts because the courts make him, but it's very minimal—$150 a month. He's only seen his son once at six weeks old. That's the only time he has had any contact with us in four years. It's been pretty hard.

"I had made arrangements at work six months before the birth of my baby to hire my replacement and train her and get her ready to take my job. I was going to stay home for a few years and then everything fell apart; everything started crumbling around me. I had to move home to my mother's. I was without a job. After five months I went back to work and went on living with my mother until Billy was about six or seven months old, and then I found a duplex and we moved.

"I felt very withdrawn from my son in the beginning. A lot of times, I'd forget I even had a baby. I'd be sitting at work, hearing other people talk about their babies and it wouldn't even occur to me that I had one too. I felt some bonding with him, but it wasn't as it should have been because I was going through so many other things. I could feel this detachment. It was really sad. That whole first year was very difficult. But we're close now. He's four.

"I started putting things back together about a year and a half ago. We're getting by. My job is kind of a dead end, and I've been looking for another one. I'd like to make more money, to have some cushion there. As Billy gets older, the expenses are going to get greater with sports and school.

"My mom has been very supportive. She babysits at night and I have next-door neighbors who have been wonderful and have helped me a lot. I also have a lot of wonderful friends. They care about us and they are there to help. But I know they'll never really understand. Some of them have babies, and when I see the fathers with the babies, I can hardly handle it. Those fathers are so involved with their babies. I'm happy for them, but I wish so much it had been my situation. I sometimes feel sorry for myself that I have to do it all."

Just like women who are single mothers by choice, Melissa is faced with the problem of what to tell her son about his father, and what to do if Philip ever comes back into his son's life. "So far, Billy has only asked one time about his father, and I said his daddy doesn't live here. It was at his birthday party and the little girl sitting next to him said, 'Is his daddy dead?' and I said, 'No, he isn't dead.' She said, 'He doesn't have a daddy.' I said, 'Yes, he does, he just doesn't live here.' She said, 'Did he send him a birthday present?' I said, 'No, honey.' Billy just kind of watched me, but that's all he asked. I don't know what I'll say if he asks why his father isn't here. I've thought about it a lot, but I keep changing my mind about what to say. I do know I don't want to say anything mean about Philip. I don't want to damage that relationship in case it ever develops. Even though he neglected us early on, if Philip ever came back into Billy's life, I wouldn't stop them from having a relationship.

"So far, Billy is very confused about what a daddy is. He'll see friends with a daddy and he'll say, 'Where's Daddy?' Billy just doesn't understand. A month ago I heard a friend ask him, 'What's your daddy's name?' and he said Big Bill, which is what he calls the man I'm dating. He does not understand what a daddy means."

Unlike Melissa, many of the divorced women were in marriages that they knew weren't sound even before they got pregnant. After their child was born, they tried to stay with their husbands, but eventually initiated the move to end the marriage, taking on single parenthood as part of the deal.

For Grace, forty, the head of reference at a university library, a change in her career circumstances convinced her to get pregnant even though she was not happy in her marriage. "When I was growing up I had always thought I would have children, but I had been married for eight years when my daughter was born. My ex-husband was the emotionally fragile type—prone to depression—and I felt he was not a good role model for a child.

"We both worked in a large university. I loved my job and became very good at it while my husband struggled with the 'publish or perish' attitude of the university. Although he was a conscientious instructor and gradually made a name for himself doing research in his chosen field, he did not develop professionally at a fast enough rate for the university and his contract was not renewed at the end of his fourth year. He spent a year out of work while he 'job-hunted' and continued his research. He did nothing part-time to bring in money and I supported us both with my salary and the savings we had put aside.

"At this time I never even considered having a child because I was afraid to depend financially on him while I was out of work having the baby. I was not happy with him and felt a child would complicate life too much. Eventually, he was offered a teaching position in a four-year college and we planned to move. I gave up my job with great reluctance. In fact, I even toyed with the idea of leaving him and staying at the university. But finally I decided to go with him. We bought a house and I faced the fact that in a small town I could not find a job. So I became pregnant. I knew that once I went back to work I would not want to take time off to have a baby so this was the perfect time. I was out of work for three years altogether before a suitable job opened up in the library of the college where my husband taught.

"My husband was doing well in his new position and got promoted, but I never felt financially secure and I was still not happy. One of my reasons for going back to work was so that I could support myself, take my daughter, and leave my husband. He did not want me to go back to work and said he would do nothing to help me. That crystallized my resolve to leave him as soon as I could afford to do so. I thought his attitude was incredible. When I started work, my daughter was two and a half, and as soon as I could, I left." Since then, Grace has remarried, and has a baby boy with her second husband.

For some women, divorce, however hard it has been, has turned out to be what they needed in order to live full, successful lives. "I have two gorgeous girls, aged five and six," says Corinne, thirty-one, a regional assistant. "I've never regretted having them even though it was tough when I was first divorced—they were two and three at the time. I know many aspects of my life, both professional and social, would be less complicated without them, but I can't imagine feeling wholly satisfied and happy with my life if it weren't for them. I've come a long way since my divorce, both personally and professionally, and quite frankly, I wouldn't have it any other way."

Audrey, thirty-six, a sales manager and divorced mother of two, expresses many of these same feelings. "How do I feel about having children? I love it. While it hasn't been a cakewalk—I put my career on hold for years in order to be with them when they were tiny, and the three of us went through a gut-wrenching custody battle which lasted two years and cost $20,000—motherhood makes everything else possible. It's allowed me to grow mentally and spiritually. It's forced me into making tough decisions I wish I could have avoided. My children provide the constant courage and willpower that make my challenging career possible. They told me I could succeed when I doubted I could. Last year, I earned more money than I ever dreamed of."

13

Single Mothers
And Baby Makes Two

All across the country, single women are getting tired of waiting for a husband in order to start a family, and are going ahead on their own. Out-of-wedlock births to white women increased by 17.6 percent in 1980 alone. Chapters of Single Mothers by Choice are springing up in cities from Maine to Oregon.

An astonishing 20 percent of the mothers surveyed for this book have gone this route and had babies without being married. For some of these women, single motherhood was premeditated. Ten percent, for instance, had artificial insemination (AI). But over three quarters of them got pregnant by their boyfriends, and in many cases, pregnancy was accidental, or the result of letting nature take its course—not exactly planned, but not prevented either. This is not to say that these women didn't want to have babies. Two thirds of them had always dreamed of having a child, and when they found out they were pregnant, they chose not to have an abortion. But they did not necessarily plan on this course of action.

Many of these women are strong, independent thinkers who have not been slowed down by fear or by responsibility. Some stood up to angry boyfriends who demanded they get an abortion. Half of them have managed without any involvement from the father at all. He walked away and has never been heard from again and they have coped on their own—emotionally and financially. Many have friends who have pitched in. Others have moved back to their hometowns to be near their families. Thirty percent of the men who fathered their children have maintained some contact, but in most cases the mothers are the only daily parent, managing all the demands, stress, and anxiety without support. They have no one to turn to when child care falls through, no one to take over when they are exhausted, and no one with whom to share the joy of their child. And they do without the safety net of a partner's income.

However, in spite of the difficulty of their position, the single mothers are happy they have had a child; they would not undo what they have done, and they believe they can make a good life for their child. Those who are entirely alone are far happier with their lives than those in situations where the father is still involved in some way. Being the sole provider has given many of these women the impetus to pursue more challenging and lucrative jobs—almost 40 percent have done so, compared to only 23 percent of the married mothers. Many others were already established in their careers and motherhood has not affected their status. Nearly a third of the single mothers are professionals, and another third are in management or supervisory positions.

Having a child by themselves has not necessarily meant the end of romance. The fathers may have walked away, but other men have come into their lives. Almost 20 percent of them have found the right guy and gotten married. Over 10 percent are living with a man. But the rest have remained unattached, and some of them intend to stay that way—they have no desire to ever get married, or remarried. Surprisingly enough, over 40 percent of the single mothers had been through a bad marriage and were divorced before getting pregnant and deciding to go it alone.

Just like many married mothers, single mothers usually do not seem to have a very long-range vision about their children. It's the weeks and months immediately ahead that count—orchestrating child care and work schedules, and enjoying the time they have together. They don't really want to think about the difficulties their child may experience later on because they don't have a father. In fact, some of these mothers seem to want to believe a father is not that important—since they can't go out and simply find one. Most of them have thought about what they will tell their child about his or her father and why he isn't there, but these musings are purely theoretical until the questions actually get asked.

Here are a few of their stories. Some women have given birth in recent months; others have toddlers or older children. Some are alone in the world with this great responsibility, while others are negotiating with the fathers over their role. And some have established a relationship for their child with the father, if not for themselves.

The Father Walked Out

Fern, thirty, a police officer, and Milly, thirty-five, a supervisor of municipal finance, both were entirely alone as they set forth into the land of motherhood. The fathers disappeared from their lives as soon as they heard they were pregnant.

FERN'S STORY

Fern's son is now two and a half months old. She is out on maternity leave, and expects to return to work in six weeks. "The father is married. He and I were really good friends," she says. "We were intimate, but we were also good friends. I didn't plan to get pregnant, but I didn't do anything to prevent it. It took a few months. I was two months pregnant when I told him. I wasn't going to tell him at all, but then at the last minute I decided to, and I shouldn't have. He cursed and hollered at me and screamed that he would never speak to me and that he wanted to spit in my face and hated me for going through with it. He felt used. He says he was set up. He wants nothing to do with either of us. I think if I hadn't told him so early, he would have found out on his own and we would still be friends."

Fern's own father took the news a lot better. "I had pretty much prepared him ahead of time—and my sister had already done the same thing. My niece was born almost exactly a year before my son. Sometime during the summer before I got pregnant, I mentioned to him that I wanted to have a baby and he said, 'You're old enough to do what you want, but it's a big decision. You better think about it first.' So when it was time to tell him, he guessed."

Fern's female friends also know that this was something she had wanted for a long time, and, she says, "they were happy for me. Male friends, for the most part—and I was surprised—didn't try to stay away from me for fear of being labeled the father. The father stayed away, but even his best friend would dance with me when I went out. I said he better not do that because someone might think he was the father and he said, 'What's the difference? It will keep them guessing.'"

But the problem was that people did want to guess. They kept asking her who the father was when she went out. "I got real sarcastic toward the end when they'd ask that. It seemed so ridiculous. I'd say, 'Hey, I don't ask who you sleep with.' Someone asked me, 'Whose is it?' I said, 'Excuse me?' And he repeated the question, and I said, 'It's mine.' He said, 'I know that.' And I said, 'Then why did you ask?' And at that point, he kind of caught the hint: 'She knows what I mean but she's not going to tell me.' That got on my nerves a lot."

Luckily, Fern did not experience any of this sort of harassment at work. "I got pregnant when I was off work on disability because I was injured in an auto accident while on the job," she says. "When I went back, I was out on the street for about a week, and then I took them my little doctor's note saying I was pregnant, and they put me inside at a desk. I didn't want to stay out on the street because I didn't think I'd be safe, or the baby would be safe. I was assigned an office where I knew absolutely nobody, so I had all new people to work with, and they were pretty good to me. They treated me well, and went out of their way to help me. If I needed a glass of water, they'd get it for me."

Fern worked up until two days before the birth of her son. "I got off work at midnight Tuesday and I had Wednesday off and my waters broke that night. My best friend and another friend coached me through labor and my best friend was in the delivery room with me. It was the most wonderful experience of my life. They induced me about 10 A.M. and he was born around 6 P.M. I was ecstatic at the birth and during the first few days. I felt really confident. I had wanted to have a child for a long time, and I just knew I could take good care of him. My only fear concerned my work schedule.

"We work rotating shifts and there is no way in the world I can go back to that schedule because I have no one who can watch the baby on that schedule —even members of my family. And even if I found some poor soul who would do that from midnight to 8 A.M., how am I supposed to sleep and take care of the baby during the day? So I'm going to try to finagle a day-work job. But I'm not sure I'll be able to do it. There are no women who have done it for this reason. I know of men who have gone to their commanding officers and said, 'Look, I'm in trouble. My wife left me and I'm stuck with the kids. I need a steady shift,' and they've gotten it. But whether or not they'll do it for me, I don't know. I've been there almost six years. I'm going to speak to my commanding officer in a couple of weeks. If I have to crawl in on my hands and knees with the baby in one hand and a handkerchief in the other, that's what I'll do. I don't know what my chances are. He's a captain I haven't worked for because he was transferred in while I was in the other office. I don't know what he's like."

Meanwhile, Fern has found someone to babysit for her on the assumption that she'll go back on a regular day shift. "A friend of mine had been telling me for a year, 'Fern, if you decide you want to have a baby, go ahead and get pregnant, and I'll watch the baby.' She has two of her own. Then right after I got pregnant, she called me up and said, 'You're going to hate me, but I'm pregnant again.' That cut her out. Shortly after my son was born, I was at the house of a good friend who also recently had a baby and we were talking about going back to work and not knowing how I would handle it and her mother offered to do it. I was really glad."

Although worries about her work are paramount for Fern, she also is concerned about what she will tell her son about his father. "I haven't heard from him since the birth," she says. "I sent him a birth announcement—I figured, why not? He was a friend before this. I talked to him once after our screaming match. When I was about seven months pregnant, I called to ask him, 'Do you still hate me?' When he answered the phone, and I said it was Fern, he was very cordial and courteous. I could hardly believe it. He said, 'Oh, hi. How are you doing?' and he asked how I was feeling and how much weight I had gained, and all sorts of nice questions. He also asked when I was taking vacation and I said I wasn't taking any, and he asked why not and I said I'd be taking it in September when the baby was due. He said, 'Oh, yeah.' I was almost tempted to ask him if he really knew who this was on the phone because I expected him to hang up on me and tell me he despised me. It threw me for a loop. I'm hoping at Christmas time he'll break down and bring over a gift, but we'll see. If he wants to come over and see him once a week, or once a year, or once a day, that's up to him. I would never prevent him from seeing his son.

"If he came back into our lives and he wanted me to let my son know he's his father, I would. But if he didn't, I wouldn't tell until my son is a lot older. If he stays away, I would tell my son that his father is a very good man, a very decent man, and because of his responsibilities to another family he couldn't be around. He just couldn't be. His marriage is not going to end. If he told me once, he told me a hundred times how much he loves his wife and he could never envision leaving her, or her leaving him, and he'd be devastated if she did. I kept asking him, 'Then why are you doing what you are doing?' and he'd say, 'I don't know.'

"I never want to get married. Since I've had the baby, it's firmly reinforced my notion of never getting married. I've run across a hundred men in the last ten years who say, 'My wife is a rotten this and that . . .' and they play around. But to see the father of my son, a man who loves his wife so much, or at least professes to, and he's also playing around. . . . I'm surely not the first, and I know I'm not the last. I can't see myself as another one of those wives—the poor woman who's been married for twenty years and the husband has been playing around behind her back and she thinks everything is great and she doesn't suspect a thing. I would never want to be put in that position because I'd kill him. I'd rather avoid the whole situation and never get married. I'd live with someone. It's just that I couldn't make a commitment because there is no man I know in this day and age who could keep that commitment, except my father."

MILLY'S STORY

Milly began her life as a single mother eight years ago in similar circumstances to Fern's—but a lot has changed since then. "I was nearly twenty-eight when my daughter was born," she says. "The pregnancy was an accident and I considered having an abortion, but I didn't because of my age. I couldn't justify doing it and at the same time really wanting to get pregnant before I was thirty. I had a feeling I'd go out and get pregnant again on purpose, just to have a child, so I decided to go ahead.

"I knew what the father's attitude would be—get an abortion—so I waited until I was over four months pregnant to tell him. We saw each other during that time, but we weren't living together, so when I was vomiting, he wasn't there. When I told him, he left, which was fine with me. I knew he was going to do that, and I really didn't give him much choice. I said, 'I'm having this baby. You do what you want to do.' "

That was the last contact Milly ever had with the father. She soon moved back to Maryland from California to be near her family but even with their support, the months of her pregnancy were not easy ones. "I was frightened," she says. "Had I realized how hard single motherhood would be, I would have been more frightened. I was too stupid. As it got closer to my due date, I got more scared, especially because by then I was unemployed. I had been doing secretarial work as a temp, so no one I worked with knew I wasn't married and I kept it that way. People kept telling me, 'God, it's so hard to have a baby, even with a husband. What are you going to do without a husband?' And I kept saying, 'There are divorced women who do it all the time. They love their kids and they raise them. If they can do it, I can do it.' But it's different when you're alone through the whole thing."

Milly was even alone for the birth because her sister didn't make it on time. "It was just me and the nurses and the doctor," she says. "It was the best experience of my life. It was wonderful, just wonderful. But then we got home. The first months could best be described as a disaster. I went on welfare because I wasn't working. Financially, it was very difficult. But I don't think that bothered me as much as being totally responsible all the time. Linda was not a very cooperative baby. She screamed for the first five months, which made me say, 'You fool! They were right. You should not have done this.' My family was around, but all my sisters were working, and my mother couldn't do a lot, and I was alone. I remember having five huge plastic bags of garbage sitting in my kitchen waiting to go to the dumpster, which was way back behind my apartment, and I just did not have the energy to get back there. Simple things like that—like mailing a letter—were a real physical drain. Everywhere I went, Linda had to go. It's just so much work. The physical and psychological are all intertwined. You know when she's screaming and it's two o'clock in the morning, that you are the only one there. You are the only one who can get the bottle and feed the baby. And the physical exhaustion makes the responsibility seem even heavier.

"It was a good sixteen months before I was physically recovered. Linda didn't sleep through the night until she was over two. She stopped screaming finally, and by sixteen months, she only woke once a night. By then, I was working steadily and I didn't have to worry financially so much. I was also away from her for those hours, and that made a difference."

When Linda was eighteen months old, Milly met a man and her life changed. "We met at a pool party given by a friend. I can't say it was love at first sight, but I did know the first time I went out with him that I would marry him. It was really strange, since I had no intention of getting married. The one thing that disappointed me about staying single was that Linda would not have any brothers or sisters. I come from a family of seven and my sisters are very important to me. I felt bad for her that she wouldn't have those kinds of relationships. I also realized that there would be many awkward situations for her as she got older. It's difficult for little kids to lie and say that their parents are divorced when they know that's not true. But marriage itself had never appealed to me.

"And then I met Joe. I guess I had never met anyone I wanted to be married to before. He changed my mind about it. It was serious for him right away too. We got married a year later when Linda was two and a half. Joe was very family-oriented. He was interested in having a family, so it was almost perfect for him—here was an instant family.

"Joe has adopted her. She knows she's adopted. She knows there was what she calls 'the first father.' But she really hasn't asked that many questions about it. It normally doesn't come up in conversation. It's not something I would ever lie to her about, and I will still have to tell her who he was and why he left and exactly what happened. There are too many people who know that I was single when she was born, and I wouldn't want her finding out from someone else. She can't go looking for him, because he died in an accident. That alleviated a lot of problems for the future, and it made it easier for my husband to adopt."

Since her marriage, Milly has had a second child, a son, who is now three, so she has seen motherhood from both perspectives. "It is a hundred times more difficult when you are alone," she says. "The second time around was so much easier psychologically because there was someone else to share the responsibility with, someone else who had total responsibility for that child too. It was his as well as mine. He was there."

Negotiating a Father's Rights

The man who inadvertently fathered the child of Olive, thirty-eight, a psychiatrist, was extremely angry at her for refusing to have an abortion. But communication was not entirely broken off, and after the birth she began a process of negotiation as to what the father's involvement—if any—in time and money, would be.

OLIVE'S STORY

Olive had known the father of her seven-week-old son for only three months when she found herself accidentally pregnant because her diaphragm didn't work. "My period was three days late and I looked at myself in the mirror and I said, 'You're pregnant.' I did a home pregnancy test, and then I had it confirmed with a blood test. I was really excited. I had wanted to have a baby. But I kept putting my cutoff date up another year, and if it hadn't happened this way, I don't know how long I would have gone, but I probably would have had artificial insemination in another year or two.

"I waited until after the real test to tell Peter, the father. He vehemently wanted me to get an abortion. He screamed and yelled and had temper tantrums. I vaguely considered an abortion because I hate to make other people unhappy, but I realized it was either him being unhappy or me being unhappy. Our relationship seemed to end the minute I told him, but he was around for two or three weeks screaming at me. It's hard to deal with someone yelling at you as if you were a terrible person. He said it was the worst thing that had ever happened to him, and I was ruining his life and how could I do this to him. I felt as if he were this little boy, about fifteen years old. He said, 'I don't love you. I don't want to marry you. I don't want anything to do with this, and if you have this baby, don't expect me to have anything to do with it because I won't.' I just said, 'OK, if you want to be that big an idiot, go ahead.'

"Peter had been married for ten years and then gotten divorced. They never had any kids because he was never sure if it was the right person or the right time. When I got pregnant, he said, 'It's not the right time.' I said, 'Jeez, if everyone waited until it was the right time to have kids, there would be a lot fewer kids in the world. Besides, you may think it's the right time, but then you can lose your job, or get sick—anything can happen. You can think your life is all planned and you can get exactly what you want, but then something changes.' He's thirty-seven years old and he says he wants to get married and have a family, but when? My biggest fear while I was pregnant was that he'd get married to someone and four or five years later he'd want to have a child and discover she didn't want to, or couldn't and he'd come back looking for his only kid."

Peter pulled out of Olive's life, but he kept calling her up during her pregnancy and making her very angry. "He kept working this whole thing out in his head, what he was going to do," she says. "I had told him he could do what he wanted to do, that I wasn't going to go after him for child support and he could do what he goddamn pleased. So he would intermittently call me up and tell me he thought we should meet, or that he'd decided that he should always let me know if he was out of town so I'd know where he was so that if in three or four years an emergency came up, I could find him. And I said, 'Gee whiz, I'm kind of more worried about an emergency in the next few months.' And he'd say, 'Oh, I guess so.' Then later, he called up and said he'd be real noble and helpful and make sure I got to the hospital when I was in labor, and he'd call my girlfriends who were my coaches and wait until they got there and then leave. I told him that if I wanted a cab, I'd call a cab. If it wasn't an emergency, I could certainly get a cab, and that if he were going to walk out on me again, I didn't want to have him around. He had a real good knack for saying the wrong thing and setting me off on screaming binges about what a selfish human being he was."

Aside from these phone calls from Peter, Olive's pregnancy went fine. "I had periods of being real lonely," she says, "but it's easier to be alone than to have someone around who isn't supportive, who refuses to deal with it, or is stupid. I sometimes worried, 'How are you going to handle it? How is every-one going to react and what are you going to do?' But basically I figured it would work out. My family reacted OK. My brother lives about a hundred miles away and he was fine, and my mother was really supportive, which surprised me. When I told her I was pregnant, she said, 'Oh, fine. Whatever you want to do.' My friends were great. A good proportion of them are married with teenaged kids. I really didn't have any friends who were preg-nant. Most of my girlfriends are my age and single. The guys who are friends still came around pretty regularly. They either have no kids, or are divorced and have older kids. Because it wasn't going to be their responsibility, they were supportive.

"Physically, I didn't have any problems at all. I was exhausted in the early months, but that went away. I went to pregnancy fitness class at the YMCA and I swam almost every day for the last six months. I decided I wasn't going to gain a lot of weight and I put on only thirty pounds. I even went white water rafting in my little inflatable kyack when I was seven months pregnant. I didn't worry about the baby because I had CVS testing so I'd know early if something was wrong. If something had been wrong, I would have had an abortion. I knew the results in three days. They gave me the choice of know-ing the sex and I said, 'If you know, I'm going to know.' I didn't have a preference for a boy or a girl—I couldn't decide if having a boy without a father or a girl without a father would be easier."

Olive's friends were there for her right through the birth. "One girlfriend went to classes with me," she says. "When Peter made his noble offer to drive me to the hospital, I asked if he wanted to come to any classes, but he couldn't deal with that. My friend's twelve-year-old daughter came to the birth. Another girlfriend also stayed with me through the whole thing. I was a week late and I was going to have a nonstress test, but I ended up leaking fluid. I went to the hospital and they kept me there. Labor just wasn't pro-gressing, and the bag ruptured fully and there was some fetal distress, so I had a C-section at 1 A.M. I had an epidural so I was awake. It didn't bother me to have the section. The baby was fine—that's what was important. I felt, 'I'm not a supermom, and whichever way is the best, I don't really care.'

"After they checked him out, they gave him to my girlfriend, who gave him to me to hold. When I held him I felt like, 'Oh, my goodness, he's really here.' I think I spent a good portion of the whole nine months thinking it wasn't really happening. Then all of a sudden, here was this real baby. I could sort of recognize what Peter was going through, because to him, it really wasn't real. And I was pregnant, and still not dealing that well with something that was going to happen."

Once she was a mother, however, Olive settled quickly into this new role. "Jason was born Friday at I A.M. and I went home on Monday. I was bored in the hospital. I didn't have anyone at home to help me, so I arranged for a girlfriend to come over for two nights, and then my mother came up. Being alone with him, it was the first time I decided it was a good thing I'd gone to medical school and done neonatal intensive care because I was at least familiar with taking care of babies, so it wasn't as bad as it could have been. He was also a very good, very mellow baby. He slept well almost from the first night I brought him home. He'd wake up just once, at 3 A.M. or 4 A.M., and he wasn't fussy. Feed him, and he'd go right to sleep. He wasn't the kind of baby who would make you nervous. I am breast-feeding, and after the first day or so, we got the hang of it and it was fine. It's certainly more convenient, and it's closer, and you feel more important. But it does make it harder to leave the baby with anyone else."

One person with whom Olive has left Jason is his father. "Peter has babysat for me once," she says. "It went fine. He lives a block from the YMCA where I swim. I dropped Jason off with his diaper bag and miscellaneous goodies and gave Peter a few little instructions on what he was supposed to do. I came back two hours later and Peter was sitting on the couch and Jason was asleep on his chest. He said, 'We danced to MTV. We rocked. We watched a little boxing. Then we looked out at the lights of the city, and then he got sleepy so I sat down and he went to sleep.' He's going to baby-sit again this week while I swim. I also have a plan, which Peter doesn't know about yet, to ask him to take care of Jason one night during the week, Friday night, and one weekend day a month so I can go out and try to meet people.

"Peter has been in therapy these nine months and he's changed. He has decided that perhaps it isn't the most terrible thing that ever happened to him. He's a lawyer who works for the federal justice department on a case out here which could take ten to twenty years. He's from the East, and he'd lived here for only a few months when he met me. He'd come out to do this case. When I told him I was pregnant, he was in the process of studying for the California bar, which he failed. He'd rather live in California, or back East, but he hasn't taken the California bar again because he's decided he has to figure out his emotional state—this has really thrown a hooker into it.

"I think now that he will be there for his son in some way. If not, I'm going to try to find a man who will be because I think it's important for children to have a male figure in their lives, and to have someone else they can depend on besides their mother. It can get too intense if Mommy is the only person in their life—for them and for you. Also, a man plays with them differently—rougher—and he does different activities with them. He gives them different feelings about themselves, and he gives them a different idea of what people do in life, and he looks at the world in a different way. I think Peter is trying to be that person for Jason."

Just recently, Olive has begun to think about formalizing their relationship. "When Jason starts to talk, I'm beginning to wonder about what we should call Peter. Just Peter, or Daddy. Because as far as I'm concerned, until Peter signs a piece of paper saying he's the father, I don't want Jason to call him Daddy. Peter has not admitted paternity. I haven't pushed him. That's where he is going to get a shock. In about five or six months, after he's established a relationship with Jason, I'm going to say, 'Hey, Peter, put up something here.' I wouldn't mind a little financial assistance—$100 or $200 a month. I don't have to have it to live, but it would be nice. So far, he hasn't volunteered anything except babysitting. But I think he is slowly moving in that direction. Eventually, he'll have to commit to something because I don't think it's right for him to have the fun of taking care of Jason and watching him grow and not admit any responsibility."

Olive is also leaving open the possibility of a relationship for herself and Peter. "He eliminated that, I didn't," she says. "It's weird, because he's always telling me how much he likes me as a friend, as a person. The ball is in his court. It's too much trouble to push him."

But if Peter does pull out of their lives, Olive is ready. "I'm going to take some pictures of Peter and Jason together," she says. "That way, he'll have a record that his father knew him. And I think I'll be pretty honest about it. I'll say his father left. Back when Peter wasn't around at all, I figured Jason would ask to meet his father eventually, and I'd give him the information about how to find him, and let Peter do the rejecting. I wasn't going to be the bad guy because a kid can put you in that position—'It's your fault my father's not around.' I also figure it won't be as bad as it would have been fifteen or twenty years ago because everyone is divorced anyhow. There are lots of kids around who are two or three years old who don't have fathers at home. In some sense, it's better because he's not growing up in a household with the parents screaming at each other. This way, there is no horrible custody battle and he won't feel he has to choose, or end up in the middle, or feel guilty that he broke up the marriage."

All these musings are somewhat removed from the here and now of single motherhood with an infant. Olive's life was immediately changed in all respects. She went back to work almost at once, but she cut back her schedule. "I do psychotherapy and I couldn't leave patients without treatment for weeks and weeks and have any patients left," she says. "So what I cut down on was in-patient psychiatry, which I'm not going back to for another month. I also stopped being on call on weekends until January. Monday I work from 8:30 A.M. until 5 or 6 P.M. Tuesday I'm off. Wednesday I work all day again, but sometimes I have free hours and I go to his baby-sitter and feed him. Thursday I work in a mental health clinic out of town all day. Friday I work for about two hours in the morning. Work has a different importance to me now. It's obviously important because I need the money, but I'm not going to work as many hours as I used to. Before, if someone needed an appointment at night, I was free to set one up if I wanted to. Now I can't do that because there's no baby-sitter, and I've been gone all day and it's more important to come home and play with him. He's more important."

Of course, being a single mom means having to orchestrate all these maneuvers alone, which may be the part of her situation which bothers Olive the most. "It would be nice to have another person to do things—like drop Jason at day care and pick him up—so I wouldn't feel so rushed all the time, so I could get away once in a while. I can't just go out. I can't just pick up one thing I forgot in the supermarket. It sometimes drives me a little bit crazy because I was used to doing things on the spur of the moment. I was going to go to a movie last week, but then he was sleeping at the time I'd have to leave and it hardly seemed worth it. It's those times I wish there were someone else around. Going grocery shopping is a pain in the neck with the baby. If there were someone else around, they would watch the baby and I could go grocery shopping, or vice versa. I've even thought of getting a roommate, but I'm so used to living alone, I think I'd resent it more having my privacy invaded than I'd appreciate the relief. I do have lots of nice girlfriends, and they are a support system. They always tell me that they want to help, and when they are coming over I should tell them what to bring and they'll be happy to get it. But I tend not to ask them for favors.

"It can also get pretty lonely, especially on weekends. During the week, people are more apt to make plans to do things with you and be with you, but on Friday and Saturday night, and on Sunday, they are going to be with their families, or out on dates."

So far, Olive has not resumed dating. "My main social life has been going out to dinner with male or female friends, and Jason. I haven't even been to a movie. I do folk dancing and square dancing and pretty soon I'm going to take Jason with me because I can wear him in a snuggly on my chest or put him down someplace to nap. The people who do it are pretty mellow, and family-oriented. But the truth is that social life is less important to me now."

Having Jason has also changed the kind of man she would get involved with. "I used to look for someone who was going to be fun," she says. "Now I want someone who wants to be around a baby. I look at men as fathers now. They have to be able to get along with Jason and like kids and they have to be a little less selfish perhaps and a little more willing to give. I haven't given up hope of getting married, and having a baby has changed that too. Before, I went out with a lot of guys who had had vasectomies and that eliminated them. But now it doesn't. We could get married—Jason is already here. It's up front."

Despite her current lack of mobility, Olive doesn't feel that becoming a mother at age thirty-seven is going to hamper her at all, and she doesn't worry much about the future. "Being an older mother, I'm more relaxed," she says. "I've already done a lot of things in my life, so I don't feel I'm missing out, which I think you would in your early twenties, especially if you didn't have friends who were having babies and you felt like the whole world was passing you by. I'm looking forward to all these family-oriented activities I've never done. I'm going to take Jason to the children's museum. They have a little class. I'm going to take him swimming at the Y at six months, and when he's three I'm going to take him to learn how to ski. It's a whole new world that has opened up. I feel I'm readier for those things, and willing to experiment. I've done all the vacations, and traveling, and singles clubs, and I can again by the time he's two or three if I want to. I can go to Europe with a baby. I wouldn't spend as much time looking at architecture—I'd do different kinds of things. If you're younger, I think you feel the baby restricts you more and I don't think it has to. I'm also more relaxed in feeling that I can take Jason with me. At this age, he's real portable. I have a medical meeting Monday night at six and he's coming with me. I'll just breast-feed him there and to hell with what other people think."

Because Jason was not planned, Olive has also come to understand the wisdom of letting come what may instead of trying to control everything. "We're all so used to having everything come when it's supposed to, that it's real hard to deal with things that don't arrive on schedule," she says, "but you can't plan that everything is going to work out right, or that the baby is going to be OK, and you can't know what is going to happen when you are forty. There's so much obsessive intellectualizing among women about when to have a baby. It's like Peter—they want to have guarantees. I was that way too—waiting for the perfect, right time for a baby to come into my life. I had hit thirty-seven and I hadn't done anything about having a baby. I kept saying I'd wait another year, I'd wait another two years to see what would happen. And then I got pregnant by accident, which took all the planning away. Ironically enough, I was doing this fellowship in child psych half-time so for the last umpteen years I've been working fifty or sixty hours a week and I'd actually told people that when I finished the fellowship, I'd try to get pregnant because then I'd be able to juggle my life so I could have a baby. And as soon as I was psychologically ready for it, I got pregnant. It was certainly something I wanted."

Boyfriends as Fathers

Some of the single mothers had their children by men with whom they had long-standing relationships; often they were living together. But if the relationships have not been solid, they have made their lives as single mothers more difficult. This was the case for Sunny, thirty-three, a manager of computer operations.

SUNNY'S STORY

Sunny, thirty-three, had never thought she wanted a child, and she didn't have a change of heart until she discovered she was accidentally pregnant by a married man with whom she was living—a sailor who was often away from home. Her son is now three, and she has gone far in resolving her relationship with his father, and in getting her professional life firmly on track. But the journey hasn't been easy.

"I had always been interested in a career in management, but I had never been interested in having a child," she says. "I came from a home of child abuse and I was probably afraid of continuing this tendency even though I had put myself through three years of successful therapy. If I hadn't gotten pregnant accidentally, my feelings might have changed. I might have tried to get pregnant, depending on the man I met. I just don't know."

In fact, Sunny didn't even know she was pregnant until five and a half months had elapsed. That sounds impossible, but there were good reasons for it. "I had never been pregnant," she says, "and I was too busy to consider that I might be, and I never even had any symptoms. I had always had

irregular periods and I still had a period during the pregnancy. It was different, but considering what I was putting my body through, it wasn't unusual
for me. I was working two jobs, one as an operations supervisor for the
management information systems department of a large computer company,
which took sixty-plus hours a week, and the other a part-time night job in a
liquor store lifting heavy boxes and stocking the refrigerator because the man
who owned the store had muscular dystrophy. I was also going to school, and
renovating the house I owned.

"I began having fainting spells and I went to one doctor and he told me it
was all stress and he wanted to give me tranquilizers. Not being a pill person,
I said, 'No thank you. If it's just stress, I'll deal with it.' A little while later, I
had heart palpitations, and I went to another doctor and he examined me and
took a urine test and he told me I had progressive heart disease. He gave me
pills to control it, but he said to stay off them as long as possible because I'd
get dependent on them. I left his office thinking I was dying.

"Finally, one night I had this dream, believe it or not, with this voice
yelling at me, 'You fool! Don't you know when you are pregnant!' I said,
'What? Gee.' I was married for eight years and didn't get pregnant. I was
beginning to think I couldn't. The next day I went down to Planned Parenthood and got a test. It was positive. They wanted to give me a pelvic exam,
but it was a Friday and I said I'd see my doctor the next week. So I had that
whole weekend to think about what I wanted to do. Based on when my last
period was, I thought I was at the most two months pregnant. I thought I had
the option of having an abortion. Charles was out at sea. There was no way I
could call him and talk to him. It was my decision. I talked to my friends and
there were some who were against it and some who thought I should have
one. I finally decided I would probably have the baby.

"The next Tuesday I went to my doctor and he asked me why I thought I
was pregnant. I told him I'd had a positive test and all the other stuff that had
happened. He said, 'You might not be pregnant. It might be something else.
We'll have to check this out.' He started to do an internal and his words were,
'Christ! You are at least four months pregnant!' I said that was impossible and
he said, 'No, the baby is all the way up to your naval.' He sent me to another
doctor who thought I was more like five months pregnant and he sent me to
have a sonogram and I was five and a half months.

"Because of the circumstances, they were still willing to do an abortion in
the next two weeks, but I decided to have the baby. I'm a real metaphysical
person, and I thought that considering what I had put this child through—
lifting all those boxes, and working all those hours—without having a miscar-

riage, he must want to be born awfully bad. But it was pretty scary. I didn't have any money. I was barely making ends meet as it was. I knew I'd have to sell my house. I had stopped having roommates because Charles had moved in with me, but he had started to get a little flaky on me about money so I was often behind on my payments. I didn't know what would happen, but I wanted to go for it."

When Charles came home from sea, he found Sunny seven months pregnant. "It shocked the hell out of him," she says. "I must have been four months when he left. I had flown down to San Diego to see him off and we had traipsed all over the city and I was very out of breath. He started giving me flack about being out of shape because I was huffing and puffing. Looking back, it's kind of hysterical."

If so, it was the only funny thing about her pregnancy. It was, says Sunny, "probably one of the most stressful periods of my life. I remember one day feeling as if my head were going to explode because I was under so much stress. Charles was around for a little while, but he basically deserted me. I had to cut back on my overtime at work, quit school, and cut out my second job. Money was really scarce. I suffered from malnutrition because I didn't have the money to buy good food—it was all going just to pay the bills until I could sell the house. So I was eating hot dogs and God knows what I did to myself. I was in and out of the hospital a number of times because they were concerned about the effect of the stress on the baby. I ended up with pre-eclampsia. But I went on working until four days before he was due. I was supposed to be off for a month because I was having so many problems. If I stood for more than an hour, I would start bleeding. So they took this couch and moved it into the computer room, and I stayed on the couch and kept my feet up."

The delivery was also difficult, and Sunny went through it alone. Charles wasn't there. "I went into labor at six in the morning and I started pushing at 3 P.M., but he wouldn't come into the birth canal at all. We couldn't tell what was wrong. At 5 P.M., they decided to do a cesarean, but they couldn't get me an operating room because there were so many people giving birth that night. Finally, at 8 P.M., they were just about to wheel me in when they asked me to give it up because the woman next to me had a baby with the cord around its throat. Of course, I said yes. By the time Matthew was born, it was 10 P.M. I was so tired, I just said, 'Get this child out of me!' The epidural block didn't work, so they put me out, with the knife poised above me to get him out as fast as possible."

It took Sunny a while to feel comfortable and bonded with her son. "Because I was under the anesthesia when he was born, there wasn't that instant bonding. And when I first saw him, his forehead was all bruised from pushing and his nose was pushed in. I felt fear. I didn't know what to do with this child, how to care for him—even though I'd been to all the classes and had read all the books. It had been a long time since I'd been around kids. I felt like a real thimble fingers for about three days. I was up and walking the first day because I thought that the faster I got moving, the faster I'd be able to care for him. Then, the third day I had him moved into the room with me. I figured, as long as I could take care of him there, I would feel better about it when I left. Breast-feeding was also much more work than I ever thought it would be. I didn't understand, and no one ever told me, that it's something the baby has to learn. It doesn't come naturally. Fortunately, I had this nurse in the hospital who was an expert and she came in and sat with me when it was time for him to be fed, to make sure everything was going OK. We were in there a week, and by the time we left, the bonding had started, but he still felt like this foreign little thing. When we got home, because I didn't have any help and because of the cesarean, I was scared to death he'd choke or something would happen and I wouldn't be able to get to him fast enough, so he slept on my stomach all night for about three weeks. That bonded us."

Through all of this, Sunny had the support of her friends, and she doesn't know how she would have coped without them. "When I was pregnant, I'd come home from work and find a bag of groceries on the doorstep," she says, "and after Matthew was born, a bag of diapers. One day I found a Christmas tree. Someone had asked me if I was going to buy a tree, and I said that since the baby was too young to understand it, I'd rather buy something for him. So they bought the tree for me. And after he was born, people would show up at my front door with a vacuum under their arm, and they'd clean my house."

Her family was also behind her emotionally, but they couldn't do much to help physically. Her brothers and sisters all worked, and her mother was dying of cancer. "She had a real nasty bone cancer, multiple mylenoma—the worst you can get. She lived about forty minutes away and she was as supportive as she could be, but she couldn't really help me at home. She couldn't even lift the baby. She died a year ago. My brothers and sisters did what they could, and I knew that if worse came to worst, I could have moved in with one of them."

Things did get pretty bad financially for Sunny, but she didn't have to take that step. One of the problems was that it took her over a year to sell her house because interest rates were high and they affected the market. She is just now getting the bills paid off. In addition, shortly before getting pregnant, she had gone through a career change from sales to inside management, and in order to get started, she had taken a relatively low-paying job, earning just under $20,000 a year. Then, six months after she went back to work, when Matthew was eight months old, she got laid off with 250 other people.

Although this increased Sunny's immediate financial problems, it turned out to be the best thing that could have happened to her—both personally and professionally—because it allowed her to explore her feelings and her motivations and to change her behavior based on what she learned. In fact, motherhood for Sunny has been a constant process of self-examination and learning. "I was feeling a great deal of guilt over not being a proper mother," she says. When I was still working, I felt so badly over not being with Matthew enough that I was even taking him to work with me during my overtime hours. He would sleep in my lateral file drawer. So when I got laid off in November, I decided I wouldn't look for a job until the first of January and I would spend the two months with my son. We went to visit my sister in Texas for the holidays. We got to spend a lot of time together. I got to see his first steps, which was great because I had really been resentful that other people were getting to see his first everything, and I wasn't there. I'm really grateful we had that time together, but I learned something about myself—I was bored to tears being home all the time. I loved my baby and I loved being with him, but I found myself being mechanical, doing things out of habit and not really enjoying him when I was with him, not really appreciating him the way I did before when I'd come home from work and feel, 'I'm so glad to see you.' It was just routine. I wasn't giving him the kind of attention I'm giving him now."

Having learned this about herself, Sunny felt much more at ease when she started looking for work in January, and her financial problem gave her the impetus to push for more lucrative jobs. "I had never believed enough in myself to think I could get a job like this, but I found I was very qualified and employers were very willing to pay me well," she says. "During the interview process, I leveled with my employer. Although legally he could not ask about my personal life, I told him I was a single mother with a baby. I said, 'When he's sick, I want to be with him. And I want to be up-front and tell you that because that's how I'm going to feel. But if you are the person who understands that and gives me a little leeway on that side, I'll work 200 percent for you. You won't find a better employee."

This is the way it has worked out. Her employer has willingly granted her "child days" for illness, or child care emergencies. In fact, she says, "they have encouraged me to take days off because of my willingness to work overtime. After two years, and two extremely good reviews, I have received a major management promotion, doubling my responsibilities with a hefty salary increase. I'm now making twice as much as I used to. I remember when making $2,000 a month was so much money I couldn't imagine it. Now, within a couple of years, I'm looking at getting up to $50,000 a year. It's a major difference for the two of us. I've got headhunters calling me now, trying to recruit me for other jobs. I just see the sky's the limit."

Working at such demanding jobs and being on her own have made finding good child care particularly important for Sunny. Like most mothers, she has had her son in a number of situations, and she has learned that reliability is only part of the package. "I first had a lady who was referred to me, and who took care of a number of children," she says. "I thought it was OK, but I've learned to trust my instincts—even if I can't pinpoint why I don't feel good about a situation. Babies, no matter how young they are, will tell you whether they are in a good situation or not. Matthew was in a room with three or four other cribs and she also had a room with toddlers. I found out she really wasn't giving the kids enough attention. She wasn't bad to them or anything, but she had so many kids that they were starved for attention. He was always cranky when I came to get him. I think he was bored, that he needed more people contact. It was just a feeling I had. But I didn't trust it then.

"I pulled him out of there when I was laid off, and when I went back to work, I put him into a different group care situation. The woman seemed very qualified and she had good references, but that situation is what really taught me my lesson. He didn't want to go there. He had a fit every day. But I blamed it on myself. I thought that I was too protective and overpossessive and he was picking up on my feelings, that it wasn't anything he was trying to tell me.

"She had several children there in a little room with all these toys and a TV. The thing that did bother me was that every time I went there, she'd be lying on this cot in the room reading. She wasn't really participating, and there was always someone crying. One day, when Matthew was about eighteen months old, I came to get him and all the way out in the street I could feel him crying—even before I could hear him—which is unreal. I ran into the house and I ran into the playroom and he wasn't there, and the woman wasn't there. So I started going through her house. I finally found her in the back room with all the cribs and she was making up a playpen and he was standing there with a bottle of orange juice—I had told her he wasn't to have any orange juice because he was allergic to it—and he was crying. I said,

'What's wrong?' and she said, 'Oh, he doesn't know what he wants.' I said, 'Yes, he does. He wants a hug.' I picked him up, and he stopped immediately. Then I saw what was in the bottle. I said, 'I told you he wasn't to have orange juice. . . . Oh, just forget it.' And I walked out the door and promised him he'd never have to go back there and I'd always listen to my instincts.

"I started looking again and I decided that no matter how much I liked a person I was going to talk to all the available babysitters—five or six people and not stop because I thought one was good. That way I'd have comparisons. I also decided to take Matthew with me and spend time there and see how he reacted to the environment. Fortunately, I ran into this school-type situation—a house that had been converted to a little school—for toddlers. What I liked was that there was always a child in someone's arms, or holding someone's hand. When kids cried, I liked the way they comforted them. Matthew was drawn right into the environment. He stayed there for a year and a half, and then I sold my house and we moved so I had to look again. I found a Montessori school, which is where he goes now in the morning. In the afternoon he's cared for in a home situation, but I'm looking for an afternoon sitter, because his current one is pregnant and is due next month."

Once Matthew started the Montessori program, Sunny also needed a morning sitter to feed him breakfast and take him there because she left for work at 6:30 A.M. She found a very nice older woman who worked for her until recently. "Unfortunately, she got a little senile and she thought she was in charge. She wouldn't listen to my wishes. She decided Matthew was a neglected child, and I had to fire her."

Sunny has had a hard time finding a new morning sitter, so she's been staying home later in the morning and taking Matthew to school herself. It's turned out to be wonderful for both of them. "I had been used to getting into work an hour early and getting all revved up and doing all this overtime," she says. "But I've really been enjoying taking him to school, and the teacher tells me it's changed his whole mood for the day. It sends him off really happy, and it's carried through the whole day. Before, there would be days when I wouldn't even see him in the morning. It was tough on both of us. I mentioned to my boss the other day that I had to take a couple of days off to interview morning sitters, and she said, 'Why don't you just keep taking him to school.' I said, 'I'm supposed to be here at 9 A.M. and I'm rolling in ten or fifteen minutes late, and I'm not setting a good example for my staff, plus it feels like noon since I'm used to being here so early.' She sat me down and said, 'Look, you're different. Those are hourly people. You just told me you came home at 10:30 last night. You don't get paid for those hours. Stop thinking that way.' So I'm going to go on taking him to school at least for another month and see how it goes."

During these three years, Charles has moved in and out of Sunny's and Matthew's lives. His absence at the birth, Sunny says, "sort of started things rolling downhill for our relationship. He came back soon after that, and he was here off and on. He's probably been around for a total of a year of Matthew's life. Matthew knows that Charles is his father and he has a very positive image of him. Our problems are not Matthews's problem, and I feel he deserves to be proud of his father no matter what. I even send him stuff in the mail and pretend it is from his father. But there are problems, especially after Charles visits. Matthew asks, 'Why is my daddy gone?' I'm trying to better prepare him ahead of time. Charles is probably going to come and visit him after Christmas and I've been telling him that his daddy and I aren't married like so and so, or so and so, so we don't live together and Daddy has another home and that's OK. But their relationship is difficult to solidify because Charles is living out in the Cook Islands, so it's tough to arrange visits. My hunch is that he's probably going to move back to the states. At that point, I have no concern about setting up something regular. If Charles is here, my feeling is that anytime he wants to see him, it's great, as long as he's not going to try to sail off with him. We also are very close to Charles's mother and sister and brother. They have a farm near here and Matthew has a pony there and we spend a lot of time up there."

Sunny's own relationship with Charles has been more difficult than her son's, and she finally ended it eight months ago. "I still love Charles very much," she says, "but he's got a problem—he needs to grow up and accept responsibility—he's got to deal with that. But he just sent me an eight-page missive and I'm finding myself weakening about having ended the relationship. My friends are starting to get their hackles up and say, 'Sunny, you just can't do this to yourself.' And I say, 'I'll do what I want.' But I read an article recently that said the way to tell about whether a relationship is good for you is to ask the questions: 'Are you better off with him, or without him?' and I have to honestly say that it is without him. Every time he is here, things start going downhill for me financially. I'm just recovering from him again. I don't think we'll get back together, but I may break down for a little while. I'd like to remain friends. I feel strongly about any man I've had a relationship with—I want to remain friends afterward. My husband and I are still good friends."

At this point, Sunny feels she has control over the relationship with Charles, and she has her financial feet firmly on the ground—things have come together for her as a single mother. Obviously getting to this high ground has meant going over some pretty rough emotional and financial terrain, and there are still bumps in the road ahead. One problem she will probably always have to deal with is guilt over her long working hours and whether she is doing a good job raising her son. But now that Matthew is older, she is getting good reports back from school, and that has helped her feel that she is doing all right by him. "One teacher I think a lot of has told me that Matthew has high self-esteem, that he talks positively about his father in school, that he is happy, that he is not disruptive. They've told me that they have to turn away kids every so often who come from two-parent families—kids that have these problems. I figure he is out there in the world, and he's doing OK, and it would be showing up in his behavior if I weren't doing OK as a parent. I'm beginning to accept the fact that I'm going to have guilt for being away so many hours a day. Taking him to school in the morning is helping that, and I'm trying to plan my life so that I take days off on a regular schedule to be with him."

Her long work hours also mean that Sunny feels badly if she takes any time away from Matthew in the few hours she has with him. "It's really difficult to get out in the world and do something on my own or have a night out to myself when I haven't seen him all week," she says. "How can I do that? Also, if I'm in a bad mood, or work isn't going well, I can't go away and be by myself. I don't have much space. I have to come home and be on again. The commute helps me because I have almost an hour to settle my head. But if he's in a bad mood too, and it's taking a lot out of me to deal with it, I sometimes find myself taking my mood out on him. So what I do then is sit down and talk to him about it. 'Mommy is a person. Mommy has had a bad day and I'm sorry I yelled at you too much.' He does well understanding it, and even if he doesn't really understand all of it, he gets the emotion."

The emotion Sunny gives out is love. And it is love tempered in the fire of self-knowledge. "Matthew is the most important thing in my life," she says. "I'd like to say he's everything to me, but that's not completely true. My self-esteem, my feelings about myself, are important too. I can't be a good mother to him if I don't feel good about myself. It's going to show in the way I treat him. So ultimately it all comes down to him, but I have a life too. When I was pregnant, I had no idea he'd be as important as he is. He's taught me so much about myself—just seeing myself through him, hearing him repeat things I've said to him. I love animals, and I consider myself a loving person, and to see him up on the farm, touching baby animals and the way he cares about them and the relationship he's setting up with them, and with his pony—it makes me feel good about myself. He's opened up a quality of love I didn't know I had. I cry now so much more quickly than I used to. I feel things more deeply now.

"I thought I wanted a girl, but I believe the world gives you what you need when you need it. I needed to get in touch with the part of me that wasn't used to being around boys, that experienced fear because of the abuse of my father. Having him has helped me get in touch with that abuse. My older sister told me that when she had her two children she relived the childhood she never had through them. I'm finding the same thing is true for me. The abuse is the reason I thought I didn't want to have children, because I was afraid I'd do it. But what I've found is that being aware you have the potential nullifies it. When he acts up and I go into an automatic reaction mode and am afraid, I find I don't abuse him. I yell at him, and that's OK. I'll give him a swat on the behind every once in a while, and it's never going to go further than that.

"Single motherhood has been a struggle for me—emotionally and physically—but the rewards are great, and I have a philosophy which has gotten me through the bad times. I keep a quotation by Charles Kingsley next to my bed which says it all—'Thank God every morning when you get up that you have something to do which must be done, whether you like it or not. Being forced to work, and forced to do your best, will breed in you a hundred virtues which the idle never know.' I feel I am living my life to the fullest, and I keep thinking back to what I would have missed if I'd had an abortion.

"I believe other single women who want to have a child should seriously consider it, as long as they don't expect any financial or emotional support from the father. If you keep your expectations low, anything you do receive is extra. But I don't know about finding a man to have a child with and checking him out or having artificial insemination. As many problems as we've faced—'Where's my daddy? Why isn't he here?'—at least he exists. Matthew is my little love child—a manifestation of the love I felt for his father. I've kept the letters Charles has sent me when he's been out at sea and I'm seriously considering giving them to Matthew when he grows up. I can look him in the eye and say, 'I kept you because I wanted you. I loved your father.' And he can see it right in the letters—his father and myself talking about him being born, and what we'd name him. I'd have a tough time growing up knowing I came from a test tube."

Opting for Artificial Insemination

Many of the women who are considering single motherhood reject one of the easiest ways available—artificial insemination—to the point where, if that is the only alternative, they say they will not have a baby. But Theodora, forty-three, a clinical psychologist in private practice, had no hesitation about using AI in order to conceive her child, a boy who is now almost four.

THEODORA'S STORY

Theodora, forty-three, came to AI after considering other options and deciding they were too complicated. When she was thirty-six, she even had an abortion—for reasons these other single mothers thought were inadequate. "It wasn't the right time," she says. "I was in the throes of a dissertation in my last year of graduate school. The father of the baby absolutely did not want any more children. If I had gone ahead and had his child when he didn't want a child, it would have been an unethical and unfair thing to do to him. I didn't feel it was fair to bring someone else's child into the world who felt so strongly that he didn't want a child. And I also could not have supported a child alone in a way I would have wanted."

Two years later, things had changed. It seemed to Theodora that it was "absolutely the right time. Everything else in my life was together." At first she considered inviting a man to coparent with her. "I went so far as to ask one man, and he gave it very serious thought and then declined. But at the same time, it was beginning to seem very complicated to do that. All the men I considered were living far away. It would mean all the problems inherent in a divorce—who does the child spend time with? What are your values in child rearing? I was worried about sharing a child, and the heartbreak of a child's being torn between wanting to be with two people. And if we didn't have a relationship to begin with, it would be worse. So I decided to go to a sperm bank."

But not just any sperm bank. Theodora investigated a number of them. "At that time, sperm banks assumed you were lucky to get the sperm from them, and they didn't need to give you any kind of information about the donor. They only gave race and religion, but those things were not important to me. I had had an earlier miscarriage of a black child, and it was offensive to me that those things were all they would tell me.

"My research led me to the Repository for Germinal Choice, which really tells you everything but the actual identity of the person—the background, interests, hobbies, education, profession, appearance, siblings, any other children they have had, likes and dislikes. Now a lot of sperm banks are giving this information because many of them are consumer-oriented and women have come to believe they have a lot more rights about the selection of a donor.

"It cost $176 for a one-time insemination at my physician's office. I had an early miscarriage the first time. Then it took nine months before I got pregnant with my son. Once I decided on the father, I used his semen every time. I learned to inseminate myself. They supplied me the semen and the equipment. It wasn't a cold experience at all. To me, inviting a soul into the world who is very much wanted and loved is an act of love. It was always done in a loving way with meditation, and incense burning, and music playing. It was a celebration ritual."

When she found she was pregnant, she was elated, and she describes her pregnancy as "an emotional high" even though she was nauseous for the whole nine months. "I wasn't alone and I was very, very positive," she says. "It was a period of extreme ecstasy and excitement. All women who set out to have a child alone have this sense of being in control of their lives, and really feeling joyous about it.

"I had support from every side—my family, my friends, my colleagues, the sperm bank—it was as if this child had a hundred relatives. My mother and brother live nearby and I discussed it with them before going ahead. My mom thinks I'm a pioneer. She couldn't have been more pleased that I chose to do it this way. My brother had a hard time initially, which some men do, because AI has a kind of implication that men are obsolete, but once there was a real child, he forgot that."

Theodora's own sense of the realness of the baby was increased when she had amniocentesis and discovered she was carrying a boy. "I wanted a boy and I never doubted that he would be a boy," she says. "I can't understand why anyone would choose not to know the sex with amniocentesis because the bonding is so much more intense knowing the sex. You can picture the baby much more clearly and talk to the baby. I had the amnio to find out the sex as much as anything. If there had been Downs syndrome, I would not have had the baby because I feel that it's hard enough to bring up a normal, healthy child. A Down's child would usurp all your energy. I would chose quality of life."

The support Theodora had during her pregnancy extended through the birth of her son. "I had three women coaches. One was my cousin, and the other two were close friends. One of them has subsequently had a girl by the same sperm donor I used so that our children would be family, so that they would be able to say, 'my brother,' 'my sister,' which they do.

"I had nonprogressive labor and it turned out his cord was too short and he couldn't descend, which I guess is not that uncommon. So I ended up with a cesarean. But I was awake and I got to hold him right away. I was screaming, 'Give him to me right now!' I was ecstatic. It was wonderful. He wasn't a stranger. We talked to each other. He was finally here. It was only a matter of his coming from the inside to the outside."

Once the baby was "outside," however, Theodora had a difficult time because of his personality. "He is very intense," she says. "He's driven to intensity, which in infancy made him cry a lot because he was feeling everything intensely. He couldn't relax easily. It was hard on me because I didn't want him to cry and I felt as if I wasn't meeting his needs. If I had another child who was like that, I think I'd understand better that it was the only way they had of expressing their feelings. But as a first-time mother, it was hard for me. I'd breast-feed him, and walk him up and down. I'd rock him; I'd go for a ride in the car. I'd do anything that seemed to help. I could not just leave him to lie there and cry."

But even being solely responsible for such a difficult baby, Theodora says, "I had a feeling of ecstasy the whole time, a feeling of oneness, of merging together, and physical closeness. For the first three years, it was totally consuming. I knew before I had him that I'd feel that he would be the most important thing in my life, but not to the extent that he is. He's ten times more important than I had thought possible. I've never had a relationship I felt so intensely. There's an intimacy with him I didn't know was possible. I know other single parents, and divorced parents, who feel the same way—that they didn't even know what intimacy was until they found themselves alone with their child."

Of course, being a single parent also means being the sole financial support, and in this regard, Theodora was considerably better off than most women in her position because she was earning well over $50,000 a year. This enabled her to hire live-in help, and her career offered her considerable flexibility to arrange her practice hours to suit her child's schedule. She began seeing a few patients at night two weeks after Duncan was born, and then she built her practice back up slowly. Having live-in help made her schedule a breeze. "His nanny was a wonderful Latin woman who just loved him. She was a wonderful surrogate mother for the first two years, but then he needed a lot more intellectual stimulation. He was so active and inquisitive and she was into holding and cuddling, so I put him into a school situation when he was two."

At that point, Theodora also cut her hours back so she could spend more time with Duncan. "I really feel he needs me more now than during his first year," she says. "I work only twenty-five hours a week—Tuesday, Thursday, and Saturday. I teach one day a week at his school. I've loved having that experience, being with him while he's with his peers. He only goes a full day on the days I work. On the others, he goes for a few hours and then I pick him up."

Probably because of their close relationship and the school Duncan goes to, in which they are a lot of children with single parents, Duncan has yet to inquire about his father. But when he does, his mother is ready. "When he asks, I'll tell him the truth," she says. "The truth to begin with is that his father doesn't live with us. He lives far away. Usually the 'why' question doesn't come for a while. It's just like questions about sex—you don't answer more than is asked for.

"I think his situation is comparable to a child's whose grandparents died before he was born—it would have been interesting to know them, but you don't grieve for them. There's a loss, but not the loss of someone you loved and were attached to. A child doesn't miss them in a deep, devastating way because he never knew them. I think the loss is felt when you have someone and then you lose them. People project: 'What would I have done without my father? It would have been terrible.' But that is because they knew their father.

"Also, because of the sperm bank I used, I know what his father is like, and I can tell Duncan. So I don't know how different his situation is than that of a child who lost a father in a war before he was born. I also think there is a strong possibility he will meet his father. I can arrange a meeting. The local press did a story on sperm banks and they tracked him down and one of the TV stations let me know how I could reach him."

Theodora also doesn't worry about role models or substitute fathers for Duncan. "He has my brother, and he has close colleagues of mine that we do a lot of things with and there are a lot of men on the staff of his school—good nurturing men who have chosen early childhood education. He probably has more male contact in his life than most children with conventional fathers who work a great deal and come home late."

Because these matters do not worry her and she has had such a wonderful experience as a single mother, Theodora is considering having a second child on her own—the only single mother interviewed who would do so. But she isn't ready yet. "I think there are a lot of advantages to waiting until the first is five or six years old," she says, "because you avoid a lot of sibling rivalry and being torn between the two, so I'm quite happy to wait another year. I have forty vials of sperm from the same donor so I can give Duncan a full brother or sister. I'll be forty-four or forty-five, but that doesn't seem a problem for me. My health is excellent and the health of the fetus has a lot to do with your own genetic background, and there are a lot of late births in my family."

Would she advise other women to follow in her footsteps? Yes—with two qualifications. "It would be a very different experience without enough money," she says. "I don't want to underplay how important this is. If I did not make the money I do, I would have had a much harder time seeing this as a totally positive experience. It takes a lot of money to bring a child up in a good way, and I'm finding out it takes even more than I thought—it's at least $1,000 extra a month for Duncan to have the kind of schooling, and toys and food and child care that I want him to have. It's not that I couldn't do it for a lot less, but I think if you are going to do something, you need to do it the best way possible. I make a lot of money compared to the national average and I feel as if I'm just scraping by. I don't know how people do it who are making less.

"Another important factor is whether a woman has lived alone and likes living alone, because you can't expect a child to fill an empty part of your life. If anything, you need to be more secure in your emotional economy to have a child. I'd discourage single women from having children who have not felt good living alone."

14

When All Is Said and Done

How would you feel if you never had a child? It's a difficult question to answer, both for women who very much want to become mothers and those who are still torn by indecision. Just as a woman can't see into the future and know that having a child will make her life more fulfilling, that she will be happier, that her career won't suffer, that she'll be glad she did it, she also can't know with any certainty how she would feel if her life continues as it is, and she devotes her energies to her work, her important relationships, and her other interests—travel, hobbies, fitness, community projects—whatever they may be. There are no guarantees either way.

Even being happy with life today doesn't seem to have much to do with how a woman thinks she will feel if her future is childless. Two thirds of the clock-watchers are very satisfied with their lives, yet almost 60 percent of them believe they will be unhappy if they don't have a child someday. Close to another third believe they will have mixed emotions if they remain childless.

A Sense of Loss

Married women who definitely want to be mothers—whether they are ready and trying to get pregnant, or still postponing the time to begin trying— almost universally speak about a sense of loss. What would be lost, of course, depends on what is important about having a child—the special bond between mother and child, the experience of family life, the continuation of the blood line, the sense of oneself as a woman, sharing parenting with one's husband.

Nina, thirty-one, a secretary who is trying to start her family after a number of years of postponement, says, "If I were never to have a child, I'd feel an emptiness. I'd feel that I would be missing an experience that would be very fulfilling and enriching to my life—that I'd never have the chance to create and raise, with my husband, a human being that would, hopefully, turn out to be the best of both of us and more. And that there would be no seed to carry on, no mark left on this earth, no continuity to life."

For Fran, thirty-six, the director of a preschool, it's missing out on the whole parenting experience that she'll regret—and she doesn't know if her financial situation will ever improve enough to allow her to have a child, even though she wants one very much. "I think I would feel a sense of loss of the parent-child relationship I never had," she says, "of the final step of 'growing up' one takes in becoming a parent oneself, of a family closeness in the later years of my life, of the learning and understanding I would never have in a personal sense about parenting, of the sharing and fun of a family, of the new and special relationship I might have had with my husband in our new role as parents."

Even though they believe they will feel this sense of loss, most of these women, a number of whom are facing possible infertility, have come to some kind of terms with the future, some way of seeing their lives without children in them, or of compensating for the loss of that experience. Natalie, thirty-one, a marketing consultant, speaks of her situation in these terms. She got pregnant by accident and miscarried at four months, which devastated her and her husband because the pregnancy itself had totally changed their view of having a child. Since the miscarriage, she has tried for a year to get pregnant without success. "If it doesn't happen, I'll always feel a little cheated," she says. "But I've got such a wonderful marriage and such a good home and everything else I've ever wanted in life that I wouldn't go around sulking all the time. But it would always be a tender spot. I would always feel sad at times like Christmas. Friends of our parents who are childless have told us that if you get into your forties and you are childless, most of your friends' kids are grown, so it's a little easier to take because all of a sudden there are lots of couples who can do things together, and there aren't a lot of babies around."

Virginia, now forty-one, a director of development, has finally come to terms with the fact that she will not have a child—not because of infertility but because her husband is absolutely opposed. "When I was thirty-seven, I found myself suddenly suffused with a passionate desire to have a child," she says. "But the man with whom I was living, a divorcé of forty with a little girl, who was then twelve, was adamant about not wanting another child. It came down to a choice between having a child and having him, and I chose him over motherhood. Having been 'on the market' throughout my twenties and through half my thirties, I realized how excruciatingly difficult it was to find a halfway sane, decent, reasonable, intelligent human being who also cared for me. Don was the best of the bunch and I decided I wouldn't give him up and face the search again for anything—even for a baby!

"But the desire to have a baby stayed with me and wouldn't go away. It haunted my dreams. It arose when I was with friends who had babies, when I saw babies in carriages on the street. I can think of no endeavor more exciting than nurturing the growth of another human being—certainly not my job, as interesting as it is. And the curious and ironic thing about this desire was that I had never felt it before becoming involved with Don. I came to see having a child as the culmination of our love. And being a weekend 'stepmother' made me poignantly aware that no matter how close Don's daughter and I became, she was always his child and not mine.

"Of course, we had countless discussions about having a child and I didn't get anywhere. After we got married in 1981, I continued to try to change his mind about having a baby, but he remained adamant. I didn't give up until the end of 1984 when it became obvious that going ahead and having a child against his wishes would wreck our marriage.

"I will always have an inner grief about not having children, and this grief will not just waft away. Part of me will never be reconciled to not being a mother. I have suffered a lot, and cried a lot and made Don very unhappy and guilty. I finally understood that this was an issue on which he just couldn't compromise. Now a lot of the grief is in the past and I feel I can leave this issue and move on in my life. In a lot of ways, it is a great relief. I was expending a lot of emotional energy on the subject and now I can redirect that energy."

Questions, Questions

Married women who are still hung up about deciding whether to have children tend to ask themselves a lot of questions about how they will feel ten years or so down the road if they remain childless. Jennifer, thirty, who has her own writing business, had never wanted to have children, but when she answered the survey, she was beginning to question that decision. "I'm coming to believe I will live to regret it if I don't have this important component in my life. At times I think that having plenty of money and freedom to travel, etc., will be enough for a full life, but at other times it seems as if that will wear thin in time, and that my values will change. Do I want to be old and completely alone with nothing to show for my existence except used plane tickets? I don't think so."

"Am I going to regret it later? That's my biggest worry," says Sally, thirty-six, a personnel officer and compensation analyst, who has been married for fifteen years and thinks a lot about how she would feel without children. "In a way, the thought of never having one is frightening to me. If I don't, I will probably be wondering about it for the rest of my life. If I knew early in our marriage what I know now, I would have gone ahead and had a child then. It would be fun to have an older child around now."

Mary, thirty, a sales and marketing manager, who has been postponing year by year through ten years of marriage, also wonders how she will feel when the possibility has gone. "I hope I would be comfortable with it," she says. "That's one of my main questions. If I don't have a kid, will I wake up one day and say, 'God what a waste of my life!' And I guess I keep telling myself that if it's meant to be, I'll know it, and if not, I'll go along with all the things I do and be content with the life I have. Sometimes I think about being old and not having a family or anyone around to take care of me. And then I think, 'Isn't there some other reason you want to have kids than that?' "

That Lonely Future

More single women than married women believe they will be very unhappy if they don't have a child—perhaps because they lack a close, intimate relationship in their lives. When they project a future for themselves without a family, they often see a picture they don't particularly like. For Theresa, forty, a project consultant who is involved with a man eight years younger than herself who isn't ready to make a commitment, a future without children is a selfish future. "I can't bear the idea of always thinking about me, although it's been my focus for so long as I've tried to get my act together," she says. "I just cannot imagine not having children. I project into the future a lot. Ten years? Twenty years? To be basically doing the same stuff, which is life maintenance stuff, rather than having a life, doing things for other people. It feels unfinished, incomplete, not to be a part of a family. In many ways, it feels like not having grown up."

When they imagine their futures, some single women think of older women they know who have lived out their lives alone, and they pull back from identifying with them. This happened to Melanie, thirty-five, an art director, who doesn't have any man in her life and does not think she would become a single mother even though she feels sad at the thought of not having a child. "I recently went to a family party of a friend of mine," she says, "and I met an aunt of hers, a woman in her seventies. I could hear her talking and I felt as if I was looking at myself in the future. I got the sense that she had never had children and wasn't married. She said little sarcastic things that gave you the impression she was trying to be brave and be an independent person but underneath she was hurt by never having had children. We took an instant liking to each other because we felt we were similar kinds of people. But it kind of spooked me because I felt I was looking at myself."

Because she does not want to see herself as old and alone, Joan, thirty-eight, a systems analyst, has created a fantasy of forging a new life if she doesn't find a man who wants to have children. "It goes like this," she says. "When I'm forty, I'll join the Peace Corps and I will go live in Central America and learn how to dig good latrines, or whatever, for two years—do something really different from anything I've ever done, and hard. And then I'll come back and find someone who doesn't want to have children."

A Sense of Fate

Many of the single women seem to feel that whether or not they have a child is out of their hands—if it's meant to happen, it will; if not, not. This attitude brings with it a certain peace of mind, especially for women who very much would like to have a child. Rita, thirty-eight, a clerk-typist who wants to be a single mother and is negotiating with a man to be the father of her child, says, "If I don't have a child, I'll probably feel regret, but not despair, because I'll assume it wasn't meant to be. I'm not a religious person, but that serenity prayer always made a lot of sense to me: 'God grant me the serenity to accept the things I cannot change and the courage to change the things I can and the wisdom to know the difference.' "

Karla, twenty-eight, a data manager and an actress, is faced with infertility because of endometriosis and she, too, has come to a fatalistic view. "If I were never to have a child," she says, "I would wonder if I had made the right choices in my life. My focus was elsewhere in my early twenties and now I question whether I was chasing dreams and rainbows when I should have been considering the larger picture. Then again, things may happen the way they are supposed to happen."

This life view isn't a means of copping out of making decisions about the future; rather, it allows a woman to remain happy with who she is right now instead of struggling against herself. Alexandra, thirty-six, who owns her own company, came to this conclusion about her life. "There is no way to know how I would really feel if I never had any children," she says. "How can you know if the grass is really greener on the other side? I've thought about it a lot, and I've come to the conclusion that I don't think it matters one way or the other. I am content with who and what I am. I don't feel a void, or a need to have a child. Maybe having my own business is like having a baby— needing time and energy and attention—and if I didn't have the business I would feel differently, but I think not. My life offers me the opportunities and challenges to grow every day. I think my life is as it is supposed to be and if I am supposed to be a mother, then a man who will be the father will come into my life and the decision to have children will be as natural as the decision to marry that man."

Joining the Motherhood Club

Motherhood is the ultimate secret society. A woman becomes a pledge when she is pregnant but is only ushered in as a full member when she has her baby in her arms. It's a society that requires a lifetime membership, and that obviously extracts high dues. However, members may also reap untold and countless rewards. How do women feel who have joined—has it been worth it? These late mothers answer a resounding "yes" to that question—92 percent of them are very satisfied with motherhood, and no one is unhappy

(8 percent have mixed emotions). And they are also more satisfied with their lives than the clock-watchers—(80 percent versus 65 percent).

Mothers have a lot to tell the clock-watchers about what motherhood means to them—and they tell it well. "It's a great chance that a woman takes," says Gretchen, thirty-one, who has a six-month-old daughter and is at home working on a novel. "You don't know what your child will be like, or just how much time she will really take. You can count on one thing though —you will love your child if you let yourself. It's a natural feeling of awesome strength that pours out of you. And motherhood will give you a sense of fulfillment and purpose that you have never before experienced. You feel as if you have joined the slow turns of the wheel of time. You become very aware of your own mortality just as life becomes more precious than ever before, and each moment becomes a bright spark of eternity that you have reached out and captured in your hand."

Many women speak about the immense satisfaction and joy of being a mother and of the added dimension children bring to their lives, but some mothers also note that their lives were not incomplete before they had a child —they're simply more complete now. "It's the most fulfilling thing that's ever happened to me," says Denise thirty-nine, who married at age thirty-seven and is the mother of a sixteen-month-old daughter. "She's just a great kid, and I'm part of a great family. Motherhood gives me warmth, and security and happiness. But I also feel that if I hadn't met someone and gotten married and had a child, I would still be happy. That's my nature. And I don't feel as if my life wasn't anything without my husband and child. But having a family and having a child are extremely fulfilling."

Eleanor, forty-six, a psychotherapist and writer who was forty-one before her daughter was born, echoes Denise when she says she could have lived her life happily without a child. "But it was an experience," she says, "I would choose not to miss if I could help it. I enjoy life more now, and I always have the feeling that if all else fails, I have this happy little creature in my life. It gives me a sense of security. And motherhood has certainly added a tremendous dimension to my life, most of all in terms of intimacy. Having and raising a child is such an intimate experience."

Mothers also speak of their children as the center of their world—a center around which they have reconstructed their lives. As Elizabeth, thirty, a part-time financial economist and the mother of a seven-month-old daughter, puts it, "Motherhood is the basis of my life, the axle upon which everything else turns. I love my baby and I'm happy to be able to keep my foot in the door of my profession so I can open it wider later on."

Surprised by New Feelings

The intense emotions a child elicits can almost never be anticipated. Over and over again, mothers say they had no idea how they would feel about their children until they had them. "Our decision to embark upon parenthood after eight satisfying years of marriage was rational and not emotional," says Carolyn, thirty-two, an assistant director of career services who has a two-year-old daughter. "My feelings about becoming a mother had ranged from sheer terror when we married to raging ambivalence as age thirty approached, and my husband's feelings mirrored mine. When at last we faced the question squarely and measured pros against cons, we made a decision to take the plunge, not because we were starry-eyed over the notion of parenthood, but because it seemed the logical 'next step' for us as a couple. How prosaic we were! Our daughter has been a revelation to us from the moment of her birth. It is unfathomable to me that we might have decided the cons outweighed the pros and chosen not to have this child who lights up our lives with her presence."

Some women were particularly surprised by the feelings they experienced with their own babies because they were never attracted to other people's. This was certainly true for Emma, thirty-four, an advertising executive who has a three-year-old son and is planning a second child. "I remember people saying, 'There's just a special feeling you have for your own child. You just can't imagine what it's like until you have your own.' They were absolutely right. It really is a special relationship. I still am not crazy about kids generically, but I'm absolutely foolish about mine. We're very glad we waited, but we're very glad we did it. Our son is a delight and motherhood is, to my surprise, fun."

A Mixed Blessing

Naturally, there are women for whom motherhood is not a totally positive experience. They have to really work at it. Sometimes they even find themselves wishing they could step back in time—if only for an hour or two. "I don't love motherhood, not at this point," says Myra, thirty-four, a marketing consultant, whose son is nine months old. "I have not taken to it, but because of my work with child abuse, I know how bad some kids have it, and I can safely say that I may not be a perfect mother, but my son is getting a hell of a lot from me emotionally that many kids don't get from their mothers. If I didn't know that, I'd be worrying more about why I enjoy getting away from him so much.

"I do feel more positively now, but I still have ambivalence about being a mother. I wonder if I'll ever completely get over that. There are days when I come home from my office and I'd like to open up my mail and read it, but I can't. There's this little person there who needs my attention. I wouldn't trade him for the world. I love him dearly, but there are moments when I think: 'What have I done?'"

If a woman finds herself pregnant accidentally when she didn't think she ever wanted to have a child, her reaction to motherhood can be more negative. This was the situation Beatrice, thirty-five, a recreation therapist, found herself in. Her husband had been trying to convince her to have a child, and she did not believe in abortion, so she went through with the pregnancy and had a daughter who is now three and a half. "It's been hard work developing my nurturing, maternal feelings," she says. "About six months ago I went into therapy because I was still struggling with it. I discovered that a lot of it has to do with a bad relationship with my mother, and I'm working on that.

"But there are times that I really resent the fact that our budget is tight because we have to pay for child care. If I didn't have to spend all this time being a parent while my husband is in school, I wouldn't be so tired, and everything would be a lot better. That's one of the things I'm working on in therapy: Why am I blaming her?

"She is very active, and she is also in love with me. It's unfair. Dan really wanted her and she prefers me. I wish she preferred him. People say, 'Oh, you wouldn't like that.' But I say, 'Oh, yes I would. I wouldn't be jealous.' When I've had it up to here with her, I leave the house. I go grocery shopping, which I don't even like.

"I'm still growing into the relationship. The therapy is helping me deal with some of these negative feelings, and she's also getting a little more independent and playing by herself a little bit more, and she's more enjoyable. I find myself liking her more. We're developing a relationship and we have these intimate little talks and I feel really good about those. When I'm not tired, I feel more positive about motherhood. But when people ask me, 'Aren't you glad you have her?' I can't always say, 'Oh, yes,' the way everyone else does."

Advice to the Uninitiated

No woman can tell another whether to have a child, whether it will be worth it to cancel a childless future and take a journey to motherhood. But some mothers are willing to offer advice about making that enormous decision.

"Motherhood is an important step in your life and should be made only when you are ready, not so much financially, but emotionally," says Roberta, thirty-seven, an administrative assistant who is the mother of a three-year-old son. "To me, being a mother is a wonderful feeling . . . and I was ready for it! I look at my son as an individual. He is a little kid, but I treat him with respect and love because he is a person."

"It gets to a point where you know," says Margie, thirty-five, a Ph.D. chemist and mid-level manager who is now the mother of a three-year-old son. "You know that a child is something you want in your life, that there will be something missing until you have this child. Unless you feel that way about having a child, don't do it. It totally changes your life, and unless you have totally committed yourself to the decision that this is what you want, the stress, the juggling, the trade-offs, the things you have to give up because there are just so many hours in the day, can make you really bitter.

"The baby experience is not positive when they are screaming at 2 A.M., or when you are falling asleep in a meeting the next day because you didn't get any sleep the night before. The bond with the baby is what gets you through."

Wendy, thirty-four, a customer communications specialist who procrastinated about having a child but is now the mother of an eighteen-month-old daughter has the opposite view about the decision-making process. "I think women analyze it too much," she says. "There are so many choices, and people have become more analytical than they were fifteen or twenty years ago. And it's so easy to just put it off. That may have happened to me if it weren't for my husband. I'm glad it didn't.

"Parents can be very specific about the negatives. Yet almost all the people I know who have children, tell you all the bad stuff—how the kids have been so crabby today, and they've been up all night, and they are dead tired, and they can't do this, and they can't do that—but then say, 'I wouldn't trade it for the world.' I think it's a very special experience. We wouldn't trade our daughter for the world. We wouldn't go back for the world. It's just like anything else—be it your career, or whatever. The more you work for something, the more you appreciate it and the more special it becomes. But by the same token, if you are really not willing to make the sacrifices, don't do it. It's not for everybody."

15

An Epilogue
My Own Journey to Motherhood

I am a clock-watcher who became a mother for the first time before I ever felt I was up against it—even though I was thirty-four. My mother had had me when she was forty and my father was forty-seven, and having "elderly" parents had never particularly bothered me. In fact, there were real advantages in terms of what they could offer in wisdom and material comfort. So even in my early thirties I didn't feel pressured. I knew I wanted to have a child "someday"—that I'd be missing out on a significant experience if I didn't do so—but I also assumed that day would come later on.

What I had felt pressured about in my thirties was getting married, but it wasn't so I could have a child; it was so I could feel settled and secure. But I hadn't always wanted marriage either. When I was in my twenties I wanted romance, to be loved, and even though marriage would mean a culmination of that love, it also seemed that it would close off some part of the world. When I graduated from college in 1967, I was madly in love with a guy who had flunked out of Lafayette and been drafted, and was down at Ft. Benning, Georgia, waiting to find out if he was going to be cannon fodder in Vietnam. If he'd asked me to marry him, I'm sure I would have. But I also remember feeling that spring that all the girls in my dorm with their engagement rings from M.B.A. candidates at Dartmouth were missing out on something. By not getting married, I would have a chance to be out on my own exploring the world, working, being independent as my mother had before me.

I went off to Cambridge, Massachusetts, where I shared an apartment with a college friend and worked for a magazine at the business school at M.I.T. Through my job I met the next man in my life, an M.B.A. student from Oregon with whom I was involved for over four years. Jim kept getting close to a commitment, but he was too busy exploring the world and finding himself to be ready.

Bambinos

It was during the years of that relationship that I came to know, and care about, babies for the first time in my life. As an only child of parents whose contemporaries had long since finished with childbearing—or never begun—I had had no contact with babies, or even done any baby-sitting. My only experience had been at age sixteen, when I spent one full day as a mother's helper up in New Hampshire, where we had a summer cottage. There were four children, aged one, three, five, and eight. I had not the slightest idea what I was doing. When I was unable to find clothes for the baby, I left the three-year-old guarding him and took the eight-year-old upstairs with me to look. When I wanted to go swimming, I left the five-year-old with the two little ones while the eight-year-old and I swam out to the float. I lost track of the baby and he crawled under the hot water heater and blew out the pilot light. Result: no hot water for baths. For dinner, I shucked three dozen ears of corn, and then went home and collapsed.

Now in my mid-twenties I was around babies for the first time as an adult. One of Jim's good friends had a four-month-old daughter named Andrea, whom I watched grow up during weekend visits. I was fascinated by the nursing process—the closeness of mother and child—and by the way she reached out to make contact with the world as she grew. I liked to carry her around, and sometimes if we were out, I'd be mistaken for her mother. But it was their son, born two years later, who was the first baby I was crazy about. Jim and I had abandoned New York for one of his adventures—an "On the Road"–Jack Kerouac–type trip to the West Coast—and for a few weeks we stayed with his friends who had moved to Albuquerque. Jordan was ten months old and a delight. When he would wake up from his nap, he'd stand up in his crib and laugh and "talk" until I came to get him. Then he'd wrap his little arms around my neck. He was delicious.

Yet there was something about the role of mother that bothered me. It seemed so confining. Jordan and Andrea's mother had no existence beyond that. Their father moved in and out of his close family world and the larger world beyond, but she did not. I didn't know any mothers who did. My friend Charlotte, who lived outside San Francisco, had a two-year-old daughter and was expecting another baby. I spent a lot of time with her on that trip—living off and on at her house for four months. I could see little appealing about her life. She had no independence at all—she was even on an allowance—and no life beyond the confines of her family. Motherhood seemed to be a big trap.

Yet it was also during that time that I began to dream about babies—and realized that I didn't feel like a whole woman—I felt barren; I had a flat, unused belly. I imagined my eggs rolling down my fallopian tubes like useless ball bearings. Motherhood seemed one way to bar death from the door, to renew myself, to be alive forever.

Mr. Right

In the fall of 1972, a year after that West Coast trip ended and Jim and I were back in New York, he got married to someone else. I was close to twenty-eight. I had my own studio apartment, a low-level management job in a publishing house, which I hated, and the poetry I'd been writing since college, which was beginning to get published. Away from the children of my friends and the loneliness of the California landscape, I had stopped having strange dreams about babies.

Three weeks after Jim's wedding I was fixed up on a blind date with Bill, the man who eventually became my husband. I worked with the wife of Bill's best friend from college, Tom, who said he'd take me out himself if he weren't married. Bill decided that was a good enough endorsement. We were a pretty exclusive couple almost from the beginning, and started living together a little over a year later. Bill was committed to the relationship in a way Jim never had been, and I was the happiest, the most secure, I'd been in my whole life. But after a year or so, I began to want more—marriage—and when I was thirty-two, I decided to press the issue. We were planning a trip to Spain in the spring and I told Bill if we weren't going there on our honeymoon, I wasn't going at all, and not only that, when he came back, he'd find he wasn't living in our apartment anymore. I didn't know if I'd really go through with it, but I said it and then let the subject drop. That was in October. At Christmas he gave me a ring, and we were married in May, 1978. One year later, almost to the day, our son was born.

Big with Child

That was not the plan. We had talked a little bit about having kids—enough so I knew Bill wanted one also. But it certainly wasn't a big issue. We'd gotten a dog three years before and Bill had joked that if I did a good job raising her I could have a baby someday. Someday could certainly have been a few years off. I was at that point managing editor of a national magazine, and earning the bulk of our family income. He was just breaking into the big time as a book reviewer and magazine writer, and had a part-time job as book review editor of the magazine where I worked. The career and financial aspects all said, "Wait." But I no longer felt that motherhood would be a trap. I felt mature, and successful, and I knew I would continue to have an outside life. I wouldn't *just* be a mother.

The only thing pressuring me to go ahead soon was the sudden fear that I might have a problem getting pregnant. I began to talk about it with Bill, to explain that it might take me six months or a year to conceive. We finally negotiated that we'd start to try in the fall. But in July I didn't get my period. I had an IUD, so I didn't think I could be pregnant and I wasn't. But missing my period made me worry that maybe the IUD was wreaking some unknown havoc within. I decided to have it removed.

That was that. We used foam that next month, but again I didn't get my period. I didn't really think I was pregnant right away because I wasn't counting the days. But at around forty days I realized my breasts were sore, I was going to the bathroom a lot, and something was different. I went to the doctor and had a blood test. The results were due on Friday. I called from work. Yes, the test was positive, the secretary said. "Are congratulations in order?"

"Yes," I said. Deep breath. Bill's office was next door to mine, but he shared it with another editor, so I called him on the phone. "Guess what?"

"What?"

"I'm pregnant."

"Ohhh, no . . . ." He hung up. The next thing I knew, he was in my office, athletic bag in hand. "When?"

"May second."

"I'm going to play squash," he announced abruptly, and left. I would have hated to be his opponent that afternoon.

I had a very easy pregnancy—little nausea, no headaches, or backaches, exhaustion for the first few months, but no medical problems of any kind. I was naïve. I didn't think about anything going wrong and nothing did. I gained forty-two pounds, and looked as if I'd swallowed a watermelon. By the end, I felt sort of like a life-support system, a space suit for the baby. My body certainly served no other purpose.

We were living in a big apartment on the Upper West Side of Manhattan, and everywhere I went on the street, people would tell me I was having a boy. I wanted a boy, and that made me feel great. When I passed mothers with babies or toddlers in strollers, I would look at them in a new way, and when the mothers caught my eye, they welcomed me into a special club, a sisterhood of mothers. I'd never seen that look before. It was exciting.

Delivery

On May 14, almost two weeks after my due date I went to work as usual, but I was exhausted. I told my boss I was going to leave early and I went home and napped. At 6 P.M. I woke up and went to the bathroom. On my way back to bed, I felt something running down my leg. I tightened my pelvic floor muscles, but it didn't stop, and I realized my water had broken. If I'd stayed at work, I probably would have been on the subway when it happened.

I called Bill at the office and could hear my secretary screaming down the corridor, "Molly's waters broke!" He came rushing home and we drove down to my doctor's to make sure the baby was in the right position and the cord was not hanging down. Everything was fine, and I was told I'd probably go into labor in the next few hours. We went home again. There was only one problem. I loved my doctor, but I didn't like his partner, and I didn't want him to deliver the baby. They alternated days, so which one I got was all a matter of timing. I called the office, and found out that my doctor wasn't on delivery duty that day, and wouldn't be on until 9 A.M. the next morning. I decided to have a stiff drink, which in Lamaze class I'd been told could hold off, or slow down, labor, and hope to wait it out.

That's exactly what happened. I had an uneventful night, and by the next morning could feel mild, mild cramps, like I would occasionally get with a period. I called my doctor right at 9 A.M. and was told to go into the hospital. By the time we got there, registered, were settled into our labor room, and I'd been given an enema and shaved and strapped into the monitor, it was noon. Then the bad part began. They induced me with Pitocin because my labor hadn't begun. They attached an IV and it began dripping into my vein. Immediately I started to have contractions. They were two minutes apart from the start. At first I could read through them, but as the resident increased the dosage, the pains got worse. I did my breathing, and Bill held my hand, and soon I just lay there exhausted in between. The afternoon wore on. Another increase in dosage, and another. Now I slept between them. Bill would watch the monitor and when he could see another contraction coming, he'd rouse me and I'd start breathing again. While I breathed, I could see myself in a mirror at the end of the bed which some thoughtful soul had hung up so that women in labor could reassure themselves that they were still human and had not turned into a gigantic, ugly blob of pain. Then I'd collapse in sleep.

At one point, we could hear a woman in the delivery room bellowing and a doctor yelling, "Push, push." She'd bellow again. Then there would be silence, and I'd think, "The baby must be out now." But no. Again the voice would yell, "Push, push, push." Again she would cry out. The cry, and the command to push, seemed to go on forever until at last came the high-pitched cry of the baby. Bill and I looked at each other in disbelief. Were we going to go through that?

At 6 P.M. they decided to examine me internally to see how I was doing—something they hadn't wanted to do before because once the waters are broken, they are afraid of infection. Bad news. For six hours I had labored in vain. I hadn't even effaced. My cervix hadn't thinned out, let alone opening even one centimeter. It was at this point that a midwife told me my doctor would probably recommend a cesarean because I wasn't getting anywhere and twenty-four hours after the water breaks, the baby is no longer protected against infection. But my doctor wasn't going to be there for another two hours. Jolly. Maybe something would happen in those two hours. Maybe I'd still get somewhere.

I was wiped out, and I didn't have the mental commitment anymore. Why was I going through all this pain when I'd just end up with a section? Why hadn't someone told me (and no one had) that there was this twenty-four-hour cutoff? I'd have come in last night. Those two hours were the worst. When my doctor arrived, I still hadn't effaced, and he said that they could shut off the Pitocin and see if I got somewhere on my own, but that I was risking the baby's life and the loss of my reproductive organs. He recommended an immediate section. I said, "Great, just get me off this damn Pitocin and do it."

Relief. When they took that stuff out of my IV, it was just great. I was back to a few mild cramps—just as I'd had that morning. It was also 8 P.M., and the New York Rangers hockey team was playing Montreal in the Stanley Cup finals. Game two. The Rangers had won game one. Bill had played hockey for Colgate and I had gotten hooked through him. I'd even brought a tiny portable radio with me to the hospital—naïvely thinking I could listen to the game while I labored. Now I could. But even better, the West Indian orderly who showed up to wheel me down to the OR was also a hockey fan, and he had a much better radio with him. I held it on my stomach and we twisted and turned through the serpentine corridors of the hospital. Alas, the Rangers, who had been leading when we left my room, were behind by two goals by the time we got to OR, and they eventually lost that game and the series. But my orderly provided some comfort. He stayed there while the epidural was administered, and he said to me, with some precognition, it turns out: "You will have a son and he will be a hockey player." Two winters ago, Nicky played on his first team, coached by his dad. They went from an 0–5 start, to the finals of the town's elimination tournament, where they beat the team with the best record by scoring two goals in the final two minutes of the game. The champs!

After the epidural, I was numb from the waist down. I remember lying there flat on my back, and feeling tremendous pressure, as if someone was pushing my stomach to see how much it could bear. And then suddenly the pressure was released, and the baby was crying big lusty cries. "It's a boy," my doctor said. "He's a loud one. I'm glad I don't have to take care of him." They showed him to me briefly and then wisked him away to the nursery, where Bill also got to see him but not to hold him.

Suddenly, a Mother

I didn't get to see my son again until the next afternoon. I woke up that morning asking for my baby, and was told he'd be right in. I'd drift off to sleep and wake to realize he wasn't there. I'd call again and ask for him, and he wouldn't appear. Finally, my doctor arrived to check on me and I told him I still hadn't seen the baby. He found out what was going on: the baby had a little tremor, and they had put him in an isolet to observe him. My doctor said there was nothing wrong with him, they were just being nervous. And he got him released from the nursery in the isolet and wheeled into my room. He was fast asleep, his face turned away from me. I couldn't hold him, but I could reach through this round opening in the side, like a cat port, and touch him. I noticed his ear looked just like mine. I stroked him through that little opening, but it was so removed, and I was still so exhausted, and hurt so much, it all seemed to be happening in another time warp. I remember that Bill came in while the baby was with me and jumped at the sight of him: "He's in here. . . ." I don't think either of us thought of him as ours yet, as part of our family. We still hadn't held him.

Later that day, a female resident pediatrician, came in and asked me what drugs I'd taken during my pregnancy—hoping to pin this quiver on me. I told her I hadn't even taken an aspirin. She left. A nurse came in to see me while I was struggling to get myself to the toilet and gleefully announced that my son, whom I wanted to breast-feed, had drunk half a bottle of formula. Thanks a lot. My pediatrician came to see the baby and said he was just fine and if they hadn't released him from the isolet by the next day he would request it.

The next day Nicky was still in the isolet, and no move was being made to free him. They wouldn't even let him make a return visit to my room. I was getting wild. I wanted my baby. It was as if a part of me had been amputated; I didn't feel whole. I called my pediatrician, and after a considerable delay, he got him released. While all this was going on, a nurse from the nursery came to my room to say that while she couldn't bring the baby to my room, I could come to the nursery to nurse him. The nursery was down my corridor and around a corner and down that corridor. No wheelchair was offered. I didn't care. I would have crawled if I'd had to. It wasn't quite that bad. I walked holding on to the walls, inching my way forward, stooped over, panting for breath. I got there and sat down, and she handed Nicky to me. He was so small. Even though he was a big baby at eight pounds nine ounces, I was overcome by how tiny he was. He opened his eyes and looked at me and bellowed. He was hungry. I started to nurse him, and in the middle, the call came through that he could be released to me, so the nurse told me to return to my room and she'd bring him down. I toddled back, and Nicky was brought in a few minutes later. We were left alone together—mother and son. At last he was mine.

All this was over eight years ago, but it is still crystal clear in my mind, although I have no diary from that era and no notes. I remember the night in the hospital when I felt we were a family for the first time: Nicky was nursing, and Bill came in for his visit, wearing his white doctor's smock. He lay down across the foot of the bed and we talked. When Nicky had finished and was drowsed out on my chest, I picked him up and carefully passed him to his dad. He went back to sleep on his father's chest, and I watched his dad gently stroke his back and his cheek, and get to know him. That night, and many other times back then, I remember being overcome by a feeling which still hasn't gone away, and I hope never will—the miracle of having together created this person. He didn't exist. We had made him from nothing.

Back to Work

But wonders aside, I wasn't going to disrupt my career life for my gorgeous baby boy. My excuse, of course, was that we needed my money. In fact, we couldn't live without it. I was pulling in two thirds of the family income, and we'd just bought a cooperative apartment in New York. I thought I had worked out a reasonable schedule with the magazine. I would take off two months, but spread it out over five. At three weeks I was back part-time, and by two months I was back four days a week, but I was compressing my workday in the office so that I got in about 11 A.M. and left at 5:30 P.M. so I could be home to breast-feed at 10 A.M. and at 6 P.M. I took a lot of work home with me, however, and even did editing on my days off.

This would probably have worked out fine if I'd been a senior editor, who didn't need to be physically present all the time. But it did not work with my job. It didn't matter to the magazine that I had been editing a story since I finished the 6 A.M. feeding. The only point they cared about was that I wasn't there when some crisis had to be solved on Wednesday when I was on leave, or at 7 P.M. on one of my workdays. As managing editor I was responsible for putting out the magazine on time, which meant that I either had to be there, or not be there and let someone else handle it. My schedule had left them in limbo. I don't know what I was thinking of when I devised this schedule, and I don't know what my boss was thinking of when he said OK. It was great for the baby and me personally. We both got to gradually adjust to being apart, but it was dreadful at work.

The arrangement lasted only three months. At that point I was told there was going to be a new order, and I wasn't part of it. I was kicked to the side, into a position with no power on the fringe of the editorial operation. The only thing I didn't lose was my salary. What I gained by my superfluousness to the operation was control over my schedule. Since what I did was so unimportant, it didn't particularly matter when I was there.

During these first crazy months back at work, Nicky was cared for by a young woman from Harlem who had two small children of her own she'd often bring with her. Ruby would stay just until I got home and then race out the door. By the time I arrived, Nicky would be ravenous, screaming for his dinner. I would need him as much as he did me. Often on the subway home, my shirtfront would become saturated with milk. Occasionally, Bill would be stuck with the chore of pacifying Nicky until the "Moo Mom" arrived. It was no easy task, and when I'd come in the door, he'd practically throw him at me. Once, he was so angry and upset by Nicky's half hour of relentless crying that he marched right out the door to a bar and didn't come back until after 8 P.M. How life had changed.

My own realization of that fact occurred one night when Nicky was about two months old. For once, I'd made an effort to cook a nice dinner—lamb chops, mashed potatoes, and salad, and we had a good bottle of red wine. I looked forward to a pleasant, civilized meal. It was not to be. We brought trays into our bedroom to watch television while we ate, and within seconds, Nicky, who was asleep there in his carriage, woke up and began to cry. I had nursed him only an hour or so before, but I knew that was the best way to calm him down. So Bill cut up my meat for me, and while Nicky ate his dessert from my body, I ate my dinner over his body, raising small forkfuls of food carefully to my mouth—with tears running down my cheeks. I knew then that my life was not my own—it belonged first to him, then to me.

Of course, this fact was confirmed over and over in his infancy. The first day I was alone with him in the apartment, he was asleep and I got on the phone and called my office. Within minutes he was awake and howling for no reason. End of phone call. On days when I worked at home, Nicky made this a habit—waking up as soon as I got into the middle of a business call and crying as I talked. He'd fall asleep when I wanted to go out, and if I tried to put him into a cuddly sack, he'd wake up and bellow. He demanded things on his terms, which were usually not my terms, and he told me in no uncertain way that he said to hell with my terms.

The Nanny

A good chunk of my life came back to me when Nicky was six months old, and I hired a live-in nanny because Ruby turned out to be very unreliable.

It was the most wonderful thing I ever did for myself. It was like having a wife—the house was clean; the baby was cared for; the wash was done. I was luxuriously free. It allowed me to be a mother only when I wanted to be one, and only on my terms. My other life continued almost as it had before Nicky was born. Within three months of hiring my first nanny, I accepted a job as managing editor of another magazine and I was back in the swing of things. I negotiated my hours up front—9:30 to 5:30 except when a production crisis was at hand. Bill and I were able to go out for dinner or the movies whenever we wanted without arranging a baby-sitter.

During the week, I usually rolled in exhausted, and more often than not I didn't spend quality time with Nicky. I wanted to put my feet up and watch the news, not get down on the floor of his room and play with blocks or help him stuff plastic pieces through appropriately shaped holes or stack doughnuts in the right order. When I could get myself past the exhaustion barrier and concentrate on him and what he wanted to do, I enjoyed it. But those evenings were too rare—for both of us.

Even on weekends I hung back from total commitment to him. It was as if I were on the outside watching myself take care of him. I wasn't centered or focused on him. I loved him, but I had a very hard time making the change-over from my responsible adult, career-oriented self to my mother self. I was there in body, but often not in spirit. We'd spend a lot of time at the playground in the park when the weather was nice, partly because there he could do activities that didn't directly involve me. But getting there was often more of a hassle than it was worth. We also spent a lot of time at my in-laws in New Jersey, where I could hand him over to his grandparents and his aunts, who were crazy about babies—and especially about him—and sit back in my observer role and watch them doing the loving and the caring. His grandfather had endless patience for sitting in a car in the driveway and letting Nicky honk the horn, turn the wheel, and pull and push all the buttons.

By Sunday afternoon of a normal New York weekend, I was tired and grouchy and wanted some peace and quiet and most of all a nap. Of course, my son was never tired then. He wanted to play. He wanted me. He was a bundle of energy who had sapped whatever strength I had once possessed. I certainly didn't have the strength to be a consistent disciplinarian, so he got away with almost everything. And on Monday, with a sigh of relief, I went back to my "real" life, and left him to the nanny.

My first nanny lasted only three months, but after that I was lucky. Other women I knew went through six or eight a year. But when my first one went back to Trinidad to be with her children, she convinced a friend to take her place. Fran stayed with us from the time Nicky was ten months old until shortly after he turned three. She became his other mother—someone he cared for just as much as he did me, and sometimes more. She was there for him much more than I was. There were nights when I'd be late from my work that he'd turn around in his high chair when he heard my voice, sort of glare at me, and then turn his back. I could see what he was feeling, but it didn't make me change—not then.

The Transformation

When Nicky was just over three, Fran got her working permit and found a job in the accounting department of an advertising agency. She also found another nanny for me—the mother of one of her best friends from Trinidad. At the same time the new nanny was taking over, I started a new job as a senior editor of a high-powered weekly magazine, a job that looked great on my résumé, but one that I grew to hate in fairly short order. I can't pinpoint the moment when I knew that something was askew in my little corner of the world, but I know when I voiced it. Bill and I were driving to Newport, Rhode Island, in late December 1982 for an annual New Year's get-together with close friends at which each person makes a "presentation" of what they have been doing, and where their careers and lives are taking them. Just knowing that I was going to have to explain myself to seven good listeners brought my inner musings to the surface, and I told Bill that I realized that my work didn't hold the center place in my life anymore. Obviously, it's hard to believe your work is really important when at the same time you loathe it. But I also realized that a good deal of the reason I wasn't happy was because I felt I was missing out on Nicky, who by then was three and a half.

We had just moved from the city out to the suburbs, and I left for work every morning on an 8:34 bus, which gave me perhaps one rattled, chore-filled hour with him. I arrived home between 6:30 and 7:00 P.M. to find him and his nanny in the front hall waiting for me, toys covering the carpet. He'd rush to me for hugs the moment the key turned in the lock. God knows how long they'd been there waiting. It was a pathetic scene. By this point he was very verbal and a lot more fun to be with, and I wanted more time than the two hours a day my work schedule allowed. They just weren't enough. At the time I didn't even understand how little that really was.

By April 1983 I had had enough at the magazine and decided to launch myself into a new career, one that would suit my desire to have the flexibility to spend time with Nicky—consulting and free-lance writing from a home office. But the change of career did more than give me time with Nicky, it gave me time to examine what was really important in my life, and when I did so, it changed me.

For over four years now I have worked out of an office on the second floor of our home, writing this book and monographs and articles and newsletters and annual reports and speeches. I'm paid well and I keep busy. I no longer have live-in help, but I have the time to be with my boy. I'm there to kiss him as he gets onto his morning school bus, and to hug him when he gets off in the afternoon. My workday conforms pretty much to his school day unless I'm under a deadline crunch, which can necessitate going back to work later on.

But changing my schedule was just the beginning. Having time with my son, and responsibility for him, caused a fundamental shift in my sense of myself, and my relationship to him. When I began working at home he was a bright, funny, inquisitive—and spoiled and stubborn—four-year-old who desperately wanted my attention—proof of my love—and had found that whining, screaming, and throwing fits were some of the best ways to get it. I was raising a savage, a little boy who had developed very little control over himself because there had never been any consistent control over him by his nannies or by me. His demands for attention and his clinging to me showed deep insecurities about how much I loved him. There was a great deal less of that almost immediately because there was time for the attention he was craving. And there was time for the most basic things I couldn't (or wouldn't) do before: disciplining him when he acted up; knowing his friends because they came to play in the afternoon; giving him his bath; fixing dinner and eating it with him. I was happy just to be with him, doing things he wanted to do, or things we planned to do together. No longer was I thinking with half a mind of all the things I wanted to be doing that I was giving up for him. When I looked at him, I could really see this person I helped to make—in all his shining wondrousness. I had at long last become his mother in more than body.

I had also never worked harder at anything in my life. My career has been child's play by comparison; this was the real stuff. In the beginning, each area of his life—getting dressed, eating meals, going to bed and getting up, even playing—presented an opportunity for conflict. As soon as he knew I meant what I said about his behavior in one area, he'd move his attention to another to see what he could get away with there. For instance: lunch. One might think it would be a simple meal. Wrong. I'd offer him the choice of two sandwiches, and he'd pick. I'd make it. He'd come to the kitchen to eat it and say he didn't want it. He wanted the other one, the one he hadn't chosen. In the past, I'd sometimes given in to food demands—fixing him something different for dinner than I planned—because it was less trouble than fighting with him. And I began to realize that his last nanny had consistently done this: throwing away his dinner when he refused to eat it and making him something else. Being home all the time, not just on weekends, made me much less tolerant of such behavior. So I told Nicky that he'd picked this kind of sandwich and he was going to eat it. Cries, screams—"I won't eat it." Fine, I'd say, and I'd grab his arm and march him upstairs to his room. "You can come down when you'll eat your lunch nicely, or you can go hungry." Ten minutes would go by, in the beginning punctuated by screams and bangs from above, and then he would come down the stairs, humming, and sit and eat his lunch as if nothing had happened. This went on at every lunch he had at home for six weeks before he gave in.

Over the four years I've been working from home, these incidents have happened less and less frequently. The results of the loving attention, and the consistent discipline, have been noticeable not just to Bill and me but to friends, neighbors, and teachers. Nicky is now a pleasure to be with. Now that he knows there are firm limits—rules of the house—he has learned to accept them with a fair degree of equanimity. He's usually cooperative. He listens. And I can truly say that being Nicky's mother has been more significant to me than any work I've done in my life.

I can still remember back when this wasn't true. Once, when he was about two and a half, I called home around 7 P.M. to tell the nanny I was going to be late and she should put him to bed. He got on the phone to talk to me. "Nicky," I said, "Mommy's stuck at work." There was a long pause, and then he said with worry in his voice, "Stuck?" I realized he was thinking of glue, and perhaps imagining that I was pasted to my desk and would be there forever. What I didn't realize back then was that in some sense his image was absolutely correct. I was "stuck" at work, stuck in that mind-set, where my career and my time and my needs came first.

Baby Lust

What these new feelings about motherhood also did for me was make me want another baby. I'd always thought I wanted two children because I'd been an only and felt that loneliness, and that pressure to do and be the best, and the abundant worry surrounding my every move. It was all too intense. I didn't want Nicky to go through that, or to be the odd one out. Every time I saw parents with their one child I thought about how isolating it is: two of them and one of you. And then, when you grow up, there's no one with whom to share your memories, no one who's been through it too, who can help you explain it to yourself. As an adult I'd craved family. Part of Bill's appeal was his big, close-knit family.

Yet I hadn't had any driving desire to have a second baby. It was easy enough to put it off, especially since my various career changes had made it more difficult. Working at home, of course, my situation was now ideal. My schedule was mine. I could call my own shots. But there was one big problem: Bill did not really want another baby. He was now a senior writer at a weekly magazine three days a week and trying to write a second book the other four. He worried about getting sucked into all sorts of baby care. Nicky was just getting to be easier to handle, and why go through all that again? And how would I get any work done if I had a baby? Even though he now brought in the bulk of our income, we still needed my earnings to meet our expenses.

I kept bringing it up periodically to let him know that it was something I really did want, not just some whim of the moment. Nicky was growing up so fast. I could hardly fit him on my lap anymore. He was still a glutton for hugs and kisses, but there is nothing like that baby love, and I craved it. I also craved the excitement of pregnancy—of growing someone new from nothing. I found myself really attracted to babies. One afternoon a friend of mine came over with her four-month-old daughter to pick up her son, Reuben, who was a friend of Nicky's. Her baby was in her arms, and I rushed over to her. I had this wild desire to smell the baby, to sniff in that special baby smell.

But Bill kept hedging. The money issue was always his big card. And it did worry me too. I put in a full six to seven hours a day, and I needed that time in order to earn a decent living. But I also knew I could make adjustments to my schedule—working after the 6 A.M. feeding, working during nap time on the weekends, and at night, to make up for time lost during the day. Other women who worked at home managed it. I could too. When the idea for this book came up and I wrote my proposal, Bill finally said that if I got a contract we could have another baby, but it was a real concession; it still wasn't anything he wanted to do.

It was September 1984. I was going to be forty in January. I was hitting the wire.

The Babies That Were Not to Be

I got pregnant the first month we tried. I went for a blood test even before missing my period—that's how sure I was that I was pregnant. It was positive. I found out on a Friday. On Sunday, when I was five weeks along, I started to bleed. That was it. The next test was negative. I was told to wait three months before trying again. I willed myself not to cry, but the grief did not go away so easily. There had been a life inside me. I knew something had to be terribly wrong for it to end like that, and that I should be glad it did. But for months I thought about that person I'd never know.

When February came around, we were able to start trying again, and again I got pregnant right away.

Things seemed to go all right with this pregnancy. I had an ultrasound at eight weeks because I had thought I'd like to have chorionic villi sampling (CVS) to make sure the baby was OK, instead of waiting for amniocentesis.

The ultrasound was done to determine exactly how pregnant I was. On the screen I saw the peanut-shaped amniotic sac, and within it the form of the fetus, and the tiny dot of a heart beating. The technician said, "Isn't that amazing!" And truly it was. There was a life in there. The other thing the picture showed is that I have a retroverted uterus, which makes it difficult to do CVS and increases the risk of a miscarriage. Seeing that tiny heart made me decide to play it safe and wait for the amniocentesis, which would be done at the end of May.

The spring passed in its usual fashion, but the pregnancy was a lot harder than the one with Nicky. I felt lousy from about 3 P.M. to 7 P.M. each day—nauseous without getting physically sick. The thought of cooking dinner was repulsive. I was also exhausted. I could have spent most of my time in bed, but I wouldn't let myself because I had too much work. I also worried, but not only because I'd had a previous miscarriage. I found myself racked by ambivalence about having a second child. What was I doing to my nice orderly world? How I was going to manage my work with all the extra baby duties? How would I divide my love between two children? How was Nicky going to take this intrusion? Would it shatter his cozy little world?

In the middle of April, when I was through the first trimester and felt I could relax about a possible miscarriage, we told Nicky we were expecting a baby. He didn't react right away, but a few nights later he told me his heart was breaking. I asked him why, but he couldn't tell me. At last he said that it wasn't breaking now, but it would break when the baby came. I could not console him with descriptions of how much I loved him. The next night I brought it up again, and he said he still felt his heart was going to break. Then he asked if he would be seven when the baby came, and I said, he'd be six and a half, and that I thought he'd be so busy with school and his friends, and sports that the baby wouldn't bother him at all. "Like Reuben?" he said. I said yes, like Reuben. And then I had a brainstorm. I told him that Reuben's sister Rebecca loved Reuben and wanted to be with him all the time. It was as if a light bulb came on in Nicky's head: his baby would be another person who loved him, not someone who would just take away love. He got all excited about what he could teach the baby, and how he could play blocks with the baby and build towers. He was bouncing around his room looking for appropriate baby toys.

At sixteen weeks of pregnancy, right before my amniocentesis, I was examined by my doctor, and everything was normal. Except he couldn't hear a heartbeat. He wasn't worried, however, because that often happens. And he didn't send me for an ultrasound because I'd be having one the next week with the amnio. It was scheduled for 9 A.M. on May 29. There was lots of traffic into the city, but we made it early and had coffee and split a bran muffin at a coffee shop near the hospital. I didn't feel any apprehension about the procedure itself, but I remember telling Bill I worried a bit they'd find something wrong on the screen—like a missing arm or leg, or the head too small. It was just a nagging little tick I'd been thinking about all week, and it felt good to get it out.

Then we sauntered up to the hospital, still early, and rode the elevator to the second floor and walked to the end of the corridor to the ultrasound room, past a very pregnant woman with dark hair, belly jutting out, in a white hospital gown. I felt a camaraderie with her—me a few months ahead.

We were ushered inside right away and after I signed two consent forms I lay down on the table, pulled my dress up and my panties down, and had my stomach dabbed with some cold greasy conductive stuff just as they had used before. Bill stood a little away from me; it wasn't his show.

The technician switched on the ultrasound machine and put the matchbox-sized receptor on my stomach. She didn't immediately come up with a picture. A little concern. Then she found the sac. It didn't look very big, not that much bigger than when I had been here before. Now it was like a two-to-three-inch peanut with tendrils growing out of the middle.

"Have you been bleeding?" she asked.

"No."

"Are you sure about your dates?" she said. "You don't look very big."

"Yes. I was here in March to be tested for CVS." Odd, I thought, I felt big.

Maybe not as big as I'd been with Nicky, but then I'd gained a lot more weight with him than I had this time.

"Oh," she said.

I was growing cold. Something wasn't right; the sense of it was seeping into me. I could see Bill off in the shadows but I couldn't bring myself to reach out to him. I didn't want to admit that what was wrong could be so wrong that I would need his comfort or he would need mine.

"I think I better get the doctor," she said.

In a second he was there, and from the chart on the desk she was telling him when I'd had the previous ultrasound and that the dates were correct.

He found the sac right away, and moved the little crosses of light to each end to measure it. He pressed a button and read the number. That was all he had to do; there were no other calculations necessary. "I'm sorry," he said. I reached out for Bill's hand, drawing him to the table. The worst that could be wrong was wrong.

"The fetus isn't growing," he said. "There isn't a heartbeat," he said. "It's already disintegrating," he said.

I asked questions, questions in the guise of statements, questions that were supposed to make him look again and recant all those words. "But I was the right size for sixteen weeks when I went to the doctor last Monday—how could that be? But I still feel pregnant? But I haven't been bleeding?"

He had answers—the wrong answers. They changed nothing. "The amniotic fluid can keep being made even when the fetus has died, and therefore the uterus seems to be the right size. . . . The hormones of pregnancy are still being produced by the placenta, which is why you still feel pregnant. . . . Fifteen to twenty percent of all pregnancies end in miscarriage."

It was over. He said he would call my doctor. He said the usual procedure now would be for me to have a D&C. He said we could try again in two months.

Someone wiped my stomach, and I pulled up my underpants, slid down my dress and climbed off the table. I put on my coat and we left, sliding through the door, and down the corridor. The pregnant woman was no longer there— my future self was gone. Bill put his arm around me and I put mine around him, hugging so close there was no space between us, walking silently like that up to the end of the corridor, where at the doors of the delivery rooms doctors chatted about patients. We stood as one, waiting for the elevator, and down in the elevator, and out into the world which was still there, still busy with traffic and dog walkers and people on errands.

But a totally different world for us. I don't remember the ride home except that I cried and stopped and cried again, and I kept reaching out for Bill and he for me and there was nothing to say except, "Why? Why? What did I do?"

We were home by 11 A.M. Bill thought I should lie down, but I knew that if I did, I'd be lying in a lake of my tears, so I worked at my computer, and cried, and worked some more. Around lunch time I went downstairs and announced that what I wanted was not food, but a stiff drink. "Go ahead," said Bill, so I made myself a vodka on the rocks. It didn't matter anymore what I did to my body. Taking good care of myself hadn't protected the life within.

I wanted to know why so I began to read everything I could about miscarriage. My menstrual cycles over the past couple of years had shortened down to twenty-three or twenty-four days from twenty-eight to twenty-nine. I found out that was a sign that I was entering the premenopausal period. Was it the reason for the two miscarriages? Was my hormonal system too weak to support a pregnancy? Did I have what they call a luteal phase defect? But why had the pregnancies ended at such different times?

Just like every other woman who has had a miscarriage, I was also full of self-recrimination—making lists of all the possible things that had gone wrong—fertilizing the lawn, having the trees sprayed (even though I had stayed indoors); using the microwave oven; having a bad fall on the water slide we had bought Nicky. The baby had been my responsibility, mine to protect and nurture, and I'd failed. My body had failed.

I was also overwhelmed with loathing for the deadness that was inside me. I wanted it out. In one day I had gone from feeling protective to wanting to destroy. I also wanted it out of me because the sooner it was, the sooner I could try again. If anything, the miscarriage had made me more determined to have another baby. It had also changed Bill. He had gotten used to the idea with this pregnancy, but still wasn't thrilled. Now he wanted it too.

The D&C two days later went off without a hitch, but the next six weeks were pretty dreadful. I didn't sleep, waking up over and over again during the night. I didn't eat. I drank too much. Over and over I counted the days until I would have had two normal periods and we could try again to make a baby. But in the middle of July, my work load got so heavy that I managed to forget, and by the time I realized what date it was, I'd gotten another period (this time with a 28-day cycle) and we could try once more.

Pregnant Again

It took three months this time, causing me incredible anguish. I took my temperature every morning and even made Bill take a later bus into the city on a couple of occasions because it had gone up a few tenths of a degree. I'd wait for my period and expect it not to come and it would come. The first month I assumed I was miscarrying and lay down, that's how nuts I was. The second month I had a blood test before it came and when it was negative I couldn't believe it—I had convinced myself that I had the symptoms of pregnancy. After I got that period, I decided I was not going to drive myself crazy, but was going to lose the last seven or eight pounds I'd gained and concentrate on that. I counted calories and lost the weight. I also took my temperature and waited for the bleeding not to begin. This time it didn't. I was pregnant.

I decided to make a new beginning by getting a new doctor, Irwin Merkatz, who is chairman of the Department of Ob/Gyn at Albert Einstein College of Medicine. Throughout the pregnancy, he ran every test in the book to make sure I felt positive. I had an ultrasound at seven weeks, and again at thirteen weeks, just before Christmas—to reassure me so I'd have a happy holiday. I watched the tiny fetus move its arm up to its head and then back down. He performed the amnio himself at sixteen weeks and I got the good news at nineteen weeks. When we told Nicky that the baby was OK and it was a girl, he was upset because he wasn't getting a brother. But he got used to the idea, and loved to sit with his hand on my stomach waiting for her to kick—and kick and punch she did, giving constant reassurance to her father and me.

By April 1986, I was thirty-one weeks along and weighed in at 160. But despite a ravenous appetite for root beer floats and mint Girl Scout cookies, I didn't gain any weight from then on. I could still waddle out to play catch with Bill and Nicky in the backyard, but it was becoming increasingly difficult to walk around for any length of time, or to lift anything. My belly button area was already stretched to the splitting point, and the ligaments along my hips were tender to the touch at the end of the day. Sometimes I felt as if my stomach, which looked like a basketball attached to the front of my body, was going to fall off. Pregnancy at age forty-one was definitely more exhausting than at thirty-four. Until then, I hadn't really felt what the years had wrought. Samantha was due June 28 and I was scheduled to have another section on June 19. After everything I'd gone through, I didn't want to risk the perils of labor. As Bill said, "Let them cut on the dotted line and get her out of there."

We didn't bring the crib or any of Nicky's baby clothes down from the attic until close to the end of May. And I never did go shopping for toys for babies from birth to six months, or little pink stretchie suits. Both of us worried that doing such things might be tempting fate.

It's funny how you react when things don't go as expected in your life. It makes you pull back a little from experience, from involvement in your world. You can't allow yourself to be as open as you would be. You hang on the outside, looking in. It made me worry that when Samantha was born I might not be able to leap with both feet into love, into being her mother.

Sam's Birth

I was admitted to the hospital the day before the section after spending a sleepless night. I put Nicky to bed thinking, "This is the last night I'll ever do this as the mother of one." I crawled into our bed thinking, "This is the last night I'll sleep here as the mother of one." It seemed like doomsday, with life beyond the hospital to be irreparably changed. There would be no going back. "What if she's not a great kid?" I thought. "What if I don't love her the way I love Nicky? What if she doesn't love me? I adore him so much, what if I'm wrecking that in some way?" And most of all, I wondered, "What if something is wrong with her?" By the next morning as we prepared to drive to the hospital, the friction and tension were palpable. Bill yelled at me about something, and I called him an "ungrateful wretch" because he complained about some work I'd done for him over the weekend. We both realized how scared we were and talking about it cleared the air.

The section was to be at 11 A.M. the next morning and Bill got back to the hospital at 10. There was a sense of unreality about it all—being scheduled to have a baby, to be anesthetized, cut open, and have her pulled out of me. A nurse came to get us about 10:30, and we walked with her to the other end of the floor where the operating rooms are. After I was given the epidural, the room started to fill up with people—including Bill, all gowned and masked, with a cap over his hair, only his eyes letting me know him, and Dr. Merkatz. It was like the opening act of a play, everyone hustling onto the stage and taking their assigned places. Bill's was to be by my side, and after a bit of chitchat with Dr. Merkatz, there he was, holding my hand.

Dr. Merkatz greeted me warmly, but then he was all business, asking for a particular arrangement of instruments, a particular placement of the draping over my legs and abdomen. They put up the "screen," a curved tube over which they hang a cloth, so I couldn't see.

Then it began, orchestrated and lectured through by Dr. Merkatz, telling Dr. Cantu, the resident who was assisting, exactly what he was doing, asking for instruments, having Dr. Cantu do this and then do that. Bill looked at me and I at him. What was happening below that screen seemed to be on another planet. The reality of Samantha's imminent arrival was lost on us both.

Then suddenly Dr. Merkatz said, "Look now, here comes the baby. Get that screen down so she can see. Get it *down.* Lift her head. *Lift it.* Get the camera ready." Bill handed it over to a nurse with quick instructions. My head was hoisted up, and by God, there she was, first just her head, all white and slimy, covered in vernix with a few tiny drops of blood clinging to her, and then her upper body with the long, slippery coils of cord. I know I was speechless. Bill said, "Oh my God, my God," but later he didn't even remember uttering those words. Total awe. Our baby.

"Take pictures, take pictures," said Dr. Merkatz, and he clamped the cord and grabbed her upright to his chest. "It's a girl. This is the shot." Then he handed her to a nurse to be cleaned, and Bill went with her, drawn like a magnet. Dr. Merkatz said to me, "What do you think? Heh? A big, beautiful baby. A girl. She's terrific, huh? A beautiful baby. You know, I could never give this up, delivering babies. It's too wonderful. The greatest profession ever."

Then he was back to work, lecturing on technique again, all business, expressing the placenta, sewing me up. And Bill and Samantha were back too. She was cleaned up, wrapped in blankets and wearing a little white cap on her head. He was holding her close and looking at her, and I could tell he was overwhelmed, in love, flying. When I was pregnant, she was much more just my baby—he had made his momentary contribution and now I was doing the rest. But now, seeing him hold her, feeling his joy, she had become his baby too.

I could see he didn't want to give her up, but I wanted her badly. I don't know if I had a chance to say so before Dr. Merkatz told Bill to hand her over, and they unstrapped one arm and Bill put her down next to me, with her little face against my face, and my hand, IV and all, holding her. She was funny and beautiful all at once. Mottled skin, with some vernix still on it, dark pink eyelids, scratches on her cheeks. But a beautiful square forehead, and delicate pursed mouth and button nose. I loved her so much, so quickly, that it was overwhelming. She cried occasional long, soft cries. Bill said, "She's inconsolable." I talked to her gently, "Sam. Hello, Sam. You're here now. Open your eyes, honey. Come on, Sam, look at Mommy." Gradually the crying ceased, but her eyelids stayed shut. After about ten minutes, Dr. Merkatz told me she should go to the nursery to be warmed up, and Bill took her from me and handed her to the nurse and said, "Goodbye, Samantha" to her. It felt as if part of me was gone too.

After I was all stitched up and a painkiller was put in through the epidural, I was taken to recovery, where I'd been promised I could have Sam back. I was freezing cold. I shook and shook, and they kept piling heated blankets on to me. I was also lonely, even though Bill was right there. I wanted my baby. Her absence was like a hole in my heart. I was also worried about her because of what had happened with Nicky. I asked one nurse and she came back to tell me that maybe later I could have her. Time went by. My legs started coming back to life. I'd move my knee an inch and my leg would shoot up on the bed like a puppeteer had jerked on a string. I asked again, and I explained to the nurse why I was worried. She came back soon to tell me that everything was fine, that Sam was still in the special warming isolet and she'd come to my room later, showing me consideration that was duplicated by the nursing staff many times during my stay. Soon I was back in my room, and soon after that Sam was brought in and handed over to me. I held her close and put her to my breast, and she started to suck, eyes still tightly shut, little fists clenched, and I fell even more in love with her.

Two days later, Nicky came with his dad to see his sister for the first time. He was radiant, shining. I had missed him so much and expected he would come right to me, but he was drawn to her little bassinette. "Look, look how tiny she is," he said as he stared down at her. Then he came and kissed me, and Bill kissed me. I was crying, I was so happy, having my family—expanded—all together. I asked Nicky to wash his hands before he touched her and he went to do it right away—no arguments, no saying "But . . ." Then Bill picked up Samantha and after a few minutes handed her to Nicky, who was waiting on a chair with a pillow in his lap. He was so quiet and gentle with her—pointing out to us her delicate hands and feet and her satin skin. When I got up and went in the bathroom, he said to Bill, "I feel like I'm in a dream." And indeed, the afternoon had the quality of a dream. The room itself was suffused with a glow from the afternoon sun reflecting off the peach-colored walls. The curtains billowed in a soft wind. And the love for our new baby glowed around us.

I had worried so much about how I would love two when I already loved Nick so much, and seeing them together it all seemed so simple. I loved them differently—they pulled from different love sources, and I gave to them in different ways. And it was also true that I had expanded. I had more love now to give, just as I told Nicky I would. I had told him my love was like a balloon. When the baby came, I said, I would blow up the balloon of love even further. My love for her wouldn't take from him. And it was true.

A Mother of Two

Having a seven-year-old and a baby has been wonderful and easy. Nicky is very busy with his own life, and when he's here he's usually cooperative and helpful. During the summer he went to day camp five days a week from 8:15 A.M. to 4:45 P.M., and in September, he started second grade, leaving on the school bus at 8:30 A.M. and coming back at 3:45 P.M. During the summer I had a mother's helper for five hours a day five days a week, and when she went off to college, I hired a young mother of a fourteen-month-old who works twenty hours a week and leaves her son with her own mother.

And Sam is a good baby. She isn't fussy, and she doesn't cry for no apparent reason. I can tell when she's tired, and if I put her in her crib, she'll go to sleep. I don't always nurse her to sleep as I tended to do with Nicky. I can tell when she's bored, and I change her position or take her into a different room or get out a different toy. The long and short of it is that I understand her, much better than I did Nicky at this age. Maybe because of that, she's more fun. I enjoy being around her. I don't want to get away from her, and when I am away, there's still that little hole in my heart. I can imagine her crying.

Having a competitor for my attention has been a bit hard on Nicky, especially on the two nights Bill doesn't get home until late. But because he's older, he can tell me about it. One night I asked him how he felt about Sam and he said, "Sometimes I get angry because you have to spend so much time with her." Another afternoon, the mother of one of his friend's told me he had crossed a street on his bike when a car was coming. When he got home, we talked about how important it is to make sure for yourself whether a car is coming, and I told him how I would never get over it if he got hurt or something happened to him. He said, "But you have Samantha." That broke my heart—that he would feel she could replace him. Because, of course, no matter how much I love her, she can't. Which is what I told him.

Meanwhile, there has been a work life after this second motherhood. I wrote seven chapters of this book before having Sam, but the rest has been written in the five months since. As soon as the babysitter arrives, I head for the computer and shut the door. I take a break only to nurse Sam if she refuses the bottle. On the days when I don't have help, I work during her naps. I won't let myself do chores or errands no matter how much they need to be done. Those are reserved for when she is awake. I've vacuumed the upstairs while she rides on my shoulders in a backpack. I take her on walks to the local shopping area for bagels and hardware supplies or dry cleaning. She's sat peaceably in her stroller while her dad and I have raked leaves.

And what of Dad, that reluctant participant in making a baby? Back when I was trying to convince Bill to have another, I promised him that his life wouldn't change—I would have promised anything. But in truth, the only change has been that he's fallen in love with his daughter—the product of my female macho, he jokes. He gets just as much work done on his writing as he would have if she weren't here. Since she won't always take a bottle, I can't leave her if she might be hungry, so she goes everywhere with me—the supermarket, the department store, the library. There have been only rare occasions when he's been stuck with an unhappy Sam and not able to work.

As for me, having a second baby at this, the eleventh hour of my baby-making days, has filled me with wonder. When I look at Samantha, so new and wide-eyed and perfect, so happy to be with her people, smiling and "talking" to us, I know the meaning of the word "miracle." For that is surely what she is. That one sperm out of millions meets and enters one egg and in nine short months the cell they formed together has become a perfect and totally unique baby, made of billions upon billions of cells, all in the right place, doing the right job, is wondrous. In making Samantha, Bill and I have become miracle workers again—creating another life from nothing.

And when I look at Nicky, so big and grown up by comparison, mastering one skill after another and making ever-widening explorations of our complicated world, that sense of the miracle of it all is just as strong. I hope it never goes away. The two of them have opened up love in me I didn't know I had. They have expanded my world and made it full of possibilities—because they see through new eyes and open my eyes, and because their lives will go many directions mine did not, and they will take me along for part of their journey.

But motherhood is more than this. Being part of a family I helped to create brings me a joy I don't think I could have found in any other way. The other night, as I was preparing dinner surrounded by my family, I realized how exquisitely happy I was with my life. Instead of watching the news on TV, we had put on the classical music station on the radio and Bill had Samantha in the backpack and was dancing her around the room, sometimes dipping her down so I could give her a kiss. Nick had been very fresh the day before and as punishment was forbidden television for a week, so he was reading a new book I'd bought him at the school book fair, *Something Queer at the Lemonade Stand,* and giving us the blow-by-blow of the mystery as it unfolded. I was chopping cucumbers for the salad, or doing some other mundane dinner task, when it struck me that it was one of those special moments in my life that I'd always remember. We were all together, all happy, all feeling glad to be with each other, and I loved everyone in that room so much. It was the kind of time that makes having a family worth all the trouble it sometimes is.

Appendix
Cast of Characters

A

Abigail, 30, an assistant manager in a regional office of a federal agency
Agatha, 33, vice president and commodities broker
Alexandra, 36, president of her own company
Alexis, 29, pricing manager
Amber, 28, officer in the Air Force
Anita, 34, director of community services
Anne, 30, director of marketing
Ariel, 38, programmer analyst
Audry, 36, sales manager
Augusta, 34, case manager in a social service agency

B

Barbara, 29, dean of students
Beatrice, 35, recreation therapist
Beth, 36, flight attendant
Betty, 36, business development representative
Beverly, 37, M.D., orthopedic surgeon

C

Caitlin, 32, video program coordinator
Camille, 31, assistant director of career services
Candy, 30, executive assistant
Carol, 37, Ph.D., coordinator of degree program in biology
Carolyn, 32, assistant director of career services
Carrie, 38, managing editor of industry publication
Charlotte, 34, part-time counselor of graduate students
Cheryl, 31, assistant director of an industry council
Clara, 38, public health adviser
Colleen, 42, graphic designer with her own business
Connie, 36, sales representative
Corinne, 31, regional assistant
Cynthia, 30, regional sales manager

D

Dana, 30, corporate attorney

Daphne, 32, account supervisor in market research firm

Dean, 31, program officer at a foundation

Deborah, 37, vice president and director of marketing

Denise, 39, full-time mother, starting her own business from home

Diana, 29, executive director, human services agency

Dina, 32, lieutenant in the Navy

Dolores, 38, nurse-midwife

Donna, 35, associate general counsel with the federal government

Doreen, 29, staff accountant

Dorothy, 29, joint data base coordinator

E

Eleanor, 46, psychotherapist and writer

Elizabeth, 30, financial economist

Ella, 32, part-time actress

Ellen, 31, artist and illustrator

Emily, 35, former director of patient services; full-time mother

Emma, 34, advertising executive

Erica, 30, architectural designer and personnel consultant

Evelyn, 39, program analyst

Evonne, 28, division manager of interior design department

F

Faith, 29, management consultant

Fern, 30, police officer

Flora, 30, programmer analyst

Fran, 36, early childhood educator

G

Gail, 33, finishing doctorate in psychology

Germaine, 37, documentary filmmaker

Gerry, 32, stock market analyst

Gillian, 28, office administrator

Gina, 32, division secretary

Ginger, 37, director of personnel

Grace, 40, head of reference in university library

Gretchen, 31, former librarian; writer

Gwen, 29, artists' representative with her own business

H

Hannah, 28, real estate salesperson

Harriet, 35, artist and jeweler

Heather, 35, senior marketing representative

Heidi, 27, occupational health consultant

Helene, 32, secretary

Hillary, 28, proprietor of a store
Holly, 31, production scheduling supervisor

J
Jackie, 35, bureau supervisor in police department
Janet, 39, writer and professor
Janis, 36, sales planning manager
Jennifer, 30, public relations writer with own business
Jessie, 36, Ph.D. instructional assistant
Joan, 38, systems analyst
Joyce, 36, sales representative
Judy, 31, research assistant
Julia, 28, secretary

K
Karen, 32, full-time mother
Karla, 28, data manager
Kathleen, 29, vice president of a commercial bank
Kim, 35, head medical librarian
Kitty, 32, manager of computer operations
Kristin, 28, juvenile court officer
Kyle, 33, ethics director

L
Lana, 30, computer sales representative
Laura, 31, marketing director and family therapist
Leslie, 30, trade broker
Letty, 38, writer and publicist with her own business
Libby, 33, secretary and receptionist
Lorraine, 31, budget analyst
Louisa, 32, teacher
Lydia, 32, senior secretarial specialist

M
Maggie, 30, social worker
Marcy, 31, sales representative
Margaret, 31, former director of marketing for hotel chain; works for husband's business
Margie, 35, Ph.D., chemist and mid-level manager
Martha, 27, insurance agent
Mary, 30, sales and marketing manager
Maryanne, 34, vice president
Mathilda, 36, full-time mother
Maude, 34, manager of marketing
Melanie, 35, art director
Melissa, 32, secretary
Meredith, 39, bookkeeper with her own business
Milly, 35, supervisor of municipal finance

Mindy, 30, pilot
Miranda, 29, advertising and sales promotion director
Myra, 34, marketing consultant with her own business

N
Nancy, 27, software editor
Naomi, 31, marketing research consultant with her own business
Natalie, 31, marketing consultant with her own business
Nina, 31, secretary

O
Olive, 38, M.D., psychiatrist

P
Pam, 28, looking for a job
Pat, 37, copywriter
Patricia, 40, congressional investigator
Penelope, 40, Ph.D., college professor
Phoebe, 37, program manager
Polly, 30, educational program manager
Priscilla, 33, mid-level manager

R
Rachel, 35, supervisor
Regina, 32, free-lance writer
Renee, 36, regional administrator
Rita, 38, clerk-typist
Roberta, 37, administrative assistant

S
Sadie, 36, financial administrator
Sally, 36, personnel officer
Samantha, 35, weaver
Sandy, 27, management associate with a bank
Sarah, 35, manager of information systems
Sophia, 32, ballet teacher
Stephanie, 35, former teacher; full-time mother
Sunny, 33, manager of computer operations
Suzanne, 29, systems engineer
Sybil, 36, attorney with federal government
Sylvia, 30, sales representative

T
Tammy, 28, former administrative manager; full-time mother
Tessie, 28, software engineer with her own business
Theodora, 43, Ph.D., clinical psychologist
Theresa, 40, project consultant with her own business

V

Valerie, 34, sales coordinator

Victoria, 32, M.D., anesthesiologist

Virginia, 41, director of development

W

Wanda, 31, accounting supervisor

Wendy, 34, customer communications specialist